Learn HTML

Third Edition

Send Us Your Comments

To comment on this book or any other PRIMA TECH title, visit our reader response page on the Web at **www.prima-tech.com/comments**.

How to Order

For information on quantity discounts, contact the publisher: Prima Publishing, P.O. Box 1260BK, Rocklin, CA 95677-1260; (916) 787-7000. On your letterhead, include information concerning the intended use of the books and the number of books you want to purchase. For individual orders, turn to the back of this book for more information.

Learn HTML

In a Weekend

Third Edition

STEVE CALLIHAN

PRIMA TECH

A DIVISION OF PRIMA PUBLISHING

A Division of Prima Publishing

Prima Publishing and colophon are registered trademarks of Prima Communications, Inc. PRIMA TECH and In a Weekend are trademarks of Prima Communications, Inc., Roseville, California 95661.

Publisher: Stacy L. Hiquet
Marketing Manager: Judi Taylor
Managing Editor: Sandy Doell
Acquisitions Editor: Debbie Abshier
Project/Copy Editor: Kezia Endsley
Technical Reviewer: Michael Johnson
Interior Layout: Marian Hartsough
Cover Design: Prima Design Team
Indexer: Johnna VanHoose Dinse

Microsoft, Windows, Internet Explorer, Notepad, VBScript, ActiveX, and FrontPage are trademarks or registered trademarks of Microsoft Corporation. Netscape is a registered trademark of Netscape Communications Corporation.

Important: Prima Publishing cannot provide software support. Please contact the appropriate software manufacturer's technical support line or Web site for assistance.

Prima Publishing and the author have attempted throughout this book to distinguish proprietary trademarks from descriptive terms by following the capitalization style used by the manufacturer.

Information contained in this book has been obtained by Prima Publishing from sources believed to be reliable. However, because of the possibility of human or mechanical error by our sources, Prima Publishing, or others, the Publisher does not guarantee the accuracy, adequacy, or completeness of any information and is not responsible for any errors or omissions or the results obtained from use of such information. Readers should be particularly aware of the fact that the Internet is an ever-changing entity. Some facts may have changed since this book went to press.

ISBN: 0-7615-2694-3
Library of Congress Catalog Card Number: 00-106664
Printed in the United States of America

00 01 02 03 04 II 10 9 8 7 6 5 4 3 2 1

To my best pal, Jerry

ACKNOWLEDGMENTS

The creating of any book is much more than just a one-person job. Any author owes a large debt to the many helpers who perform many of the necessary tasks required to produce a quality and, hopefully, successful book. Much appreciation is due to Kezia Endsley (Project Editor), Debbie Abshier and Stacy Hiquet (Acquisition Editors), Michael Johnson (Technical Editor), Jason Haines (CD-ROM Producer), Marian Hartsough (Layout), and Jeannie Smith (proofreader) for their strong efforts and very real contributions to this book.

ABOUT THE AUTHOR

Steve Callihan is a freelance and technical writer from Seattle. He is the author of several other books published by Prima Tech, including *Create Your First Web Page In a Weekend, 3rd Edition, Create Your First Mac Web Page In a Weekend*, and *Learn HTML In a Weekend, 3rd Edition*, as well as the co-author of *Create FrontPage 2000 Web Pages In a Weekend* (with C. Michael Woodward). He has also had articles published in major computer magazines, including *Internet World*, and has extensive experience writing and producing hardware and software user guides.

CONTENTS AT A GLANCE

Introduction . . . . **xx**

FRIDAY EVENING
Getting Oriented **1**

SATURDAY MORNING
Learning the Basics **19**

SATURDAY AFTERNOON
Dressing Up Your Pages **79**

SATURDAY EVENING (Bonus Session)
Working with Tables **127**

SUNDAY MORNING
Working with Frames **165**

SUNDAY AFTERNOON
Working with Forms **197**

SUNDAY EVENING (Bonus Session)
Working with Graphics **225**

APPENDIX A
HTML Quick Reference 273

APPENDIX B
XHTML/XML Compatibility Guide 311

APPENDIX C
Non-Keyboard Characters. 315

APPENDIX D
Using Relative URLs 325

APPENDIX E
Using Cascading Style Sheets. 333

APPENDIX F
Completing Your Wish List 349

APPENDIX G
Transferring Your Pages to the Web. 375

APPENDIX H
What's on the CD-ROM 391

Glossary 399

Index 404

CONTENTS

Introduction . . . . **xx**

FRIDAY EVENING
Getting Oriented **1**

What Is HTML? 3

What Is Hypertext? 4

What Is a Markup Language? 5

Why Learn HTML? 6

HTML: The Evolution of a Standard. 8

    The Initial Versions of HTML 8

    HTML 2.0 9

    Ad Hoc HTML: Netscape and Microsoft Extensions 9

    A Failed Initiative: HTML 3.0 10

Take a Break. 11

    HTML 3.2 11

    HTML 4.0 12

    HTML 4.01 13

What Are XML and XHTML?. 14

    XML 1.0 14

    XHTML 1.0 15

    Impact on Web Publishers 15

Other HTML Developments 16

Wrapping Up. 17

SATURDAY MORNING
Learning the Basics 19

What You Need 21
   Using a Text Editor to Create HTML Files. 21
   Using a Web Browser to Preview Your Work. 22
Installing the Example Files from the CD-ROM. 23
Anatomy of an HTML Tag 25
   Tag Attributes 26
   Don't Overlap HTML Tags. 27
Saving Your HTML File 27
Turning Word Wrap On in Note Notepad 29
Starting Your HTML File 29
   The HTML Tag 29
   The HEAD Tag 30
   The TITLE Tag 30
   The BODY Tag 31
Using a Starting Template 32
Working with Headings, Paragraphs, and Line Breaks. 33
   Using Headings to Structure Your Page 33
   Working with Paragraphs 35
   Horizontally Aligning Headings and Paragraphs 38
   Inserting Line Breaks 39
   Spacing, Tabs, and Returns: For Your Eyes Only 41
Highlighting Your Text. 41
   Using Italic and Bold Highlighting. 41
   Embedding Monospaced Text 42
   Adding Superscripts and Subscripts 43

Other Highlighting Tags 44

Inserting Non-Keyboard Characters 45

Using Reserved Characters 46

Adding Comments 48

Using Block Quotes 48

Using Preformatted Text 50

Take a Break 52

Creating Lists 52

Creating Bulleted Lists 52

Nesting Bulleted Lists 53

Creating Numbered Lists 54

Mixing Lists 55

Creating Definition Lists 56

Creating Hypertext Links 57

Anatomy of the A (Anchor) Tag 58

Linking to Another File 59

Linking to a Place in the Same HTML File 60

Linking to a Place in Another HTML File 64

Creating Link Lists 65

Creating a Simple Link List 65

Adding Descriptions to Your Link List 66

Using Inline Images 67

Providing Alternative Text 68

Specifying the Width and Height of Images 69

Vertically Aligning Inline Images 70

Using Horizontal Rules 71

Changing the Size and Width of a Horizontal Rule 72

Turning the Shading Off 72

Signing Your Work 73

Centering Your Address Block 74

Other Things Your Can Include in Your Address Block 76

Saving Your Work 76

Wrapping Up 76

SATURDAY AFTERNOON
Dressing Up Your Pages 77

What Your Need 80

Using the Starting Template 81

Saving Your HTML File 82

Using a Banner Image 82
Horizontally Aligning Images 85
Using Graphic Rules 85
    Resizing a Graphic Rule 86
Flowing Text around Images 87
    Flowing Text between Images 89
    Adding Horizontal Spacing 90
    Flowing an Image between Two Other Images 91
    Creating a Drop-Cap Effect 92
Working with Image Links 93
    Using an Image Link by Itself 93
    Controlling the Image Link Border 94
    Creating Navigational Icons 95
    Creating Thumbnail Image Links 95
Creating Custom Lists 98
    Creating Custom Bulleted Lists 98
    Creating a Multi-Level Outline 99
    Inserting Paragraphs 101
Take a Break 102
Creating Icon Link Lists 102
    Creating Indented Icon Link Lists 104
Changing Font Sizes 106
    Setting Absolute Font Sizes 106
    Setting Relative Font Sizes 108
    Setting the Base Font Size 109
Using the BIG and SMALL Tags 110
Changing Font Colors 111
    Setting Font Colors Using the 16 Color Names 111
    Setting Font Colors Using RGB Hex Codes 112
Changing Font Faces 112
Using Background Colors and Images 116
    Using a Background Color 117
    Using a Background Image 119
Adding the Final Touches 121
    Changing the Font Color and Face of Your Level-One Heading . . . 122
    Changing the Font Face of Your Whole Page 123
    Using a Transparent Banner Image 123
    More Things Your Can Do 124
Saving Your Work 125
Wrapping Up 126

SATURDAY EVENING (Bonus Session)
Working with Tables **127**

What You Need 129
Using the Starting Template. 130
Saving Your HTML File 130
Starting Your Table 131
Defining Columns and Rows 131
Adding and Controlling Borders 132
Setting Spacing and Padding 133
Adding Column Headings. 134
Adding a Caption 134
Centering a Table 135
Setting the Table Width 136
Doing More with Your Table 136
Adding Row Headings 137
Horizontal Aligning Cell Contents 138
Setting Column Widths 139
Inserting an Image 140
Vertically Aligning Cell Contents. 140
Spanning Columns 141
Spanning Rows 142
Setting Row Heights 143
Take a Break 144
Controlling Fonts, Colors, and Backgrounds 144
Changing Font Sizes and Colors 145
Assigning Background Colors. 146
Removing Borders and Cell Spacing 148
Using Background Images 149
Controlling Border Colors 152
Creating Icon Link Lists Using Tables 152
Flowing Text and Other Elements around Tables 154
Flowing Text around a Table. 154
Displaying Side-by-Side Tables 155
Adjusting the Horizontal Position of Side-by-Side Tables 156
Saving Your Work 157
Take a Break 157
Creating Two-Column Layouts Using Tables 157
Using a Two-Column Background Image. 158
Setting the Column Width with a Spacer Image 158

Including a Banner Image 160
Adding Vertical Spacing. 160
Creating a Vertical Button Menu 160
Adding the Content to the Right Column 162
Saving Your Work. 164
Wrapping Up 164

SUNDAY MORNING
Working with Frames 165

Pros and Cons of Using Frames 167
What You Need 169
Creating Two-Column and Two-Row Frame Pages 169
Creating a Two-Column Frame Page 170
Creating a Two-Row Frame Page. 178
Take a Break. 182
Creating a Combo Row/Column Frame Page 183
Creating Your Frameset Page 183
Creating the Navigation Bar Page 184
Creating the Other Pages. 184
Checking Out Your Frame Page in Your Browser 184
Creating a Nested Row/Column Frame Page 187
Keeping Things Straight. 187
Creating Your Top-Level Frameset Page 189
Creating Your Top Bar Menu Page 189
Creating the Initial Nested Frameset Page 190
Creating the Content of the Initial Nested Frameset 190
Pages I've Created for You. 191
Checking Out Your Nested Frame Page in Your Browser 192
Using Background Images to Dress Up Your Frame Pages 195
Wrapping Up. 196

SUNDAY AFTERNOON
Working with Forms 197

What Your Need. 199
Creating Mailto and CGI Forms 200
Starting Your Form Page 201
Setting Up the FORM Element 202
Creating Input Controls. 202
Creating Text Boxes 202

Creating Radio Buttons 206
Creating Check Boxes 208
Other Input Controls 209
Creating List Menus 210
Allowing Multiple Selections 211
Creating Text Area Boxes 212
Creating Submit and Reset Buttons 214
Using an Image as a Submit Button 214
Using the BUTTON Tag 215
Take Break 215
Testing Your Form 216
Handling Form Responses 216
Setting the Content Type 217
Using Mailto Form-Processing Utilities 218
Creating CGI Forms 218
Using Your WEB Host's Form-Processing CGI Script 218
Using a Remotely Hosted Form-Processing CGI Script 219
Creating Your Own CGI Scripts 219
Where a Find Form-Processing CGI Scripts 220
Software Programs That Create CGI Scripts 221
Creating Secure Forms 221
Using JavaScript with Forms 222
Wrapping Up 223

SUNDAY EVENING (Bonus Session)
Working with Graphics 225

What You Need 227
Installing Paint Shop Pro 6 228
Running Paint Shop Pro 6 229
Starting Your Image 229
Creating the Banner Text 230
Creating Transparent and Interlaced GIF Images 233
Setting a Transparent Color 234
Saving Your Image as an Interlaced GIF 236
Checking Out Your Image in Your Browser 237
Using Paint Shop Pro's Undo Feature 238
Using Fill Effect 240
Using Solid Color Fills 241
Using Pattern Fills 242

Using Gradient Fills 245
Take a Break 27
Working with Layers. 247
Creating Drop Shadow Effects 249
Saving Your Image as a Paint Shop Pro 6 Image 251
Creating an Optimized Color Palette. 251
Creating Transparent Drop Shadow. 253
Against a Light Background Image with White
as a Major Color. 253
Against a Non-White Background 254
Take a Break. 259
Creating 3-D Buttons 259
Starting a New Image 259
Filling the Background with a Pattern Fill 260
Applying the Buttonize Effect. 260
Creating a Text Label for Your Button 261
Creating 3-D Text Using the Cutout Effect 262
Adding a Drop Shadow Effect. 263
Placing the Label Text on a Separate Layer 264
Saving Your Image 264
Using Your 3-D Button in a Web Page 265
Optimizing Your Images. 265
Optimizing GIF Images 265
Optimizing JPEG Images 268
Wrapping Up 271

APPENDIX A
HTML Quick Reference **273**
Attribute Legend 273
Document and Head Elements 273
Block Elements 281
Inline and Other Non-Block Elements 291
The FRAMESET Element (4.0) 305
General Attributes 308

APPENDIX B
XHTML/XML Compatibility Guide **311**
Main Differences between XHTML 1.0 and HTML 4.01 312
Guidelines for Making Your HTML Documents XHTML-Friendly 313

APPENDIX C
Non-Keyboard Characters. 315

Reserved Characters. 316
Unused Characters 317
Displayable Characters 318
Unicode Characters 321

APPENDIX D
Using Relative URLs 325

What Is a Relative URL? 326
Benefits of Using Relative URLs. 326
Examples of Using Relative URLs. 327
Linking to a File in the Same Folder 328

APPENDIX E
Using Cascading Style Sheets. 333

The STYLE Element 334
Typing Style Declarations 335
Creating a Simple Style Sheet 335
Adding to Your Style Sheet 340
Finding Out More about Styles. 347

APPENDIX F
Completing Your Wish List 349

Adding Background Sound 350
Adding a Hit Counter 356
Adding a Guestbook. 357
Adding a Message Board. 358
Adding GIF Animations 358
Adding Image Maps 362
Adding a Search Form 265
Adding JavaScript Scripts 366
Adding Java Applets 367
Adding Dynamic HTML Effects 370
Adding Streaming Media 371
Adding Interactive Animations 373

APPENDIX G
Transferring Your Pages to the Web **375**

Finding a Web Host 376
Transferring Your Web Pages to a Server 380
Using WS_FTP LE to Transfer Your Web Page Files 382

APPENDIX H
What's on the CD-ROM **391**

Running the CD-ROM Interface 392
The Prima Tech License 392
The Main Page 393
Installing the Example Files 393
Installing the HTML Templates 394
The Software Programs 395

Glossary **399**

Index **404**

INTRODUCTION

Probably one of the most common questions asked in job interviews these days is "Do you know HTML?" Knowing some HTML is rapidly becoming a requirement not only for computer professionals, but also for anyone who works with a computer and a modem. A friend of mine recently told me about a job ad for an executive secretarial position that listed HTML knowledge as a requirement. Becoming "functionally literate" in HTML is fast becoming one of the keys to future success in all sorts of fields.

Advancing your career is not the only reason to learn HTML. Although for many people just surfing the Web is enough, many others yearn to publish their own Web pages, but just don't know where to start or what is required. The Web is a dynamic two-way medium and the real fun starts when you start becoming a producer, and not just a consumer, of Web content. The door is open to anyone to publish their own pages on the Web, but many just don't know what or where the key is to open that door. That key is HTML.

There are many software tools—various WYSIWYG HTML editors and Web publishing suites—that purport to allow you to create your own Web pages without having to learn HTML. However, it would probably take you longer to learn to use one of those tools than it would take you to just learn HTML in the first place.

If you know HTML, you don't need any special software tools—all you need is a text editor, such as Windows Notepad, a browser, and an FTP program to transfer your Web page files. You also don't have to fork out extra bucks every year or so to upgrade your software, because you either already have what you need or it is available for free on the Web.

Even if you do decide to use a software tool to create your own HTML files, already knowing HTML helps you to maximize your results. And if something goes wrong (which it will!), you'll know how to look "under the hood" and fix it yourself. Learning HTML is essential when you're serious about publishing your own Web pages.

This book uses a graduated fast-track approach that cuts down the task of learning HTML into manageable bite-size chunks. This book is dedicated to the proposition that learning HTML should be a fun and exciting experience!

Who Should Read This Book

One assumption this book makes is that you have interests that complement your computer skills. The computer is a tool that enables people to do stuff, not an end in itself. So, also, should the Web and HTML be this way. The Web, via HTML, should serve as an extension of your interests and purposes. What tends to get in the way is that many people think they need to know more than is necessary. Don't make the mistake of thinking HTML is only for computer professionals and programmers. HTML is for everyone!

Also, HTML isn't something you learn first and do later. It's more like riding a bicycle, because you'll learn by doing. Don't worry about making mistakes. Mistakes are just experimental results by another name. Play around with it, experiment, and try new and different things. That's the only way you're going to truly learn.

Although this book and CD-ROM are optimized for Windows, users of other platforms should also be able to use this book to learn HTML. If you're not using Windows, look for notes in the text that'll direct you to what you need to do to get set up and running.

NOTE If you're using a Macintosh, I've got a Mac-specific version of this book available, *Learn HTML On the Mac In a Weekend*, also from Prima Tech. You can find out more about it at **www.callihan.com/learnmac/**.

What You Can Do in a Weekend

You might look at this book and wonder, "How can I possibly do all that in a weekend?" Although a surprising number of my readers have managed to soak up everything I've thrown at them in a single weekend, I don't expect that everybody will complete everything in this book in a single weekend. The book includes many bonus or optional sessions and sections that you need to do over your first weekend only if you have the time and energy. In fact, one session, Saturday Morning, covers *everything* you need to know about HTML to be able to start creating your own Web pages right away. Feel free to take all day, or all weekend, to do just that session. Everything else, in other words, is frosting on the cake.

Exactly how much you'll be able to complete this weekend depends on your learning style, the time you put in, and the effort you put forth. Regardless, by just putting in the minimum effort and time required, by the end of the weekend you should be able to say with confidence, "I know HTML!"

A basic understanding of HTML is all that's required to create many of the Web pages you've visited while surfing the Web. The point is that you don't need to know a lot about HTML to get started actually using it. In other words, you don't need to know *everything* first! The more you learn, of course, the more you'll be able to do, and the more sophisticated the Web pages you create can be.

What You Need to Begin

Besides a computer, you need only three things to learn HTML and start publishing your own Web pages: a text editor, a Web browser, and an FTP program. If you want to create your own Web art images, you also need an image editor capable of creating GIF and JPEG format images.

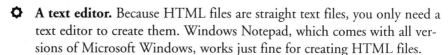

- ✿ **A text editor.** Because HTML files are straight text files, you only need a text editor to create them. Windows Notepad, which comes with all versions of Microsoft Windows, works just fine for creating HTML files.

- ✿ **A Web browser.** Just about any graphical browser installed on your system should be suitable for doing the Saturday Morning tutorial on the basics of HTML. I've also included some Web browsers on the CD-ROM that you can use. For the other tutorials, I recommend using either Netscape Navigator 4 (or higher) or Internet Explorer 4 (or higher).

- ✿ **An FTP program.** You use an FTP program to transfer your Web page files to your site's server on the Web. I've included a number of FTP programs on this book's CD-ROM. See Appendix G, "Transferring Your Pages to the Web," for tips on finding the right Web host for your pages, as well as a tutorial on using WS_FTP LE, an FTP program that's included on the CD-ROM, to upload your files to your site's folders on the Web.

- ✿ **An image editor.** If you want to create your own custom Web art images to dress up your pages, you'll need an image editor. Several shareware and trialware image-editing software tools are included on the CD-ROM. The Sunday Evening session features a tutorial using Paint Shop Pro 6 (an evaluation version is included on the CD-ROM) to create Web art special effects.

• •

NOTE Because many of the programs included on the CD-ROM, such as Paint Shop Pro 6, have evaluation periods during which you can try them, you should wait to install them until you're ready to use them. For instance, to maximize the amount of time you have to try Paint Shop Pro 6, don't install it until you're ready to start the Sunday Evening session, "Working with Graphics."

• •

Readers of all levels of experience, from total beginners to computer professionals, have used my books in the past to learn HTML and create their own Web pages. Although some degree of prior computer experience and a working knowledge of basic Windows operations, as well as some familiarity with using a Web browser, are helpful and will make your learning curve a little less steep, even a complete computer dunce can, with a modicum of patience and persistence, learn everything needed to start creating Web pages—in a weekend!

NOTE All the example files used in this book are included on the CD-ROM. See the start of the Saturday Morning session, "Learning the Basics," for instructions on installing these files from the CD-ROM to your computer's hard drive.

What This Book Covers

This book breaks down the process of learning HTML into easily achievable modules:

- **"Learning the Basics"** covers everything you need to know about HTML to start creating your own effective Web pages right away, including adding headings, text highlighting, lists, links, link lists, inline images, image links, horizontal rules, and more.

- **"Dressing Up Your Pages"** covers adding wrapping text, banner images, graphic rules, font size and face changes, colors, background images, icon link lists, and other design features to your Web pages.

- **"Working with Tables"** covers everything you need to know to start working with tables in your pages, including defining rows and columns, controlling borders, adding column and row headings, aligning cell contents, spanning rows and columns, setting background colors and images, and more.

- **"Working with Frames"** covers everything you need to know to start creating your own "framed" Web sites, including creating two-column, two-row, combination row/column, and nested row/column framed Web sites.

- **"Working with Forms"** covers everything you need to know to start using client-side forms in your Web pages, including adding text boxes, radio button lists, check boxes, drop-down lists, comment boxes, Submit and Reset buttons, and more.

- **"Working with Graphics"** covers everything you need to know to start creating your own Web art images, including creating special effects in Paint Shop Pro 6 (transparency, drop shadows, gradient fills, and so on), creating GIF animations in GIF Construction Set, and creating image maps in Mapedit.

To learn enough HTML to start creating your own Web pages, it is only necessary for you to complete the Saturday Morning session, "Learning the Basics," this weekend. In that sense, everything else is optional! Feel free, in other words, to try to follow the schedule that's laid down, but don't get frustrated if doing a particular session takes longer than the time allowed. If doing the Saturday Morning session takes all Saturday to do, just do the Saturday Afternoon session on Sunday. Any sessions you don't manage to complete this weekend can be saved for another weekend.

After you've completed all the sessions scheduled for this weekend, you'll find additional material in the appendixes that you can read when you have the time:

- Appendix A, **"HTML Quick Reference,"** organizes and describes all the tags and attributes included in HTML 4.01 in an easily accessible A-to-Z format.

- Appendix B, **"XHTML/XML Compatibility Guide,"** covers everything you need to know to make your pages forward compatible with the newest Web publishing standards, XHTML and XML.

- Appendix C, **"Non-Keyboard Characters,"** covers inserting non-keyboard characters in your Web pages from both the ISO 8859-1 and Unicode character sets.

- Appendix D, **"Using Relative URLs,"** provides a rundown on using relative URLs to link to pages and images within a multi-folder Web site.

- Appendix E, **"Using Cascading Style Sheets,"** introduces you to using style sheets to control the appearance and layout of your Web pages.

- Appendix F, **"Completing Your Wish List,"** covers adding various "wish list" features, such as background sounds, hit counters, guestbooks, JavaScript roll-over buttons, streaming media, Java applets, and interactive animations.

- Appendix G, **"Transferring Your Pages to the Web,"** covers using an FTP program, WS_FTP LE, to transfer your pages to the Web.

- Appendix H, **"What's on the CD-ROM,"** covers how to use the CD-ROM, as well as details on what's on the CD-ROM, including example files, HTML templates, Web art collections, and a broad selection of freeware, shareware, and trialware software programs.

You'll also find a convenient glossary of Web publishing terms and definitions at the back of this book.

What's New in the 3rd Edition

Although the responses to the previous editions of *Learn HTML In a Weekend* have been very positive, there's always room for improvement. The 3rd Edition has been thoroughly updated and revised, reflecting many of the suggestions and responses I've received from readers of the previous editions. Here are some of the improvements to this edition:

- All the Saturday HTML tutorial sessions have been reorganized and updated, using all new code and graphics examples.

- The Sunday Morning and Afternoon sessions, covering using frames and forms, have been redesigned as straight HTML tutorials, replacing the "software" tutorials (using software utilities from the CD-ROM) that were included in the previous editions.

- The Sunday Evening session, covering creating graphics for your Web pages, has been thoroughly updated and now features Paint Shop Pro 6. You'll also find tips for using Adobe Photoshop LE, as well as updated tutorials on creating GIF animations and image maps.

- The HTML quick reference appendix has been thoroughly updated to reflect the latest standard, HTML 4.01. Code examples have been added to make it easier to see how particular elements and attributes are used.

- The appendix covering adding non-keyboard characters to your Web pages now also covers inserting Unicode characters.

- An XHTML/XML compatibility guide has been added to the appendixes. It covers how to write your HTML code so it is forward compatible with the latest XHTML and XML Web publishing standards.

- Coverage of using style sheets in your Web pages has been expanded and consolidated in its own appendix.

- Coverage on how to add many much-requested features to your Web pages, including background sounds, hit counters, guestbooks, roll-over buttons, streaming media, Java applets, and interactive animations has been added to the appendixes.

- A tutorial for using WS_FTP LE, an FTP program included on the CD-ROM that transfers your HTML files to the Web, has been added to the appendixes.

- The CD-ROM has been updated with the most recent versions of freeware, shareware, and trialware Web publishing, graphics, and multimedia software utilities.

- All the HTML templates included on the CD-ROM have been thoroughly updated and improved.

Special Features of This Book

This book uses a number of icons and typographical conventions to make your job easier as you work through the sessions. They're used to highlight and call your attention to notes, tips, cautions, buzzwords, additional resources located on the Web, and programs or other resources included on the CD-ROM. Here are some examples of what you'll see.

 NOTE *Notes* are food for thought as you work through the tutorials. They bring up points of interest and other relevant information you might find useful as you develop your abilities with Web publishing and HTML.

 TIP *Tips* offer helpful hints, tricks, and ideas to apply as you progress in the learning process.

 **CAUTION** *Cautions* warn you of possible hazards and point out pitfalls that typically plague beginners.

 BUZZ WORD *Buzzwords* are terms and acronyms that you should keep in mind as you develop and expand your Web publishing skills.

FIND IT ON ▶ THE WEB This icon marks resources or tools located on the Web that might be helpful to you in your Web publishing endeavors.

ON THE
CD This icon marks resources or tools located on the CD-ROM that might be helpful to you in your Web publishing endeavors.

Visit This Book's Web Site

Be sure to visit my Web site for *Learn HTML in a Weekend, 3rd Edition* at **www.callihan.com/learn3/**. You'll find many additional features and resources there that are not included in the book or on the CD-ROM, including the following:

- All the example files and HTML templates included on the CD-ROM can also be downloaded from this book's Web site, in case the CD-ROM becomes damaged or is not available. You'll also find additional downloads available that are not included on the book's CD-ROM, including a collection of Web art images that I'll be periodically updating.

- A collection of Web site promotion tips and tricks, covering using META tag descriptions and keyword lists to snag search engines, announcing your Web site, and submitting your Web site to the major search engines and directories.

- An FAQ (Frequently Asked Questions) page that includes answers to questions that have been frequently asked by readers. If you run into problems, check here first.

- A Readers' Page featuring links to Web sites that have been created by readers of my Web publishing books—a great place to get ideas and inspiration for creating your own pages. When you're ready to show off your own stuff, request to have your page listed too.

- Links to various other support pages I've created, including my Web Hosts site (find a Web host for your pages), Web Links site (find Web publishing resources), and Web Tools site (find Web publishing software tools).

- If you run into any problems that are not addressed in the FAQ (or other resource and support pages), you'll find an e-mail link where you can personally query me, the author.

Are You Ready?

You should now have a good idea what you'll be learning and the tools you'll be using. Although I've scheduled the different sessions included in this book so they can be done over the course of a weekend, that is only a suggestion. You'll find lots of bonus and optional material included, so don't feel that you have to do absolutely everything in a single weekend. Also, feel free to arrange your own schedule if you want—nothing says you can't do one session a day over the course of a week, for instance.

Just start out with the Friday Evening session. It is purely a reading session that provides background information on what HTML is and how it became what it is, so you don't have to set up or install anything to do that session. Just flip to it and start reading!

Getting
Oriented

- ✿ What Is HTML?
- ✿ What Is Hypertext?
- ✿ What Is a Markup Language?
- ✿ Why Learn HTML?
- ✿ Evolution of the HTML Standard
- ✿ What Are XML and XHTML?

It's Friday evening—at least if you're following the schedule. Yes, for the purposes of this book, Friday evening constitutes part of the weekend. Okay, maybe that is fudging a bit, but if you're going to learn HTML in a weekend, I thought you might first want to get oriented—get a look at the of the lay of the land—rather than just jump right into learning how to write HTML code.

What Is HTML?

HTML stands for *HyperText Markup Language*. HTML is a language of codes (called *tags*) used to specify the formatting of text documents for display on the World Wide Web as Web pages. When surfing the Web, every Web page you've visited was created using HTML.

What Is Hypertext?

The term *hypertext* was first coined by Ted Nelson, way back in 1965 when he was a graduate student at Harvard. At that time he conceptualized it simply as "non-sequential writing," the idea being that any object (a word or phrase, an image, the text itself), can be linked to any other object within the "docuverse" (a term also coined by Ted Nelson). The original idea was to create a computer program, called Xanudu by Nelson, that facilitated this non-sequential access to documents, thus enabling readers to easily create their own non-sequential path for learning and understanding a subject. Although he worked on it for many years, Nelson never completed his Xanudu system. Besides coining the term *hypertext*, Nelson also coined the term *hypermedia* to denote dynamically linked media, such as movies in which viewers can choose alternative plot paths, for instance.

The concept of a computer-based hypertext system actually goes back even further, having been first proposed by Vannever Bush in an article, "The Way We Think," in the July 1945 issue of *Atlantic Monthly*. In that article, Bush proposes a system called a *memex* which he described as "a device in which an individual stores all his books, records, and communications, and which is mechanized so that it may be consulted with exceeding speed and flexibility. It is an enlarged intimate supplement to his memory." This system was to operate along the lines of the working of the human mind, which Bush characterized as formed along the lines of an associative "web of trails": "The human mind . . . operates by association. With one item in its grasp, it snaps instantly to the next that is suggested by the association of thoughts, in accordance with some intricate web of trails carried by the cells of the brain."

Although Nelson coined the essential term *hypertext*, several others were contemporaneously working along similar lines. As early as 1985, Xerox developed the NoteCards hypertext-based system. The OWL Guide, another hypertext system, was released in 1986. In 1987, Apple released the Hyper-Card system, invented by Bill Atkinson.

The HyperCard system, originally developed in 1987 and bundled with Apple's Macintosh computers, helped to popularize the notion of non-sequential textual applications that allowed readers to find their own way by choosing which branch or path they wanted to follow. A clone of the Hyper-Card system, Asymmetrix Toolbox, was developed for Microsoft Windows.

The full potential of the idea of hypertext, however, had to await the invention of the World Wide Web (or *the Web*) by Tim Berners-Lee, first proposed by him in 1989 and released in 1991 by CERN *(Conseil European pour la Recherche Nucleaire* or *European Organizaton for Nuclear Research)* in Switzerland. When he first proposed the idea of the Web, he described it as "a wide-area hypermedia information retrieval initiative aiming to give universal access to a large universe of documents." Today, Berners-Lee is more liable to describe the Web as "the universal space of all network-accessible information." It shouldn't pass notice, I think, that these descriptions are relatively exact, if somewhat more wordy, equivalents to Ted Nelson's wonderfully apt term, *docuverse.* It is, of course, no accident that the term *hypermedia*, originally coined by Ted Nelson, is prominently featured in Berners-Lee's initial description of his proposed World Wide Web.

Berners-Lee originally conceived the World Wide Web as a means for scientists and academics to collaborate and share research results over the Internet. It has since evolved way beyond that original conception, becoming rapidly a cybernetic "global village" (a term coined by Marshal McLuhan) within which anyone can actively contribute as a producer of online content, and not just as a passive surfer. With access to the Internet and the Web proliferating, whether through connections at home, work, schools, libraries, or Internet cafes, no one need feel shut off from actively contributing to the Web.

What Is a Markup Language?

The idea of a markup language actually comes from the field of desktop publishing. HTML, at least in its original formulation, was intended as a subset of SGML *(Standardized General Markup Language)*, which is used to mark up computer-based (or "electronic") documents for publishing on a printing press. Similarly, HTML is also used to mark up computer-based documents, but for publishing on the Web.

A markup language works by defining a set of codes (or tags) that are then used to specify the format or function of a particular object or element, be it a section of text, a line, a paragraph, a heading, a list, a table, an image, and so on. A program or application is then required to interpret the markup language and apply the correct formatting. For HTML, this program is a Web browser, which interprets the markup tags in an HTML document (or Web page) and then displays the page in its window.

In addition, HTML includes the capability to code non-sequential links within and between documents, which enables visitors to a Web page to jump from one location to another within a document, to an entirely different document or object, or even to a specific location in a different document, within your own site or anywhere else on the Web. It is this capability that makes HTML a *hypertext* markup language.

Why Learn HTML?

You might be wondering why you need to learn HTML at all. After all, there are many WYSIWYG HTML editing and Web publishing programs (such as Microsoft FrontPage or Macromedia DreamWeaver) that purport to enable you to create your own Web pages without knowing any HTML. Many current word processing and desktop publishing programs also enable you to save a file in HTML format that can then be displayed on the Web. Here are some of the reasons why you might want to learn HTML, rather than just use a WYSIWYG HTML editor, to create HTML documents:

- **Learning HTML can be easier and quicker** than learning all the ins-and-outs of an HTML editor or a Web publishing program. Just because it is an acronym, there is no need to be intimidated by HTML. HTML is not all that terribly difficult to learn. You don't need to be a computer techie to learn HTML. Just about anyone, when willing to put in a minimal amount of time and effort, can learn HTML.

- **Only a code-level familiarity with HTML can assure the creation of compatible and efficient Web pages.** Knowing what's standard and what's not is the key to creating Web pages that are cross compatible with all browsers. Also, in the hands of someone ignorant of HTML, a Web publishing program is much more likely to produce bloated Web pages that are crammed with incompatible and nonstandard *spaghetti* *code.* Using a word processor to save a document in HTML format will likely produce the same inefficient and bandwidth-wasting result.

- **You don't need anything other than a text editor to create your own HTML files.** Windows Notepad is included with Windows, and it is free! Other platforms should also include free text editors. There are also many additional text editors available over the Web that offer extra bells and whistles, such as spell checking and search-and-replace, for instance, either for free or at a small cost. You'll also never have to upgrade a text editor to handle new developments in HTML, because a text editor is a generic tool, rather than a specialized tool (like an HTML editor or Web publishing program).

- **Knowing HTML can help maximize your results even if you later decide to use a Web publishing program.** Even if you eventually decide to use a Web publishing program to create your pages, knowing HTML helps to maximize your Web publishing results. Anyone who wants to get serious about Web publishing *must* have a good understanding of HTML, regardless of the tool they decide to use.

- **If things go wrong with your page, you need to be able to stick your head under the hood to fix it.** Even the best Web publishing program can't guarantee that you'll be able to create trouble-free Web pages. When things go wrong (which they will!), you need to be able to stick your head under the hood and decipher and correct your page's HTML code.

- **Advance your career or impress your friends and family.** Being able to say, "I know HTML!" with confidence can be a big factor in helping to advance your career. Many job positions, and not just computer job positions, now require some knowledge of HTML and Web publishing. At the least, you'll gain a newfound respect from your friends and family.

- **Add to your own sense of personal achievement and reward.** Learning to use HTML to create your own Web pages can be empowering. The Web is the ultimate medium for self-expression—by learning HTML you can start taking advantage of it!

- **Have some fun!** Seeing your own efforts materialize on the Web, especially when you've created everything yourself from scratch, can be a real blast. If you think surfing the Web is a lot of fun, just wait until you start creating your own pages for others to surf!

HTML: The Evolution of a Standard

HTML has come a long way since Tim Berners-Lee first proposed it. In many ways, the development of HTML resembles the layers of an onion because within each further development of the HTML standard, the earlier standards are still largely preserved. Part of the reason for this is the need for *backward-compatibility*, which allows documents produced using earlier versions of HTML to remain fully readable and accessible by means of later versions.

The Initial Versions of HTML

The initial version of HTML was exceedingly simple and lacked many essential features that were added later. Still, it was a fully functional hypertext system with the following main features:

- The capability to specify a title, a hierarchy of headings, and paragraph elements within an HTML document.
- The inclusion of hypertext *anchors* within an HTML document, either defining a jump to another document or object on the Web, or defining both ends of a jump from one location to another location within the same or two different documents.
- The specification of bulleted lists and glossary lists.
- Insertion of non-keyboard character entities.
- The denotation of an included section of text as an *address block,* in which authorship and contact information can be provided.

Because of the limited scope of the initial HTML specification, it didn't take long before *user agents* (Web browsers) began to incorporate unofficial "extensions" to HTML. In 1993, Tim Berners-Lee and Dan Connolly proposed a draft proposal for the standardization of current HTML practice. In 1993, the HTML+ standard was proposed by Dave Raggett as a means for standardizing and proposing further extensions to HTML.

Although neither of these proposals was ratified as a formal standard, they played a crucial role in formulating the elements that were later to become part of both the HTML 2.0 and HTML 3.2 standards.

HTML 2.0

In 1995, Tim Berners-Lee and Dan Connolly proposed the HTML 2.0 standard. Part of the rationale behind the proposal was to standardize "the capabilities of HTML in common use prior to June 1994." As indicated previously, HTML 2.0 incorporated much, although not all, of what had been included in the HTML+ proposal. New features incorporated into HTML 2.0 included the following:

- Elements to hierarchically structure an HTML document (the HTML, HEAD, and BODY elements), which identify it as an HTML document containing separate heading and body elements within it.
- The paragraph element is now treated as a container element (with an implied ending), rather than as a paragraph separator. The capability to insert line breaks is added.
- Bold, italic, and monospace character emphasis.
- The display of inline images.
- Use of horizontal rules for separating sections.
- Use of numbered lists (bulleted, or unnumbered, lists were included in the original version of HTML).
- Other additions such as block quotes, comments, preformatted text, character entity names, and input forms.

Ad Hoc HTML: Netscape and Microsoft Extensions

Both Netscape and Microsoft developed their own special extensions to HTML for use in their browsers. These can be used in any Web document, but they translate into special formatting only when users view the Web page in the particular browser for which they were created (unless the other browser's manufacturer provides support for the extensions, too).

An early example of an unofficial extension to HTML is the IMG tag for displaying inline images, which was first introduced in the Mosaic browser and then later incorporated into the HTML 2.0 standard.

Later, extensions to HTML were also implemented by Netscape in its Navigator browsers and by Microsoft in its Internet Explorer browsers. Many, but not all, of these extensions have been incorporated into later versions of standard HTML (HTML 3.2 and 4.0). Netscape's BLINK tag (causing text to blink) and Microsoft's MARQUEE tag (causing text to scroll horizontally from right to left on a line) are examples of unofficial extensions to HTML that have never been incorporated into any standard version of HTML.

A Failed Initiative: HTML 3.0

HTML 3.0 was proposed as the next standard for HTML following HTML 2.0. However, the ambitiousness of HTML 3.0 ultimately proved its downfall—coming to an agreement on how to implement it simply was impossible. Ultimately, the World Wide Web Consortium (W3C) abandoned HTML 3.0 in favor of a much more modest proposal, HTML 3.2.

NOTE   The World Wide Web Consortium (also known simply as the W3C) is the organization responsible for developing protocols and standards (including HTML) for the Web. It was founded in October 1994 by Tim Berners-Lee, the inventor of the Web, in collaboration with CERN, where the Web originated. You can find out more about the W3C's activities and mission at **www.w3.org/**.

A number of HTML 3.0 features, however, found support in Web browsers—the most notable of which were tables. Other proposed HTML 3.0 elements that gained the favor of Web browsers to one degree or another include superscripts and subscripts, font-size changing (with the BIG and SMALL tags), and underlining. Many tags and attributes that were first proposed as part of HTML 3.0 have since been incorporated into the HTML 3.2 and HTML 4.0 standards.

Take a Break?

If your eyes are starting to droop a bit from all this reading I'm having you do tonight, get up and refocus your eyes, stretch a bit, and get your circulation going again. If you feel you need a picker-upper, feel free to take the time to fix yourself a cup of tea or pour yourself a glass of lemonade (or whatever will perk you up). I'll see you back here in five to ten minutes.

If your eyes are just getting too droopy, feel free to come back and read the rest of this session's material at another time. You don't need to read the remainder of this session's material in order to continue to the next session.

HTML 3.2

HTML 3.2 was released in January 1997. A large part of the HTML 3.2 specification is a rubber-stamping of what originally were Netscape's unofficial and *ad hoc* extensions to HTML. The rest of the HTML 3.2 specification covers features of the previously proposed specification, HTML 3.0, which had already gained wide acceptance and implementation (tables, for instance) in Web browsers. HTML 3.2 offered little that hadn't already been widely implemented in browsers. Here are some of the primary features included in the HTML 3.2 standard:

- Creation of tables.
- Insertion of Java applets.
- Use of background images, as well as definition of background, text, and link colors.
- Specification of font sizes and colors.
- Flowing of text around images.
- Controlling (and turning off) of image borders.
- Specification of the height and width of images (so browsers can allocate space for them and not hold up display of other elements).
- Horizontal alignment (left, center, or right) of paragraphs, headings, and horizontal rules.

- Insertion of superscripts, subscripts, and strikethroughs.
- Specification of document divisions.
- Inclusion of client-side image maps.
- Provisions for style sheets (using the STYLE tag), left otherwise undefined.

HTML 3.2 should be fully supported by all current graphical Web browsers.

HTML 4.0

HTML 4.0 was released in December 1997. Like HTML 3.2, HTML 4.0 is a mix of the old and the new. Included in it are elements that were previously either Netscape or Microsoft extensions (frames and font-face changes), as well as a number of entirely new elements and capabilities. Here are some of HTML 4.0's primary features:

- Frames, including inline frames.
- Cascading style sheets.
- New form elements, including the BUTTON element, which provides for the creation of graphical form buttons.
- New table elements, including the capability to apply formatting to column and row groups.
- New text-markup elements, including elements for making insertions and deletions, striking out text, adding quotations, and adding formatting to a "span" of text.
- The capability to specify font faces for the display of text (formally a Microsoft extension).
- The capability to attach styles and actions to specific elements or a class of elements so that passing the mouse over or clicking on an element, for example, triggers an action executed by a script.

Although current browsers support much of what is included in the HTML 4.0 standard, there are a number of features that have yet to be supported. Some features, such as frames, had already been implemented widely in current browsers, but others, such as the Q tag for formatting inline quotations for instance, have yet to be supported by any browser.

Also, support for style sheets, the most important feature included in the HTML 4.0 standard, is still inconsistent and incomplete in current browsers. The result is that the same style sheet can have radically different results depending on whether it's displayed in Internet Explorer or Navigator, for instance. Style sheets can be used effectively to design Web pages for display in today's Web browsers, but they must be used wisely and with circumspection. (For further information on using style sheets, see Appendix E, "Using Cascading Style Sheets.")

Of course, newer browser versions will undoubtedly more fully support the use of style sheets, as well as other yet to be implemented, or yet to be fully implemented, features included in HTML 4.0.

HTML 4.01

The HTML 4.01 recommendation was released in December 1999. It primarily fixes some bugs and clarifies obscurities in the HTML 4.0 specification. The W3C has no plans currently to continue the development of the HTML standard beyond version 4.01. This might actually be a good thing, in that it should help to stabilize the current feature set (elements and attributes), thus providing browsers with a single stable version of HTML that they can universally support. In the meantime, developments in the area of cascading style sheets, scripting technologies, and dynamic HTML (the Dynamic Object Model, or DOM) should continue to extend the capabilities of HTML for many years to come.

The W3C's future development efforts in the area of markup languages will be primarily focused on the new XML/XHTML standards. For further discussion of the practical impact this might have on Web publishers, see the "Impact on Web Publishers" section later in this session.

NOTE

FIND IT ON ▶
THE WEB

After you have some practical experience working with HTML this weekend, you might want to check out the actual specifications for HTML at the W3C's HTML Web page at **www.w3.org/MarkUp/**. You can find links there to the HTML 4.01, 4.0, 3.2, and 2.0 specifications. Checking out the earlier specifications for HTML can give you an in-depth understanding of why and how HTML has become what it is today.

What Are XML and XHTML?

The W3C has stated that future development efforts in the area of markup languages will be focused on the development of two new standards, XML (Extensible Markup Language) and XHTML (Extensible HyperText Markup Language).

XML 1.0

The XML 1.0 specification was released in February 1998. XML is not strictly a markup language as much as it is a *meta-language* that allows for the further development of other markup languages—XHTML, MathML, and SMIL (Synchronized Multimedia Integration Language) are just three instances of this. Academic groups, for instance, should be able to create and publish their own markup languages for displaying academic and scientific papers and articles, including footnotes, citations, bibliographies, figure captions, and so on. In conjunction with XML, the W3C has also developed XSL (Extensible Stylesheet Language).

The promised benefits of XML are several. Primarily they fall into two areas:

✪ Allowing a single document to be tagged for multiple presentations. For instance, the same document can be displayed in a Web browser, printed on a printing press, printed on a laser printer, displayed on a wireless communication device, presented through a Braille browser, spoken through a speech browser, and so on. Organizations and businesses will conceivably no longer have to maintain multiple instances of the same document, one for the Web, one for hard copy publishing, and so on.

✪ The capability to extend access to many more data formats than are currently available through straight HTML. Conceivably, any interested group can create its own markup language, publish an SGML-conforming DTD (Document Type Definition) on the Web, and then have it instantly recognized by any XML-compatible Web browser. The phrase "the decentralization of HTML" has been used to describe this capability of XML.

XHTML 1.0

XHTML (Extensible HyperText Markup Language) is intended as a version of HTML that has been brought entirely into conformance with XML (and thus with SGML), as opposed to the "Wild West" variant that has finally evolved into HTML 4. The recommendation for XHTML 1.0 was released in January 2000.

Impact on Web Publishers

Ultimately, the proof in the pudding is what's supported by current Web browsers. Right now, current browsers haven't even supported everything included in HTML 4.01, let alone in XHTML 1.0. There is no guarantee that future browsers will ultimately support everything that's included in the new XHTML/XML standards.

The W3C has committed itself to maintaining the character of HTML as a "language that the ordinary person can use" and its accessibility to individuals who "still find value in writing their own HTML from scratch." You should be assured, in other words, that your documents written in HTML will continue to be compatible with future browsers. HTML will likely remain the markup language of choice for individual Web publishers, especially for those who want to exercise the ultimate control of writing their own code. XHTML, on the other hand, is more likely to appeal to corporate users who need a more "industrial strength" solution for distributing not just documents, but interactive data and media, over the Web.

With millions of HTML documents currently residing on the Web, there is little possibility that Web browsers will ever drop support for HTML. Also, the capabilities of HTML, through the development of cascading style sheets and the Dynamic Object Model (DOM), will continue to evolve and change. These developments alone will ensure that the capabilities of HTML will continue to evolve for many years. It is unlikely that any new HTML tags or attributes will be added any time soon, which might not be such a bad thing.

Understandably, most Web publishers will be resistant to recoding HTML documents that have already been created and published to the Web, simply to be in conformance to XHTML and XML—especially when the recoding will have little or no real impact on how those documents are displayed in current or even future Web browsers. Appendix B, "XHTML/XML Compatibility Guide," provides some simple guidelines on how you can insure that your HTML documents will be forward-compatible with XHTML and XML.

FIND IT ON ▶
THE WEB To find out more about XHTML and XML, see **www.w3.org/TR/xhtml1/** and **www.w3.org/XML/**.

Other HTML Developments

There's much more going on in the HTML area than just XML and XHTML. Here are some of the current initiatives afoot to expand and extend HTML:

- ✿ **Cascading Style Sheets, levels 1 (CSS1) and 2 (CSS2)**—Style sheets conforming to CSS2 enable you to specify fonts on the Web that can be downloaded with a Web page, create rectangular regions containing other elements that can overlap and be positioned anywhere on a Web page, and define multiple style sheets for a single Web page that can be used by different media types (such as speech synthesizers, Braille printers, handheld devices, and so on).

- ✿ **The Dynamic Object Model (DOM)**—Development and agreements in the area of the DOM are keystones for the full implementation and development of dynamic HTML, allowing the dynamic addressing of any objects in a Web page through scripts or programs. Right now, Netscape and Microsoft are supporting different versions of the DOM and Dynamic HTML, but they have agreed to standardize on the same DOM in their next generation of browsers.

- ✿ **Mathematical Markup Language (MathML)** provides complex formatting capabilities for equations and formulas.

- **Synchronized Multimedia Integration Language (SMIL, pronounced "smile")** provides non-programmers with the ability to create their own multimedia presentations on the Web.

- **Scalable Vector Graphics (SVG)** provides for the inclusion of vector-based scalable graphics in Web pages. SVG graphics are currently supported by Adobe Illustrator 9 and Jasc Software's Trajectory Pro, with others sure to follow.

- **Mobile Access**—A number of proposed specifications are in the works to facilitate the display of Web content on mobile and wireless devices, such as cellular phones and personal digital assistants (PDAs). These include the Wireless Application Protocol (WAP) and various "navigation" markup languages that propose additional HTML tags or attributes to facilitate browsing through mobile communication devices.

- **Voice browsers**—The W3C is currently working on proposals for standardizing interaction with Web sites through spoken commands.

Wrapping Up

You should now have a good understanding of the origin and nature of HTML. If you want to further investigate any of the subjects that were broached in this session, check out any of the Web addresses that I've included.

Tomorrow morning in the Saturday Morning session, "Learning the Basics," you'll be doing a tutorial on the basics of HTML. This tutorial covers everything you need to know to start creating your own Web pages using HTML. Although that session is scheduled for Saturday morning, feel free to take all day, or even all weekend, to do it, if you want.

If you decide to further check out any of the Web addresses provided in this session, don't stay up too late! I've got lots of stuff for you to do starting tomorrow morning, so be sure to get a good night's sleep.

Learning the Basics

- ✪ Anatomy of an HTML Tag
- ✪ Working with Headings, Paragraphs, and Line Breaks
- ✪ Adding Bold, Italic, and Monospaced Text
- ✪ Inserting Non-Keyboard Characters
- ✪ Creating Lists, Hypertext Links, and Link Lists
- ✪ Inserting Inline Images

L ast night you read up on what HTML is, how it became what it is today, and where it's heading in the future. Even if you didn't take the time to read everything included in the Friday Evening session, you should still have a good idea of what HTML is.

NOTE Although this session is scheduled for Saturday morning, feel free to take as much time as you need to complete it. Everyone has a different learning style. Go at your own speed. Feel free to take all day, or even all weekend, to complete this one session. This session covers *everything* you need to know to start using HTML to create your own Web pages, so even if you only complete this one session this weekend, you'll still be able to say, with confidence, "I know HTML!"

What You Need

There are only two minimal requirements in order to complete this morning's session: You need a text editor and a graphical Web browser.

Using a Text Editor to Create HTML Files

You don't need anything special to create HTML files—a plain text editor will do. That's because HTML files are just ordinary text files. Windows Notepad comes free with Windows and works just fine for creating HTML files. Most other operating systems also include free text editors that you can use to create HTML files.

ON THE

CD

You can use any text editor that you want. You'll find an excellent text editor, EditPad Classic, included on the CD-ROM. It lets you open and edit more than one HTML at the same time, without having to run multiple instances of the program, as you have to do with Notepad. It also has a Find and Replace feature,✗ which can be very handy when working with HTML files. EditPad Classic is "postcardware," so you're free to use it for free, but the author requests that you send him a postcard or a used phonecard. If you like EditPad Classic, you might check out EditPad Pro—you can

FIND IT ON ▶
THE WEB

download an evaluation version at **www.editpadpro.com/**. For even more text editors that you can try out, check out my Web Tools site at **www. callihan.com/webtool/**.

✗ This feature also available in Notepad Version 50+ with Windows 2000.

Using a Word Processor

I don't recommend using a word processor, such as Word or WordPad, to create HTML files. You usually can't keep your HTML file open in both your word processor and your Web browser at the same time, which is essential if you want to be able to dynamically preview and debug your HTML code while creating it. Starting out, I also don't recommend that you use an HTML editor, at least until you've gained some familiarity with HTML by directly typing in the codes yourself.

Using a Web Browser to Preview Your Work

In this book's sessions, you'll be using a Web browser to dynamically preview and debug the HTML files you create. For this session, any fairly recent graphical Web browser should work fine. Even if you're still using Internet Explorer 2.0 or Netscape Navigator 1.1 as your browser, you shouldn't need to upgrade your browser just to do this session.

For the other sessions in this book, however, I recommend that you have Internet Explorer 4 (or higher) or Netscape Navigator 4 (or higher) installed, if you want to be able to try all the examples. All the figures shown in this book use Internet Explorer 5.01 or Netscape Navigator 4.73.

> **TIP** By default, Windows hides the file extensions for known file types, showing only the file-type icon to help identify the file type. In this book, I'll be including the file extension for all file names. To turn on display of file extensions in Windows 98, click on Start, select Settings and Folder Options, and click on the View tab. Under Files and Folders, make sure that the check box, "Hide file extensions for known file types," is not checked. In Windows 95, double-click on the My Computer icon on your Desktop, select View and Options, click on the View tab, and make sure the check box, "Hide MS-DOS file extensions for the file types that are registered," is not checked.

Installing the Example Files from the CD-ROM

I've included example files on the CD-ROM that are used in this and in all the other sessions in this book. Windows users can use the CD-ROM interface to install the example files to their hard drives (if you don't have access to the CD-ROM or are a non-Windows user, skip ahead to the following note):

1. Insert the CD-ROM into your CD-ROM drive. If Prima Tech's user interface doesn't automatically run, do the following:

    A. Click on the Start button, and then select Run.

    B. In the Open text box, type **d:\start.htm** (where **d:** is your CD-ROM's drive letter) and click on OK.

2. Read the license agreement and click on I Accept to accept its terms.

3. At the next page, if you're using a 32-bit version of Windows (95/98/NT/2K/Me), click on the "Continued to the Main page" link. (If you're not using a 32-bit version of Windows, click the "Read the nowindow.txt file" link to get instructions on how to install the example files on your computer.)

4. In the CD-ROM interface's Main page, click on the Examples option in the sidebar.

5. Click on the link, "Click Here to Install the Example Files to Your Hard Drive."

If Internet Explorer 5 is your default browser, follow these steps:

1. In the File Download window, select the radio button, "Run this program from its current location." Click on OK.

2. At the Security Warning window, telling you that the Authenticode signature is not found, just click on the Yes button (the self-extracting *.exe file was created by me, in case you're wondering). (Earlier versions of Internet Explorer also provide a security warning, although a different one. For those versions, just click on the Open button.)

If Netscape Navigator 4 is your default browser, follow these steps:

1. In the Save As window, click on the Save button to save examples.exe to your My Documents folder.

2. Click on the Start button, select the Run option, and then in the Open box, type **C:\My Documents\examples.exe**. Click on OK.

For both browsers:

1. At the WinZip Self-Extractor window, click on the Unzip button to install the example files to an Html folder on your C drive (C:\Html). (If you want to install these files to a different drive or folder, just edit the "Unzip to folder" box.)

2. After the files have been unzipped, just click on the OK button, and then click on the Close button. To close the CD-ROM interface, just select File and Close.

If you installed the example files to the default drive and folder, you'll find them in an Html folder on your C drive (C:\Html).

NOTE If you don't have a CD-ROM drive or don't have access to this book's CD-ROM, you can download the example files from this book's Web site at **www.callihan.com/learn3/**.

Anatomy of an HTML Tag

In HTML, a *tag* is a code that defines an element (such as a heading, a paragraph, a list item, and so on) within an HTML file. A related term, *tag element*, refers not just to the HTML code involved, but also to the text or other elements that are enclosed within the tag.

There are two kinds of tags: *containers*, which bracket or contain text or other tag elements, and *empty tags*, which stand alone (sometimes referred to as *stand-alone tags*). A container tag actually consists of two codes, a start tag and an end tag, which bracket the text or other elements they affect. An empty tag functions as a single stand-alone element within an HTML document, and thus doesn't bracket or contain anything else.

HTML tags can also be distinguished in two additional fashions: as being either *block elements* or *inline elements*. A block element defines a separate "block" in an HTML document, with vertical spacing added above and below it. An inline element is displayed *inline*—that is, "in a line"—no vertical spacing is added above or below an inline element to separate it from other elements.

HTML tags are inserted into a document between less than (<) and greater than (>) symbols (also referred to as left or right angle brackets). For instance, a start tag of a container tag or an empty tag element looks like this:

```
<tagname>
```

To distinguish a container tag's end tag from its start tag, a forward slash (/) is inserted at the beginning of the end tag:

```
</tagname>
```

To mark a section of text with a certain tag, you bracket it inside a start tag and an end tag. For instance, text contained in a level-one heading tag looks like this, where `<h1>` is the start tag and `</h1>` is the end tag:

```
<h1>This is a Level-One Heading</h1>
```

Whenever I refer to "a level-one heading tag," for instance, I'm referring to both the start and end tags. When I want to specifically refer to a start tag or an end tag, I refer to "the start tag" or "the end tag." Note, however, that a few tags look like empty tags, but are actually container tags that have *implied* end tags (I'll let you know which ones when you get to them, in today's HTML sessions).

Tag Attributes

Attributes enable you to specify how Web browsers treat a particular tag. An attribute is included within the actual tag (between the left and right angle brackets), either within a start tag or an empty (stand-alone) tag. End tags can't contain attributes. Most of the tags covered in this tutorial don't use attributes, but you'll use them to include images or hypertext links in a Web page toward the end of this tutorial.

Most attributes are combined with a value to enable you to specify different options for how a Web browser treats the attribute. Here's the format for including an attribute value in a tag:

```
attribute="value"
```

For instance, to specify that the middle of an image be aligned with the line of text it is on, you include the following attribute value inside the IMG (Image) tag:

```
align="middle"
```

NOTE   Tag names and attributes in HTML are case-insensitive, so you can type them in either lowercase or uppercase. XHTML 1.0, the new XML version of HTML, however, requires that all tag names and attributes be typed in all lowercase. In this book, all tag names and attributes in the code examples are presented in all lowercase.

In HTML, the placing of quotes around attribute values is often optional, but XHTML requires that all attribute values be quoted. In this book, all attribute values are quoted.

For other things you can do to help ensure that your HTML files are future-compatible with XHTML, see Appendix B, "XHTML/XML Compatibility Guide."

Don't Overlap HTML Tags

You should always *nest* HTML tags, and never overlap them. For instance, always do this:

```
<b><i>Always nest tags inside each other.</i></b>
```

Notice that the `<i>...</i>` pair is nested within the `<b>...</b>` pair. Never overlap tags so that the outer one ends before the inner one:

```
<b><i>Don't overlap tags like this.</b></i>
```

HTML operates in a hierarchical, top-down manner. A tag element can have other tag elements nested in it or be nested within other tag elements. If you overlap two tags, a browser can't tell what falls inside of what, and the browser might not be able to display your page correctly, or at all. Be kind to your browser and to your potential visitors: don't overlap tag elements.

 The model that this tutorial employs resembles a "scratch pad" approach. Think of your text editor as a scratch pad. As you do this morning's session, enter the example tags and text as though you were jotting them down on a scratch pad; in other words, you don't have to clean the slate each time you move on to a new section. Just move on down the page, leaving everything you have already done in place. Doing so also leaves you with a sample file that you can return to and reference later.

Saving Your HTML File

To get started, you need to run your text editor and then save your file. Starting out, I recommend that you use Windows Notepad. (If you're not using Windows, use whatever text editor is available on your system.) To run Windows Notepad and start your scratch pad HTML file, just do the following:

1. Run Windows Notepad: click on the Start button and select Programs, Accessories, and Notepad.

 For a shortcut to run Notepad, just click on the Start button, select Run, type **notepad**, and then press the Enter key.

2. Save your file as **scratch.html** in the same folder (C:\Html) where you installed the example files earlier. If you don't know how to do this, just follow these steps:

A. In Windows Notepad, select File, Save As.

B. In the Save As dialog box, click on the Save in list box, and then click on the C drive icon [C:].

C. In the folder window, scroll over (if necessary) and double-click on the Html folder.

D. Type **scratch.html** in the File name box and then click on the Save button.

NOTE   You can save HTML files using either an .html or an .htm extension. (The latter originates from MS-DOS and Windows 3.1 systems being restricted to using eight-character file names with a three-character extension.)

SOME CONVENTIONS

In this book, I present numerous HTML code examples that you can type into your text editor as examples. I use the following formatting conventions to help you interpret these examples:

- ✿ Example code or text that is `bold` and `monospaced` should be typed by you into your "scratch pad" HTML file.

- ✿ Example code or text that is `monospaced` should not be typed by you—it indicates either text that you've already typed or text that is presented for example purposes only.

- ✿ Example text that is *`italicized`* and *`monospaced`* should not be typed as is, but represents placeholder text. *`Your Name`*, for instance, indicates that your actual name should be typed.

◆◆◆◆◆◆◆◆◆◆◆◆◆◆◆◆◆◆◆◆◆◆◆◆◆◆◆◆◆◆◆◆◆◆◆◆◆

CAUTION In order for the example graphics to show up when you preview your scratch pad HTML file in your browser, you must save scratch.html in the same folder where you installed the example files (in C:\Html, unless you installed the example files in another location).

◆◆◆◆◆◆◆◆◆◆◆◆◆◆◆◆◆◆◆◆◆◆◆◆◆◆◆◆◆◆◆◆◆◆◆◆◆◆

Turning Word Wrap On in Notepad

By default, Word Wrap is turned off in Notepad. To turn Word Wrap on, just select Edit, Word Wrap (after Word Wrap is turned on, the Word Wrap option will be checked). With Windows 95, you have to do this every time you run Notepad. In Windows 98, Word Wrap will remain on until you turn it off. *In Windows 2000 this is in the 'format' menu.*

Starting Your HTML File

Whenever you start a new HTML file, begin by including these tags:

- ✪ The HTML tag
- ✪ The HEAD tag
- ✪ The TITLE tag
- ✪ The BODY tag

The following sections provide examples of using each of these tags.

The HTML Tag

Recall that a tag defines a structural element within an HTML document. The HTML tag defines the topmost element, the HTML document itself, thus identifying it as an HTML document rather than some other kind of document. The HTML tag is a container tag that has a start and end tag, and all other text and tags are nested within it.

In your scratch pad file in Notepad, type the start and end HTML tags, placing a single hard return between them, like this:

```
<html>
</html>
```

NOTE   Remember that the HTML start tag (`<html>`) must remain at the very top of your file, and the HTML end tag (`</html>`) must remain at the very bottom of your file. Everything else must fall between these two tags.

The HEAD Tag

The HEAD tag contains information about your HTML file. It also can contain other tags that help identify your HTML file to the outside world. The HEAD tag is nested within the HTML tag. Type the HEAD tag inside the HTML tag now, as follows:

```
<html>
<head>
</head>
</html>
```

There is only one tag that must be contained within the HEAD tag: the TITLE tag. Other tags also can be contained within the HEAD tag, but of these, only the META, BASE, and LINK tags are particularly useful.

NOTE   See Appendix A, "HTML Quick Reference," for descriptions of the META, BASE, and LINK tags. You'll also find a link on this book's Web site (**www.callihan.com/learn3/**) to a page of Web site promotion tips and tricks that also includes coverage of the META tag.

The TITLE Tag

The TITLE tag is nested inside the HEAD tag and is used to specify the title of your page. Although the content of your title is not displayed as part of

your page, it is displayed in a browser's title bar. The TITLE tag is officially a required element that should be included in any HTML file. No browser I know of will refuse to display a page if a title is missing, but you should *always* include a title in your HTML files.

Your title also identifies your page to the rest of the world. For instance, many directories and search engines, such as Yahoo!, AltaVista, and WebCrawler, display your title as the link to your page. Think of your title as your welcome mat—it is the first thing a prospective visitor to your page is likely to see. For this session, however, don't spend time trying to think up a title—just enter the dummy title included in the example:

```
<html>
<head>
<title>Your Title: Describe Your Title</title>
</head>
```

The BODY Tag

The BODY tag is the complement of the HEAD tag and contains all the tags, or elements, that a browser actually displays as the body of your HTML document. Both the HEAD tag and the BODY tag are nested inside the HTML tag. Note, however, that the BODY tag comes after the HEAD tag; they denote separate parts of the HTML document.

Type the BODY tag following the HEAD tag, but inside the HTML tag, as follows:

```
<html>
<head>
<title>Your Title: Describe Your Title</title>
</head>
<body>
</body>
</html>
```

You have started your HTML file. All HTML files begin the same way; only the titles are different.

Don't bother trying to check this out in your browser yet. All you'll see is a blank page, but with the title displayed on the browser's title bar (as shown in Figure 2.1). A little later on, after you've added some example codes and text to your HTML file that will appear in a browser window, I'll show you how to open and preview your page in your browser.

Using a Starting Template

Because all HTML files start the same, with only the title being different, you can save your HTML file as it stands now as a starting template for creating future HTML files. That way, you don't have to retype the same stuff every time you start a new HTML file. To save you the trouble of saving a starting template, I've already saved it for you—you'll find it as start.html in the example files (in C:\Html, if that's where you've installed the example files). In the future, when starting a new HTML file, just open the starting template in your text editor and then resave with a new name.

Title

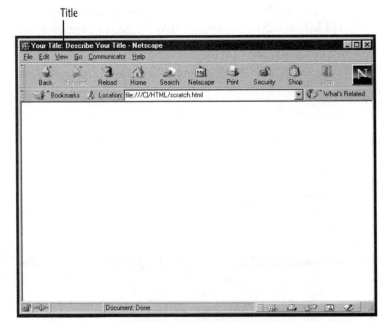

Figure 2.1

When an HTML file with only a TITLE element is loaded into a Web browser, the title is displayed on the title bar, but otherwise you see a blank page.

Working with Headings, Paragraphs, and Line Breaks

The tags for creating headings and paragraphs are probably the most commonly used HTML tags. Think of them as the basic building blocks of any Web page. In this section, I also cover using line breaks to break up your paragraphs or headings into separate lines.

Using Headings to Structure Your Page

You use headings to organize your Web page into hierarchical levels. The top-level heading (denoted by the H1 tag) is the title that's displayed at the top of your Web page. (Don't confuse this with the title that appears in the browser's title bar, which you just set up using the TITLE tag.) Because the H1 tag functions as the title (or top-level heading) for a Web page, each Web page should have only one H1 tag.

You use a second-level heading (denoted by the H2 tag) to define a major division in your page, and a third-level heading (using the H3 tag) to define a sublevel division within a major division. Within the BODY element that you typed earlier, type the six heading-level tags, like this (see Figure 2.2):

```
<body>
<h1>This is a top-level heading</h1>
<h2>This is a second-level heading</h2>
<h3>This is a third-level heading</h3>
<h4>This is a fourth-level heading</h4>
<h5>This is a fifth-level heading</h5>
<h6>This is a sixth-level heading</h6>
</body>
```

As a practical matter, you probably will seldom use more than four heading levels. Displayed in a browser, different heading levels appear as different font sizes, from large to small.

OPENING YOUR HTML FILE IN YOUR BROWSER

If you don't know how to open your HTML file in your browser, just follow these instructions to do so:

1. In your text editor, save your current changes to scratch.html. In Notepad, select File, Save (pressing Ctrl+S does not work in Notepad). *→ Does in Windows 2000.*

2. Run your Web browser. If prompted to connect to the Internet, or if your dialer starts to connect, click on the Cancel or the Work Offline button (depending on which is displayed).

3. In Netscape Navigator 4, if prompted that "Netscape is unable to locate the server..." (or something similar), just click on OK. (That just means that Navigator can't open your start page, because you're not connected to the Web.) When unable to display your starting page, Internet Explorer 5 displays a page with the heading, "Web page unavailable offline."

4. Open your page in your browser. In Netscape Navigator 4, select File, Open Page, and click on the Choose File button. In Internet Explorer 5, select File, Open, and click on the Browse button.

5. Go to C:\Html and double-click on scratch.html to open it. To do this, click on the "Look in" box and then on the C drive icon (C:), double-click on the Html folder, and then double-click on scratch.html. In Navigator, make sure the Navigator radio button is selected, and then click on the Open button. In Internet Explorer, just click on OK. Figure 2.2 shows scratch.html opened and displayed in a browser window.

6. After checking out your page in your browser, just leave your page open in your browser, and hop back over to your text editor. (To do this, just hold down the Alt key and tap the Tab key until the Notepad icon is selected, and then release the Alt key.)

You can also open a local HTML file in your browser by dragging the HTML file from Notepad's open dialog box and dropping it on your browser's window.

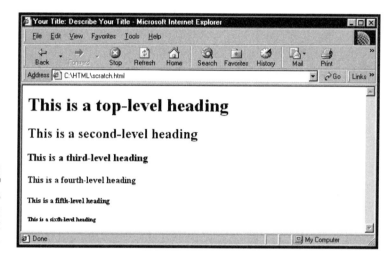

Figure 2.2

Web browsers
display heading
levels in different
font sizes.

 NOTE In order to make the content of the illustrations easier to see, I've resized the width of the browser window to 640 pixels in all the illustrations in this book. There is no need for you to resize your browser window to match—just realize that what you see in your browser might not exactly match what is shown in the illustrations.

Working with Paragraphs

You can't just type text into an HTML document. Everything in an HTML file must be tagged, even ordinary paragraph text. You tag paragraph text using the P (Paragraph) tag. The P tag is a container tag that brackets any regular text paragraphs in your HTML file.

As shown in the following example, insert the example text paragraphs following the first two heading level examples (see Figure 2.3):

```
<h1>This is a top level heading</h2>

<p>Paragraph text adds vertical space above and below. Paragraph
text adds vertical space above and below. Paragraph text adds verti-
cal space above and below.</p>

<h2>This is a second level heading</h2>
```

```
<p>Paragraph text adds vertical space above and below. Paragraph
text adds vertical space above and below. Paragraph text adds verti-
cal space above and below.</p>
```

Nesting Paragraphs

Although in most cases you'll be nesting your paragraphs inside the BODY
tag, you can also nest paragraphs inside of many other block elements,
including block quotes, glossary definitions, list items, and address blocks
(all of which I cover later in this session). You cannot, however, nest a paragraph (or any other block element) within a paragraph.

HOPPING BETWEEN YOUR TEXT EDITOR AND YOUR BROWSER

While doing this and the other HTML sessions in this book, you should frequently hop back and forth between your text editor and your browser to
check out your results in your browser. The following steps assume that
you've already followed the steps in the previous sidebar to open your HTML
file in your browser:

1. After hopping back from your browser using Alt+Tab, make further
   changes to your HTML file and then save it again (select File,
   Save). (Note: Ctrl+S does not work in Notepad.)

2. Use Alt+Tab to hop back over to your browser and refresh the dis-
   play of your page. In Navigator, click on the Reload button; in
   Internet Explorer, click on the Refresh button. (You can also press
   Ctrl+R in either browser to do this.) (See Figure 2.3.)

3. After previewing your HTML file in your browser, hop back over to
   your text editor and make further changes to your HTML file. As
   you go through this and the other HTML sessions in this book,
   repeat these steps frequently to dynamically preview and debug
   your HTML files. (Use the illustrations as prompts to hop over to
   your browser.)

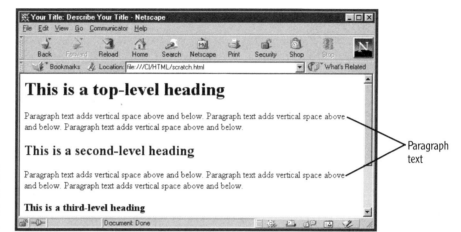

Figure 2.3

The P (Paragraph)
tag is used to tag
paragraph text.

The Question of the P End Tag

In the original version of HTML, the P tag was treated as a stand-alone
element that functioned as a paragraph separator. Later, it was redefined as a
container element, but with an implied ending. HTML 3.2 confirmed this,
continuing to allow the </p> end tag to be omitted, but HTML 4.0
discourages leaving off the end tag. The latest "post-HTML" standards,
XML and XHTML, prohibit leaving off the end tag.

There also are a number of cases where leaving off the P end tag will cause
problems in certain earlier browsers, such as where a list (UL or OL tag) follows a paragraph, for instance. The easiest way to avoid these browser
"quirks" is to always add the P end tag.

Don't Use Multiple P Tags to Add Blank Lines

Generally, a P tag that contains no text has no effect. No browsers that I
know of let you add blank lines by simply adding P tags. To illustrate this
point, following the text paragraph you just typed, add three P tags, followed
by another text paragraph (see Figure 2.4):

```
<p>Paragraph text adds vertical space above and below. Paragraph
text adds vertical space above and below. Paragraph text adds verti-
cal space above and below.</p>

<p></p>
```

```
<p></p>

<p></p>

<p></p>

<p>There are four blank P (Paragraph) tags between this paragraph
and the paragraph above. Multiple blank P (Paragraph) tags should
not be displayed in most browsers, so don't try to use them.</p>
```

Go ahead and hop over to your Web browser to see what this looks like. Multiple P tags, with or without their end tags, should have no effect. Most browsers completely ignore them, as shown in Figure 2.4. Even if some browser out there does display them, you don't want to code your page exclusively for that browser anyway.

Horizontally Aligning Headings and Paragraphs

The ALIGN attribute can be used to center or right-align headings and paragraphs. Just insert `align="center"` to center a heading or paragraph and `align="right"` to right-align a heading or paragraph (see Figure 2.5):

```
<h1 align="center">Top-Level Heading</h2>

<p align="center">Paragraph text adds vertical space above and
below. Paragraph text adds vertical space above and below. Paragraph
text adds vertical space above and below.</p>

<h2 align="right">Second-Level Heading</h2>

<p align="right">Paragraph text adds vertical space above and below.
Paragraph text adds vertical space above and below. Paragraph text
adds vertical space above and below.</p>
```

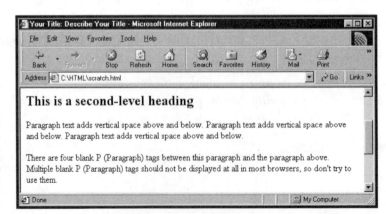

Figure 2.4

Empty P paragraphs should be completely ignored by all browsers.

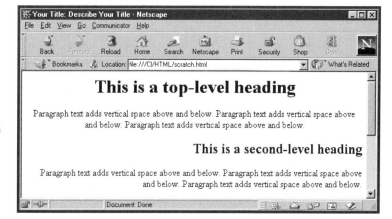

Figure 2.5

The ALIGN attribute lets you center and right-align headings and paragraphs.

The ALIGN attribute started out as a Netscape extension before being incorporated into HTML 3.2. All but the oldest of browsers support it.

Inserting Line Breaks

The BR (Break) tag is an empty, or stand-alone, tag that simply inserts a line break. Following the last heading level example, type three text lines separated by BR tags (see Figure 2.6):

```
<h6>This is a sixth-level heading</h6>
<p>These lines are separated by BR (Break) tags.<br>
These lines are separated by BR (Break) tags.<br>
These lines are separated by BR (Break) tags.</p>
</body>
```

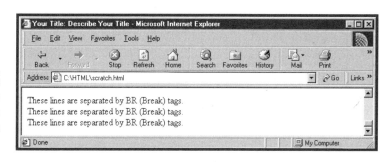

Figure 2.6

Use the BR (Break) tag to insert a line break at the end of a line.

NOTE   You can use the BR tag almost anywhere you have text, not just inside of P tags. You can put them inside an H1 or H2 tag to force a heading to show up on two lines, for instance.

Avoid Using Multiple BR Tags to Add Blank Lines

Although according to the HTML standards, you're not supposed to be able to do it, you can use multiple BR tags to add blank lines to your page. To see what happens when you try this, type a line of text followed by four BR tags:

```
<p>Four BR (Break) tags follow this line.<br>

<br>

<br>

<br>

Four BR (Break) tags precede this line.</p>
```

According to the official HTML specifications, this shouldn't be allowed—multiple BR tags should be treated as a single BR tag, just as is the case with empty paragraph tags. However, Netscape Navigator has always let you get away with this, and the latest versions of Internet Explorer also let you do it, as shown in Figure 2.7.

Because this is non-standard HTML and, despite current browsers supporting it, is not universally supported by older browsers, avoid using multiple BR tags to space down in an HTML file. There is no guarantee that it will be supported in the future.

Figure 2.7

Both Navigator and Internet Explorer display multiple BR tags, but in contravention of the standards for HTML.

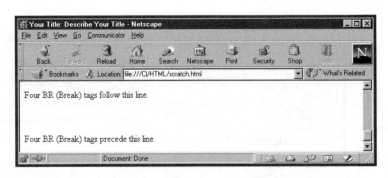

Later in the "Using Preformatted Text" section is a tip that shows you a perfectly legal way of inserting blank vertical spacing in your HTML file.

Spacing, Tabs, and Returns: For Your Eyes Only

In HTML, the tags themselves do all your page's formatting. A browser ignores more than one space inserted into text (two, five, or ten spaces all appear as if they are a single space), as well as all tabs and hard returns (unless they're inside a PRE tag). Any formatting of your HTML file using extra spaces or tabs and returns is *for your eyes only*. So feel free to use all the extra spaces, tabs, and returns you want to make your raw HTML files more readable as you work on them.

Later in the "Inserting Non-Keyboard Characters" section is a tip that shows you how to use nonbreakable space characters to insert blank horizontal spacing in your HTML file.

Highlighting Your Text

Just as in a normal book or report, an HTML document can use text highlighting to clarify the text's meaning. For instance, you can easily bold or italicize text in an HTML file to emphasize particular words or phrases.

Using Italic and Bold Highlighting

HTML has two ways to include italic or bold text on your Web page. The first way involves using "literal" tags: the I (Italic) and B (Bold) tags. The second way is to use "logical" tags: the EM (Emphasis) and STRONG (Strong Emphasis) tags. Most browsers should display the I and EM tags identically, just as they should display the B and STRONG tags identically.

So what's the difference? None, really. The basic philosophy behind HTML is to logically represent the elements of a page rather than literally describe them. The browser can freely interpret the logical elements of an HTML page and display them as it sees fit. Thus, the philosophically correct method is to use logical tags rather than literal tags. On the other hand, in this case the literal tags (I and B) require fewer keystrokes than the logical tags (EM and STRONG), so if you're going to be making liberal use of bold or italic highlighting in a page, the more practical method in this instance, I think anyway, is to use the literal, rather than the logical tags. Either way, you'll get the same result. You can also nest these tags inside of each other to get bold italic text (or emphasized and strongly emphasized text).

As an example of using the I, B, EM, and STRONG tags for text highlighting, type the following lines of text using these tags, as shown here (see Figure 2.8):

```
<p>The tags for <i>italic text</i> and <b>bold text</b> are "liter-
al" tags. The tags for <em>emphazized text</em> and <strong>strongly
emphasized text</strong> are "logical" tags.</p>

<p>You can combine the BOLD and ITALIC tags to get <b><i>bold italic
text</i></b>. You can also combine the EM and STRONG tags to get
<strong><em>emphasized and strongly emphasized
text</em></strong>.</p>
```

Embedding Monospaced Text

You might want to embed monospaced text within a paragraph to, for example, request keyboard input or to represent screen output. A *monospaced font,* also called a fixed-pitch font, is a font in which all the characters occupy the same amount of space on a line. (In a *proportional font,* on the other hand, each character occupies a unique amount of space on a line.) For example, the following line uses a monospaced font:

```
This line uses a monospaced font.
```

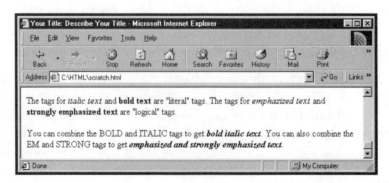

Figure 2.8

You can use literal tags (I and B) or logical tags (EM and STRONG) to italicize or bold text.

The most widely used tag for embedding monospaced text is the TT (Tele-type) tag. It appears as a monospaced font in all Web browsers. You can think of it as a general-purpose monospaced text tag that you can use whenever you want to embed monospaced text within a paragraph. Type the following as an example of using the TT tag (see Figure 2.9):

```
<p>This is regular text. <tt>This is an example of the TT (Teletype
or Typewriter Text) tag.</tt> This is regular text.</p>
```

NOTE To insert monospaced text as a separate text block rather than embedding it inside a paragraph, see the "Using Preformatted Text" section later in this session.

Adding Superscripts and Subscripts

The SUP (Superscript) and SUB (Subscript) tags enable you to add superscripts and subscripts to your HTML document. These tags were originally Netscape extensions and are widely supported by all but the oldest browsers. To try out these tags, type the following example in your scratch pad HTML file (see Figure 2.10):

```
<p>This is regular text. <sup>Use SUP for superscripts.</sup> This
is regular text. <sub>Use SUB for subscripts.</sub> This is regular
text.</p>
```

Figure 2.9

Text tagged with the TT (Teletype) tag is displayed in a monospaced font.

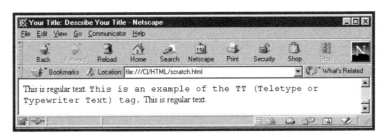

Figure 2.10

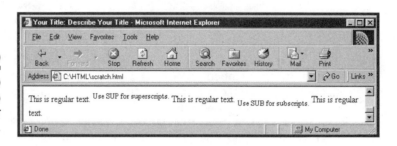

HTML 3.2 and 4.0 enable you to superscript or subscript text.

TIP

In older browsers that don't support the SUP or SUB tags, the results can be less than pleasing. `Hoogles<sup>TM</sup>`, for instance, is displayed as "HooglesTM" in browsers that don't support superscripting. A workaround, although not perfect, is to place parentheses around the superscripted text; `Hoogles<sup>(TM)</sup>`, for instance, is displayed by non-supporting browsers as "Hoogles(TM)."

Other Highlighting Tags

There are other highlighting tags, besides those for bold, italic, and mono-spaced text, that you can use in HTML documents. Of these, only the STRIKE (Strikethrough) and U (Underline) tags are useful at this point. The STRIKE tag draws a line through nested text, whereas the U tag draws an underline under nested text. The U tag, however, is not supported by versions of Netscape Navigator earlier than 4.0, and so most likely should be avoided on that account alone.

The other highlighting tags—the KBD (Keyboard), CODE (Program Code), and SAMP (Sample Text) tags—display in almost all browsers exactly the same way as the TT tag. The CITE (Citation), VAR (Variable), and DFN (Definition) tags all display exactly the same way as the I or EM tags (the DFN tag is only supported by Internet Explorer).

HTML 4.0 has introduced a number of additional text highlighting tags. These include the S (Strike), DEL (Delete), INS (Insert), ABBR (Abbreviation), ACRONYM, and Q (Quote) tags. Of these, the S and DEL tags are supported by only the latest versions of Internet Explorer and Netscape Navigator, but display exactly the same way as the more widely supported

STRIKE tag, whereas the INS tag is supported only by the latest version of Internet Explorer (and displays exactly the same way as the U tag).

For now, your best bet is to stick to using the I or EM tags for adding italic text, the B or STRONG tags for adding bold text, and the TT tag for adding monospaced text. Avoid using the U tag, because earlier versions of Netscape Navigator don't support it. Underlined text on the Web can also be easily confused with hypertext links, which are usually underlined by browsers.

Inserting Non-Keyboard Characters

Not every character that you might want to use is included on the keyboard. For western European languages, the ISO 8859-1 character set (also called the Latin1 character set) defines all the characters that are displayable in a Web browser.

There are two means for inserting a non-keyboard character into a Web page: *numerical entity codes* and *named entity codes*.

A numerical entity code is inserted in the following format (where *number* is the number of the character from the ISO 8859-1 character set):

`&#number;`

A named entity code is inserted in the following format (where *name* is the name of the character from the ISO 8859-1 character set):

`&name;`

In this section, I'm providing some examples of inserting numerical and named entity codes, so you'll know how to insert them. For a full list of all of the allowable numerical and entity names in the ISO 8859-1 character set, see Appendix C, "Non-Keyboard Characters."

◆ ◆

CAUTION Versions of Netscape Navigator earlier than 4.0 only support using the named entity codes for the copyright symbol (`&copy;`), the registered symbol (`&reg;`), and any of the accented characters (`&agrave;`, for instance, for inserting a lowercase *a* with a grave accent). For any other characters, stick to inserting them using their numerical entity codes.

◆ ◆

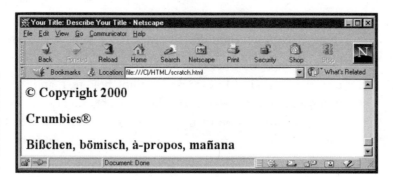

The following example demonstrates inserting several non-keyboard characters, including using both named and numerical entity codes (see Figure 2.11):

```
<h2>&copy; Copyright 2000</h2>

<h2>Crumbies&reg;</h2>

<h2>Bi&#223;chen, b&#246;misch, &agrave;-propos, ma&#ntilde;ana</h2>
```

TIP Other than inserting a totally transparent image, the only way to insert multiple horizontal spaces in your HTML file is to use nonbreakable space characters. You insert these into an HTML file by entering either the numerical or named entity code for the nonbreakable space character: ` `. To simulate a paragraph tab, for example, you insert ` ` three times at the start of a paragraph:

```
   
```

This works in virtually all Web browsers, although some X-Windows Web browsers display nonbreakable spaces as zero-width characters.

Using Reserved Characters

Several keyboard characters are reserved for use as part of HTML codes. These include the <, >, &, and " characters, which are used to parse, or interpret, an HTML document for display. Except for angle brackets, you rarely need to automatically replace these characters with their entity codes:

- Angle brackets (< and >) should always be replaced by their corresponding entity codes when you want to display them "as is" in an HTML file.

- Double quotes (") should only need to be replaced when they're part of an HTML tag that you want to appear "as is" rather than as interpreted by a browser.

- Ampersands (&) signal the beginning of an entity code, but only need to be replaced when they're part of an HTML entity code that you want to appear "as is" rather than as interpreted by a browser. You should never need to replace stand-alone ampersands (an ampersand followed by a space).

For an easy reference, Table 2.1 lists the named entity codes for inserting HTML reserved characters. Because all browsers support these named entity codes, there is no need to show or use the corresponding numerical entity codes for these characters.

Enter the following example to get some practice inserting reserved characters in your HTML document (see Figure 2.12):

```
<h2>This displays the &lt;EM&gt; tag and the &amp;copy; named entity
code in a Web page.</h2>
```

TABLE 2.1 HTML RESERVED CHARACTER ENTITY CODES

Character	Entity	Code
Less Than	<	&lt;
Greater Than	>	&gt;
Ampersand	&	&amp;
Double Quote	"	&quot;

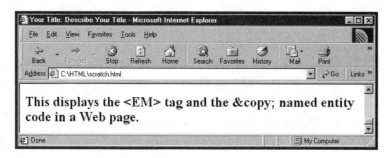

Adding Comments

You can also add comments to annotate your HTML files. The comment tag is a stand-alone tag that enables you to include messages, for future reference, that are not displayed in a Web browser in your HTML files. What is a little confusing about this tag, however, is that no "name" is included in the tag. Instead, a comment always begins with a `<!--` and ends with a `-->`.

Any text inserted between these codes is comment text that a browser completely ignores. Here's an example of the form in which you enter a comment into an HTML file:

```
<!--Put your comment here-->
```

Now, go ahead and type a comment between two lines of text, like this:

```
<p>This line is followed by a comment.</p>
<!--Comments are not displayed by a browser.-->
<p>This line follows a comment.</p>
```

The previous two paragraph lines appear in a Web browser without any additional vertical space between them (other than the space normally added between the two paragraphs). The browser ignores any text inside the comment tag.

Using Block Quotes

The BLOCKQUOTE (Block Quote) tag double-indents a block of text in from both margins. You normally use it to display quotations, as the name

of the tag implies. But you aren't limited to using it for quotations; you can use it to double-indent any block of text.

Type a paragraph of text, followed by a paragraph of text inside a BLOCK-QUOTE tag (see Figure 2.13):

```
<p>In <em>The Theory of the Leisure Class</em>, Thorstein Veblen
points out the degree to which comfort may be sacrificed to taste
in order to maintain a decent level of conspicuous consumption:</p>

<blockquote>

<p>It is true of dress in even a higher degree than of most other
items of consumption, that people will undergo a very considerable
degree of privation in the comforts or the necessaries of life in
order to afford what is considered a decent amount of wasteful
consumption; so that it is by no means an uncommon occurrence, in
an inclement climate, for people to go ill clad in order to appear
well dressed.</p>

</blockquote>
```

To increase the amount of the double-indent, just nest a block quote within a block quote.

Web publishers often use the BLOCKQUOTE tag purely as a formatting device to double-indent sections of a Web page (or even a whole Web page). However, because of inconsistency in how some earlier browsers treat this tag (Internet Explorer 2.0, for instance, still used by lots of surfers, displays block quotes in a bold and italic font), you might want to avoid using a block quote as a formatting device.

Figure 2.13

The BLOCKQUOTE tag is used to double-indent text from the margins.

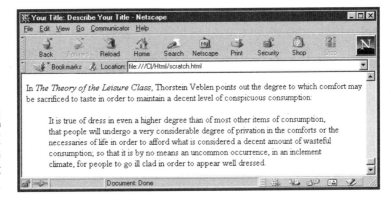

TIP

By using BR (Break) tags to add line breaks at the ends of the line, you can use the BLOCK-QUOTE tag to display indented poetry stanzas or song lyrics. To increase the indentation, just insert the text inside of two nested BLOCKQUOTE tags.

Using Preformatted Text

You use the PRE (Preformatted Text) tag to display text in a monospaced fixed-pitch font. As its name implies, you use the PRE tag to display text as is, including all spaces and hard returns. The primary use for this tag is to display text in a tabular or columnar format—because multiple spaces are displayed as is, instead of being collapsed to a single space, you can use them to vertically align columns in a PRE element.

CAUTION

Always use spaces, not tabs, to align columns when using the PRE tag because different browsers can display tabs in PRE tagged text differently.

Actually, the PRE tag is the original "tables" tag for HTML. Unlike the TABLE tag (part of HTML 3.2 but not HTML 2.0), all Web browsers support it, which is a real advantage. It can be particularly handy for displaying worksheets or reports. Another common use is for displaying program code or output.

CAUTION

When typing tabular or columnar text to be tagged with a PRE tag, make sure that you have a monospaced fixed-pitch font such as Courier turned on in your text editor or word processor. Notepad automatically displays all text in a monospaced font. Word processors, however, by default normally use a proportional font. Many HTML editors automatically display PRE tagged text in a monospaced font, but some don't.

For an example of using the PRE tag, type a table using rows and columns (see Figure 2.14):

```
<pre>
                        John Johnson's Portfolio
                        First Quarter, 2000


               Prev Qtr  January  February   March    Balance   Gain (Loss)


IBM   (20)    $107.75  $112.25  $102.50  $118.00  $2,360.00  $   307.50

INTC  (30)     82.88    98.54   113.00   131.25   3,937.50    1,451.10

CSCO  (10)     53.56    54.75    66.09    77.31     773.10      237.50

MSFT  (25)    116.75    97.88    89.38   106.25   2,656.25  (  262.50)


Totals:                                           $9,676.85  $1,733.60

</pre>
```

◆ ◆

CAUTION   Don't forget to include the `</pre>` end tag at the end of the previous example. If you forget this, or if you mistakenly type the following examples before, rather than following, the PRE end tag, anything you enter is treated as "preformatted text," which means word wrap doesn't work and hard returns are displayed rather than ignored, for instance.

◆ ◆

Figure 2.14

The PRE tag displays text blocks in a monospaced font, preserving all spaces and line breaks in columnar and tabular text.

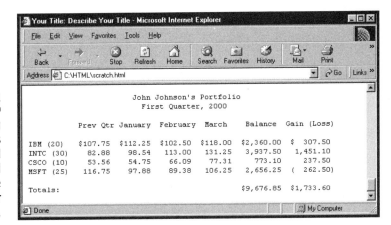

A perfectly standard way to add vertical spacing in a Web page is to insert hard returns inside of a PRE tag:

```
<p>Inserting a PRE tag containing hard returns will add extra space
between paragraphs.</p>
<pre>


</pre>
<p>This line should be three lines down.</p>
```

Take a Break

This seems like a good place to take a break. Get up and stretch those arms and legs. Pour yourself another cup of coffee. Or take the dog for a walk. I'll see you back in five or ten minutes for the remainder of this session, when you learn how to create lists, hypertext links, inline images, and more.

Creating Lists

Only headings and paragraph text elements are used more commonly than lists. Many Web pages are nothing but lists of hypertext links. You, like anyone else surfing the Web, have been on that merry-go-round a few times—going from one page of lists to another page of lists to another. If you're going to create Web pages, you need to know how to make lists! There are two types of lists: bulleted lists and numbered lists.

Creating Bulleted Lists

The UL (Unordered List) tag defines a bulleted list of items. The LI (List Item) tag is nested inside the UL tag and defines each item within the list. Create a bulleted list as follows (see Figure 2.15):

```
<h2>Entertainment</h2>
<ul>
<li>Television
<li>Movies
<li>Video Games
</ul>
```

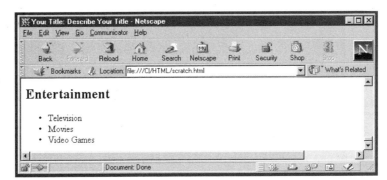

Figure 2.15

The UL (Unordered List) tag, in combination with the LI (List Item) tag, creates a bulleted list.

Nesting Bulleted Lists

When you nest a UL tag within a UL tag, your browser automatically varies the bullet type. To create a nested bulleted list, edit the bulleted list you just created as follows (see Figure 2.16):

```
<ul>
<li>Television
   <ul>
   <li>Sit-Coms
      <ul>
      <li>Ozzie and Harriet
      <li>The Brady Bunch
      <li>Friends
      </ul>
   <li>Game Shows
   <li>Soap Operas
   </ul>
<li>Movies
<li>Video Games
</ul>
```

NOTE

In the Saturday Afternoon session, "Dressing Up Your Pages," I show you how to specify the type of bullet you want to use in a bulleted list.

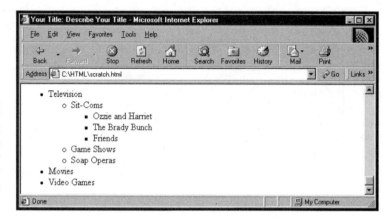

Figure 2.16

When you nest
bulleted lists, the
browser
automatically
varies the
bullet type.

Creating Numbered Lists

The OL (Ordered List) tag defines a sequentially numbered list of items. The LI (List Item) tag is nested inside the OL tag and defines each individual item within the list.

Create an ordered list to see how these tags work together (see Figure 2.17):

```
<h3>The Roman Empire</h3>
<ol>
<li>The Julio-Claudian Dynasty
<li>The Civil Wars
<li>The Flavian Dynasty
</ol>
```

NOTE The LI (List Item) tag is actually a container tag with an implied ending. Leaving off the end tag is customary in this instance and approved by the latest HTML standards.

NOTE In a nested numbered list, unlike in a bulleted list, the number type is not automatically varied—all the nested levels display the same number type (Arabic numerals). In the Saturday Afternoon session, I show you how to manually vary the number type to create a multi-level outline.

Figure 2.17

The OL (Ordered List) tag creates a numbered list.

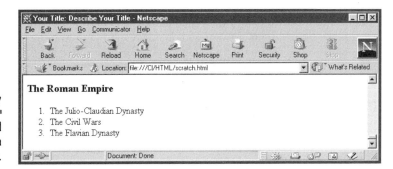

Mixing Lists

You can nest an ordered list within an unordered list, or vice versa (see Figure 2.18):

```
<h3>The Roman Empire</h3>
<ol>
<li>The Julio-Claudian Dynasty
   <ul>
   <li>Julius Caesar
   <li>Augustus
   <li>Tiberius
   <li>Gaius (Caligula)
   <li>Claudius
   <li>Nero
   </ul>
<li>The Civil Wars
   <ul>
   <li>Galba
   <li>Otho
   <li>Vitellius
   </ul>
<li>The Flavian Dynasty
   <ul>
   <li>Vespasian
   <li>Titus
   <li>Domitian
   </ul>
</ol>
```

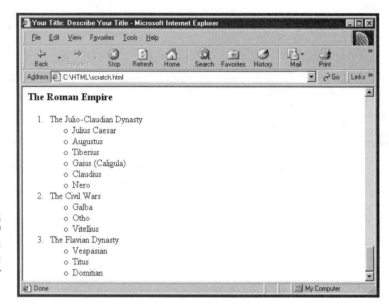

Figure 2.18

You can nest a
bulleted list inside
a numbered list, or
vice versa.

Creating Definition Lists

The DL (Definition List) tag enables you to create a definition list (also
called a *glossary*), which is a list of terms and definitions. A definition list
actually consists of three tag elements that all work together: the DL tag
defines the list, the DT (Definition Term) tag defines the terms, and the DD
(Definition Description) tag defines the definitions. Set up a short definition
list now (see Figure 2.19):

```
<dl>

<dt>bandwidth

<dd>The transmission capacity of a network, but also the amount of
capacity consumed by a connection.

<dt>binary file

<dd>A non-text file, such as an image or program file. Also called a "raw data"
file on the Macintosh platform.

<dt>bookmark

<dd>A way in Netscape Navigator to "bookmark" a Web page so it can
easily be returned to later. In Internet Explorer, this is called a
"favorite."

</dl>
```

Figure 2.19

A definition list (or glossary) is created using three tags: the DL (Definition List), DT (Definition Term), and DD (Definition Description) tags.

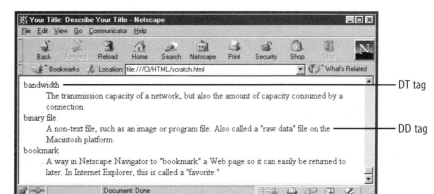

As you've probably noticed, the end tags for the DT and DD tags are implied, the same as for LI end tags in a regular list. The only difference is that a definition list has a two-part item (both a term and a description) rather than a one-part item. As long as you keep this in mind, you should have no trouble creating glossaries.

By itself, a definition list is a bit bland. You can dress it up by adding emphasis or tagging the definition terms with a heading tag. Here is an example of adding bold italic emphasis to a definition term:

```
<DT><I><B>bandwidth</B></I>
```

Here is an example of tagging a definition term using an H3 heading tag:

```
<DT><h3>bandwidth</h3>
```

Creating Hypertext Links

If you've surfed the Web at all, you should be familiar with hypertext links. You've probably used hypertext links not only to jump to and view another Web page or jump to a specific place in either the same or another Web page, but also to display an image, download a program, send an e-mail message, play an audio or video clip, run a script, access a database, and so on. You can use hypertext links to jump to anything that has an address on the Internet (not just on the Web), as long as you don't need a password. Of course, what happens after you make the jump depends on where you go.

The three basic kinds of hypertext links are as follows:

○ **Links to other HTML documents or data objects.** These links enable you to jump from one Web page to another, as well as to any other object that has an address on the Internet (not just the Web), such as an image, a script, a Gopher file, an FTP archive, and so on.

○ **Links to other places in the same HTML document.** These links enable you to jump from one place to another within the same HTML document. These kinds of links are often used to create a table of contents or a menu to make it easier to access an HTML document with many or lengthy subsections. They can also be used to create loop-back links that jump back to the top of a document and links that function like cross-references, connecting related or associated parts of a document.

○ **Links to places in other HTML documents.** These links combine the two other kinds of links: first jumping to another HTML document, and then jumping to a location within that HTML document. If you've clicked on a hypertext link and then jumped to some point halfway down another Web page, you've used this type of link.

Anatomy of the A (Anchor) Tag

Think of a hypertext link as being composed of the following three elements:

○ The start and end tags
○ The link target
○ The link text

Figure 2.20 illustrates the three parts of a hypertext link.

Figure 2.20

A hypertext link has three parts: the start and end tags, the link target, and the link text.

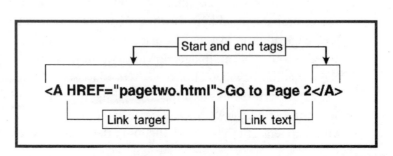

In Figure 2.20, the HREF (Hypertext Reference) attribute specifies the URL, or address, of the object of the link, which here is simply another Web page. Note that the full address (URL) is not given, just the file name. This means that the object of the link, most commonly another Web page, is located in the same folder as the Web page from which the link is being made. If you want to link to a Web page somewhere else on the Web, you have to include the full URL (`http://www.somewhere.com/somepage.html`, or something like that), rather than just the file name (somepage.html). For more information on using the A tag's HREF attribute, see the following section, "Linking to Another File."

Linking to Another File

You can form an HTML link to anything on the Web that has an address. To create a hypertext link that jumps to a file that is somewhere on the Web (as opposed to a folder included in your own Web site), you include the whole URL of the file to which you want to jump. Type the following example to create a real hypertext link that links to the World Wide Web Consortium's home page (see Figure 2.21):

```
<p>Visit the <a href="http://www.w3.org/">World Wide Web Consor-
tium</a> to find out more about the World Wide Web and HTML.</p>
```

Feel free to hop over to your browser to check this out. You'll have to go online to check out the link to the W3C site, however.

Figure 2.21

The underlining flags a hypertext link to the home page of the W3 Consortium.

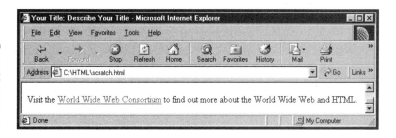

NOTE It used to be considered proper *netiquette* to request permission before linking to someone else's Web site or page. One of the reasons for this was the skimpy traffic allowances and bandwidth restrictions that were typical not that long ago. These days, however, most people want to get as many links to their sites as they can (within reason, of course). It is a good policy, however, to notify someone when you link to their site or page, which enables you to ask for a link in return (a *reciprocal link*). Also, if you're linking to a subpage within another person's site, it is good manners to also link to the site's top-level page, as well—top-level pages are also much less likely to suffer from *link rot* (the tendency of links to cease functioning over time because the pages they're linked to disappear or are moved).

TIP On Web servers, index.html is often designated as an "index" page. Other default index pages are also used, depending on the server. This enables you to leave off the index page's file name in a URL, if you want. For instance, `http://www.myserver.com/index.html` and `http://www.myserver.com/` represent the same URL. You can create index files, not only in your root folder, but also in any other folder in your site. (This only works on a Web server, however—it doesn't work on your local machine.)

Linking to a Place in the Same HTML File

Linking to another place in the same HTML file requires two anchors, an HREF anchor and a NAME anchor (or target anchor). An HREF anchor that links to a NAME anchor has a special form:

```
<a href="#anchorname">anchortext</a>
```

In an HREF anchor, the # sign indicates that the following is the name of a target anchor—the # sign combined with the anchor name is called a *fragment identifier*.

Any time you create a hypertext link using a fragment identifier to link to another location in your Web page, you need to also insert the corresponding target anchor. Target anchors are inserted in the following format:

```
<a name="anchorname"></a>
```

Just remember that your linking anchor uses an HREF attribute and has a # character preceding the anchor name, whereas the target anchor uses the NAME attribute and doesn't have a # character preceding the anchor name. Anchor names are case-sensitive, so the two anchor names (in the linking and target anchor) must match exactly, including any uppercase characters. Target anchor names must also be unique (if you have more than one target anchor with the same name in an HTML document, your link won't work).

The following HTML code shows you how to create a menu or table of contents for the top of a Web page that links to subheading sections located lower on the same Web page. To save you some typing, this is a somewhat compressed example (in a real Web page, the subsections are usually much longer). Enter this example at the top of your HTML file, just below the <body> tag (feel free to cut and paste to create the text for the section paragraphs), as shown here (see Figure 2.22):

```
<body>
<h2>Table of Contents</h2>
<p><a href="#one">Section One</a><br>
<a href="#two">Section Two</a><br>
<a href="#three">Section Three</a></p>
<h3><a name="one"></a>Section One</h3>
<p>This is the text following the first subheading. This is the text
following the first subheading. This is the text following the first
subheading. This is the text following the first subheading. This is
the text following the first subheading. This is the text following
the first subheading. This is the text following the first subhead-
ing. This is the text following the first subheading.</p>
<h3><a name="two"></a>Section Two</h3>
<p>This is the text following the second subheading. This is the
text following the second subheading. This is the text following
the second subheading. This is the text following the second sub-
heading. This is the text following the second subheading. This
is the text following the second subheading. This is the text
following the second subheading. This is the text following the
second subheading.</p>
<h3><a name="three"></a>Section Three</h3>
```

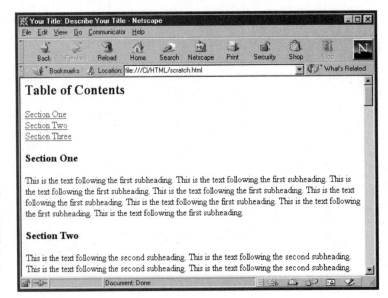

Figure 2.22

You can create a
table of contents
using hypertext
links that jump to
subheadings within
your document.

```
<p>This is the text following the third subheading. This is the text
following the third subheading. This is the text following the third
subheading. This is the text following the third subheading. This is
the text following the third subheading. This is the text following
the third subheading. This is the text following the third subhead-
ing. This is the text following the third subheading.</p>
```

Be sure to hop over to your browser to check this out. Figure 2.22 only
shows part of what this looks like, plus you'll want to test how the table of
contents links jump to the different subsections. Click on the Back button
to return to the table of contents.

Creating Loop-Back Links

If you have a lot of subsections, or your subsections are fairly long, you might
want to add loop-back links that loop back to the table of contents or the
top of the document when they're clicked. A loop-back link here works the
same as the table of contents links you just created, except they go in the
opposite direction (see Figure 2.23):

```
<body>

<h2><a name="top"></a>Table of Contents</h2>

<p><a href="#one">Section One</a><br>
```

```
<a href="#two">Section Two</a><br>

<a href="#three">Section Three</a></p>

<h3><a name="one"></a>Section One</h3>

<p>This is the text following the first subheading. This is the text
following the first subheading. This is the text following the first
subheading. This is the text following the first subheading. This is
the text following the first subheading. This is the text following
the first subheading. This is the text following the first subhead-
ing. This is the text following the first subheading.</p>

<p>Return to <a href="#top">Top</a>.</p>

<h3><a name="two"></a>Section Two</h3>

<p>This is the text following the second subheading. This is the
text following the second subheading. This is the text following the
second subheading. This is the text following the second subheading.
This is the text following the second subheading. This is the text
following the second subheading. This is the text following the
second subheading. This is the text following the second subhead-
ing.</p>

<p>Return to <a href="#top">Top</a>.</p>

<h3><a name="three"></a>Section Three</h3>

<p>This is the text following the third subheading. This is the text
following the third subheading. This is the text following the third
subheading. This is the text following the third subheading. This is
the text following the third subheading. This is the text following
the third subheading. This is the text following the third subhead-
ing. This is the text following the third subheading.</p>

<p>Return to <a href="#top">Top</a>.</p>
```

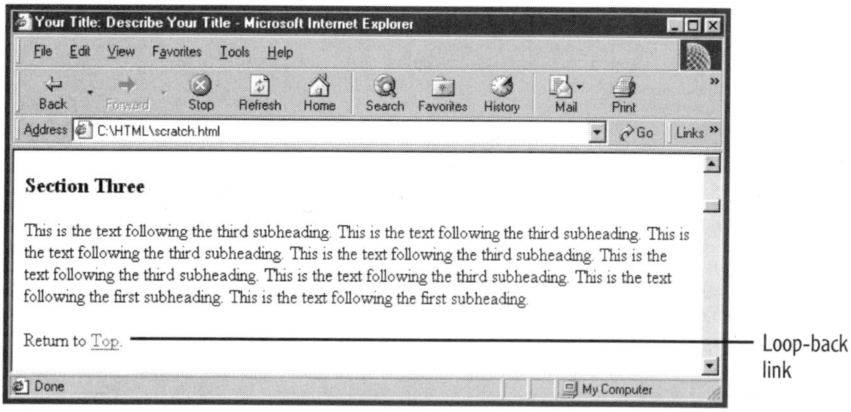

Figure 2.23

A loop-back link jumps back up to a table of contents or the top of a page, depending on where the target anchor tag is inserted.

Linking to a Place in Another HTML File

Just as you can make a hypertext link to a place in the same HTML file, you can link to a place in another HTML file. Both links work the same way, except in the second instance the NAME anchor (your landing spot) is placed in an entirely different HTML file from the one where the link is being made. The form for an HREF anchor that links to a place in another HTML file is as follows:

```
<A HREF="address#anchorname">anchortext</A>
```

This actually combines the forms for linking to another page and linking to a place on a page. In this example, *address* refers to the URL of the HTML file that the link jumps to (this can be a full URL or just an HTML file name if it is located in the same folder, for instance); *anchorname* refers to the anchor name assigned in the target anchor; and *anchortext* refers to the text that is displayed as the hypertext link. Move back down to the bottom of your HTML file and enter the following example, just above the </body> end tag. This creates a hypertext link that jumps to a place in another HTML file (see Figure 2.24):

```
<p>Go to <a href="example.html#part2">Part Two</a> of the <a
href="example.html">Example</a> Web page.</p>

</body>
```

This example uses an example file, example.html, included with the example files that you installed this morning. If you open that file in a separate copy of Notepad, you'll see that the location that the first link jumps to is marked by a <a name="part2"></a> code, which is the target anchor for the link (the landing spot).

Figure 2.24

The first link jumps to a location in the linked Web page, whereas the second link jumps to the Web page itself.

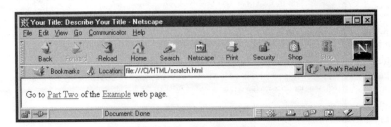

Creating Link Lists

So far, the discussion has focused on creating lists and creating links but hasn't explained creating link lists. A *link list* is a list of hypertext links, usually bulleted but sometimes numbered. Because link lists are so ubiquitous, everybody should know how to create them.

Creating a Simple Link List

A simple link list includes the hypertext link and the link text, without any following text that describes the links. Include whatever you want as the link text, but it should be informative and descriptive of the page you're linking to, because you're not adding any descriptive text outside of the links. It is a good idea to use the title or the level-one heading of the Web page you're linking to as the link text, although occasionally you might need to expand or abbreviate it. For practice in doing this, create a link list of online newspapers (see Figure 2.25):

```
<h2>Online Newspapers</h2>

<ul>

<li><a href="http://www.nytimes.com/">The New York Times</a>

<li><a href="http://www.washingtonpost.com/">The Washington Post</a>

<li><a href="http://www.seattletimes.com/">The Seattle Times</a>

</ul>
```

Figure 2.25

A link list combines an unordered list and hypertext links.

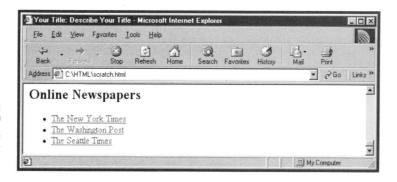

Adding Descriptions to Your Link List

Although sometimes a hypertext link is sufficient to describe what the object of the link is, often you'll want to add additional text to describe the link (see Figure 2.26):

```
<h2>Online Newspapers</h2>

<ul>

<li><a href="http://www.nytimes.com/">The New York Times</a> Read
the greatest newspaper in the world. A great source for internation-
al, national, and financial news.

<li><a href="http://www.washingtonpost.com/">The Washington Post</a>
Read the newspaper that broke the Watergate story. A great source
for political news from the capital of the most powerful nation in
the world.

<li><a href="http://seattletimes.nwsource.com/">The Seattle Times</a>
Read the top newspaper from the Pacific Northwest, home of
Microsoft, Boeing, and Weyerhauser.

</ul>
```

Using Inline Images

The IMG (Image) tag enables you to display inline images on your Web page. The term *inline* here means that an image is inserted at a particular location in a line within a Web page.

The IMG tag is an empty, or stand-alone, element. Its form is:

```
<img src="imagefile">
```

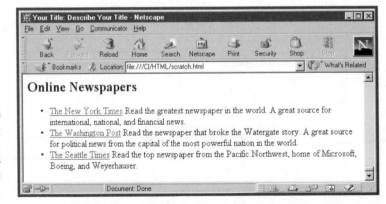

The SRC (Source) attribute is a required attribute. If the image file is located in the same folder as the HTML file, only the file name of the image needs to be specified as the SRC value. If the image and the HTML file are located in different folders within your site, you need to use a relative URL (see Appendix D, "Using Relative URLs"). In the following example, you use the image's file name as the SRC value, because the image, image.gif, and your HTML file are located in the same folder (C:\Html). Now, insert an inline image into your HTML file (see Figure 2.27):

```
<p>An inline <img src="image.gif"> is displayed <i>inline</i> (or
"in a line").</p>
```

Stick to using GIF (.gif) or JPEG (.jpg) images in your Web pages. A newer standard image format, the PNG (.png) image format, is allowed, but is supported only by the latest browsers. Internet Explorer also displays a number of additional image formats, such as BMP (.bmp) image files, but these should be avoided because other browsers do not support them.

See the Sunday Evening "bonus" session, "Working with Graphics," for detailed advice on how to make the most out of using GIF and JPEG images in your Web pages.

◆ ◆

In most cases, linking to someone else's Web page is okay. However, you should never link directly to image files located on someone else's server, rather than on your own, unless you have explicit permission to do so.

◆ ◆

Figure 2.27

All graphical Web browsers can display inline images.

FIND IT ON ▶   Check out this book's Web site at **www.callihan.com/learn3/** for a collection
THE WEB   of Web art images that you can download and use.

Providing Alternative Text

When someone views a page using a browser with display of images turned
off, or is using a text-only or a Braille browser, for instance, they can't see the
content of your images or know what their functions are. The answer is to
use the IMG tag's ALT attribute to provide "alternative text" that's displayed
in place of your images when the display of images is turned off or not
available.

Many browsers, including the latest versions of Netscape Navigator and
Internet Explorer, also display the content of the ALT attribute when the
mouse pointer is passed over an image, which lets you provide supplementary information to help explain an image. (You want to keep this somewhat
short, however, because Navigator doesn't wrap the text, but displays it all on
a single line.) Enter the following to create an example of an inline image
with an ALT attribute (see Figure 2.28):

```
<p>An inline <img src="image.gif" alt="This is an example image.">
is displayed <i>inline</i> (or "in a line").</p>
```

NOTE   You don't need to hop over to your browser to turn off display of images, just so you can
check this out. If you want to try this anyway: In Internet Explorer 5, select Tools and Internet Options, click on the Advanced tab, and then under Multimedia, clear the Show Pictures
check box. Click on OK and then click on the Refresh button. In Netscape Navigator 4, select
Edit and Preferences, click on the Advanced option, and then clear the "Automatically load
images" check box. (For this to take effect, you have to exit and rerun Navigator after turning display of images off, but you'll only have to click on the Reload button after turning it
back on.)

CAUTION   If you turn display of images off, don't forget to turn it back on!

Figure 2.28

Including alternative text can help to identify an image when display of images is either turned off or unavailable.

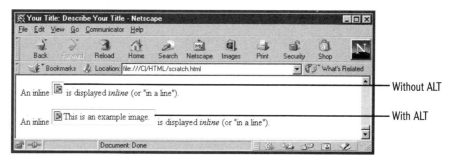

TIP

If an image is purely decorative and serves no informational purpose, insert an ALT attribute with a blank attribute value: `alt=""`. That way, you won't clutter up a Web page in a text-only browser with `[Image]` references. Also, if you're using icon images to create list bullets, include this ALT attribute to cue users of text-only browsers that the image functions as a bullet: `alt="*"`.

Specifying the Width and Height of Images

The IMG tag's WIDTH and HEIGHT attributes are used to specify the width and height of an image. When these attributes are present, a browser uses these attributes to allocate space for your image, allowing adjacent text, for instance, to be displayed while your images are still being downloaded. For this reason, it is a good idea to add these attributes to your IMG tags, except possibly for the smallest images (such as for icon bullets).

Just open an image in your image editor to determine its width and height in pixels. For an example of doing this, just edit the previous example you created, adding WIDTH and HEIGHT attributes to the IMG tag:

```
<p>An inline <img src="image.gif" width="125" height="65" alt="This
is an example image."> is displayed <i>inline</i> (or "in a
line").</p>
```

Stick to using the WIDTH and HEIGHT attributes to specify the actual size of an image and avoid using these attributes to resize an image, up or down, within a browser. Decreasing the size of an image in a browser is a waste of bandwidth, whereas increasing the size of an image in your browser is the waste of a good image. Resize your images in your image editor, in other words, not in your browser.

Vertically Aligning Inline Images

The ALIGN attribute enables you to vertically align an inline image relative to the line of text that it is on. You can set top-, middle-, and bottom-alignment for an image (bottom-alignment is the default). Enter the following as an example of using the IMG tag's ALIGN attribute to vertically align inline images (see Figure 2.29):

```
<p>The image on this line <img align="top" src="align.gif"> is top-
aligned.</p>

<p>The image on this line <img align="middle" src="align.gif"> is
middle-aligned.</p>

<p>The image on this line <img align="bottom" src="align.gif"> is
bottom-aligned.</p>
```

NOTE In the Saturday Afternoon session, I cover more things you can do with inline images, including horizontally aligning them, wrapping text around them, and creating image links.

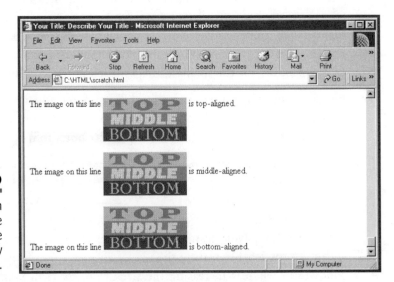

Figure 2.29

Inline images can be aligned relative to the baseline of the line they are on.

Using Horizontal Rules

The HR (Horizontal Rule) tag is an empty (or stand-alone) element that enables you to add horizontal rules to your Web pages. Set up a text paragraph followed by an HR tag (see Figure 2.30):

```
<p>A horizontal rule is displayed below this line.</p>
<hr>
```

Changing the Size and Width of a Horizontal Rule

You can use the HR tag's SIZE and WIDTH attributes to control dimensions of your horizontal rule. Edit the horizontal rule you just created by adding these attributes (see Figure 2.31):

```
<hr size="10" width="75%">
```

You can also set the WIDTH value using a pixel value. Always set the SIZE value using a pixel value instead of a percentage value. When no WIDTH value is set, the default width is 100% (of the browser window).

Figure 2.30

A horizontal rule can be used to separate different sections of a Web page.

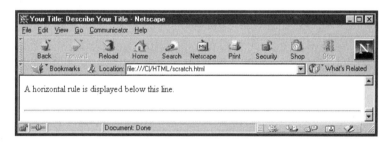

Figure 2.31

You can change the size (height) and width of a horizontal rule.

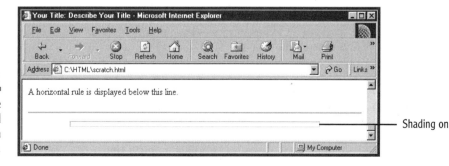

Shading on

When the width of a horizontal rule is less than the width of the browser window, it is centered by default. (Include an `align="left"` or `align="right"` attribute in the HR tag to left-align or right-align it.)

Turning the Shading off

You can also use the NOSHADE attribute to turn off the rule's shading (see Figure 2.32):

```
<hr size="10" width="75%" noshade>
```

This actually has the effect of filling the horizontal rule with a gray tone—the shading that is turned off is actually around the outside of the rule. Also, although Netscape Navigator rounds off the corners of a rule with shading turned off, Internet Explorer leaves them squared.

Signing Your Work

In HTML, the ADDRESS tag is used to define an "address block" for your page. Although it is not required, it is a good idea to use the ADDRESS tag to identify the author or owner of a Web page (or the person responsible for maintaining the page), as well as to provide a means by which that person can be contacted.

The most common way for visitors of your page to contact you is by using a Mailto link. In browsers that support Mailto links, a visitor to your page only has to click on the link to send you an e-mail message—a message composition window pops up with your e-mail address filled in.

Figure 2.32

You can turn off a horizontal rule's shading, which has the effect of filling it with a gray tone.

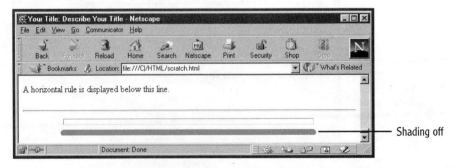

Shading off

Because browsers don't do anything special to format text nested in an ADDRESS tag other than italicize it, it is a good idea to insert a horizontal rule before the ADDRESS tag.

Enter the following at the bottom of your scratch pad HTML file to add an address block to your page (see Figure 2.33):

```
<hr>

<address>

Janet Doe<br>

E-Mail: <a href="mailto:youraddress@yourdomain.com">
youraddress@yourdomain.com</a><br>

</address>

</body>
```

TIP To add more vertical space above a horizontal rule that precedes an ADDRESS element, precede it by a paragraph start tag, like this:

```
<p><hr>
```

This is an instance where including the `</p>` end tag following the HR tag can yield an undesirable result, adding more vertical space below, as well as above, the horizontal rule.

Not all browsers support Mailto links. Users of Internet Explorer 2 can't use Mailto links, whereas users of Internet Explorer 3 and 4 need to have Internet Mail or Outlook Express installed, respectively, in order to be able to use Mailto links. For that reason, as shown in the previous example, always include your e-mail address both in the HREF attribute and as the link text—that way, if someone can't use your Mailto link, they can still copy and paste your e-mail address into their mail program if they want to contact you.

Figure 2.33

An address block can identify and provide a means for contacting the author or owner of a Web page.

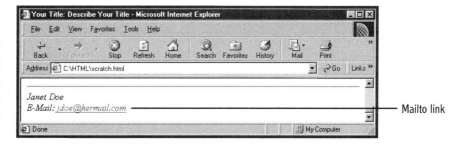

PREVENTING SPAM

Unfortunately, someone always comes along to spoil the party—in this case, the spammer. Some spammers use spiders to roam the Web just looking for Mailto links, so they can grab and resell the included e-mail addresses.

I personally have Mailto links to my e-mail address on scads of pages and, although I do get spammed on a daily basis, I don't feel that I'm overwhelmed by it. Apparently, however, this is a worse problem for AOL users, who seem to be more likely to be targeted by spammers.

One way to provide a means for visitors to contact you, without having to include your name or e-mail address on your page, is using a guestbook. A *guestbook* allows visitors to your site to sign in, or leave a message that you and other visitors to your site can read. AOL provides a free guestbook that AOL users can easily add to their pages. There are also many free guestbooks available on the Web that you can easily add to your pages. (To get a listing of free guestbook providers, just do a search on "guestbooks" at Yahoo (**www.yahoo.com/**).

FIND IT ON ▶
THE WEB

Another option is to get a free temporary WebMail address through HotMail, Yahoo! Mail, or some other WebMail provider and include that e-mail address on your pages. With a WebMail address, you generally log in to a Web site to read and reply to your mail messages, rather than using your e-mail program. If your WebMail address then starts to get overly spammed, just get another one! You can then keep your permanent e-mail address private, reserving it only for family, friends, and business associates.

(To get a listing of free WebMail providers, just search for "free e-mail" at Yahoo! (**www.yahoo.com/**).

FIND IT ON ▶
THE WEB

Centering Your Address Block

By default, text nested inside the ADDRESS tag is left-aligned. To center it, just nest the text inside a CENTER tag (see Figure 2.34):

```
<hr>

<address>

<center>
```

Figure 2.34

For a different look, you can center your address block.

```
Janet Doe<br>

E-Mail: <a href="mailto:youraddress@yourdomain.com">
youraddress@yourdomain.com</a><br>

</center>

</address>

</body>
```

Other Things You Can Include in Your Address Block

There are a number of other things to consider including in your address block:

- If you're creating a page for a business, you might want to include the name of your business, your street address, and your 800 or fax number. You can also include your title.

- If the page is a subpage within your site, you can also include a link back to your home page.

- You can also include a copyright notice, if you're concerned about others stealing your text or images and then claiming them as their own. (For further security, register your copyright.)

Saving Your Work

Save the HTML file you just created. You can use it later as a reference. When you first saved it, you named it scratch.html. If more than one person is going to be doing this tutorial and you want to make sure that this file doesn't get overwritten, you might want to give it a new name (jm-scratch.html, for instance, if your name is John Miller or Jill Moore).

Wrapping Up

This session has covered everything you need to know to start using HTML to create your own Web pages. Everything else is, literally, frosting on the cake.

If you've managed to complete everything I've thrown at you in a single morning, you're a real hot shot!

If it has taken you longer to complete this session, that's perfectly okay. Even if you've taken all day, or even all weekend, to complete just this one session, that's okay. Remember, it is the tortoise, not the hare, who often wins the race. That's because how much you've learned is not anywhere near as important as how well you've learned it. Getting a good grip on the "basics of HTML" lays the foundation for anything else you'll want to do with HTML.

If you've completed this session in a single morning and are ready for more, take a lunch break in order to refuel! I'll see you back in an hour or so for the Saturday Afternoon session, "Dressing Up Your Pages."

If you've taken most or all of the day to complete this session, you have the option of continuing on this evening, if you want. Just take a break for dinner and then do the Saturday Afternoon session in place of the Saturday Evening "bonus session." If you don't have the energy left, or you've got other things scheduled for tonight, feel free to save the Saturday Afternoon session until Sunday morning.

Regardless of whether you're a tortoise or a hare, be sure to complete the Saturday Afternoon session before going on to any of the other sessions.

Dressing Up Your Pages

- ✿ Using Banner Images and Graphic Rules
- ✿ Flowing Text around and between Images
- ✿ Creating Image Links, Navigational Icons, Thumbnail Galleries, and Custom Lists
- ✿ Changing Font Sizes, Colors, and Faces
- ✿ Using Background Colors and Images

In the Saturday Morning session, "Learning the Basics," you learned everything you need to know about HTML to start creating your own Web pages. The emphasis in that session, however, was on using HTML to structure, organize, and highlight the content of your page, without much emphasis on controlling the "visual look" of your pages. This afternoon, if you're following my schedule, you'll be learning how to gain much more control over the visual look and design of your page. Think of what you learned in this morning's session as baking the cake; in this afternoon's session, you'll be adding the frosting.

NOTE If you haven't yet completed the Saturday Morning session, go back and complete that session before continuing on to this session.

If doing the Saturday Morning session has taken you all day, or even all weekend, that's okay. As long as you complete the Saturday Morning session, you can say, with confidence, "I know HTML!" You can do this session as your Saturday Evening bonus session or, if you've got something else scheduled for tonight, you can do it as your Sunday Morning session. Just be sure that you do this session before moving on to do any of the following sessions.

Although the original vision behind HTML was to specify the structural framework of a page and not its actual appearance or display, as HTML has evolved and grown, many features have been incorporated into it that give you much more control over the visual appearance of your pages. These include, for instance, flowing text around and between images, changing font sizes, colors, and faces, using background colors and images, and using

style sheets. In this session, you learn how to do most of these things to "dress up" and add visual appeal to your pages.

Even taking these developments into consideration, however, HTML by itself falls far short of giving you the kind of control over the visual appearance of a Web page that a desktop publishing program, or even a word processing program, gives you. Novice Web publishers, for instance, often envision elaborate designs and layouts for their Web pages, only to become frustrated when HTML does not let them do exactly what they want to do.

You should also be aware that Web browsers are increasingly becoming only one means among many others for accessing a Web page—these other means include wireless devices with much more limited visual displays, such as PDAs (personal digital assistants) and cellular phones, interactive TV devices, such as WebTV, and other devices that don't even include a visual display, such as Braille and speech browsers used by the visually impaired. Many people are also still using text-only browsers or are surfing the Web with the display of graphics turned off in their browsers. Increasingly, in other words, it is not just the difference between how different Web browsers access a Web page that matters, but also the difference between how different devices access it.

It is important, in other words, to put your initial stress on the organization and structure of your page, so that everyone, no matter how they choose to access it, can easily understand and enjoy its content. Form should follow function, in other words. Substance should come before style. After you've structured and organized the content of your page in HTML, feel free to "dress up" your page to your heart's content, adding more visual appeal or giving it more of a "designer look." In this session, I show you how to add visual appeal to your pages, while retaining the structural integrity required if your page is to remain accessible to all devices.

What You Need

For doing this session, I recommend that you have the 4.0 version or higher of either Netscape Navigator or Internet Explorer. All the illustrations in this book were created using Netscape Navigator 4.74 and Internet Explorer 5.01. However, if you're still using an older browser, you don't necessarily

need to upgrade your browser just to do this session. You can also use a recent version of Opera or NeoPlanet to do this session, if you want.

If you do want to take the time now to upgrade your browser, you can download the latest version of Netscape Navigator at **home.netscape.com/** or Internet Explorer at **www.microsoft.com/windows/ie/**.

NOTE You should have already installed the example files for this session at the start of this morning's session. If you haven't installed these files, please return to "Installing the Example Files from the CD-ROM" in the Saturday Morning session before doing this session.

Using the Starting Template

Although you didn't use it, in this morning's session I mentioned that a starting template, start.html, is included with the other example files that you installed this morning. By using a starting template, you don't have to retype the same "starting" HTML codes each and every time you start a new HTML file. To open the starting template in Notepad, just do the following:

1. Run Notepad (click on the Start button, select Run, type **notepad**, and press Enter).
2. Select File, Open. Click on the "Look in" list box, and then click on the C drive icon [C:]. In the folder view, double-click on the HTML folder to open it.
3. To make HTML files visible in the folder view, click on the "Files of type" list box and select All Files [*.*].
4. Double-click on start.html to open it.

The codes that you now see in your text editor should match what is shown here:

```
<html>
<head>
<title>Your Title: Describe Your Title</title>
</head>
<body>
```

```
</body>
</head>
</html>
```

Saving Your HTML File

You need to save your HTML file with a different name so that you don't accidentally write over your starting template later. To save your HTML file, just do the following:

1. In Notepad, select File, Save As.
2. Click on the "Look in" list box, and then click on the C drive icon [C:]. In the folder view, double-click on the HTML folder to open it.
3. In the "File name" box, type **scratch2.html**, and click on the Save button.

Using a Banner Image

A banner image is an inline image that runs along the top of your Web page. It might include your company name or logo, or a piece of art that adds graphic appeal and pizzazz to your page.

You don't have to create a banner image right now—the following example uses a sample banner image that is included with the example files (see Figure 3.1):

```
<body>

<p align="center"><img src="banner.gif" alt="My Banner Image"
width="500" height="100"></p>

<h1 align="center">Dressing Up Your Pages</h1>

<p>This is just some example text to help show what a banner image
will look like on a real page. This is just some example text to
help show what a banner image will look like on a real page. This
is just some example text to help show what a banner image will look
like on a real page. This is just some example text to help show
what a banner image will look like on a real page.</p>
```

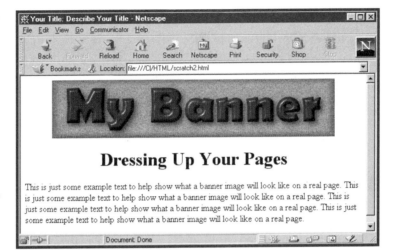

Figure 3.1

A banner image runs across the top of a Web page.

 TIP

To lessen the amount of vertical spacing that is inserted between a banner image and a following level-one heading tag, just insert the banner image's IMG tag, followed by a BR tag, inside the level-one heading tag, instead of inserting it in its own center-aligned paragraph. Here's an example:

```
<h1 align="center">"><img src="banner.gif"><br>Dressing Up Your
Pages</h1>
```

When using a banner image, it is still a good idea to also have a level-one heading for your page, even if having both seems a bit redundant. That's because many search engines place special weight on the content of your level-one heading—if you don't have one, you might not be listed as high in a Web search list. Including a descriptive ALT attribute, one that includes one or more keywords or keyphrases, in your banner image's IMG tag can also improve your position in a Web search list.

When creating a banner image in your image editor, you can format text using any font installed on your system, as well as apply many special effects, such as interlacing, transparency, gradient and pattern fills, drop shadows, 3-D edges, and more. In the Sunday Evening bonus session, "Working with

Graphics," you learn how to apply these special effects using Paint Shop Pro 6 and Adobe Photoshop LE. Also, later in this session, in the "Using Background Colors and Images" section, I include an illustration that shows an example of a transparent banner image displayed against a background image.

Even if your banner image stretches across your entire browser window, it is a good idea to place it in a center-aligned paragraph. That way, it will always be centered, regardless of the screen resolution and the size of the browser window. I also included a centered level-one heading and a dummy introductory paragraph, so you'd get an idea of what a banner image looks like "in context."

You'll also notice that, besides the SRC attribute, there are a few additional attributes included in the IMG tag. The ALT attribute assists someone who can't see your images, such as a visually impaired visitor using a Braille or speech browser, to identify the content or function of your image. The WIDTH and HEIGHT attributes express the actual width and height of the image in pixels, which allows a browser to allocate space for the image, thus freeing it to display adjacent text or other elements before the banner image has finished downloading. It is a good idea to include ALT, WIDTH, and HEIGHT attributes in all your IMG tags. For more information on using these attributes, see the "Using Inline Images" section in the Saturday Morning session.

Also, note that in the previous example only the file name of the image is used as the SRC attribute value. This requires that the image be saved in the same folder as the HTML file where it is displayed. If you want to link to an image in a different folder, you need to use what is called a *relative URL,* which states the location of the linked file *relative* to the linking file. See Appendix D, "Using Relative URLs," for a more detailed explanation of how to use relative URLs in your pages.

When creating a banner image, you want to be cognizant that many surfers are still using screen resolutions of 640 × 480 pixels. Even if someone is using a screen resolution of 800 × 600 pixels, or even 1024 × 768 pixels, the width of their browser window might be considerably less than the screen width. To help insure that your banner image is fully visible for all visitors, size your image in your image editor so it is no more than 600 pixels wide. The example banner image used in the previous example is 500 pixels wide.

Horizontally Aligning Images

Contrary to what you might think, you can't use the ALIGN attribute in the IMG tag to center or right-align an image. First, `align="center"` doesn't work at all. Second, `align="right"` may have an unexpected result, causing all following paragraphs or other elements to flow around the left side of the image (for more on this, see the next section, "Flowing Text around Images").

Because an inline image is an "inline" element, the easiest way to horizontally align it on a Web page is to nest it in a center-aligned or right-aligned paragraph. Enter the following example to insert both a center-aligned and a right-aligned image (see Figure 3.2):

```
<p align="right"><img src="right.gif"></p>

<p align="center"><img src="center.gif"></p>
```

Alternatively, you can nest your inline image in a right-aligned or left-aligned heading level tag (H1, H2, and so on). You can also nest it inside a CENTER tag.

Using Graphic Rules

Horizontal rules probably work best as simple separators. Their main advantage is that they consume very few bytes. If you want a rule that is more colorful, however, you need to use a graphic rule. A graphic rule is actually just

Figure 3.2

You can right-align or center-align an image by nesting it inside a right-aligned or center-aligned paragraph.

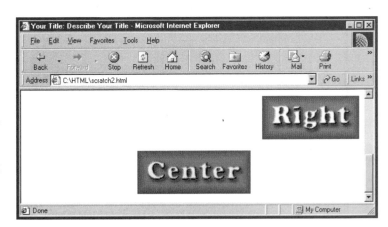

an inline image shaped in the form of a rule. The main disadvantage is that a graphic rule consumes considerably more bytes than a horizontal rule (although you can use the same graphic rule several times without taking up any additional bytes).

Go back to the top of your HTML file and enter the following example, just below the level-one heading example (see Figure 3.3):

```
<h1 align="center">Dressing Up Your Pages</h1>

<p align="center"><img src="goldbar.jpg"></p>
```

Notice in the previous code example that the graphic rule is nested in a center-aligned paragraph. Horizontal rules are centered by default, but with a graphic rule you've got to do it yourself.

Resizing a Graphic Rule

In the Saturday Morning session, I recommended that you resize your images in your image editor, not in your browser. I recommended that you use the actual height and width dimensions of your image when setting the HEIGHT and WIDTH attributes for an inline image. Every rule has an exception, however. The benefits of adjusting the height and width of a graphic rule, on the fly, in your browser simply outweigh the small

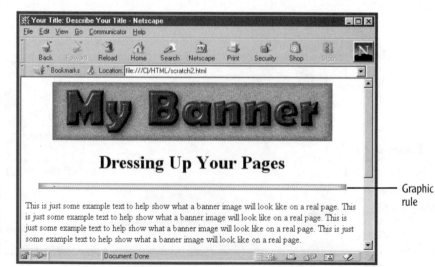

Figure 3.3

Instead of an ordinary horizontal rule, you can use a fancy graphic rule.

Graphic rule

disadvantages that might ensue. Because graphic rules usually don't have diagonal or curved edges and lines, you don't have to worry about the "jaggies" (or "staircase" effect) that can become amplified when increasing the size of an image. On the other hand, if you decrease the size of a graphic rule, the bandwidth waste is usually relatively small.

Additionally, setting a percentage width for a graphic rule can have a nice effect—dynamically resizing the graphic rule relative to the width of the browser window.

The following is an example of a graphic rule set to a width of 75 percent of the browser window (see Figure 3.4):

```
<p align="center"><img src="goldbar.jpg" width="75%"></p>
```

Flowing Text around Images

In the Saturday Morning session, you learned how to vertically align an image relative to a line of text by inserting "top," "bottom," and "middle" attribute values in the IMG tag. In addition to these attribute values, you can set two other ALIGN attribute values: "left" and "right." Although you might think that the purpose of these attributes is to align an image at either

Figure 3.4

The benefits of dynamically resizing a graphic rule in a browser are considerable, whereas the disadvantages are minimal.

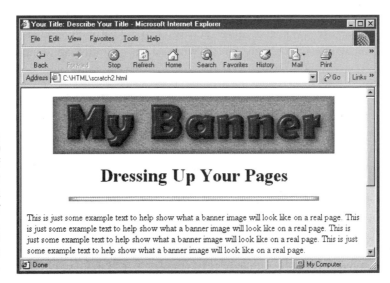

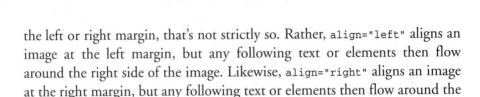

the left or right margin, that's not strictly so. Rather, `align="left"` aligns an image at the left margin, but any following text or elements then flow around the right side of the image. Likewise, `align="right"` aligns an image at the right margin, but any following text or elements then flow around the left side of the image.

The following examples make use of the same example text to help show the action of the flowing text. Instead of retyping it for each example, type it once, and then copy and paste it so you can reuse it for each example:

```
<p>This is just some example text to help show the action of the
flowing text. This is just some example text to help show the action
of the flowing text. This is just some example text to help show the
action of the flowing text.</p>
```

To cause the example text to flow around a left-aligned image, insert the following codes (see Figure 3.5):

```
<p><img align="left" src="left.gif">This is just some example text
to help show the action of the flowing text. This is just some exam-
ple text to help show the action of the flowing text. This is just
some example text to help show the action of the flowing text.<br
clear="left"></p>
```

You probably noticed the `<br clear="left">` tag. It is inserted to stop text or codes from continuing to flow around the image. In this case, it moves all following text and codes down, until the left margin is "clear" (below the left-aligned image). Because you have no control over the screen resolution or the browser window size used by a visitor to your pages, it is important to always turn off the flowing of text around an image. In the following

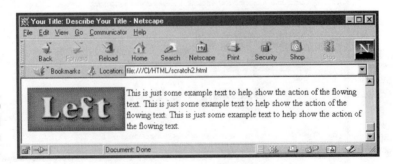

Figure 3.5

Text flows around the right side of a left-aligned image.

examples, you'll see two other variants of this, using a `clear="right"` and a `clear="all"` attribute. The first turns off the flowing of text around a right-aligned image, whereas the second turns off the flowing of text around either a left-aligned or a right-aligned image (or both).

Enter the following code as an example of wrapping text around a right-aligned image (see Figure 3.6):

```
<p><img align="right" src="right.gif">This is just some example text
to help show the action of the flowing text. This is just some exam-
ple text to help show the action of the flowing text. This is just
some example text to help show the action of the flowing text.<br
clear="right"></p>
```

You aren't limited to just flowing paragraph text around images. Any other elements, such as headings, lists, and other images, flow around a left-aligned or right-aligned image.

Flowing Text between Images

You not only can wrap text around the right or left side of an image, you can also flow text between two images. For example, enter the following (see Figure 3.7):

```
<p><img align="left" src="left.gif"><img align="right"
src="right.gif">This is just some example text to help show the
action of the flowing text. This is just some example text to help
show the action of the flowing text. This is just some example text
to help show the action of the flowing text.<br clear="all"></p>
```

Figure 3.6

Text flows around the left side of a right-aligned image.

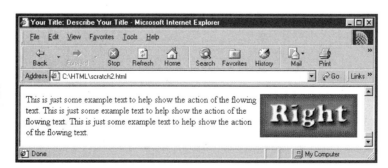

Figure 3.7

You can also flow text *between* images.

Adding Horizontal Spacing

You've probably noticed that there isn't a lot of horizontal spacing between an image and text that is flowing around it. This tends to be more of a problem with text flowing around left-aligned images. The latest versions of Internet Explorer and Netscape Navigator both just insert a "sliver" of spacing. Some earlier versions of Internet Explorer insert no horizontal spacing at all.

You can insert an HSPACE (Horizontal Space) attribute in the IMG tag, which adds additional spacing around both the left and right sides of an image. Edit the two previous examples to add ten pixels of horizontal spacing around the left-aligned image and five pixels of horizontal spacing around the right-aligned image (see Figure 3.8):

```
<p><img align="left" src="left.gif" hspace="10"><img align="right"
src="right.gif" hspace="5">This is just some example text to help
show the action of the flowing text. This is just some example
text to help show the action of the flowing text. This is just
some example text to help show the action of the flowing text.<br
clear="all"></p>
```

The only drawback to this is that the horizontal spacing is added to both sides of the image, which might not be what you want. If you're just adding a bit more spacing, however, it is not that noticeable.

There is a workaround that adds horizontal spacing only on one side of an image. It involves inserting the image inside of a left-aligned or right-aligned table, and then letting the text flow around the table instead of just around

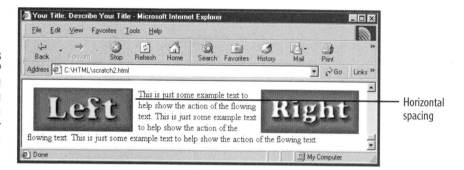

Figure 3.8

By adding horizontal spacing to an image, you can create a buffer between it and flowing text.

Horizontal spacing

the image. To increase the amount of horizontal spacing between the image and flowing text, you just increase the width of the table correspondingly beyond the width of the image. Don't try to do this right now, however—you'll be learning all about using tables in the Saturday Evening session, "Working with Tables."

Flowing an Image between Two Other Images

You can even flow a center-aligned image between left-aligned and right-aligned images. To do this, you just insert all three images in a center-aligned paragraph. For an example of how to do this, enter the following (see Figure 3.9):

```
<p align="center"><img align="left" src="left.gif"><img
align="right" src="right.gif"><img src="center.gif"><br
clear="all"></p>
```

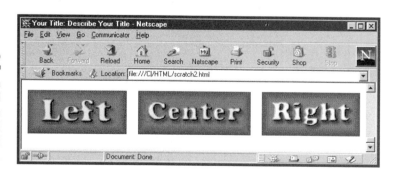

Figure 3.9

You can also flow a center-aligned image between left-aligned and right-aligned images.

Creating a Drop-Cap Effect

A neat effect that you can add to your page, using a left-aligned inline image, is a drop-cap character. To add a drop-cap character to your page, you need to have a properly sized inline image of the first character in the paragraph where you want to add the drop cap. To save you the time of having to create your own drop-cap inline image, I've created a drop-cap image of the letter "T" for you and included it with the example files you've installed into your C:\Html folder. Scroll back up to the top of your HTML file, delete the letter "T" at the start of the example paragraph (located below the graphic rule), and then enter the following to create the drop-cap effect (see Figure 3.10):

```
<p><img src="drop_t.gif" align="left" alt="drop-cap letter T"
width="50" height="50" vspace="3">his is just some example text to
help show what a banner image will look like on a real page. This
is just some example text to help show what a banner image will look
like on a real page. This is just some example text to help show
what a banner image will look like on a real page. This is just
some example text to help show what a banner image will look like on
a real page.</p>
```

If you're handy with an image editor that can create GIF or JPEG images, you can easily create your own drop-cap images. Just create an image, about 50 × 50 pixels, featuring the letter you want to use for your drop cap, and then save it as a GIF or JPEG image. In the Sunday Evening session, I show you how to create your own Web art images using Paint Shop Pro 6.

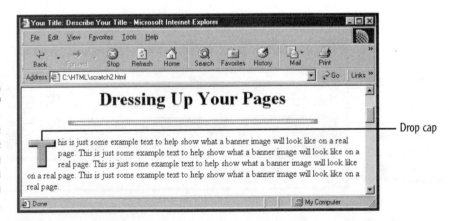

Figure 3.10

By using a left-aligned inline image of the first letter of a paragraph, you can create a drop-cap effect.

Working with Image Links

In the Saturday Morning session, you learned how to place inline images on your page, and you also learned how to create hypertext links. What you haven't learned yet is how to create an inline image that functions as a hypertext link, whereby clicking on the image activates the link. Hey, if you want to brag about knowing HTML, you've got to know how to create image links!

To activate an image as a hypertext link, all you have to do is nest it inside of a hypertext link. Scroll back down to the bottom of your HTML file and enter the following example to see how to create an image link (see Figure 3.11):

```
<p><a href="example.html"><img src="link.gif">Both the image and the
text are a link.</a></p>

</body>
```

Using an Image Link by Itself

You can nest an inline image, all by itself, inside of a hypertext link. Enter the following as an example of using an image link by itself (see Figure 3.12):

```
<p><a href="example.html"><img src="link.gif"></a></p>
```

In almost all browsers, the image displays a two-pixel border, usually blue, to indicate that it is a link. The exception to this is Internet Explorer 5 for the Macintosh, which does not automatically display a border around an image link. Instead, when the mouse is passed over the image link, it

Figure 3.11

The image, displayed with a blue border, and the link text, underlined with a blue line, are both part of the same hypertext link.

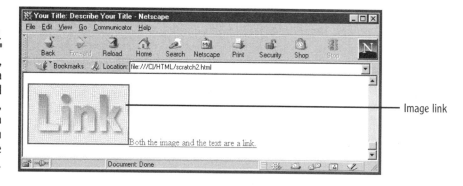

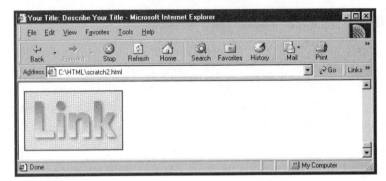

Figure 3.12

You can use an image, by itself, as a link.

displays a message in the status bar that indicates that the image is a link (to force it to display the image link border, just insert `border="2"` in the image link's IMG tag).

Controlling the Image Link Border

The default image link border is two pixels in most browsers. If you want, you can use the IMG tag's BORDER attribute to increase the thickness of the image link border, decrease it (to one pixel, for instance), or you can turn it off completely. For instance, enter the following example to increase an image link's border to 10 pixels (see Figure 3.13):

```
<p><a href="example.html"><img src="link.gif" border="10"></a></p>
```

To turn off the display of an image link's border, you just need to include a `border="0"` attribute in the image link's IMG tag. In the following section, I show you an example of turning off an image link's border.

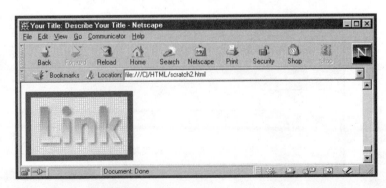

Figure 3.13

Using the BORDER attribute in the IMG tag, you can increase the width of the border around an image link.

Creating Navigational Icons

Navigational icons are image links that are often included on Web pages to assist in navigating a Web site. For instance, a "house" icon indicates that clicking on it takes you to the site's home page. An up-arrow icon usually indicates the same thing. A left-arrow icon indicates that clicking on it takes you to the previous page in a series of pages, whereas a right-arrow icon takes you to the next page in a series of pages.

Navigational icons are almost always created with the display of the link border turned off, because their function should be clearly indicated by the icon image.

To accommodate text-only browsers or graphical browsers with graphics turned off, always include ALT text in a navigational icon's IMG tag. This ALT text should indicate that it's a link and describe what it links to.

Enter the following example of a navigational icon, with the border turned off and alternative text included (see Figure 3.14):

```
<p><a href="example.html"><img src="back.gif" border="0" alt="Go to
Previous Page"></a></p>
```

Creating Thumbnail Image Links

The problem with inline images is that they can consume a fair amount of bandwidth. For that reason, if you want to display more than a few medium to larger sized inline images, you might soon find that your page is loading slower than mud flows. The solution to this problem is the thumbnail image

Figure 3.14

Navigational icons are often displayed with the image link border turned off.

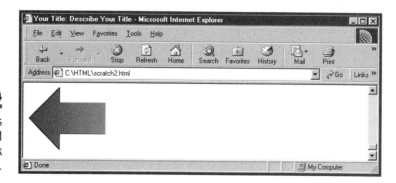

link, which uses a smaller image to link to a larger one. A visitor can then see a smaller representation of what your image looks like before they decide to click on the image link to see the larger image.

There are many ways to use thumbnail image links in a Web page. You can just include them all in a single line, letting the Web browser decide where to break the line. If you want a more ordered presentation, you can insert the thumbnail image links inside of table cells, for instance. (You'll learn about using tables in the Saturday Evening bonus session.) If you want to include more descriptive information about the images you're linking to, you can use left-alignment and right-alignment to flow text around the right or left side of your thumbnail image links.

The first thing you need to do before creating a thumbnail image link is create the thumbnail images. (Don't do this right now; I've included example thumbnail and larger-sized images that you use in the next example.) To create a thumbnail image, just open your larger-sized JPEG or GIF image in your image editor and then resize it to a smaller size. If you resize the dimensions of your image by 50 percent, your thumbnail image becomes ¼ the size of the original. To create an even smaller thumbnail image, resize the dimensions to 40 to 30 percent of the original, for instance. Then, just save your image, renaming it to indicate that it is the thumbnail of the larger image. For instance, if your larger image is named mypic.jpg, save the thumbnail image as mypic_t.jpg.

Here's an example of creating a thumbnail "gallery" to link to larger-sized images (see Figure 3.15):

```
<hr>
<h2 align="right"><a href="rocks.jpg"><img src="rocks_t.jpg"
align="right" hspace="10" alt="Sea Rocks" width="231"
height="135"></a>Sea Rocks<br>on the Washington Coast<br
clear="right"></h2>
<hr>
<h2><a href="beach.jpg"><img src="beach_t.jpg" align="left"
hspace="10" alt="Rocks and Waves" width="237" height="141"></a>Rocks
and Waves<br>on the Washington Coast<br clear="left"></h2>
```

When you click on one of the image links, the fuller-sized image is displayed directly in the browser (see Figure 3.16). Just click on your browser's Back button to return to your "scratch pad" HTML file.

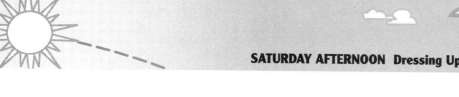

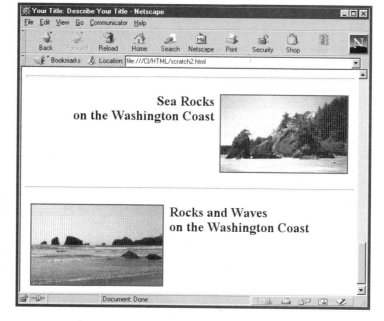

Figure 3.15

A thumbnail "gallery" is a bandwidth-friendly way to show off your photos or paintings.

Figure 3.16

After clicking on the thumbnail image link, the larger-sized image is displayed directly in the browser window.

Alternatively, you can insert your fuller-sized image in its own Web page, and then link to it through a thumbnail image link. Doing it that way enables you to center the image, add a background color, and insert a loop-back link, for instance.

Creating Custom Lists

In the Saturday Morning session, you learned about creating bulleted and numbered lists. You also learned about nesting and mixing lists. In the following two sections, you learn how to create a custom bulleted list and a multi-level outline.

Creating Custom Bulleted Lists

You're not stuck with accepting the default bullet type. Using the TYPE attribute in either the UL or the LI tag, you can specify any one of three bullet attributes: disc, circle, or square. Enter the following as an example of creating a custom bulleted list that uses a square bullet type, instead of the default disc bullet type (see Figure 3.17):

```
<ul type="square">
<li>Fiction
<li>Non-Fiction
<li>Poetry
</ul>
```

You can also change the bullet types for any nested bulleted lists. Enter the following as an example of using the other two bullet type attributes (see Figure 3.18):

```
<ul type="square">
<li>Fiction
   <ul type="disc">
   <li>Novels
     <ul type="circle">
     <li>Historical Novels
     <li>Romance Novels
     <li>Modern Novels
     </ul>
   <li>Short Stories
   </ul>
<li>Non-Fiction
<li>Poetry
</ul>
```

Figure 3.17

You can change the bullet type to give a list a different look.

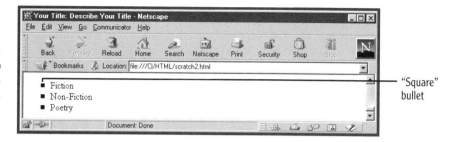

"Square" bullet

Figure 3.18

Using the TYPE attribute, you can control the bullet types for different nested bulleted list levels.

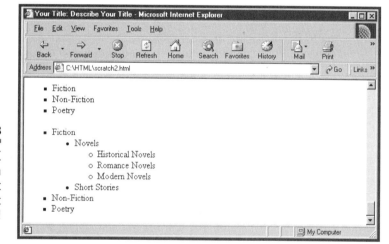

You can also use the TYPE attribute in the LI tags to vary the bullet type for individual bulleted list items.

Creating a Multi-Level Outline

By nesting OL tags and specifying the number type (using the TYPE attribute), you can create a multi-level outline. You can specify any one of five number-type attributes: A, a, I, i, and 1. Copy and paste the numbered list you just created and then edit the copy to turn it into a multi-level outline (see Figure 3.19):

```
<ol type="I">
<li>Fiction
   <ol type="A">
```

```
<li>Novels
  <ol type="1">
  <li>Historical novels
  <li>Romance novels
  <li>Modern novels
  </ol>
<li>Short Stories
</ol>
<li>Non-Fiction
<li>Poetry
</ol>
```

CAUTION

Specifying the number type in a nested numbered list is an example of an HTML 3.2 feature that might not look so hot in older browsers that are not HTML 3.2-compliant. In those browsers, the different levels of your outline will all have the same number type (Arabic numbers). Unlike with bulleted lists, no browser I know of automatically varies the number types for nested numbered lists. If you want to use this in a Web page, you might want to alert visitors to your page that an HTML 3.2-compliant Web browser is recommended.

There are two additional attributes, the START and VALUE attributes, that you can use in a numbered list's OL and LI tags. For instance, including a `start="3"` in the OL tag causes the numbering to start at 3. (If you've set the

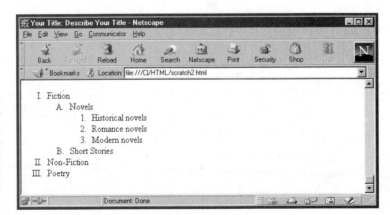

Figure 3.19

By specifying the number type in a nested numbered list, you can create a multi-level outline.

number type as "A," the numbering starts at C.) Including a `value="5"` in a numbered list's LI tag causes the numbering to restart at that number.

Inserting Paragraphs

When you insert a paragraph in a bulleted or numbered list, the paragraph is automatically indented flush with the indent of the list item. To see this in action, insert some paragraphs in the multi-level outline you just created (see Figure 3.20):

```
<ol type="I">
<li>Fiction

<p>This is just some example text. This is just some example text.
This is just some example text. This is just some example text. This
is just some example text.</p>

  <ol type="A">
  <li>Novels

  <p>This is just some example text. This is just some example text.
This is just some example text. This is just some example text. This
is just some example text.</p>

    <ol type="1">
    <li>Historical novels

    <p>This is just some example text. This is just some example
text. This is just some example text. This is just some example
text. This is just some example text.</p>

    <li>Romance novels

    <li>Modern novels

    </ol>

  <li>Short Stories

  </ol>

<li>Non-Fiction

<li>Poetry

</ol>
```

NOTE This is one of the instances in which you must include the `</p>` end tag at the end of the paragraph. If you don't, additional vertical space is not inserted between the end of the paragraph and a following list item.

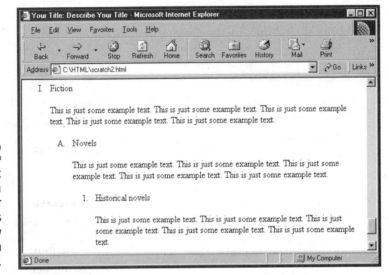

Figure 3.20

Paragraph text following a list item in a bulleted or numbered list is automatically indented flush with the list item's text.

Take a Break

Need a breather? If you need to get the kinks out, get up and stretch. Take some deep breaths. To relax your eyes, unglue them from your monitor and focus them on the horizon, if you've got a window handy. If you feel you need an energy boost, grab a snack or something to drink. I'll see you back here in 10 to 15 minutes, when you'll learn about creating icon link lists using fancy 3-D icon bullets, setting font sizes, colors, and faces, and using background images and colors.

Creating Icon Link Lists

Another way to create a link list is to use colorful 3-D bullet icon images. You don't use the UL tag to create this kind of list; instead, you use regular paragraph text separated by line breaks. To get a sense of what an icon link list looks like in a Web page, scroll back up to the top of your HTML file and enter the following example just below the example paragraph located just below the graphic rule example (see Figure 3.21):

```
<p>

<img src="icon.gif" hspace="4"><a href="http://www.nytimes.com/">The
New York Times</a>

<br>

<img src="icon.gif" hspace="4"><a
href="http://www.washingtonpost.com/">The Washington Post</a>

<br>

<img src="icon.gif" hspace="4"><a
href="http://seattletimes.nwsource.com/">The Seattle Times</a>

</p>
```

Notice in the previous code that an hspace="4" attribute was included in the IMG tags. This adds additional horizontal spacing between the icon bullet images and the link text that follows. To add more horizontal spacing, just increase the number for the attribute.

To space out the icon link list items, just use separate paragraphs, rather than line breaks, to separate the lines.

Figure 3.21

Using colorful bullet icon images is a good way to dress up a Web page.

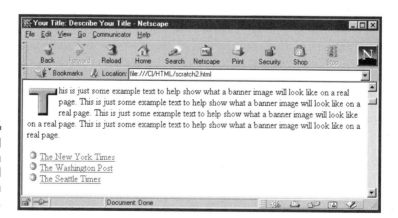

Creating Indented Icon Link Lists

The previous example is fine for a simple icon link list. However, if you want to add any descriptive text to your icon link list, you'll find that the text will wrap to the left margin. As long as you keep your descriptions relatively short, by using left-aligned icon bullet images in combination with the VSPACE (Vertical Spacing) attribute, you can create an *indented* icon link list (see Figure 3.22):

```
<p>

<img src="icon.gif" align="left" vspace="4" hspace="4"><a
href="http://www.nytimes.com/">The New York Times</a> This is just
some example text. This is just some example text. This is just some
example text.

<br clear="left">

<img src="icon.gif" align="left" vspace="4" hspace="4"><a
href="http://www.washingtonpost.com/">The Washington Post</a> This
is just some example text. This is just some example text. This is
just some example text.

<br clear="left">

<img src="icon.gif" align="left" vspace="4" hspace="4"><a
href="http://seattletimes.nwsource.com/">The Seattle Times</a> This
is just some example text. This is just some example text. This is
just some example text.

<br clear="left">

</p>
```

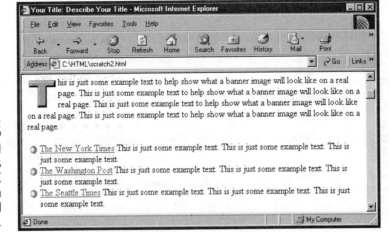

Figure 3.22

Using left-aligned icon bullet images and the VSPACE attribute, you can create an indented icon link list.

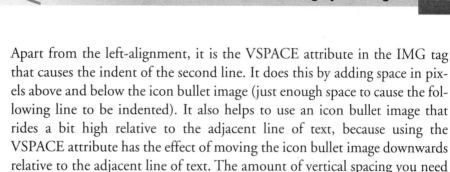

Apart from the left-alignment, it is the VSPACE attribute in the IMG tag that causes the indent of the second line. It does this by adding space in pixels above and below the icon bullet image (just enough space to cause the following line to be indented). It also helps to use an icon bullet image that rides a bit high relative to the adjacent line of text, because using the VSPACE attribute has the effect of moving the icon bullet image downwards relative to the adjacent line of text. The amount of vertical spacing you need to add might vary a pixel, more or less, depending on the specific icon image that you're using.

The primary limitation of this method is that you're limited to only two lines of indented text. A third line wraps to the left margin and is not indented. When creating indented icon link lists using this method, always test your page with your browser window set to 640 pixels across (or as close as you can get it) in order to make sure that you don't have a third line wrapping.

Another limitation of this method is that you don't have much control over how the browser aligns your icon bullet relative to the following text. The Windows versions of both Netscape Navigator and Microsoft Internet Explorer display this almost identically, but the Macintosh versions of both of these browsers display the bullet icon at least a pixel lower than the Windows versions.

If the browser doesn't support left-aligning the bullet icons, any wrapping text is displayed flush to the left margin, so you don't have to worry about this overly messing up older browsers.

TIP Someone using a text-only browser or a graphical Web browser with graphics turned off might not realize that the graphics are functioning as bullets. To clue them in, you might want to edit the IMG tags for the bullets, adding ALT="*", so they look like this:

```
<img src="redball.gif" align="top" HSPACE=5 VSPACE=5 ALT="*">
```

FIND IT ON ▶
THE WEB
Check out this book's Web site at **www.callihan.com/learn3/** for a collection of bullets, buttons, and other icons, along with other Web art images, that you can download and use.

In the Saturday Evening bonus session, I show you another method that uses a table to create icon link lists that allows for an unlimited number of indented lines.

Changing Font Sizes

The FONT tag enables you to specify the size of a section of text. The FONT tag uses the SIZE attribute to change the size of a font. You can set font sizes using absolute or relative size values.

Setting Absolute Font Sizes

Seven absolute (or fixed) font sizes, numbered 1 to 7, can be applied using the FONT tag's SIZE attribute. The default font size corresponds to a size of 3. Sizes 1 and 2 set font sizes that are two and one sizes smaller than the default font size, and sizes 4, 5, and 6 set font sizes that are progressively larger than the default font size. Generally, when it comes to the larger font sizes, 4 is the same size as an H3 tag, 5 the same size as an H2 tag, 6 the same size as an H1 tag, and 7 one size larger than an H1 tag.

(The clinker here, however, is Internet Explorer 4 for the Macintosh. It lets users bump up the Mac's relatively diminutive default font size by clicking on a Larger button, but does so simply by bumping all the font sizes up one notch, with the exception of the largest font size [7], which stays the same. As a result, if the Larger button has been clicked once, font sizes 6 and 7 will be the same size; if the Larger button has been clicked twice to bump up the font size two notches, font sizes 5, 6, and 7 will be the same size. No other browser on the Mac, however, commits these kinds of font shenanigans. Thankfully, they've fixed this in Internet Explorer 5 for the Macintosh.)

To see these different font sizes in your Web browser, scroll back down to the bottom of your HTML file and enter the following (see Figure 3.23):

```
<p><font size="1">Font Size 1.</font><br>
<font size="2">Font Size 2.</font><br>
<font size="3">Font Size 3 (the default).</font><br>
```

```
<font size="4">Font Size 4.</font><br>
<font size="5">Font Size 5.</font><br>
<font size="6">Font Size 6.</font><br>
<font size="7">Font Size 7.</font></p>
</body>
```

TIP

You can also nest font tags inside each other, so you can do something like this to switch back to the default font size in the middle of a larger set font size:

```
<font size="4">This is Font Size 4. <font size="3">This is the default size
font.</font> This is Font Size 4 again.</font>.
```

CAUTION

You might be tempted to use the FONT tag alone in place of using heading-level tags (H1, H2, and so on). This is not advisable. For one thing, browsers that are unable to display your font changes, such as text-only or Braille browsers, are left without a clue as to the hierarchical structure and organization of your page. Many search engines and Web directories also give extra weight to words and phrases included in heading-level tags when indexing your site. Nothing says, however, that you can't nest a FONT tag inside a heading-level tag.

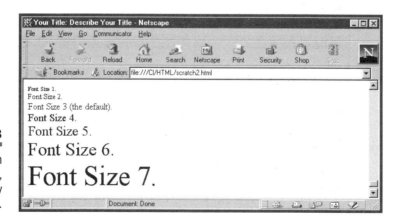

Figure 3.23

You can set seven absolute font sizes, ranging from tiny to fairly large.

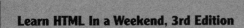

Setting Relative Font Sizes

You also can set relative font sizes. Relative font-size changes are indicated by either a plus (+) or minus (−) sign preceding the font-size number. For instance, FONT size="+1" indicates a font size that is one size larger than the base font. Because the default base font is the same as a Size 3 absolute font, a Size +1 relative font is the same as a Size 4 absolute font (3 + 1 = 4). For instance, enter the following for an example of using relative font-size changes to indicate the seven possible font sizes (see Figure 3.24):

```
<p><font size="-2">Font Size -2.</font><br>

<font size="-1">Font Size -1.</font><br>

Default Font Size.<br>

<font size="+1">Font Size +1.</font><br>

<font size="+2">Font Size +2.</font><br>

<font size="+3">Font Size +3.</font><br>

<font size="+4">Font Size +4.</font></p>
```

Notice that a relative −2 is the same as an absolute 1, −1 is the same as 2, +1 is the same as 4, and so on. The default font size, which requires no font-size change, is the same as 3.

Now, you might be asking, "If relative fonts are just another way to specify the same fonts as absolute fonts, why bother?" The next section, "Setting the Base Font Size," provides the answer to that question.

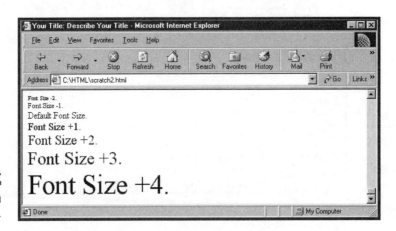

Figure 3.24

You can set seven relative font sizes.

Setting the Base Font Size

The BASEFONT tag enables you to change the size of the *base font*—the default font used in text. You can set it to any of the absolute font sizes, 1 through 7 (3 is the default). It's an empty (or stand-alone) tag. You set the base font size the same way you set an absolute font size. For instance, to increase the base font size one notch for all text following the BASEFONT tag, you set the base font to an absolute font size of 4, like this:

```
<basefont size="4">
```

Don't actually set this now. A little later on, you'll find an example that also includes using the BASEFONT tag to increase the base font size.

NOTE When you change the base font size using the BASEFONT tag, all following relative font sizes change relative to the new base font. For instance, if you change the base font size to 4, a relative font size of +1 becomes the same as an absolute font size of 5 (4 + 1 = 5).

You can insert the BASEFONT tag at any point within a Web page to set the base font to any of the absolute font sizes. It stays in effect until another BASEFONT tag changes the base font to another size. It not only affects relative font sizes, but also any SMALL and BIG font changes (described later in the session), as well as the size of all paragraph text, character rendering (italic, bold, and so on), list elements, definition lists, block quotes, predefined text, and address blocks that follow it. Headings and text set with absolute font-size tags are not affected, however.

CAUTION Don't use the BASEFONT tag to set a relative font size (`<basefont size="+1">`, for instance). Internet Explorer ignores BASEFONT relative font sizes set using negative numbers, displaying them all as minuscule size "1" fonts. With BASEFONT relative font sizes set using positive numbers, Internet Explorer treats them as if they are absolute font sizes (`size="+4"` is treated exactly the same as `size="4"`).

NOTE   If you check out the specification for HTML 4, notice that the FONT and BASEFONT tags have been *deprecated*. This just means that a more recent standard is available to achieve the same result—cascading style sheets, in this case. It doesn't mean that you shouldn't use these tags—that is the case only when they are *obsoleted*. Current and future browsers are required to support all deprecated tags but can drop support for obsolete tags.

Because of the widespread use of these tags in tons of Web pages, don't worry too much that they'll ever be obsoleted. As long as there is such a thing as HTML, these tags will continue to be supported by Web browsers.

If you want to investigate using cascading style sheets to set font display characteristics, see Appendix E, "Using Cascading Style Sheets."

Using the BIG and SMALL Tags

There are two additional tags you can use to increase or decrease the font size: the BIG and SMALL tags. These tags bump the font size up or down one step. To get even larger or smaller font sizes, you can nest BIG and SMALL tags (`<big><big>...</big></big>`, for instance). To try using these tags, enter this example (see Figure 3.25):

```
<p><small>This is a smaller font.</small> This is a regular font.
<big>This is a bigger font.</big> <big><big>This is an even bigger
font.</big></big></p>
```

Figure 3.25

You can use the BIG and SMALL tags to increase or decrease font sizes.

Changing Font Colors

You can specify a color for nested text by using the FONT tag's COLOR attribute. You can do this either by specifying a color name or by inserting an RGB hexadecimal color code.

Setting Font Colors Using the 16 Color Names

The HTML 4 specification lists 16 color names that can be used to specify colors in Web pages: black, white, aqua, blue, fuchsia, gray, green, lime, maroon, navy, olive, purple, red, silver, teal, and yellow. Enter the following for an example of specifying font colors using color names (this example omits black and white; see Figure 3.26):

```
<p><font size="7">
<font color="aqua">Aqua</font> <font color="blue">Blue</font>
<font color="fuchsia">Fuchsia</font> <font color="gray">Gray</font>
<font color="green">Green</font> <font color="lime">Lime</font>
<font color="maroon">Maroon</font> <font color="navy">Navy</font>
<font color="olive">Olive</font> <font color="purple">Purple</font>
<font color="red">Red</font> <font color="silver">Silver</font>
<font color="teal">Teal</font> <font color="yellow">Yellow</font>
</font></p>
```

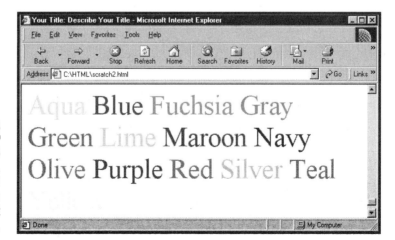

Figure 3.26

You can use 16 color names, including black and white (not shown here), to set font colors.

Figure 3.26, shown here in monochrome, gives you only a rough idea of what this looks like in a browser. Be sure to hop over to your browser to see what the colors really look like.

Setting Font Colors Using RGB Hex Codes

Setting the font color using RGB hex codes involves specifying values from 0 to 255 (00 to FF, in hexadecimal) for the red, green, and blue components of a color, providing you with a grand total of 16.7 million colors from which to choose.

If you're wondering why the RGB codes are set as hexadecimal, rather than decimal, values, the reason is that you can count in hexadecimal from 0 to 255 using only two-digit numbers. The hexadecimal equivalent to the decimal value of 159, for instance, is 9F.

You set the RGB hex code for a color in the FONT tag in this general form, where *rr* is the hex value for red, *gg* the hex value for green, and *bb* the hex value for blue:

```
<font color="#rrggbb">This is the text to be colored.</font>
```

For instance, a red color here can be specified as #FF0000, a lime green color as #00FF00, and a blue color as #0000FF. (FF is the highest hexadecimal number, equaling 255, whereas 00 is the lowest, equaling 0.) Enter the following example of assigning font colors using RGB hex codes (the example also increases the font size to 6 and adds bold highlighting so it is more visible in your browser; see Figure 3.27):

```
<p><font size="6"><b>
<font color="#ff9900">"Orange" (ff9900) </font>
<font color="#cc9900">"Gold" (cc9900) </font>
<font color="#ffcc33">"Gold-Yellow" (ffcc33) </font>
<font color="#6600ff">"Violet" (6600ff) </font>
<font color="#ff99cc">"Pink" (ff99cc) </font>
<font color="#ff9999">"Salmon" (ff9999) </font>
<font color="#cc0000">"Brick Red" (cc0000) </font>
<font color="#3399ff">"Sky Blue" (3399ff) </font>
```

```
<font color="#33cccc">"Blue-Green" (33cccc) </font>
<font color="#669933">"Olive-Green" (669933) </font>
<font color="#ff6600">"Red-Orange" (ff6600) </font>
</b></font></p>
```

Browsers on systems that can display only 256 colors use *dithering* to display colors that aren't included in the browser or system palette that is used for those systems. Sometimes this is fine, other times decidedly not. The only colors that definitely aren't dithered on 256-color systems are those included in the 216-color browser-safe palette. (The 216 colors included in the browser-safe palette are colors that are common to most 256-color systems. A Windows 256-color palette, for instance, includes colors that are not included in a Macintosh 256-color palette and vice versa.)

BUZZ WORD

◄ ◄

When a system that is limited to displaying 256 colors uses *dithering* to display a color that is not part of its system palette, it does so by combining the pixels from two or more colors present in the system palette in order to try to trick the eye into perceiving the desired color. Although this sometimes works, often the result is a grainy, splotchy color that only remotely resembles the desired color.

◄ ◄

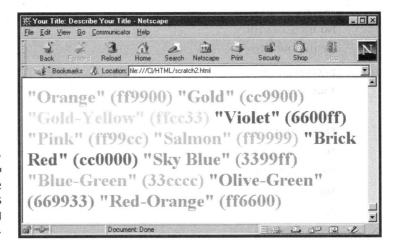

Figure 3.27

Here are just some of the many colors you can set using RGB hex codes.

TIP   If you stick to hexadecimal codes 00, 33, 66, 99, CC, and FF when inserting RGB hex codes, you'll be selecting colors from the browser-safe palette, thus helping to ensure that your page displays fine on 256-color systems. You'll also reduce the number of colors from which you must select to 216. The background, text, and link colors set in the example are all combinations of these codes.

Showing you how to count in hexadecimal or explaining how an RGB color scheme works is beyond the scope of this book. Quite frankly, unless you already know how to count in hexadecimal and have an understanding of RGB color theory, the only practical way to choose the hexadecimal color code you want is to use some kind of color chart, wheel, or cube that lets you select the color you want, along with the corresponding hex code.

A number of places on the Web have color cubes or charts that show you all the browser-safe colors and their RGB hex codes. Here are two of the best:

○ Victor Engel's No Dither Netscape Color Palette at **the-light.com/ netcol.html**

○ Doug Jacobson's RGB Color Chart at **home.flash.net/~drj2142/ pages/rgbhex.html**

I've also included a file, colors.html, along with the example files that you installed from the CD-ROM. Just open it in your browser to see a table including all the browser-safe colors and their corresponding RGB hex codes.

Many HTML editors also have color pickers, which let you choose the color you want and then insert the RGB hex code into your Web page for you. Generally, however, they don't identify the browser-safe colors.

Changing Font Faces

The FACE attribute of the FONT tag was originally a Microsoft extension. It wasn't included in HTML 3.2 but was later incorporated into HTML 4.0. It enables you to specify a font, or list of fonts, in which you want to display text. Be aware, however, that for a particular font to be displayed in a browser, it must be present on the local system where the page is being displayed. If not, the text is displayed in the default font.

One of the tricks to using this attribute is to specify a list of fonts that will snag as many computers as possible. Realize that just because a font is available on your system doesn't mean that it will be available on someone else's system. If most systems aren't likely to have a particular font, there isn't much point in specifying it. For that reason, I don't think trying to specify one particular font is the way to go, and you certainly shouldn't base the design of your Web page on having any one particular font available on someone else's system. Even if you stick with fonts that are included by default with Windows 95 or 98, for instance, realize that many of those fonts might not be available on a Macintosh or a UNIX system.

A good way to use this attribute is to specify a list of fonts that fit into the same category, such as serif, sans-serif, or monospaced fonts. For instance, to maximize the chances that the following example will be displayed in a sans-serif font, enter the following (see Figure 3.28):

```
<p><font size="6" color="blue" face="verdana, arial, helvetica">This
text will be in either Verdana, Arial, or Helvetica, depending on
which fonts are installed on a local system.</font></p>
```

You're not limited to listing only font faces that are available on your own system—Helvetica, a PostScript font face, is included in the previous example because it is more likely to be present on a Macintosh system, which is less likely to have Verdana or Arial available. Enter the following code for an example of specifying a pair of monospaced fonts (Courier New and

Figure 3.28

You can specify a list of font faces in the FONT tag's FACE attribute to increase the chance that at least one font (here Verdana) is available on a local system.

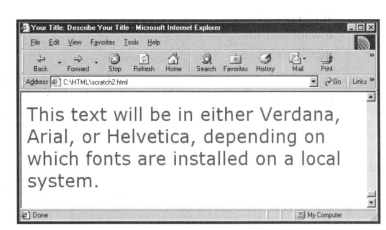

Courier) that should ensure that one or the other displays on both Windows and Macintosh systems (see Figure 3.29):

```
<p><b><font size="6" color="blue" face="courier new, courier">This
text will be in a bold Courier New or Courier font face, depending
on which fonts are installed on a local system.</font></b></p>
```

In the previous example, the FONT tag is also nested inside of a B (Bold) tag to render the monospaced font in bold.

TIP

On Windows systems, Adobe Type Manager must be installed for PostScript fonts to be finely rendered—otherwise, a lower-quality bitmap representation of the font is displayed. For that reason, when including a list of font faces in the FONT tag, always precede PostScript fonts (Helvetica, Times, Palatino, and Courier, for instance) by one or more True Type fonts (Arial, Times New Roman, Verdana, and Courier New, for instance).

Using Background Colors and Images

Using a background color or image is a great way to dress up the appearance of your Web page. In the following sections, I show you how to set a background color (as well as how to match text and link colors) and how to use a background image in your Web page.

Figure 3.29

To display a monospaced font, both Courier New (shown here) and Courier can be specified to increase the chances that both Windows and Macintosh systems display a monospaced font.

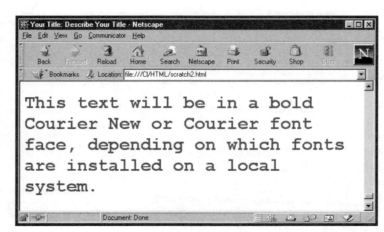

Using a Background Color

Using a background color is a simple and easy way to make your Web page look great. (Or horrible, depending on the color you choose!) In this section, I show you how to set a background color and matching text and link colors.

You can set the colors for the background, text, and links by using these attributes of the BODY tag:

- ✿ BGCOLOR sets the background color
- ✿ TEXT sets the text (or foreground) color
- ✿ LINK sets the color of hypertext links
- ✿ VLINK sets the color of visited links
- ✿ ALINK sets the color of activated links (where you click and hold down the mouse button on a link but haven't released it)

As with the FONT tag's COLOR attribute, you can set these attributes using any of the 16 color names (black, white, aqua, blue, fuchsia, gray, green, lime, maroon, navy, olive, purple, red, silver, teal, and yellow) or by using RGB hexadecimal codes.

The general form for entering these attributes as color names is shown here, where *colorname* is one of the 16 color names given:

```
<body bgcolor="colorname" text="colorname" link="colorname"
vlink="colorname" alink="colorname"
```

The general form for entering these attributes as RGB hexadecimal codes is shown here, where *rrggbb* is three hexadecimal numbers forming the RGB code for setting the red, green, and blue components of an RGB color:

```
<body bgcolor="#rrggbb" text="#rrggbb" link="#rrggbb"
vlink="#rrggbb" alink="#rrggbb"
```

The following example sets the colors for the background, the text (or foreground), and the three varieties of links—regular, visited, and activated. Your main concern when setting background, text, and link colors should be readability. If the color of your background and the colors of your text and links don't have enough contrast, or if they clash with each other, your page will end up being a strain for a visitor to read, which is not what you want.

Also, when setting the color for visited links (specified by the VLINK attribute), it is conventional to use a less bright or intense version of the same color that is assigned to links (specified by the LINK attribute). If you do it the other way around, visitors might mistake unvisited links for visited ones. You can also set the same color to both, if you want, which keeps the color of a link from changing after it has been visited.

TIP

■■■

When setting a light text color against a darker background color, it is often a good idea to bump up the base font size one notch (insert `<basefont size="4">` at the top of your page, just below the BODY start tag) to make the text font more legible.

■■■

The next example sets the background color as a dark "slate" blue, the text color as a light blue-green, the link color as a bright green, the visited link color as a less bright blue-green, and the activated link color to bright red. To help ensure that your text will be readable against the darker background, the BASEFONT tag is used to bump the base font size up a notch. Set a dark background color and complementary colors for text, links, visited links, and activated links within your page (see Figure 3.30):

```
<body bgcolor="#003366" text="#ccffcc" link="#66ff00"
vlink="#33ffcc" alink="#ff0000">

<basefont size="4">
```

TIP

■■■

Although most browsers these days default to a white background, you can't necessarily assume that will always be the case. Some browsers, such as the old Mosaic 2.0 browser as well as Netscape Navigator 4.05 for the Macintosh, default to a gray background. Even if a browser's background defaults to white, users can usually specify any background color that they want to use in their browser's preferences—if they select a pink color as their preferred background, your page will have a pink background when they view it, whether you like it or not.

To force your page's background to be displayed in white, just set "white" as the background color in your page's BODY tag, like this:

```
<body bgcolor="white">
```

This ensures that your page's background is displayed in white, unless viewers have purposely chosen to override your colors with their own.

■■■

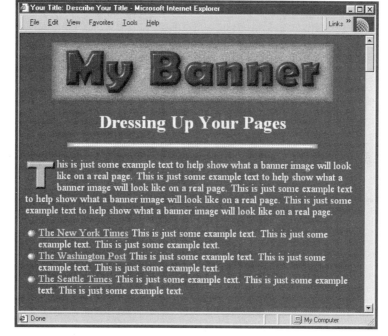

Figure 3.30

Setting the
background color,
along with colors
for text and links,
can dress up
your page.

Using a Background Image

The BACKGROUND attribute of the BODY tag lets you specify a background image. Background images are usually quite small (usually not larger than 100 × 100 pixels)—the Web browser *tiles* the image so that it fills the whole background of the browser window (similar to how tiles are laid on a bathroom wall or floor). Background images are usually created so they can be seamlessly tiled, meaning that you can't easily distinguish the seams between the tiled images; the tiled images appear to be a continuous pattern or texture.

TIP

You can create your own seamless background image instead of using one of many ready-made background images available on the Web. Paint Shop Pro 6, included on the CD-ROM, has a nifty feature that lets you select an area within an image and then convert it into a seamless background image. Just select an area in an image using the Selection tool, and then choose Selections, Convert to Seamless Pattern.

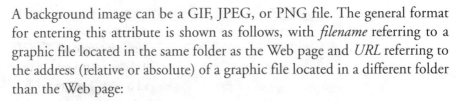

A background image can be a GIF, JPEG, or PNG file. The general format for entering this attribute is shown as follows, with *filename* referring to a graphic file located in the same folder as the Web page and *URL* referring to the address (relative or absolute) of a graphic file located in a different folder than the Web page:

```
<BODY BACKGROUND="filename or URL">
```

A key consideration when using background images is to avoid busy or high-contrast images. If you're going to use a dark background image, set the color of your text and links to a lighter color. The following example inserts a background image that is close in color and tone to the background color you added previously, so you don't have to change the other colors (see Figure 3.31):

```
<body background="backgrnd.jpg" bgcolor="#003366" text="#ccffcc"
link="#66ff00" vlink="#33ffcc" alink="#ff0000">

<BASEFONT size="4">
```

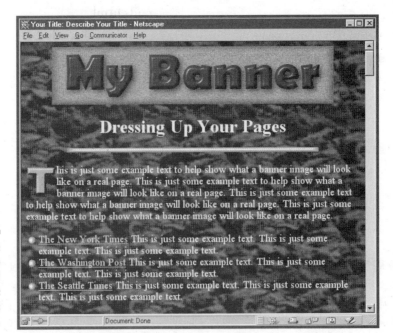

Figure 3.31

One of the more effective ways to add visual appeal to your Web page is to use a background image.

CAUTION

◆ ◆

If you set a light text color that you're displaying against a dark background image, realize that someone surfing with the display of images turned off will most likely see your light text displayed against a white background. If you've set the color of your text to white, they'll see (or won't see, that is) white text against a white background. To avoid this problem when you're using light text against a dark background image, *always* specify a dark background color, as well, that is similar at least in tone to the predominant color in the background image you're using.

◆ ◆

In the example files that you copied from the CD-ROM this morning, I've included a number of additional background images that you can experiment with (just look for images beginning with "b_"). Also, look on the CD-ROM for additional Web art collections that include background images. There are also many places on the Web where you can find background images that you can use in your pages. Here are just a few places you can download background images:

FIND IT ON ▶ THE WEB

- ❂ The Background Sampler by Netscape at **home.netscape.com/assist/net_sites/bg/backgrounds.html**.

- ❂ Backgrounds by NCSA at **www.ncsa.uiuc.edu/SDG/Software/mosaic-w/coolstuff/Backgrnd/**.

- ❂ Rose's Backgrounds Archive at **www.wanderers2.com/rose/backgrounds.html**.

Adding the Final Touches

After you've added a background image to your page, there's more you can do to help coordinate the look of your page with its background. You've already done one thing along these lines: used a BASEFONT tag to bump up the size of the default base font a notch. To make your headings stand out more against your background and from any other adjacent text, you can change the font color and font face that displays them. Additionally, you can globally change the font face of your whole page.

Changing the Font Color and Face of Your Level-One Heading

You can change the font color and font face of your level-one heading, so it stands out from the other text in your page. This is a good way to add emphasis and additional color to your page. Make the following changes to your HTML to view an example of this (see Figure 3.32):

```
<body background="rockback.jpg" bgcolor="#003366" text="#ccffcc"
link="#66ff00" vlink="#33ffcc" alink="#ff0000">

<basefont size="4">

<p align="center"><img src="banner.gif" alt="My Banner Image"
width="500" height="100"></p>

<h1 align="center"><font color="#ff9999" face="verdana, arial, hel-
vetica">Dressing Up Your Pages</font></h1>
```

In the previous example, a font list is used, listing Verdana, Arial, and Helvetica as the desired font faces. In a regular Web page, you can also change the font color and font face of any of the subheadings (H2, H3, and so on) in your page. Make sure, however, that any colors you choose complement,

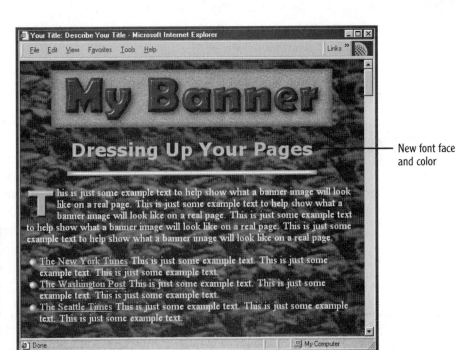

New font face
and color

Figure 3.32

Changing the font color and font face of your level-one heading is a good way to add color and emphasis to your page.

rather than clash with, the background color or image you're using. It can take several, or more, attempts to come up with just the right color combination.

Changing the Font Face of Your Whole Page

An effective means of getting the text of your page to stand out against a background, especially a dark background, is to change the font face from the default serif font face, usually a Times Roman font face, to a sans-serif font face, such as Verdana, Arial, or Helvetica, for instance. Because sans-serif font faces lack "serifs," their letterforms are generally slightly thicker than serif font faces, making them stand out more against a dark background color or image.

To globally change the font face of your whole page, bracket *everything* in your page (within the BODY tag) with a FONT tag listing your preferred font faces (see Figure 3.33):

```
<body background="rockback.jpg" bgcolor="#003366" text="#ccffcc"
link="#66ff00" vlink="#33ffcc" alink="#ff0000">

<basefont size="4">

<font face="arial, helvetica">
.

.

.


</font>
</body>
```

Using a Transparent Banner Image

Using a transparent banner image against a background image can be a good way to give your page more of a "3-D" look. In the previous examples, you've actually already used a couple transparent images, drop-t.gif and icon.gif. A GIF image is made transparent by specifying one of the colors included in the image (usually the background color) as being transparent. As a result, any background image or background color included in your page displays transparently through the image's background. In the Sunday Evening bonus session, I show you how to use Paint Shop Pro 6 to create your own transparent GIF images. Figure 3.34 shows an example of a transparent banner image displayed against a background image.

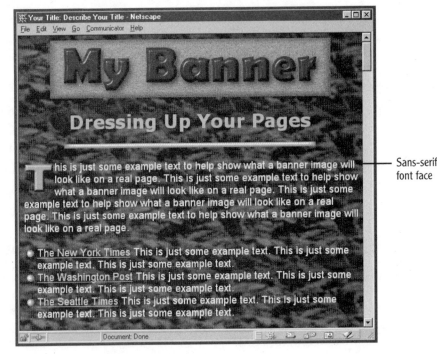

Sans-serif
font face

Figure 3.33

Changing the font
face of your whole
page is a good way
to make your page
stand out.

If you want to check this out for yourself in your own browser, the HTML
file, transpar.html, shown in Figure 3.34, is included with the example files
you copied from the CD-ROM this morning.

More Things You Can Do

There's lots more you can do to give your Web site that "special look" that
you want. In the Saturday Evening bonus session, you learn how to use
tables in your Web pages. Tables can be used for formatting tabular data in
rows and columns, but they can also be used to create multi-column Web
page layouts. In the Sunday Morning session, "Working with Frames," you
learn how to create a multi-frame Web site. In the Sunday Evening bonus
session, you learn how to create your own Web art images, as well as how to
add GIF animations and image maps to your pages.

I've also added an appendix to the book, Appendix E, "Using Cascading
Style Sheets," that gives you a quick rundown on using style sheets in your

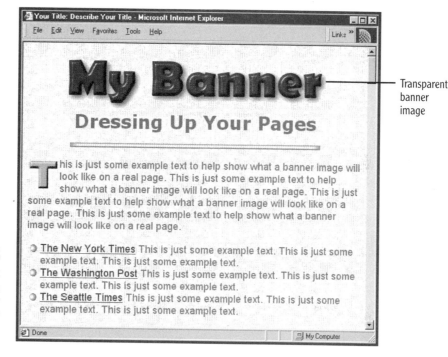

Transparent
banner
image

Figure 3.34

A transparent
banner image
can give your
page more of
a 3-D look.

pages, as well as links to several resources on the Web where you can find out
more about using style sheets.

See also Appendix F, "Completing Your Wish List," for information and guidance on how to add many popular features to your pages, such as background
sounds, hit counters, guestbooks, JavaScript roll-over buttons, GIF animations, and image maps.

Saving Your Work

You can use the HTML file you've just created later as a reference. When you
first saved it, you named it scratch2.html. If more than one person is going
to be doing this tutorial and you want to make sure that this file doesn't get
overwritten, you might want to save it under a new name (rs-scratch2.html,
for instance, if your name is Ronald Stevens or Roberta Stone).

Wrapping Up

If you've been able to complete both the Saturday Morning and Saturday Afternoon sessions before the dinner bell has rung, you're doing great! If you've taken a little longer, or even a lot longer, to complete these two sessions, that's okay. Remember, it doesn't matter how fast you've learned HTML, but how well. These two sessions, together, cover everything you need to know about HTML to be able to create effective and attractive Web pages. Even if you stop right now, you've still met your objective of being able to say, with confidence, "I know HTML!"

If you're plumb out of energy (hey, you've done a lot!), feel free to skip the Saturday Evening "bonus" session for now. You can do it tomorrow as your Sunday Morning session, or you can leave it until another weekend, if you want.

If, however, you're still hot to learn even more HTML, take a dinner break to get something nourishing into your system. Don't forget to feed your cat (or your kids, your partner, and so on). Go for a short walk, if you want, to get your circulation going. I'll see you back here in about an hour or so, when you'll learn all about using tables in your Web pages.

Working with Tables

- ✿ Defining Columns and Rows
- ✿ Controlling Borders and Spacing
- ✿ Spanning Columns and Rows
- ✿ Using Background Colors and Images
- ✿ Creating Icon Link Lists Using Tables
- ✿ Creating Two-Column Layouts

One of the weaknesses of HTML 2.0 was its inability to display information or data in a tabular format, except by including it as raw text (spaces included) inside a PRE (Preformatted Text) element—a solution that, although highly practical, was rather bland, at best. Tables were originally proposed as part of the proposed HTML 3.0 standard and were later incorporated into HTML 3.2. A few additional tags specifically designed for working with tables have also been included in HTML 4.0.

NOTE If you haven't yet completed the Saturday Afternoon session, "Dressing Up Your Pages," do so before going on to do this session.

This is a "bonus" session, which means you need to do it tonight only if you have the time, energy, and inclination. If you choose not to do this session tonight, I recommend that you do it as your Sunday Morning session instead.

What You Need

For doing this session, I recommend that you have the 4.0 version or higher of either Netscape Navigator or Internet Explorer installed. All the illustrations in this book were created using Netscape Navigator 4.72 and Internet Explorer 5.01. However, if you're still using an older browser, you don't necessarily need to upgrade your browser just to do this session. You can also use a recent version of Opera or NeoPlanet to do this session, if you want.

NOTE You should have already installed the example files used in this session at the start of this morning's session. If you haven't installed these files, please return to "Installing the Example files from the CD-ROM" in the Saturday Morning session before doing this session.

Using the Starting Template

To open the starting template, start.html, in Notepad, follow these steps:

1. Run Notepad (click on the Start button, select Run, type **notepad**, and press Enter).

2. Select File, Open. Click on the "Look in" list box, and then click on the Drive C icon [C:]. In the folder view, double-click on the Html folder to open it.

3. To make HTML files visible in the folder view, click on the "Files of type" list box and select All Files [*.*].

4. Double-click on start.html to open it.

Saving Your HTML File

Save your HTML file as scratch3a.html in your working folder (C:\Html) using these steps:

1. In Notepad, select File, Save As.

2. Click on the "Look in" list box, and then click on the C drive icon [C:]. In the folder view, double-click on the Html folder to open it.

NOTE When doing the following table examples, unless instructed to do otherwise, make all the changes to a single table, rather than trying to copy and paste to create separate tables for each example.

Later, if you want to see what the different table features do, I've included a couple of HTML files with the example files that you installed this morning that break out all the examples into separate tables, with comments added to describe the examples. After you've done this session, feel free to open tutor3a.html and tutor3b.html in your text editor and your browser to review how different features are implemented.

3. In the "File name" box, type **scratch3a.html**, and click on the Save button.

Starting Your Table

The TABLE tag needs to bracket your table. All other tags or text to be included in your table should be nested inside the TABLE tag. Enter the following HTML nested in the BODY tag:

```
<html>
<head>
<title>Your Title: Describe Your Title</title>
</head>
<body>
<p>
<table>
</table>
</p>
</body>
</html>
```

NOTE Although the TABLE tag is classified as a block element, it doesn't behave like a block element in every regard. If you include two tables in your HTML file, without any other intervening elements, they are displayed in your browser stacked one on top of the other, but absolutely no vertical spacing is inserted between the two. In some cases, this might be exactly what you want, but in other cases you might want to have adjacent tables separated by vertical spacing. The trick for doing this, as shown in this session's examples, is to nest the TABLE tag inside a P tag, to make sure sufficient space is added above and below the table.

Defining Columns and Rows

You can use the TR (Table Row) and TD (Table Data) tags to create a grid of rows and columns. Here's an example (see Figure 4.1 for an example of what this looks like in your Web browser):

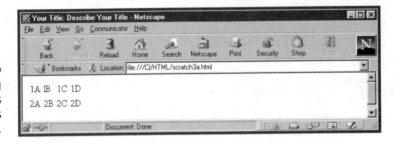

Figure 4.1

A table consisting of four columns and two rows is created.

```
<p>
<table>
<tr><td>1A</td><td>1B</td><td>1C</td><td>1D</td></tr>
<tr><td>2A</td><td>2B</td><td>2C</td><td>2D</td></tr>
</table>
</p>
```

Notice that a `<tr>` start tag and a `</tr>` end tag bracket each row.

Adding and Controlling Borders

A table hardly looks like a table without a border. Including a BORDER attribute inside the TABLE tag does the trick. Here's an example (see Figure 4.2):

```
<table border="1">
<tr><td>1A</td><td>1B</td><td>1C</td><td>1D</td></tr>
```

HTML 3.2 also recognizes the BORDER attribute by itself, whereas HTML 4.0 recognizes the `border="border"` attribute value. Both of these should have exactly the same result as `border="1"`.

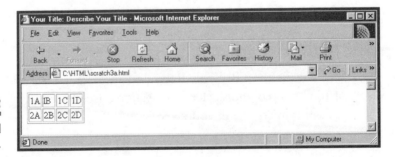

Figure 4.2

You can add borders to a table.

Increasing the value of the BORDER attribute increases the thickness of the outer border of the table, displaying it in 3-D relief; however, it doesn't affect the appearance of the interior lines of the table. Increase the BORDER value to six pixels to see what I mean (see Figure 4.3):

```
<table border="6">

<tr><td>1A</td><td>1B</td><td>1C</td><td>1D</td></tr>
```

Setting Spacing and Padding

This table looks a bit cramped, don't you think? The CELLSPACING attribute adds space between cells, whereas the CELLPADDING attribute adds space within each cell. Add six pixels of spacing and padding, like this (see Figure 4.4):

```
<table border="6" cellspacing="6" cellpadding="6">

<tr><td>1A</td><td>1B</td><td>1C</td><td>1D</td></tr>
```

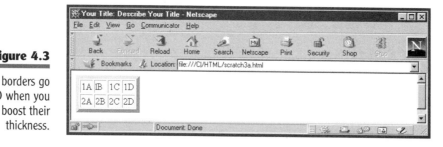

Figure 4.3

Table borders go 3-D when you boost their thickness.

Figure 4.4

You can add space between cells and padding within cells.

Adding Column Headings

What's a table without column headings, right? The TH (Table Heading) tag works just like the TD (Table Data) tag, except it defines a particular cell as a heading cell rather than as an ordinary data cell. To create a row of four column headings at the top of your table, use the TR tag to define a row; then, instead of using TD tags, insert TH tags to define the cells, like this (see Figure 4.5):

```
<table border="6" cellspacing="6" cellpadding="6">
<tr><th>A</th><th>B</th><th>C</th><th>D</th></tr>
<tr><td>1A</td><td>1B</td><td>1C</td><td>1D</td></tr>
```

You'll notice when you view this in your browser that column headings are automatically displayed bolded and centered.

Adding a Caption

The CAPTION tag lets you specify a caption for your table (see Figure 4.6):

```
<table border="6" cellspacing="6" cellpadding="6">
<caption>I. Table Example</caption>
```

NOTE Internet Explorer 5 for the Macintosh does not insert any horizontal spacing between a caption and a table, unless you nest the caption text inside a paragraph tag. I'm sure this is a browser "quirk" that'll be fixed in later versions, but if you want to make sure that your table caption will have sufficient space inserted between it and the table body in all browsers, nest it inside a paragraph tag.

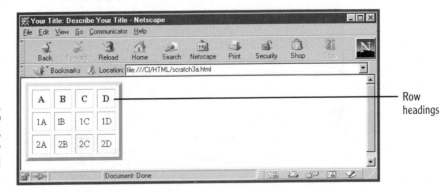

Figure 4.5

Table headings are automatically bolded and centered.

Row headings

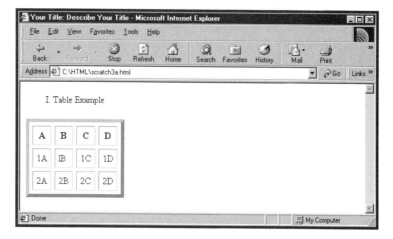

You can display the caption below the table by setting an `align="bottom"` attribute value in the CAPTION tag. The HTML 4 specification states that you should also be able to use `align="left"` or `align="right"` to display the caption either to the left or right side of a table. The only browser I know of that supports this is Opera 4.0. Internet Explorer 4/5 for Windows (but not the Macintosh version) recognizes the attributes, but merely left-aligns or right-aligns the caption text within the caption space. Netscape Navigator, for Windows or the Macintosh, completely ignores these attributes in the CAPTION tag.

TIP A trick for left-aligning or right-aligning text within the caption space, which works for all browsers, is to simply nest the caption text within a left-aligned or a right-aligned paragraph: `<caption><p  align="left">I.  Table  Example</p></caption>`, for instance.

Centering a Table

To center the table, just insert an `align="center"` attribute in the TABLE tag (see Figure 4.7):

```
<table align="center" border="6" cellspacing="6" cellpadding="6">
<caption>I. Table Example</caption>
```

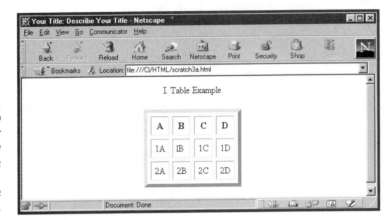

Figure 4.7

You can center
a table by
inserting the
`align="center"`
attribute in the
TABLE tag.

You can also center a table by nesting it in a CENTER tag or in a center-aligned DIV tag.

CAUTION   Don't try to center a table by nesting it in a center-aligned paragraph. Although this works fine in Internet Explorer, it doesn't work in Netscape Navigator, which still displays the table flush to the left margin.

Setting the Table Width

You can include a WIDTH attribute to specify the size of your table. You can set the width of your table using either pixels or a percentage value. A percentage value sets the width of the table to a percentage of the browser window's width. You can specify a table width of 75 percent, like this (see Figure 4.8):

```
<table align="center" border="6" cellspacing="6" cellpadding="6" width="75%">

<caption>I. Table Example</caption>
```

Doing More with Your Table

Just using the features covered so far, you can create and use many types of tables in your Web pages. I often use tables, with the border set to highlight

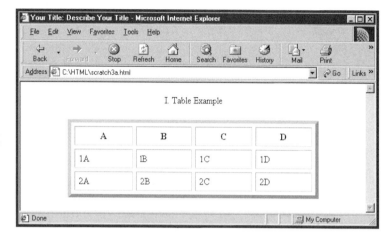

Figure 4.8

You can set the width of a table to a percentage (here 75 percent) of a browser window.

text I want to stand out from surrounding text, for instance. In the following sections, I cover some of the things you can do to create more sophisticated and complex tables.

Adding Row Headings

Now you can add some row headings. To create a row heading, just add a TH cell (instead of a TD cell) at the start of a table row, like this (see Figure 4.9):

```
<table align="center" border="6" cellspacing="6" cellpadding="6"
width="75%">

<caption>I. Table Example</caption>

<tr><th></th><th>A</th><th>B</th><th>C</th><th>D</th></tr>

<tr><th>Row 1:</th><td>1A</td><td>1B</td><td>1C</td><td>1D</td></tr>

<tr><th>Row 2:</th><td>2A</td><td>2B</td><td>2C</td><td>2D</td></tr>

</table>
```

You'll notice when you view this in your browser that row headings are formatted just like column headings—centered and bolded.

Another thing you should notice in Figure 4.9 is that when you include an empty TH (or TD) cell in a table, the cell borders for the empty cell aren't drawn. In this case, this is a desirable effect, but if the empty cell were in the middle of your table, for instance, you'd probably want to have the cell border drawn. One workaround that forces the cell borders to be drawn is to insert a non-breaking space (or) within the empty table cell.

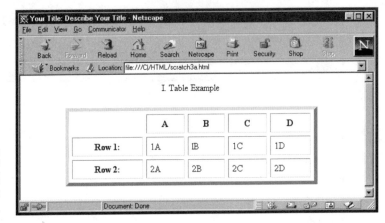

Figure 4.9

You can also add
row headings
to a table.

Horizontally Aligning Cell Contents

Right now, the text in the data cells is left-aligned. Use the ALIGN attribute
to right-align the two rows of data cells, like this (see Figure 4.10):

```
<caption>I. Table Example</caption>

<tr><th></th><th>A</th><th>B</th><th>C</th><th>D</th></tr>

<tr align="right"><th>Row 1:</th><td>1A</td><td>1B</td><td>1C
</td><td>1D</td></tr>

<tr align="right"><th>Row 2:</th><td>2A</td><td>2B</td><td>2C
</td><td>2D</td></tr>
```

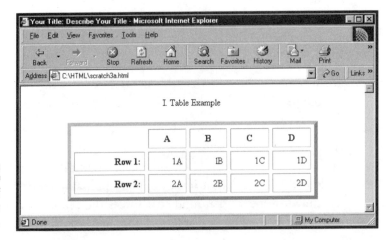

Figure 4.10

The two rows of
the table are now
right-aligned.

Besides using the ALIGN attribute in TR tags to horizontally align table rows, you can also use it in TD and TH tags to horizontally align individual table cells.

One browser I know of, Internet Explorer 5 for the Macintosh, applies the right-alignment only to the TD cells in the row, but not to the TH cells, which remain in their default center-alignment. Although this is clearly a quirk and will hopefully be fixed in future versions, if you want to ensure that the TH cells will be right-aligned as well in Internet Explorer 5 for the Macintosh, you need to insert `align="right"` in the TH tags.

Setting Column Widths

By inserting a WIDTH attribute in the top cell of a column, you can specify the width of the entire column. Column widths can be set in either pixels or percentages, or in a combination of pixels and percentages.

Setting pixel widths for table columns is relatively straightforward, but setting percentage widths can be a bit tricky. That's because Internet Explorer and Netscape Navigator calculate the width of a column differently. Internet Explorer includes any spacing set between the cells (by the TABLE tag's CELLSPACING attribute) when it calculates column widths, but Netscape Navigator doesn't.

The upshot is that, if you want to get equal columns in Navigator, you've got to deduct an allowance for the spacing between the cells. For the current table, setting a `width="18%"` attribute in the top row's TH tags does the trick. In fact, you can set any percentage value that you want, as long as it is 18 or less, and the result is the same in Internet Explorer or Netscape Navigator.

The same applies if you want to set disproportionate columns. As long as the sum total of the column width percentages includes an allowance for the spacing between the cells, the relative proportions of the column widths should be preserved in Navigator, as well as in Internet Explorer.

To test this, set each column to an equal width by inserting a `width="18%"` attribute in each of the TH tags in the top row of the table (see Figure 4.11):

```
<caption>I. Table Example</caption>

<tr><th width="18%"></th><th width="18%">A</th><th
width="18%">B</th><th width="18%">C</th><th width="18%">D</th></tr>
```

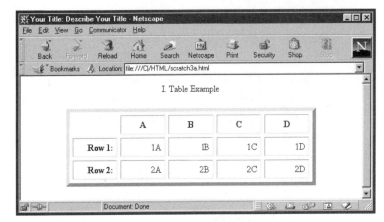

Figure 4.11

You can set equal
column widths
in a table.

That doesn't mean, however, that you can cap the width of a table column. If the content of a table cell, such as an inline image or a particularly long word, for instance, exceeds the width you've set for the column, the column width is expanded to make allowance for the cell content, and other column widths are correspondingly reduced.

Inserting an Image

You can insert an image inside a table cell. For this example, you use a graphic, one.gif, included with the example graphics. Enter the following to insert an image inside the upper-left corner cell of your table (see Figure 4.12):

```
<caption>I. Table Example</caption>

<tr><th width="18%"><img src="one.gif"></th><th width="18%">A</th><th
width="18%">B</th><th width="18%">C</th><th width="18%">D</th></tr>
```

Vertically Aligning Cell Contents

You can use the VALIGN attribute to vertically align the contents of a table row (TR), a table heading (TH), or a table data cell (TD). You can set "top" or "bottom" attribute values (middle-alignment is the default). Set the top row to be bottom-aligned (see Figure 4.13):

```
<caption>I. Table Example</caption>

<tr valign="bottom"><th width="18%"><img src="one.gif"></th><th
width="18%">A</th><th width="18%">B</th><th width="18%">C</th><th
width="18%">D</th></tr>
```

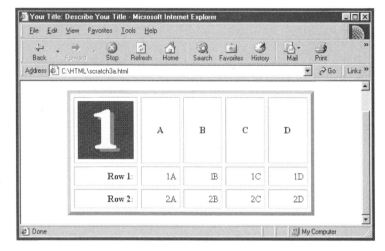

Figure 4.12

You can insert an inline image inside a table cell.

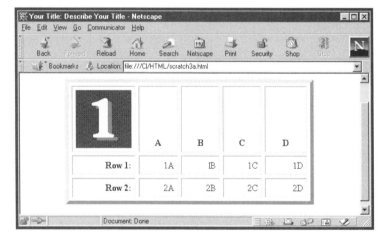

Figure 4.13

You can vertically align cell contents.

Spanning Columns

The COLSPAN attribute lets you create cells that span across columns. Add a row to your table that includes three table head cells, the last two of which span across two columns each (see Figure 4.14):

```
<tr valign="bottom"><th width="18%"><img src="one.gif"></th><th
width="18%">A</th><th width="18%">B</th><th width="18%">C</th><th
width="18%">D</th></tr>

<tr><th></th><th colspan="2">A & B</th><th colspan="2">C &
D</th></tr>
```

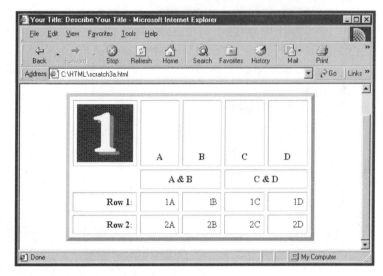

Figure 4.14

Table cells can
span columns.

```
<tr><th align="right">Row
1:</th><td>1A</td><td>1B</td><td>1C</td><td>1D</td></tr>
```

To span additional columns, specify the number with the COLSPAN attribute. Just make sure you don't exceed the total number of columns in the table. For instance, this example amounts to three cells spanning five columns (1 + 2 + 2 = 5).

Spanning Rows

You can use the ROWSPAN attribute to span rows. This can be a little tricky because you need to remove any spanned cells from any following rows included in the span. In the following example, add the ROWSPAN attribute to the first TH tag in the first row and then delete the first TH tag (shown struck through) in the second row (see Figure 4.15):

```
<caption>I. Table Example</caption>

<tr valign="bottom"><th rowspan="2" width="18%"><img
src="one.gif"></th><th width="18%">A</th><th width="18%">B</th><th
width="18%">C</th><th width="18%">D</th></tr>

<tr><th></th><th colspan="2">A & B</th><th colspan="2">C &
D</th></tr>
```

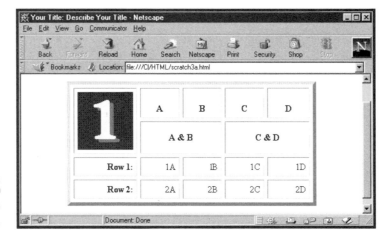

Figure 4.15

Table cells can also span rows.

Setting Row Heights

You can't set the height of a row of cells by using a HEIGHT attribute in the TR tag. Rather, to do this, you must insert the HEIGHT attribute in the first TD or TH tag in the row where you want to set the row height, unless a ROWSPAN attribute is being used, in which case the HEIGHT attribute must be inserted in the first TD or TH tag following the row-spanning cell, as shown in the following example (see Figure 4.16):

```
<caption>I. Table Example</caption>
<tr valign="bottom"><th rowspan="2" width="18%"><img
src="one.gif"></th><th height="65" width="18%">A</th><th
width="18%">B</th><th width="18%">C</th><th width="18%">D</th></tr>
<tr><th colspan="2">A & B</th><th colspan="2">C & D</th></tr>
```

You might be wondering why, in the example, the first row height is decreased, instead of the second row height being increased. The reason is that you can't decrease the height of a row beyond what it otherwise normally is, but you can increase it. Thus, in the previous example, in order to decrease the height of the second row, you had to increase the height of the first row.

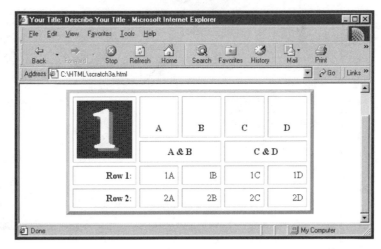

Figure 4.16

You can adjust the height of a table row.

Take a Break

Wow, if you've been at it all day, you're definitely a long-distance runner! Take a breather.

If your eyelids are drooping and your fingers cramping up, feel free to call it a night. I'll see you bright and early tomorrow morning. You can always complete the rest of this session on another weekend. You don't need to complete the rest of this session before going on to do the Sunday sessions.

However, if you're still hungry to find out more about creating tables, I'll see you back here in five or ten minutes, when you'll learn how to control the appearance of your table using fonts, colors, and backgrounds, create fancy icon link lists using tables, and flow text and other elements around tables.

Controlling Fonts, Colors, and Backgrounds

So far, you've learned how to structure your tables, adding row columns, spanning rows and columns, setting row heights, and so on. The following sections cover things you can do with your tables to make them more attractive.

Changing Font Sizes and Colors

You can change the font size and color of the contents of a table cell by inserting a FONT tag bracketing the text you want to be affected. The following example sets the font size to 7 and the color to blue for one of the cells (see Figure 4.17):

```
<caption>I. Table Example</caption>

<tr valign="bottom"><th rowspan="2" width="18%"><img
src="one.gif"></th><th height="65" width="18%"><font size="7"
color="blue">A</font></th><th width="18%">B</th><th
width="18%">C</th><th width="18%">D</th></tr>

<tr><th colspan="2">A & B</th><th colspan="2">C & D</th></tr>
```

This brings up one of the bigger bugaboos relative to tables. If you want to use the FONT tag to change the size, color, or face of text in a table, you have to set the tag in every cell where you want it to take effect. Font tags located outside of a table have absolutely no effect on text inside the table.

This is an instance where using a style sheet to control the appearance of a table can offer some big advantages. In a style sheet, it only takes a single line to define the font characteristics of every cell within a table, which beats the heck out of having to insert FONT tags inside of every table cell.

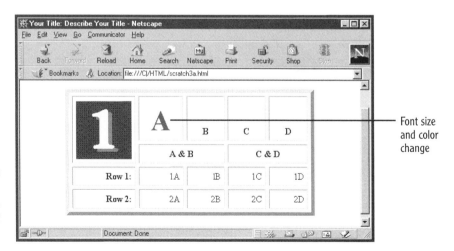

Figure 4.17

You can assign different font sizes and colors to text inside table cells.

Font size and color change

Assigning Background Colors

You can assign a background color to an entire table, a row within a table, or a single cell. For instance, a table can be made more readable by assigning different background colors to distinguish row-heading cells and table-data cells.

Assigning a Background Color in the TABLE Tag

Navigator and Internet Explorer do not handle assigning a background color to an entire table in the same fashion. In fact, Internet Explorer 5 doesn't even handle this the way earlier versions of Internet Explorer did. Navigator displays the background color only within the table's cells, but not in the spacing between the cells. Internet Explorer fills in the spacing between the cells with the background color. Earlier versions of Internet Explorer also fill in a table caption with the background color, whereas Internet Explorer 5 displays the background color only behind the body of the table. In other words, if you want to ensure your table is displayed at least similarly in these browsers, you should probably avoid setting a background color in the TABLE tag altogether. To see what it does, use the BGCOLOR attribute to set a background color in the TABLE tag (see Figures 4.18 and 4.19):

```
<table bgcolor="aqua" align="center" border="6" cellspacing="6"
cellpadding="6" width="75%">

<caption>I. Table Example</caption>
```

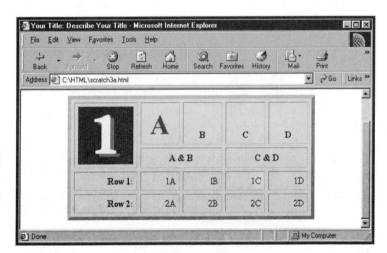

Figure 4.18

Internet Explorer displays a background color behind the whole table.

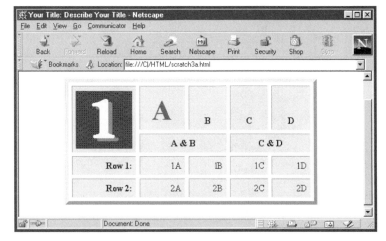

Figure 4.19

Navigator displays
a background color
only within the
table's cells.

If you want to set the background color in the TABLE tag, that's okay. However, don't assume that because it looks one way in Internet Explorer it's going to look the same way in Navigator or vice versa. If you want your table to look the same in both browsers, set background colors in the TR, TH, and TD tags, as shown next.

Assigning a Background Color in the TR, TH, and TD Tags

You can assign background colors to individual table rows (TR tags), as well as to individual table heading (TH) and table data (TD) cells. The following code assigns a lime color to the top row, red to the top-left TH cell (the one with the image in it), fuchsia to the second row, and yellow to the bottom two rows (notice that `bgcolor="aqua"` should be deleted):

```
<table bgcolor="aqua" align="center" border="6" cellspacing="6"
cellpadding="6" width="75%">

<caption>I. Table Example</caption>

<tr bgcolor="lime" valign="bottom"><th bgcolor="red" rowspan="2"
width="18%"><img src="one.gif"></th><th height="65" width="18%"><font
size="7" color="blue">A</font></th><th width="18%">B</th><th
width="18%">C</th><th width="18%">D</th></tr>

<tr bgcolor="fuchsia"><th colspan="2">A & B</th><th colspan="2">C &
D</th></tr>
```

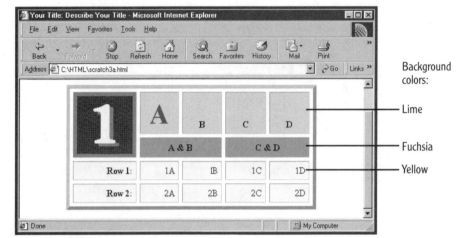

Figure 4.20

You can set
different
background colors
for rows or
individual cells.

```
<tr bgcolor="yellow" align="right"><th>Row
1:</th><td>1A</td><td>1B</td><td>1C</td><td>1D</td></tr>

<tr bgcolor="yellow" align="right"><th>Row
2:</th><td>2A</td><td>2B</td><td>2C</td><td>2D</td></tr>

</table>
```

As shown in Figure 4.20, different background colors appear behind one of
the table cells, as well as behind the top, the second, and the last two table
rows. You need to hop over to your Web browser, though, to really see what
this looks like.

Removing Borders and Cell Spacing

You might think that you can get rid of the spacing and borders between
cells just by removing the BORDER and CELLSPACING attributes in the
TABLE tag. Not so. To get rid of them completely, you have to set these
attribute values to zero, like this (see Figure 4.21):

```
<table align="center" border="0" cellspacing="0" cellpadding="6"
width="75%">

<caption>I. Table Example</caption>
```

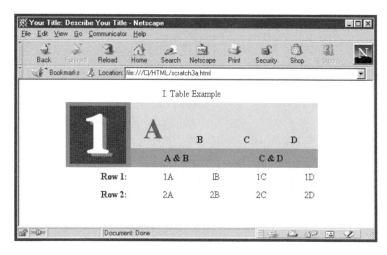

Figure 4.21

You have to set the BORDER and CELLSPACING values to zero to completely remove the borders and spacing between cells.

Using Background Images

Both of the major browsers, Internet Explorer and Netscape Navigator, do display background images inside of tables. Be aware, however, that use of the BACKGROUND attribute for tables is not included in the HTML 4.0 standard. One browser I know of, Opera, doesn't display background images in tables at all.

The main reason that the BACKGROUND attribute for tables is not included in the HTML 4.0 standard is that Internet Explorer and Netscape Navigator handle this attribute differently, and neither browser-maker was willing to budge, apparently, when the HTML 4.0 standard was being negotiated.

If you do want to include background images that display similarly in the two main browsers, here are some pointers:

○ As was the case with a background color, Internet Explorer displays a background image set in the TABLE tag behind the entire table, including behind the cell spacing. Navigator puts it only behind the individual cells.

○ Internet Explorer does not recognize background images specified in the TR tag, but Navigator does. To specify a background image for a table row that shows up in both browsers, you need to specify it for each cell (TH or TD) in the row.

✿ In Navigator, a background image specified in the TABLE tag takes precedence over any background colors set in the TR, TH, or TD tags; but in Internet Explorer, it's the other way around. Therefore, if you want to specify a background image in the TABLE tag that displays identically in both browsers, get rid of any BGCOLOR attributes elsewhere in the table.

If you decide to use a background image in a table, be aware that, if you are displaying a light font color against a dark background image, you'll end up with a light font color displayed against the background color of your whole page (most likely white) in browsers that don't support displaying background images in tables. For that reason, if you want to use a light font color displayed against a dark background image in a table, set a dark background color in your page's BODY tag. That way, if the browser cannot display your table's background image, the text in your table will still be legible against your page's background color. (If you've got a light text color set against a dark background image in your table, but vice versa in the body of your Web page, you should try to set a neutral background color in your page's BODY tag that will provide contrast for both.)

Although the BACKGROUND attribute in tables is not a standard HTML attribute, background images in tables can give a nice effect, so I wouldn't necessarily avoid using this attribute just because it hasn't got the official stamp of approval yet. Just be careful how you use it, as previously detailed. To check out what a BACKGROUND attribute set in the TABLE tag looks like, specify a background image in the TABLE tag, reset the BORDER and CELLSPACING attributes as shown, and delete any BGCOLOR attributes, like this (see Figures 4.22 and 4.23):

```
<table background="backgrnd.gif" align="center" border="6"
cellspacing="6" cellpadding="6" width="75%">

<caption>I. Table Example</caption>

<tr bgcolor="lime" valign="bottom"><th bgcolor="red" rowspan="2"
width="18%"><img src="one.gif"></th><th height="65" width="18%"><font
size="7" color="blue">A</font></th><th width="18%">B</th><th
```

```
width="18%">C</th><th width="18%">D</th></tr>

<tr bgcolor="fuchsia"><th colspan="2">A & B</th><th colspan="2">C &
D</th></tr>

<tr bgcolor="yellow" align="right"><th>Row
1:</th><td>1A</td><td>1B</td><td>1C</td><td>1D</td></tr>

<tr bgcolor="yellow" align="right"><th>Row
2:</th><td>2A</td><td>2B</td><td>2C</td><td>2D</td></tr>

</table>
```

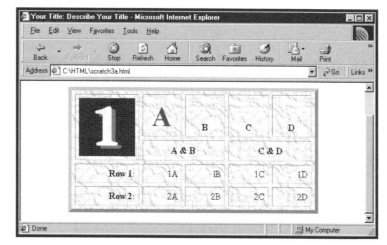

Figure 4.22

A background image in Internet Explorer is displayed behind the whole table.

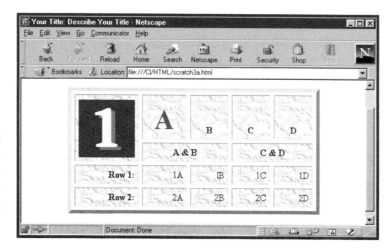

Figure 4.23

A background image in Navigator is displayed only behind the table cells.

Controlling Border Colors

You can specify colors to be used in displaying a table border by including BORDERCOLOR, BORDERCOLORDARK, and BORDERCOLOR-LIGHT attributes to the TABLE tag. You set these attributes the same way you set the COLOR attribute for the FONT tag, using either one of the 16 standard color names or an RGB hex code. These attributes are all Microsoft extensions to HTML, so support by any browser other than Internet Explorer cannot be guaranteed. Netscape Navigator 4.72 supports the BORDER-COLOR attribute, but earlier versions of Navigator do not support any of these attributes. The Opera browser doesn't support any of these attributes.

Creating Icon Link Lists Using Tables

In the Saturday Afternoon session, you learned how to create indented icon link lists using left-aligned bullet images. That method worked okay, as long as no more than two lines of text needed to be indented from the margin. In this section, I show you how to create an indented icon link list using tables. Although creating an indented icon link list using a table is a bit more involved, you're not limited to having only two indented text lines in your list item, which can make the extra work involved worthwhile.

To create an icon link list using tables, enter the following (see Figure 4.24):

```
<p><table width=100%>

<tr valign="top">

<td width="20"><p><img src="redball.gif" vspace="3"> </td><td><a
href="http://pages.nyu.edu/~tqm3413/yoyo/index.htm">Tomer's Page of
Exotic Yo-Yo</a> Dedicated to the "little-known, original, unusual,
difficult, or otherwise interesting tricks." This is one of the more
entertaining and fun Yo-Yo sites you can find on the Web.</td></tr>

<tr valign="top">

<td width="20"><p><img src="redball.gif" vspace="3"> </td><td><a
href="http://www.pd.net/yoyo/">American Yo-Yo Association</a> Read
past issues of the AYYA Newsletter.</td></tr>

<tr valign="top">

<td><p><img src="redball.gif" vspace="3"> </td><td><a
href="http://www.socool.com/socool/yo_hist.html">The History of the
Yo-Yo</a> All you want to know about Yo-Yo history.</td></tr>

</table></p>
```

Figure 4.24

Using tables, you can create an indented icon link list with no limit on the number of indented lines.

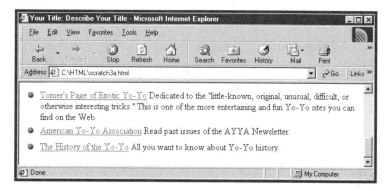

In this example of creating an indented icon link list using tables, you should pay attention to a number of things:

○ The TR tags include `valign="top"`, which sets the vertical alignment. Without this, the icon bullet images are middle-aligned, which is not what you want. You can also set this attribute value in the TD tag containing the icon bullet graphic.

○ A WIDTH attribute value of 20 pixels is set in the first cell of the top row to specify the width of the first column. This width can be increased or decreased to suit your taste.

○ A P tag is inserted in the first cell of each row, and a space is inserted at the end of the same cell. This makes allowance for older Web browsers that don't support displaying tables. The P tag causes a non-supporting browser to display the table row as a separate line, and the space is inserted between the icon graphic and the following text. Note that adding the P tag and inserting the space does not affect the display of the table in a tables-capable Web browser.

○ The IMG tags for the icon bullet images include a VSPACE attribute that sets three pixels of vertical spacing above and below the images. Rarely does an icon bullet, by itself, line up evenly with a following line of text. You can add or subtract pixels in the VSPACE attribute of the IMG tag to adjust the position of the icon bullet relative to following text. (You can also open the icon bullet image in your image editor and add or remove white space above the icon bullet to cause it to display lower or higher relative to the following text line.)

Flowing Text and Other Elements around Tables

Although tables are not inline elements, they function similarly to how inline images function. You can do many of the same things with tables that you can do with inline images, including flowing text around the right side or left side of a table, flowing text between a table, and even flowing a table between two other tables.

Flowing Text around a Table

By including either an `align="left"` or `align="right"` attribute in the TABLE tag, you can cause text to flow around the right or left side of a table.

This can be a particularly handy way of flowing text around an image, in that you can set a table's width to be wider than an image that is nested in it. This lets you add horizontal spacing to only one side of the image, allowing the image to remain flush to the left or right margin, whereas additional horizontal spacing is added only between the image and text flowing around it. Just enter the following example to see how this works (see Figure 4.25):

```
<p><table align="left" border="0" cellpadding="0" cellspacing="0"
width="140">

<tr><td><img src="image.gif"></td><tr>

</table>

This is just some example text. This is just some example text. This
is just some example text. This is just some example text. This is
just some example text. This is just some example text. This is just
some example text. This is just some example text. This is just some
example text. This is just some example text. This is just some
example text. This is just some example text.<br clear="left"></p>
```

Notice that the flowing text in the previous example is not inside of its own paragraph tag, but is nested in the same paragraph tag as the table that it's flowing around. That's because at least one browser I know of, Opera, will space down the text relative to the table if the text is inserted inside its own paragraph tag.

Figure 4.25

Using a table,
you can add
horizontal space
between an image
and flowing text
that is displayed
only on one side
of the image.

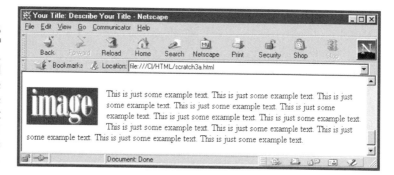

Displaying Side-by-Side Tables

This works similarly to flowing text around a table, except in this instance,
a right-aligned table is flowed around a left-aligned table (see Figure 4.26):

```
<p><table align="left" border="6" cellpadding="6" cellspacing="6"
width="150">

<tr align="center"><td height="100"><big>This is a left-aligned
table</big></td></tr>

</table>

<table align="right" border="6" cellpadding="6" cellspacing="6"
width="150">

<tr align="center"><td height="100"><big>This is a right-aligned
table</big></td></tr>

</table><br clear="all"></p>
```

Figure 4.26

You can display
tables side-by-side
by setting one as
left-aligned and the
other as right-
aligned.

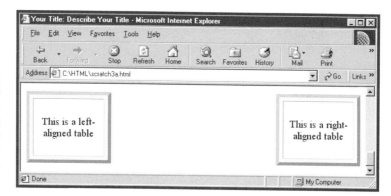

You don't want to forget the `<br clear="all">` tag at the end of the previous example. If you leave it off, any following text and elements flow between the tables, which might not be what you want.

Adjusting the Horizontal Position of Side-by-Side Tables

To adjust the horizontal position of side-by-side tables, just nest them inside of a single-cell table with the WIDTH attribute set. As long as the single-cell table has a width set to less than the width of the browser window, you'll see the nested left-aligned and right-aligned tables spaced in from the left and right margins, respectively. You can use a percentage table width to ensure that the bracketing table width is less than the width of the browser window—either that, or set the width of the table to a width value of well less than 500 pixels, to allow for visitors surfing at a 640×480 screen resolution.

Although there's no problem with setting a percentage width for the bracketing table, you shouldn't set percentage widths for the nested tables. That's because when percentage widths are used in nested tables, they tend to produce differing results in Internet Explorer and Netscape Navigator. Copy and paste the previous example's codes, and then add the following codes at the start and end of the example (see Figure 4.27):

```
<p><table align="center" border="0" cellpadding="0 cellspacing="0"
width="75%">

<tr><td>

<p><table align="left" border="6" cellpadding="6" cellspacing="6"
width="150">

<tr align="center"><td height="100"><big>This is a left-aligned
table</big></td></tr>

</table>

<table align="right" border="6" cellpadding="6" cellspacing="6"
width="150">

<tr align="center"><td height="100"><big>This is a right-aligned
table</big></td></tr>

</table><br clear="all"></p>

</td></tr>

</table>
```

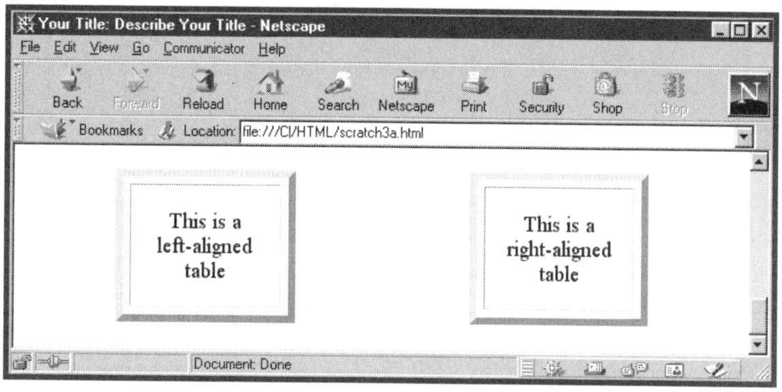

Figure 4.27

By nesting side-by-side tables inside of another table, you can adjust their horizontal positions.

Saving Your Work

You can use the HTML file you've just created later as a reference. When you first saved it, you named it scratch3a.html. If more than one person is going to be doing this tutorial and you want to make sure that this file doesn't get overwritten, you might want to give it a new name (jd-scratch3a.html, for instance, if your name is John Davis or Judy Dell).

Take a Break

Because this is an evening session, you deserve an extra break! If you feel you need it, go ahead and grab an extra breather right now.

If you're out of gas, however, feel free to save the rest of this session until another time. You don't need to complete the rest of this session before going on to do the Sunday sessions.

However, if you're up for learning even more about using tables, I'll see you back here in five or ten minutes, when you'll be learning how to create two-column layouts using tables.

Creating Two-Column Layouts Using Tables

A common use of tables on the Web is to create a layout using two or more columns. For instance, to include a sidebar menu running down the left side of your page, you can create a layout using one narrow column, with a second column set to expand to fill the browser window. An additional nice effect that you can create is to display the table against a two-tone background image, so that the left column is demarcated by one color and the right column by the other color.

To create this example, you need to create a new HTML file. Just follow the steps provided earlier to open the starting template (start.html) and then resave it as scratch3b.html to your working folder (C:\Html).

Using a Two-Column Background Image

A two-column background image displays a vertical strip in a different color or tone down one side of the page. Because you don't want this image to be tiled horizontally, but only vertically, the image needs to be wide enough to allow for the widest likely browser width. Generally, a width of 1280 pixels should be plenty wide enough, whereas the height can be kept to five or fewer pixels in order to keep the file size down. I've included an example two-column background image with the example files. To add it to your page, enter the following (see Figure 4.28):

```
<html>
<head>
<title>Your Title: Describe Your Title</title>
</head>
<body background="b_twotone.jpg">
</body>
</html>
```

Setting the Column Width with a Spacer Image

You'll want to set the width of the left column to a set pixel width, while allowing the right column to expand to fill the page. Because Navigator behaves rather quirkily if you try to combine pixel and percentage widths in a table, the way to do this is to use what is called a "spacer" image to set the pixel width of the left column. A *spacer image* is a GIF image, usually not more than one pixel high, that is completely transparent.

To set the width of the expanding right column, you just need to set a per-

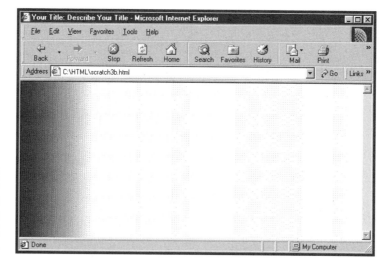

Figure 4.28

A two-column background image tiles vertically, but not horizontally.

centage width of less than 100 percent. Enter the following to set the column widths for the table:

```
<body background="b_twotone.jpg">
<table border="0" cellspacing="0" cellpadding="0">
<tr>
   <td width="100"><img src="spacer.gif" alt="" width="110"
height="1"></td>
   <td width="99%"></td>
</tr>
</table>
```

To increase or decrease the width of the left column, just increase or decrease the WIDTH attribute in the IMG tag for spacer.gif.

This won't show anything in your browser yet, because the spacer image is entirely transparent and the border, cell spacing, and cell padding values have all been zeroed. (If you do want to check out the column widths in your browser, just set a positive border value and set the height of the spacer image to several pixels.)

Including a Banner Image

Including a banner image that spans both columns can produce a nice effect. You can use the same example banner image, banner.gif, that you used in the Saturday Afternoon session. Just insert it in a table cell with a `rowspan="2"` attribute set (see Figure 4.29):

```
<table border="0" cellspacing="0" cellpadding="0">

<tr>

  <td width="100"><img src="spacer.gif" alt="" width="110"
  height="1"></td>

  <td width="99%"></td>

</tr>

<tr>

  <td colspan="2"><p><img src="banner.gif"></p></td>

</tr>

</table>
```

Adding Vertical Spacing

You can add vertical spacing to your table layout by adding a table row containing a table cell with its height set to a pixel amount. To add 10 pixels of vertical spacing below the banner image, add the following to your table:

```
<tr>

  <td colspan="2"><p><img src="banner.gif"></p></td>

</tr>

<tr>

  <td height="10"></td>

  <td></td>

</tr>

</table>
```

Creating a Vertical Button Menu

You can create a vertical button menu that links to other Web pages or to subsections within the same page. I've already created some button images

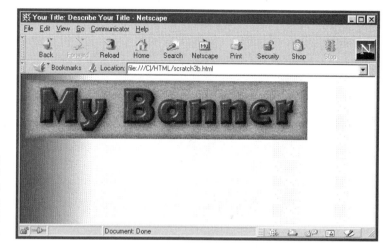

Figure 4.29

You can span more
than one column
using the COLSPAN
attribute.

for you—you'll find them included with the example images. To create a
vertical button menu, add the following to your table (see Figure 4.30):

```
<tr>
  <td height="10"></td>
  <td></td>
</tr>
<tr>
  <td valign="top">
    <a href="example.html">
      <img src="but_prod.gif" border="0" vspace="3"></a><br>
    <a href="example.html">
      <img src="but_serv.gif" border="0" vspace="3"></a><br>
    <a href="example.html">
      <img src="but_supp.gif" border="0" vspace="3"></a><br>
    <a href="example.html">
      <img src="but_cont.gif" border="0" vspace="3"></a></p>
  </td>
  <td>
  </td>
</tr>
</table>
```

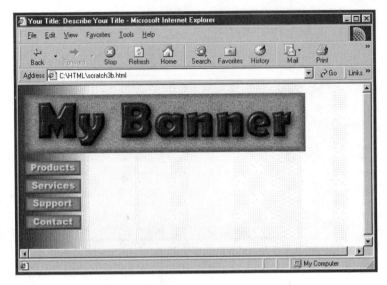

Figure 4.30

A vertical button
menu can link to
other Web pages or
to subsections
within the same
Web page.

Right now, the vertical menu buttons just link to the example page,
example.html, that I've included with the other example pages. To link to
pages of your own choosing, just edit the links' HREF attributes.

Adding the Content to the Right Column

The main content of your page is displayed in the right column. This can be
just like any other Web page, including a level-one heading, an introductory
paragraph, link lists, inline images, image links, and so on. Add the following to create some content for the right column (see Figure 4.31):

```
<tr>
  <td valign="top">
    <a href="example.html">
      <img src="but_prod.gif" border="0" vspace="3"></a><br>
    <a href="example.html">
      <img src="but_serv.gif" border="0" vspace="3"></a><br>
    <a href="example.html">
      <img src="but_supp.gif" border="0" vspace="3"></a><br>
    <a href="example.html">
      <img src="but_cont.gif" border="0" vspace="3"></a></p>
  </td>
```

```
<td valign="top">

  <h1>Two-Column Table Layout</h1>

  <p>This is just some example text to show what this will
  look like. This is just some example text to show what
  this will look like. This is just some example text to
  show what this will look like. This is just some example
  text to show what this will look like.</p>

</td>

</tr>
```

TIP

There are times when you might want to eliminate (or increase) the margin that surrounds a Web page. For instance, if you're using background colors in a table set to a 100 percent width, you might want to eliminate the margin that surrounds the table. To eliminate the margin around the page in both Internet Explorer and Netscape Navigator, you need to combine two sets of attributes in the BODY tag of your page:

```
<body marginheight="0" marginwidth="0" topmargin="0" leftmargin="0">
```

The MARGINHEIGHT and MARGINWIDTH attributes are required by Navigator, whereas the TOPMARGIN and LEFTMARGIN attributes are required by Internet Explorer. This also eliminates the page margin in the Opera browser. These attributes are unofficial extensions to HTML introduced by Netscape and Microsoft, respectively, and are not included in the official HTML specifications.

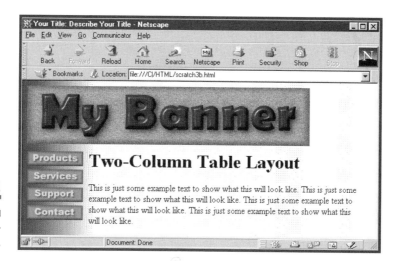

Figure 4.31

Using a table, you can create a two-column layout.

Saving Your Work

When you first saved your current HTML file, you named it scratch3b.html. If more than one person is going to be doing this tutorial and you want to make sure that this file doesn't get overwritten, you might want to give it a new name (jd-scratch3b.html, for instance, if your name is John Davis or Judy Dell).

NOTE A number of new table tags are included in HTML 4, but so far are only supported by Internet Explorer 5. These include the TBODY (Table Body), THEAD (Table Head), TFOOT (Table Foot), COLGROUP (Column Group), and COL (Column) tags. All these tags work in association with styles to assign display characteristics to horizontal or vertical table divisions. For more detailed descriptions of these tags, see Appendix A, "HTML Quick Reference." For more information on using styles, see Appendix E.

Wrapping Up

You should now be comfortable including tables in your Web pages. If you completed this whole session, you should now be able to implement a wide range of features using tables. You should even know how to create fancy 3-D icon bulleted lists using tables that have no limit on the number of indented lines, as well as create spiffy two-column layouts using tables.

If you managed to do all three Saturday sessions, you're definitely a super HTML hotshot! Get a good night's sleep. I'll see you tomorrow morning, when you'll learn how to create a "framed" Web site.

SUNDAY MORNING

Working with Frames

✿ Considering the Pros and Cons of Using Frames

✿ Creating a Two-Column and Two-Row Frame Page

✿ Creating a Combo Row/Column Frame Page

✿ Creating a Nested Row/Column Frame Page

✿ Using Background Images with Frame Pages

By now, you should have a good understanding of the basics of HTML, as well as a grasp on how to make your Web pages more colorful and attractive. If you took the time to do the Saturday Evening bonus session, you should also have a good understanding of HTML tables.

NOTE If you skipped the Saturday Evening bonus session, "Working with Tables," feel free to do that session as your Sunday Morning session, if you want. If you haven't yet completed the Saturday Afternoon session, "Dressing Up Your Pages," go back and complete that session first, before attempting to complete this session.

Although frames weren't included in the official specification for HTML until version 4.0, they've been around for some time, having first been introduced as an HTML extension by Netscape. Microsoft Internet Explorer also supported using frames long before they were officially included as a standard HTML feature.

Pros and Cons of Using Frames

Part of the reason for the popularity of frames is the "gee-whiz" factor. Separate scrollable frames, often featuring differing background images or colors and displaying menu bars, permanent mastheads or banner ads, and so on, can do much to improve the user-accessibility of a site. On the other hand, however, the injudicious use of frames can lead to a confusing and congested site that is difficult to access and navigate.

There are also a few additional "negative" factors to consider before deciding to create a frame page:

✿ Because the initial page that is loaded in a frame page lacks any content, and contains only codes, some search engine spiders have trouble indexing frame pages. This can lead to being listed further down, or not being listed at all, in a Web search response list.

✿ You can't bookmark an individual page within a frame page, but only the initial page that sets up the frames. In a more complex site, visitors can't easily bookmark a particular page in order to be able to return to it later.

✿ The use of frames in a site can make it difficult to print a particular page.

There are, however, ways to get around the drawbacks involved in using frames, although it does require extra consideration when creating your site. I cover many of these workarounds in this session, and include additional information on the Web site for this book. Here, however, is a quick rundown on what you can do to make using frames more trouble-free:

FIND IT ON ▶
THE WEB

✿ Always include META tag descriptions and keyword lists in your frame page's initial page. Many search engines use these tags to index your site. At this book's Web site, at **www.callihan.com/learn3/**, you'll find a link to a page, "Web Site Promotion Tips & Tricks," that'll show you how to include META tag descriptions and keyword lists in your pages.

✿ Always include a "noframes" section in your frame page's initial page. This not only provides a link for early browsers that are not frames-capable, but also provides a way for a search engine spider (which follows any links to other pages in your site) to index your site. In this session, I thoroughly discuss including a "noframes" section in your frame page's initial page.

✿ To counteract the bookmarking problem, if you're using frames to create a relatively complex site, break the site into several "mini-framed" sites, each with its own initial page for setting up the frames layout. Thus, if you have several major categories in your site, visitors can still bookmark (and return to) the initial page for each category.

✿ One solution to the printing problem is simply to provide links to a "printer-friendly" version of a page. This often needs to be nothing more than a link that displays the frame page's main page by itself in a full browser window.

What You Need

For this session, I recommend that you have the 4.0 version or higher of either Netscape Navigator or Internet Explorer installed. All the illustrations in this book were created using Netscape Navigator 4.73 and Internet Explorer 5.01. You can also use a recent version of Opera or NeoPlanet to do this session, if you want.

If you do want to take the time now to upgrade your browser, you can download the latest version of Netscape Navigator at **home.netscape.com/** or Internet Explorer at **www.microsoft.com/windows/ie/**.

FIND IT ON ▶
THE WEB

NOTE You should have already installed the example files from the CD-ROM at the start of the Saturday Morning session. If you haven't installed these files, please return to "Installing the Example Files from the CD-ROM" in the Saturday Morning session before doing this session.

Creating Two-Column and Two-Row Frame Pages

The easiest and simplest type of frame page you can create is one that only includes either two columns or two rows. You should first become comfortable with creating these simpler frame pages before moving on to more complex ones.

NOTE Although I use the term *frame page*, realize that a frame page is not a single page, but a collection of usually three or more pages: a page that defines the layout of the frame page and the pages that are displayed in the frames defined by the layout.

Creating a Two-Column Frame Page

The two-column frame page is often used to create a site with a sidebar menu on one side of the Web page and a fuller-sized frame for displaying the content of the site on the other side of the Web page. Included in the sidebar menu frame are links that control the content of the other frame.

To make things easier for you, I've already created the pages that'll be displayed in the main frame of the site. In this section, you'll be creating and saving two HTML files: the initial page to set up the frames and the sidebar menu page.

Defining the Column Layout

To start out, you'll be creating the page that defines the two-column frame layout. This type of page is often called a *frameset page*, because the FRAMESET tag is used to define a frame layout. Run Notepad (or any other text editor you want to use) and enter the following example:

```
<html>
<head>
<title>Two-Column Frame Example</title>
</head>
<frameset cols="20%, 80%">
</frameset>
</html>
```

Don't bother trying to check this out in your browser yet—the only thing that'll show up at this point is the title in your browser's title bar.

One of the first things you should notice in the previous example is the absence of a BODY tag. The reason is that in a frameset page, the FRAMESET tag *replaces* the BODY tag.

In the FRAMESET tag, the COLS attribute defines the actual layout of the columns. In this case, the left column is set to take up 20 percent of the browser's window, whereas the right column is set to take up 80 percent. To create additional columns, you just need to add them to the COLS attribute list (cols="20%, 60%, 20%", for instance). Just make sure that your percentage values add up to 100.

Specifying the Pages to Be Displayed in the Frames

Next, you need to use the FRAME tag to define the specific frames that form the columns of your frame page:

```
<frameset cols="20%, 80%">

    <frame src="sidebar.html" name="sidebar">

    <frame src="front.html" name="main">

</frameset>
```

You'll notice that, besides the SRC attribute that specifies the content of the frame, a NAME attribute is also used to name each frame. The name of a frame is used by links to control the content of a frame. Don't assign the same name to more than one frame; frame names must be unique.

Saving Your Frameset Page

Go ahead now and save your frameset file as frames1.html in C:\Html:

1. In Notepad, select File, Save As.
2. Click on the "Look in" list box, and then click on the Drive C icon [C:].
3. In the folder view, double-click on the Html folder to open it, and then double-click on the frames folder to open it.
4. In the "File name" box, type **frames1.html**, and click on the Save button.

Creating the Sidebar Menu Page

Next, you need to create the page, sidebar.html, that is displayed in the left column frame. Run a separate copy of Notepad and then enter the following sidebar menu example:

```
<html>

<head>

<title>Sidebar Frame</title>

</head>
```

```
<body bgcolor="#ccffcc">
<h2>Contents</h2>
<p><a href="page1.html" target="main">Page 1</a></p>
<p><a href="page2.html" target="main">Page 2</a></p>
<p><a href="page3.html" target="main">Page 3</a></p>
<p><a href="front.html" target="main">Home</a></p>
</body>
</html>
```

The main feature that you want to notice in this example, which makes this sidebar menu work within the frame page, is the `target="main"` attributes in the links (the A tags). These must exactly match the name of the frame that was defined in the frameset page (where `name="main"` is used to name the right column frame). This attribute is case-sensitive, so if you have `target="Main"` in your frameset page, but `target="main"` in the links in your sidebar menu, the links won't work.

Go ahead and save your sidebar menu HTML file as sidebar.html in the C:\Html\frames folder (for more detailed instructions on how to do this, see the "Saving Your Frameset Page" section earlier in this section).

Creating the Other Pages

Normally, you would now create all the other pages included in your frameset. In this case, these include front.html, page1.html, page2.html, and page3.html. To save you time, however, I've gone ahead and created these pages for you and included them with the rest of the example files in the C:\Html\frames folder.

Checking Out Your Frame Page in Your Browser

You're now ready to check out your frame page in your browser. Run your browser and open frames1.html from the C:\Html\frames folder. You should be familiar with doing this by now, so I won't spell out the steps this time. Figure 5.1 shows what your frame page should look like in your browser.

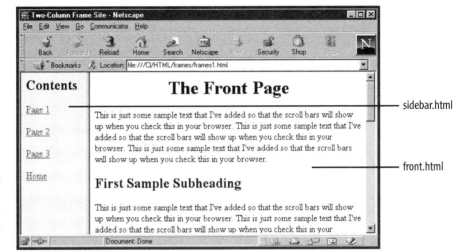

Figure 5.1

In a frame page, you can display two or more pages at the same time.

sidebar.html

front.html

If you click on any of the links in the sidebar menu, the linked page is displayed in its targeted window (see Figures 5.2 and 5.3).

When you click on the "Home" link, the front page, front.html, is redisplayed in the right frame.

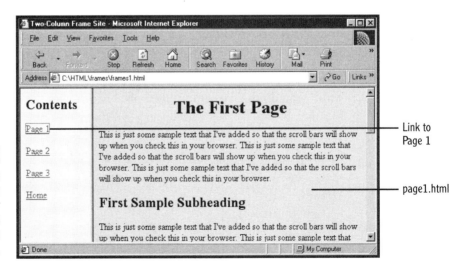

Figure 5.2

Clicking on the "Page 1" link in the sidebar menu displays page1.html in the target frame.

Link to Page 1

page1.html

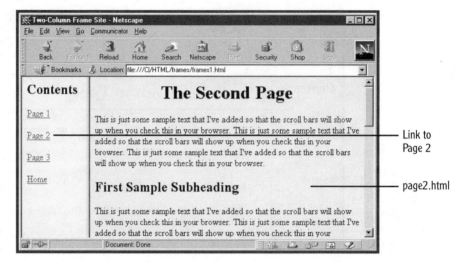

Figure 5.3

Clicking on the "Page 2" link in the sidebar menu displays page2.html in the target frame.

Combining Pixel and Percentage Column Widths

Because you have no control over the width of a browser window used to view your frame page, you might not want to set all your frame columns to percentage widths. Especially with a frame containing a sidebar menu, you might not want the width of that frame to expand or contract relative to the browser window width.

The trick is to set that frame column to a set pixel value, while leaving the other frame column free to expand and fill the rest of the browser window's width. You do this by combining a pixel width with a wildcard character (*), like this:

```
<html>
<head>
<title>Two-Column Frame Example</title>
</head>
<frameset cols="125, *">
</frameset>
</html>
```

This is my preferred way to set up a two-column (or two-row) frame layout. No matter what the screen resolution or the size of the browser window used to view your page, the width of the sidebar menu remains constant, whereas the main frame expands to fill the available space.

Using Proportional Values

Although it is outside of the scope of the current example, you can also set proportional widths when defining columns or rows. For instance, in the following hypothetical example, the middle column is set to a width of 66 percent, whereas the first and third columns occupy two-fifths and three-fifths, respectively, of the remaining space:

```
<frameset cols="2*, 66%, 3*">
```

You can also specify a pixel value in place of the percentage value in the previous example.

Controlling Other Frame Characteristics

There are a number of attributes you can use to control the appearance of the individual frames. These include:

- ✪ The FRAMEBORDER attribute turns off the border around a frame. For instance, `frameborder="0"` turns off the frame border, and `frameborder="1"` turns it on. By default, the frame border is on.
- ✪ The MARGINHEIGHT and MARGINWIDTH attributes set margins within a frame. For instance, `marginwidth="10"` sets 10-pixel left and right margins.
- ✪ The NORESIZE attribute locks in the specified frame dimensions, not allowing a visitor to resize the frames by clicking and dragging their borders. This attribute stands alone and does not require a value.
- ✪ The SCROLLING attribute specifies whether or under what conditions scroll bars are displayed on a frame. The allowable values are: yes, no, and auto. With a "yes" value, scroll bars are displayed, even when the content of the frame fits entirely within the frame dimensions. With a "no" value, scroll bars are not displayed, even when the content of the frame does not fit entirely within the frame

dimensions. An "auto" value specifies that the browser displays scroll bars only when the content of the frame does not fit entirely within the frame's dimensions.

Creating Seamless Frames

One of the questions most often asked on newsgroups covering HTML and Web publishing is how to create "seamless" frames. Seamless frames are frames where the borders between and around the frames are invisible. The principle problem is that there is no way to do this using standard HTML 4 tags and attributes that'll work in all browsers, nor even in the latest versions of Internet Explorer and Netscape Navigator. Setting `frameborder="0"`, `marginwidth="0"`, and `marginheight="0"` in the FRAME tags is the legal way to do this according to the HTML 4 specifications, but it simply doesn't work.

To achieve seamless frames, you have to take a scatter-gun approach by using various proprietary tag attributes, some of which work in some browsers, and some of which work in others. These attributes need to be inserted in the FRAMESET tag (which officially only takes the COLS and ROWS attributes). For an example of doing this, edit the FRAMESET tag in your two-column frame page (see Figure 5.4):

```
<frameset cols="125,*" border="0" spacing="0" frameborder="0"
framespacing="0">
```

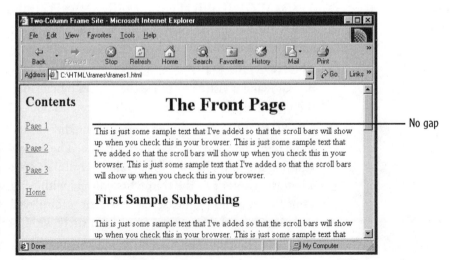

Figure 5.4

A combination of nonstandard proprietary attributes is required to display seamless frames.

Including NOFRAMES Content

The NOFRAMES tag is intended to allow Web publishers to provide content that is displayed by browsers that are not frames-capable. The basic idea behind including NOFRAMES content is that frames-capable browsers recognize the tag and ignore any content that is included in it, whereas browsers that are not frames-capable do not recognize the tag and display the content, just as they would any other positive content (non-codes) included in the page.

It is common to include in the NOFRAMES content a link to a non-frames version of your site, rather than just telling visitors that they need a frames-capable browser to see your site. This, however, can mean that you have to create and maintain a separate Web page just to service visitors using browsers that are not frames-capable. A way around this is to specify as your NOFRAMES link the "front page" of your frame page. In doing so, however, you need to design your front page so that it can function as a stand-alone Web page, rather than as just part of your frameset. An added bonus of including a link in your NOFRAMES content is that search engine spiders can use it to index your site.

Enter the following as an example of including NOFRAMES content in your frameset page:

```
<frameset cols="125,*" border="0" spacing="0" frameborder="0"
framespacing="0">

    <frame src="sidebar.html" name="sidebar">

    <frame src="front.html" name="main">

<noframes>

<p>A frames-capable browser is required to view this page. Please
click on the link to visit the <a href="front.html">non-frames
version</a> of this document.</p>

</noframes>

</frameset>
```

Linking to Pages Outside of Your Frameset

If you insert a regular hypertext link inside of a frame page, the target object of the link is displayed inside of the same frame where the linking page is displayed. In many instances this is not what you want, especially when the site you're linking to is not one of your own. Someone else might resent that you're "capturing" *their* site within *your* frameset. The way around this problem is to always include a `target=_top` attribute in the A tag for any external links you want to include within your frameset. This causes the link to display the page in the top-level browser window, without generating a new browser window. Here is a hypothetical example of a link that opens its target document in a top-level browser window:

```
<p>Go to the <a href="http://www.w3.org/" target=_top>World Wide Web
Consortium</a>.</p>
```

There are three other TARGET attributes that you can also use: _blank, _self, and _parent. Using `target=_blank` opens a new browser window to display the target document: because I find this personally to be a bit aggravating, I can't recommend using this attribute. My recommendation is that you generally stick to using `target=_top` when including external links. (The only exception is when the page you're linking to uses a re-direct that stops visitors from using the Back button to return to your page, in which case you may want to consider using `target=_blank`. Visitors then only need to close the link's browser window to return to your page.) The other two TARGET attributes, _self and _parent, display the target document in place of the current or parent frameset, and are only of use when creating more complex multi-layered frame pages.

You may also notice that I left off the quotation marks around the attribute values in this case, unlike elsewhere in this book's code examples. That's because some early, but otherwise frames-capable, browsers trip over these particular attribute values if they're quoted. Newer browsers treat them the same, whether they're quoted or not.

To display the target document in any other frame within your frame page, you must specify the name of the target frame, as shown previously in the "Creating the Sidebar Menu Page" section.

Creating a Two-Row Frame Page

You create a two-row frame page in exactly the same way as a two-column frame page, except that you use the ROWS attribute in the FRAMESET tag, instead of the COLS attribute.

Creating Your Frameset Page

Because this example works pretty much in the same way as the two-column frame page example, I won't be walking you through creating the frameset page step-by-step. Open a new Notepad window and enter the following example to create the frameset page for a two-row frame page. The top row is set to a height of 50 pixels and the bottom row expands to fill the remaining space:

```
<html>
<head><title>Two-Row Frame Site</title>
</head>
<frameset rows="50,*">
    <frame src="topbar.html" name="topbar" scrolling="no" noresize>
    <frame src="front.html" name="main">
<noframes>
<p>A frames-capable browser is required to view this page. Please
click on the link to visit the <a href="front.html">non-frames
version</a> of this document.</p>
</noframes>
</frameset>
</html>
```

You'll notice in this example that both `scrolling="no"` and `noresize` have been set in the "topbar" frame. When you have a thin frame, sometimes the space added below a block element (such as a paragraph or level-one heading tag) causes the scroll bars to be displayed, even though the text is entirely visible within the frame. Turning off scrolling ensures that the scroll bars are not displayed. The NORESIZE attribute simply insures that a viewer of the page cannot manually resize the frame dimensions.

Go ahead and save your top bar menu HTML file as frames2.html in the C:\Html\frames folder.

Creating the Top Bar Menu Page

Next, you need to create the page, topbar.html, that will be displayed in the top-row frame. Run a separate copy of Notepad and then enter the following top bar menu example:

```
<html>

<head>

<title>Top Bar Frame</title>

</head>

<body bgcolor="#ccffcc" link="navy" vlink="navy">

<p align="center"> <b> <font color="red" face="arial, helvetica">

[ <a href="page1.html" target="main">Page 1</a> ]  

[ <a href="page2.html" target="main">Page 2</a> ]  

[ <a href="page3.html" target="main">Page 3</a> ]  

[ <a href="front.html" target="main">Home</a> ]</font></p>

</body>

</html>
```

As with the two-column frame page example, you'll notice in this example that the `target="main"` attribute causes the objects of the links to be displayed in the "main" frame (which is the lower-column frame in this example frameset). For this to work, the FRAME tag in the frameset page must include `name="main"`. These must match exactly—if you've got "main" in one place, but "Main" in the other, the links won't work.

Go ahead and save your top bar menu HTML file as topbar.html in the C:\Html\frames folder.

Creating the Other Pages

Normally, you would now have to create all the other pages included in your frameset. In this case, these include front.html, page1.html, page2.html, and page3.html. To save you time, however, I've gone ahead and created these pages for you and included them with the rest of the example files in the C:\Html\frames folder.

Checking Out Your Frame Page in Your Browser

You're now ready to check out your frame page in your browser. Run your browser and open frames2.html from the C:\Html\frames folder. Figure 5.5 shows what your frame page should look like in your browser.

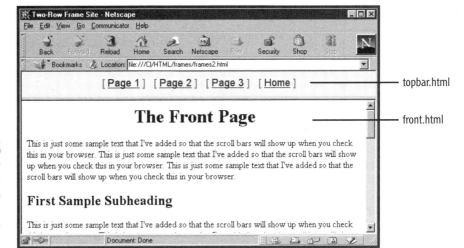

Figure 5.5

Using a two-row frame layout, you can include a top bar menu to control the contents of the bottom row.

When you click on any of the links in the sidebar menu, the linked page is displayed in its targeted window (see Figures 5.6 and 5.7).

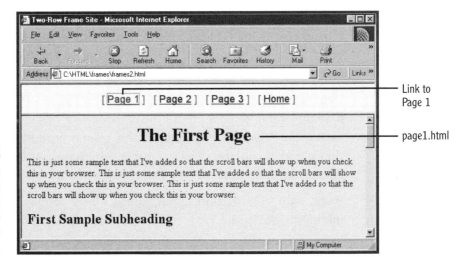

Figure 5.6

Clicking on the "Page 1" link in the top bar menu displays page1.html in the target frame.

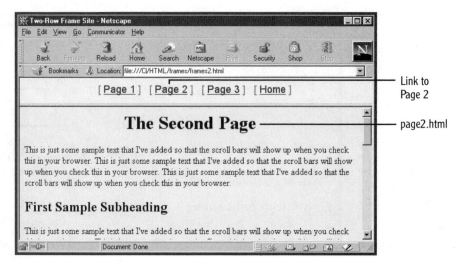

Figure 5.7

Clicking on the
"Page 2" link in the
top bar menu
displays
page2.html in the
target frame.

When you click on the "Home" link, the front page, front.html, will be
redisplayed in the bottom frame.

Take a Break

How about taking a break? Get up and walk around to get the circulation
going. Grab that second cup of coffee, if you need it. Or a bowl of cereal or
some toast, if you're hungry. Or some fruit, if you need to power up.

If doing the first part of this session has taken you most of the morning, you
have the option of going on to the remainder of this session this afternoon,
or you can leave the remainder of this session until another weekend and
skip ahead to do the regular Sunday Afternoon session, "Working with
Forms," this afternoon.

If you want to learn more about frames, I'll see you back here in five to ten
minutes, when you'll learn how to create both combo row/column frame
pages and "nested" row/column frame pages.

Creating a Combo Row/ Column Frame Page

This kind of frame page combines the two previous types you created to create a page that combines both rows and columns.

Creating Your Frameset Page

Run a separate copy of Notepad and then enter the following example:

```
<html>
<head><title>Combo Row/Column Frame Site</title>
</head>
<frameset rows="50,*">
    <frame src="navbar.html" name="topbar" scrolling="no" noresize>
    <frameset cols="125,*">
        <frame src="sidebar.html" name="sidebar">
        <frame src="front.html" name="main">
    </frameset>
<noframes>
<p>A frames-capable browser is required to view this page. Please
click on the link to visit the <a href="front.html">non-frames
version</a> of this document.</p>
</noframes>
</frameset>
</html>
```

You'll notice in this example that the second frameset is inserted inside of the first frameset, replacing the second FRAME tag that was included in the earlier two-row frame page example. The effect of this is that the second frameset (containing the two columns) is displayed as the bottom row of the first frameset. (To display it as the top row of the first frameset, just insert the second frameset in front of the "sidebar" FRAME tag.)

You'll also notice that a new file, navbar.html, is referenced as the target page in the top-row frame. You'll be creating that page in the next section.

Go ahead and save your combo row/column frameset page as frames3.html in the C:\Html\frames folder.

Creating the Navigation Bar Page

For this example, you'll be creating a simple "navigation bar" page that links to the previous two example frame pages you've created.

```
<html>
<head><title>Navigation Bar Frame</title>
</head>
<body bgcolor="#ccffcc" link="navy" vlink="navy">
<p align="center"><b><font color="red" face="arial, helvetica">
[ <a href="frames1.html" target=_top>First Example</a> ]  
[ <a href="frames2.html" target=_top>Second Example</a>
]</font></b></p>
</body>
</html>
```

You'll notice in this example that the target=_top attribute value, which was discussed earlier, causes the objects of the links to be displayed in the top-level browser window.

Go ahead and save your navigation bar menu HTML file as navbar.html in the C:\Html\frames folder.

Creating the Other Pages

Normally, you would now have to create all the other pages included in your frameset. In this case, these include sidebar.html, front.html, page1.html, page2.html, and page3.html. You've already created sidebar.html. As noted previously, I've created the other pages for you and included them in the C:\Html\frames folder.

Checking Out Your Frame Page in Your Browser

You're now ready to check out your frame page in your browser. Run your browser and open frames3.html from the C:\Html\frames folder. Figure 5.8 shows what your frame page should look like in your browser.

Figure 5.8

You can create a combo row-column frame page that includes both navigation bar and sidebar menus, along with the main frame in which the front page and other pages are displayed.

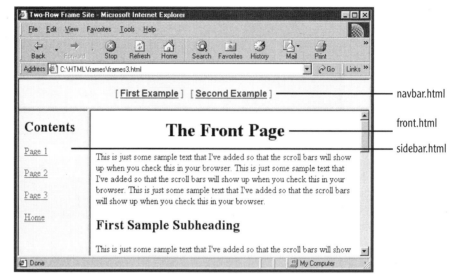

If you click on any of the links in the sidebar menu, the linked page is displayed in the "main" frame (see Figures 5.9 and 5.10).

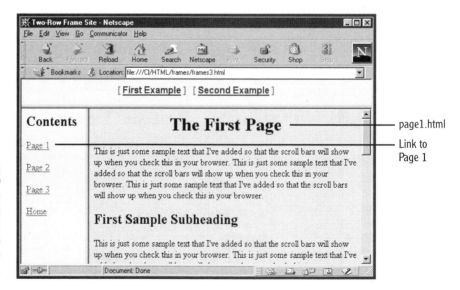

Figure 5.9

Clicking on the "Page 1" link in the sidebar menu displays page1.html in the target frame.

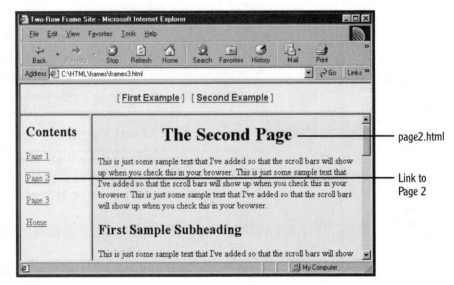

page2.html

Link to
Page 2

Figure 5.10

Clicking on the
"Page 2" link in the
sidebar menu
displays
page2.html in the
target frame.

If you click on either of the links in the navigation bar menu in the top row
of the frame page, the corresponding frame page example is displayed in the
top-level browser window, as shown in Figure 5.11.

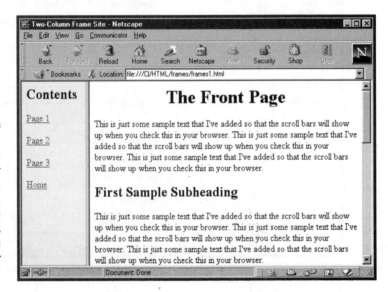

Figure 5.11

After clicking on
one of the
navigation bar
links, the
corresponding
frame page
example is
displayed in the
top-level browser
window.

Creating a Nested Row/ Column Frame Page

One of the problems with the previous example (the combo row/column frame page) is that you can't target the second frameset. That's because only frames can be targeted. Because you can't directly name a frameset, it can't be targeted.

The way around this limitation is to use what is called a "nested" frameset. To do this, instead of replacing one of the FRAME tags with the second frameset, you link the FRAME tag to a separate HTML file that includes the second frameset. By naming that FRAME tag, you can then target it in a link, which lets you use a single link to update both frames included in the nested frameset.

Keeping Things Straight

Because using nested framesets can get a little complicated, to help you keep things straight, I've listed the files here that are used (including both the files you'll be creating and the files I've already created for you).

Frameset Pages

For the previous examples' frame pages, you only had to create a single frameset file for each one. For this example nested frame page, you'll be using a total of four frameset files:

- **frames4.html**—This is the top-level frameset file. It defines a two-row frame layout, linking to topmenu.html in the top frame and to nest.html (the nested frameset) in the bottom frame.

- **nest.html**—This is the initial nested frameset that is linked to by frames4.html. It defines a two-column frame layout that is displayed in the lower row of the top-level frameset, linking to nestmnu.html in the left frame and to front.html in the right frame.

- **nest1.html** and **nest2.html**—These framesets are similar to nest.html, except that they link to nestmnu1.html and nestmnu2.html in the left frame and to page1.html and page2.html in the right frame, respectively. (To save you time, I've created these frameset files for you.)

Menu Pages

For this example, you'll be using a total of four menu files. These include one menu that remains displayed in the top frame, and three other sidebar menus that are displayed in the lower-left frame (depending on which nested frameset is displayed):

- **topmenu.html**—This menu file is displayed in the top frame of the top-level frameset file (frames4.html). It controls the content of the lower frame by targeting each of the nested frameset files (nest1.html, nest2.html, and nest.html).

- **nestmnu.html**—This menu is displayed in the left frame of the initial nested frameset file (nest.html) and links to target anchors included in the "front page" (front.html) that is displayed in the nested frameset's right frame. By clicking on the links in the menu, visitors can jump to the different subheadings included in the front page.

- **nestmnu1.html** and **nestmnu2.html**—These menus are very similar to nestmnu.html. They are included in the two other nested frameset files (nest1.html and nest2.html) and control the content of the right frame in each of them (page1.html and page2.html). (To save you time, I've already created these files for you.)

Content Pages

The "content" pages are all displayed in the lower-right frame. (A content page is any page in the frameset that is not a frameset file or a menu page.) I've created all the content pages for you (you've already used them in previous frame page examples). For this example, you'll be using three content pages:

- **front.html**—This page is displayed in the right frame of the initial nested frameset file (nest.html).

- **page1.html** and **page2.html**—These pages are displayed in the right frame of the other nested frameset files (nest1.html and nest2.html).

Creating Your Top-Level Frameset Page

Run a separate copy of Notepad and then enter the following example to create the top-level frameset page (frames4.html):

```
<html>

<head><title>Top-Level Frameset</title>

</head>

<frameset rows="50,*">

    <frame src="topmenu.html" name="topbar" scrolling="no" noresize>

    <frame src="nest.html" name="nest">

<noframes>

<p>A frames-capable browser is required to view this page. Please
click on the link to visit the <a href="front.html">non-frames
version</a> of this document.</p>

</noframes>

</frameset>

</html>
```

You'll notice in this example that the second FRAME tag now links to the nest.html file, which is the "nested" frameset file you'll be creating in the next section. You'll also notice that a new top menu page, topmenu.html, is linked to in the first FRAME tag—you'll be creating that file after you create the initial nested frameset file.

Go ahead and save the first frameset page as frames4.html in the C:\Html\frames folder.

Creating Your Top Bar Menu Page

The top bar menu page, topmenu.html, is displayed in the top frame of the initial frameset page. This page remains visible at all times and controls the content of the lower frame, switching in different nested frameset files (nest1.html, nest2.html, and nest.html), depending on which link is clicked. Open a new SimpleText window and then enter the following example to create the page in the top frame (topmenu.html):

```
<html>

<head><title>Top Menu Bar Page</title>

</head>
```

```
<body bgcolor="#ccffcc" link="navy" vlink="navy">
<p align="center"><b><font color="red" face="arial, helvetica">
[ <a href="nest1.html" target="nest">Go to Page 1</a> ]  
[ <a href="nest2.html" target="nest">Go to Page 2</a> ]  
[ <a href="nest.html" target="nest">Return to Front</a>
]</font></b></p>
</body>
</html>
```

Go ahead and save your top bar menu page as topmenu.html in the
C:\Html\frames folder.

Creating the Initial Nested Frameset Page

Run a separate copy of Notepad and then enter the following example to create the initial nested frameset page (nest.html):

```
<html>
<head><title>Initial Nested Frameset File</title>
</head>
<frameset cols="125,*">
    <frame src="nestmnu.html" name="sidebar">
    <frame src="front.html" name="main">
<noframes>
<p>A frames-capable browser is required to view this page. Please
click on the link to visit the <a href="front.html">non-frames
version</a> of this document.</p>
</noframes>
</frameset>
</html>
```

Go ahead and save your initial nested frameset page as nest.html in the
C:\Html\frames folder.

Creating the Content of the Initial Nested Frameset

The initial nested frameset links to two files, nestmnu.html and front.html,
and displays them in the left and right frames, respectively. I've already

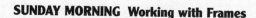

created front.html for you, so you only need to create nestmnu.html. Run a separate copy of Notepad and then enter the following example to create the initial frameset's sidebar menu file (nestmnu.html):

```html
<html>
<head><title>Nested Sidebar Menu</title>
</head>
<body bgcolor="#ccffff">
<h3>Menu:</h3>
<p><a href="front.html#first" target="main">Section 1</a></p>
<p><a href="front.html#second" target="main">Section 2</a></p>
<p><a href="front.html#third" target="main">Section 3</a></p>
<p><a href="front.html#top" target="main">Top</a></p>
</body>
</html>
```

You'll notice in this example that the sidebar menu, unlike in the previous examples, does not cause separate pages to be displayed in the "main" frame, but jumps to locations within the same page (front.html). The URLs first link to the page that is to be displayed in the "main" frame (front.html) and then use a "fragment identifier" (#first, #second, or #third) to jump to a target anchor inserted in that page. For instance, in order for the third menu link to work, a `<a name="third"></a>` target anchor must be inserted in the target page.

Go ahead and save your initial nested sidebar page as nestmnu.html in the C:\Html\frames folder.

Pages I've Created for You

I've created all the other files that are used in this example. These include the two other nested frameset files (nest1.html and nest2.html), the two other nested sidebar menu files (nestmnu1.html and nestmnu2.html), and the two other "main" frame content pages (page1.html and page2.html). All three of the nested frameset files are similar, with the only major differences being that they link to different files in their left and right frames. All the nested sidebar menu files are also similar, with the only major differences being that they target a different content page in the right frame. All the content pages are also similar, the only major difference being that they have different level-one headings.

Checking Out Your Nested Frame Page in Your Browser

Your nested frame page should now be fully operational. To test it, run your browser and open frames4.html from the C:\Html\frames folder (see Figure 5.12).

Checking Out the Top Bar Menu

To check out the top bar menu, click on either of the first two links ("Go to Page 1" or "Go to Page 2"). Figures 5.13 and 5.14 show the result after clicking on the "Go to Page 1" and "Go to Page 2" links.

Clicking on the "Return to Front" link in the top bar menu redisplays the initial nested frameset (nest.html) in the bottom row (as shown in Figure 5.12).

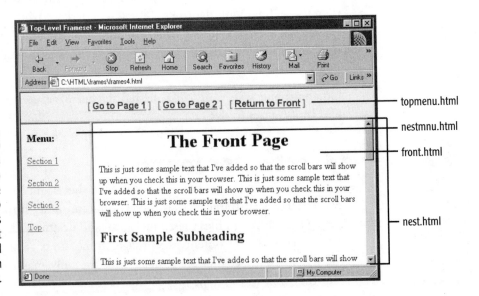

Figure 5.12

This page is composed of two frameset files, one that defines the top and bottom rows and another that defines the left and right columns in the bottom row.

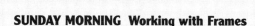

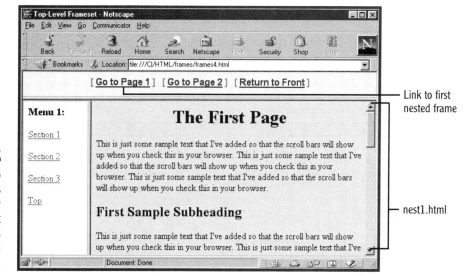

Figure 5.13

When the "Go to Page 1" link is clicked, a new nested frameset (nest1.html) is displayed in the bottom row.

Link to first nested frame

nest1.html

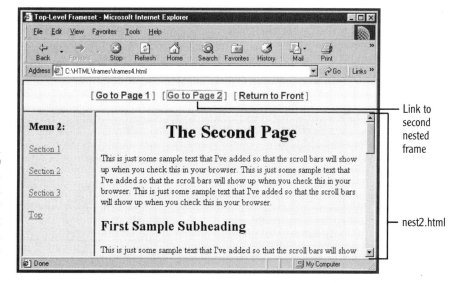

Figure 5.14

When the "Go to Page 2" link is clicked, a new nested frameset (nest2.html) is displayed in the bottom row.

Link to second nested frame

nest2.html

Checking Out the Sidebar Menu

To check out the sidebar menu, click on any of the first three links ("Section 1," "Section 2," or "Section 3"). Figures 5.15 and 5.16 show the result after clicking the on "Section 1" and "Section 2" links.

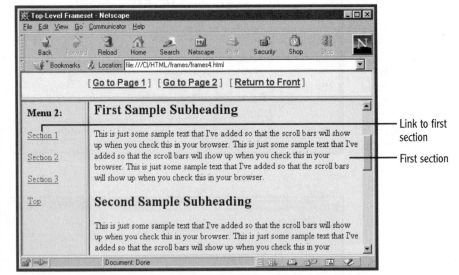

Figure 5.15

Clicking on the "Section 1" link in the sidebar menu jumps to the target anchor inserted at the first subsection of the content page.

Link to first section

First section

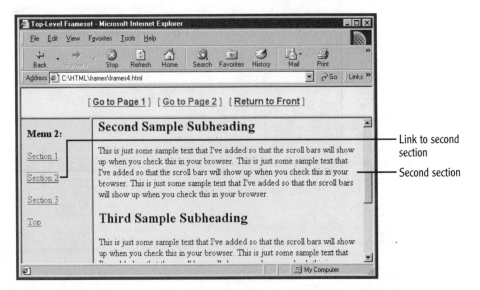

Figure 5.16

Clicking on the "Section 2" link in the sidebar menu jumps to the target anchor inserted at the second subsection of the content page.

Link to second section

Second section

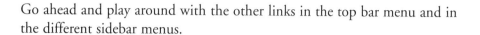

Go ahead and play around with the other links in the top bar menu and in the different sidebar menus.

Using Background Images to Dress Up Your Frame Pages

Using background images can be an effective way to dress up your frame pages. To save you some time, I've gone ahead and created the example files for you—frames4b.html, nestb.html, topmenub.html, nestmnub.html, and frontb.html—with background images set in the last three of these files. I've also reset the font colors, sizes, and faces so the text and links contrast sufficiently with and complement the background images. Feel free to open frames4b.html in your browser to see what this looks like (see Figure 5.17). To check out which codes are used, just open any of these files in your text editor.

Feel free to experiment with using different background images and color combinations. You'll find additional background images (with file names beginning with "b_") with the other example files in your working folder (C:\Html folder). Just copy any that you want to use to the frames folder (C:\Html\frames).

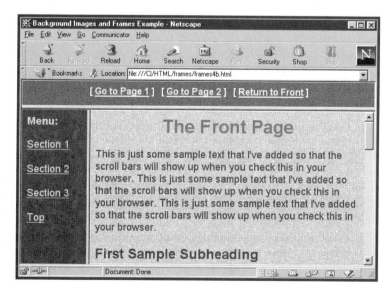

Figure 5.17

Using background images in your frame pages can make them both more attractive and more effective.

Wrapping Up

You should now have a pretty good grasp on how to use HTML frames. They're not all that difficult, once you get the basic ideas behind how they work.

If the morning session has stretched well into the afternoon, that's okay. Feel free to do either of the remaining Sunday sessions as your Sunday Evening bonus session. If you decide to skip this evening's bonus session, you can save those sessions for another weekend.

If, however, the clock hasn't yet run too far past noon, take a lunch break and I'll see you back here in a half hour to an hour for the Sunday Afternoon session, when you'll learn all about using forms in your pages. You also have the option of jumping ahead and doing the Sunday Evening session, "Working with Graphics," as your afternoon session, if you want.

SUNDAY AFTERNOON

Working with Forms

- ✿ Creating Mailto and CGI forms
- ✿ Creating Text Boxes and Text Area Boxes
- ✿ Creating Radio Buttons and Check Boxes
- ✿ Creating List Menus
- ✿ Creating Submit and Reset Buttons
- ✿ Creating Secure Forms

ey, it's Sunday afternoon! If you've done everything up to this point, you've come a long way! You've learned the basics of HTML—how to dress up your pages, and how to create tables and frames—and now you're ready this morning to tackle forms.

Don't worry, however, if you haven't completed everything up to this point. I've included lots of optional and bonus material, so I'm not expecting you to have done everything. Everyone has a different learning style and curve. So, just relax and go at your own speed.

If you haven't completed the Saturday Afternoon session, "Dressing Up Your Pages," however, you should go back and complete that session before attempting to do this session. If you've skipped the Saturday Evening session, "Working with Tables," or the Sunday Morning session, "Working with Frames," you might want to go back and complete one of those sessions before attempting to do this session.

What You Need

You don't need anything special to create the form example you'll be creating this afternoon. However, to submit an example form, you'll need the following:

✿ Any version of Netscape Communicator (Navigator and Messenger) with your e-mail account's "outgoing mail server" specified in the

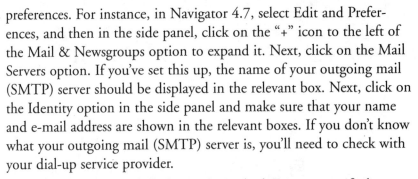

preferences. For instance, in Navigator 4.7, select Edit and Preferences, and then in the side panel, click on the "+" icon to the left of the Mail & Newsgroups option to expand it. Next, click on the Mail Servers option. If you've set this up, the name of your outgoing mail (SMTP) server should be displayed in the relevant box. Next, click on the Identity option in the side panel and make sure that your name and e-mail address are shown in the relevant boxes. If you don't know what your outgoing mail (SMTP) server is, you'll need to check with your dial-up service provider.

✿ Internet Explorer 4.0 or higher with Outlook Express specified as your e-mail program. To determine which e-mail program is specified in Internet Explorer's preferences, in Internet Explorer 5, for instance, select Tools and Internet Options, and then click on the Programs tab. As long as Outlook Express is specified as your e-mail program and it is configured to send outgoing e-mail, you should have no problem sending Mailto form responses. However, if you have a different e-mail program specified, you might not be able to send Mailto form responses.

Other browsers might also be compatible with Mailto forms, but I'm only personally aware of the two browsers described previously.

Creating Mailto and CGI Forms

There are two types of forms that you can create: Mailto and CGI (Common Gateway Interface). Mailto forms send form responses directly to your e-mail address without using any server resources, whereas CGI forms use a form-processing script located on your server to handle the form responses.

A Mailto form is, by far, easier when it comes to getting it set up and functioning. You can create and test it entirely on your local computer, for one thing. The main disadvantage of a Mailto form is that not all browsers support it (Internet Explorer 2 and 3, for instance, do not). Just to get you up and running using forms this afternoon, I show you how to create a Mailto form. At the end of this session, I give you the rundown on what you need to know and do to create your own CGI forms.

Starting Your Form Page

For this afternoon's example form, you'll be creating a visitor's questionnaire. A form is just a regular element included in a Web page. To begin creating the Web page that'll contain your form, run Notepad, or any other text editor you want to use, and enter the following:

```
<html>
<head><title>My Visitor's Questionnaire</title>
</head>
<body>
<h1 align="center">Visitor Questionnaire</h1>
<p>Please note: Although it is unlikely that you will experience
difficulties using this form, some earlier version browsers
may not be able to use this form. If you experience any difficulties
using this form, you may e-mail your response to: <a
href="mailto:yourname@yourdomain.com">yourname@yourdomain.com
</a>.</p>

<p>
I'm gathering information about visitors to my site. I"m gathering
this information solely for the purpose of being able to better
serve and respond to the needs and desires of my site's visitors.
Information you provide to me here will not be given or sold to
spammers, nor will you receive any unsolicited e-mail from me. Thank
you for your cooperation and participation.</p>
</body>
</html>
```

A couple of things need to be noted here. First, you'll notice the note at the start of the form—when using a Mailto form it is important to provide an alternative method by which visitors can contact you and send you their responses, in case their browsers can't use your form. (If you don't want to post your actual e-mail address because of concerns about spammers, just sign up for a free Web mail account for fielding your form responses.) You'll also notice that the purpose of the form and the use of the data collected are explicitly described. This provides visitors with some security that you will not misuse their data. (For even more security, you can place your form on a secure server—I'll provide more information at the end of this session about creating and setting up forms on secure servers.)

Now is a good time to save your form file. Save it as myform.html in your working folder (C:\Html).

Setting Up the FORM Element

The FORM element brackets all other elements included within your form and specifies the method to be used for handling the transmitted data. To set up your form as a Mailto form (which will post the form data directly to your e-mail address), just enter the following (remember to substitute your actual e-mail address for *yourname@yourdomain*.com):

```
<form method="post" action="mailto:yourname@yourdomain.com">

</form>
</body>
</html>
```

Creating Input Controls

There are three basic input controls that you can create in a form: text boxes, radio buttons, and check boxes.

Creating Text Boxes

The input control you'll probably make the most use of when creating forms is the text box. If you've ever filled in an online form, you've used text boxes lots of times, I'm sure. A text box provides a box of a specific size into which visitors type their information. For instance, you might specify a text box that is 25 characters in length into which visitors can type in their last names. For starters, create two text boxes into which visitors can type their first and last names (use spaces to space over, not tabs; see Figure 6.1):

```
<form method="post" action="mailto:yourname@yourdomain.com">
<pre>
<p>First Name/Initial:   <input type="text" name="First_Name"
size="25"></p>
<p>Last Name:            <input type="text" name="Last_Name"
size="25"></p>
</pre>
</form>
```

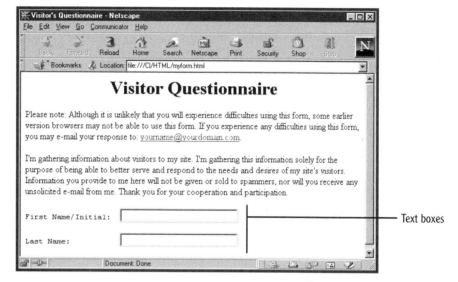

Figure 6.1

Text boxes enable visitors to type a single line of text up to a maximum number of characters (here 25).

You'll notice the following in the previous example:

❂ The INPUT tag defines the input control.

❂ The TYPE attribute specifies the type of input control that is being specified. In this case, `type="text"` specifies the input control as a text box.

❂ The NAME attribute uniquely identifies each input control. When you receive the form response, the name assigned to the form element precedes the data to identify what it is. Note: Spaces are not allowed; use underscores in place of spaces, if you want.

❂ The SIZE attribute specifies the size of the text box. Here, the size is set to 25 characters.

❂ You'll notice that the input controls for the form are nested inside a PRE (Preformatted Text) tag. This sets the text in a monospaced font and lets you use spaces to vertically line up the text boxes.

Go ahead and add some more text boxes to your form (use spaces to space over, not tabs; see Figure 6.2):

```
<pre>
<p>First Name/Initial:  <input type="text" name="First_Name"
size="25"></p>
<p>Last Name:          <input type="text" name="Last_Name"
size="25"></p>
<p>Title:               <input type="text" name="Title"
size="25"></p>
<p>Company:             <input type="text" name="Company"
size="25"></p>
<p>Address 1:           <input type="text" name="Address_1"
size="40"></p>
<p>Address 2:           <input type="text" name="Address_2"
size="40"></p>
<p>City:                <input type="text" name="City"
size="25"></p>
<p>State/Province:      <input type="text" name="State/Province"
size="25"></p>
<p>Zip/Mail Code:       <input type="text" name="Zip_Code"
size="20"></p>
<p>Country:             <input type="text" name="Country"
size="25"></p>
<p>E-Mail Address:      <input type="text" name="E-Mail"
size="30"></p>
<p>Web Address (URL):   <input type="text" NAME="Web_Address"
size="40"></p>
</pre>
```

Although it is not included in the previous example, you can also use the MAXLENGTH attribute in conjunction with text boxes. The SIZE attribute only sets the size of the text box, but does not limit the number of characters that can be typed into the box—the contents of the text box will scroll horizontally if the number of characters typed exceeds the length of the box. By using the MAXLENGTH attribute, you can limit the number of characters that can be typed into a text box.

To limit the number of characters that can be typed to the length of the text box, just enter the same value for both the MAXLENGTH and the SIZE attributes.

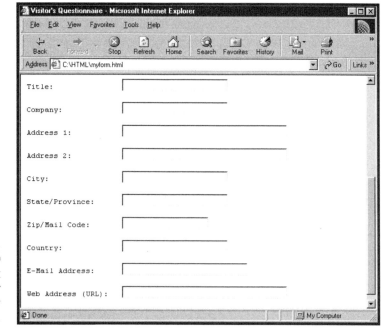

Setting Default Values

Sometimes you want a text box to be already filled out with a default value.
You use the VALUE attribute to set a default value for a text box. Go ahead
and edit the "Country" text box and set "USA" as the default value (see
Figure 6.3):

```
<p>Country:                <input type="text" name="Country"
value="USA" size="25"></p>
```

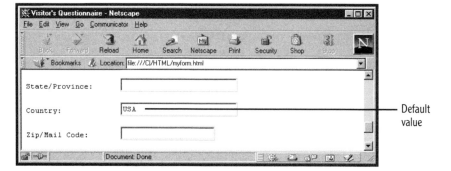

Default
value

 TIP   If your browser doesn't always automatically update the display of your page when you click on the Refresh or Reload buttons, it might be because it is reloading the cached version of your page. To force your browser to load the un-cached version of your page, just hold down the Shift key and click on the Refresh button (in Internet Explorer) or the Reload button (in Netscape Navigator).

Creating Radio Buttons

A radio button control is a circular button that is blank when unselected, but filled when selected. You can select only one radio button in a list at a time. You might be wondering why this control is called a radio button. Actually, the name comes from the radio buttons found on old car radios, which let you select a radio station by pressing a button, and then select another station by pressing another radio button (which popped up the previously pressed button). Radio buttons in forms work the same way. Selecting a button will unselect the previously selected button, in other words. Thus, only one selection can be made at any one time.

Enter the following code to create a radio button list that lets visitors select their own age group (see Figure 6.4):

 NOTE   To make it easier to create this and the following example, type the first input control, copy and paste it to create the following input controls, and then edit them to match the example.

```
</pre>
<tt>
<p>What is your age group?</p>
<p><input type="radio" name="Age_Group" value="14 and Under"
CHECKED> 14 and Under
<br><input type="radio" name="Age_Group" value="15 to 19"> 15 to 19
<br><input type="radio" name="Age_Group" value="20 to 29"> 20 to 29
<br><input type="radio" name="Age_Group" value="30 to 39"> 30 to 39
<br><input type="radio" name="Age_Group" value="40 to 49"> 40 to 49
<br><input type="radio" name="Age_Group" value="50 to 59"> 50 to 59
```

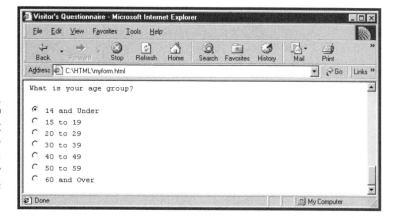

Figure 6.4

A radio button list
works similarly to
the buttons on an
old car radio. Only
one button can be
selected at a time.

```
<br><input type="radio" name="Age_Group" value="60 and Over"p> 60
and Over

</p>

</tt>

</form>
```

NOTE

In the previous example, the radio button control is nested inside a TT tag. This is done so
the typeface displayed will match that used in the text box control example, where the PRE
tag was used to allow spacing over to vertically align the boxes. Because you only want to
change the typeface here, and don't need to do any spacing over as in the text box example, the TT tag has the advantage of not rendering the hard returns at the ends of the lines.
You don't have to use a TT tag here—if you omit it, the text will be displayed in the default
proportional typeface.

In the previous example, notice the following:

○ The INPUT tag defines the input control.

○ The TYPE attribute specifies the type of input control that is being
specified. In this case, `type="radio"` specifies the input control as a
radio button.

○ In this case, the NAME attribute identifies the category to which the
whole list of radio buttons belongs, so each radio button control has
the same name ("Age_Group"). When the form response is sent, only
the value of the selected radio button is returned.

- ☼ The VALUE attribute specifies the value that is returned if the radio button is selected. For instance, if the radio button with a value of "20 to 29" is selected, only that data is included in the form response for the "Age_Group" category of radio buttons (the other radio buttons' values are ignored).

- ☼ The CHECKED attribute specifies one of your radio buttons as selected (or checked) by default. In this case, the "14 and Under" radio button is specified as already checked.

Creating Check Boxes

Check boxes work in a fashion that is similar to radio buttons, except that you can select (check) as many as you want. They are also visually different, of course, being square rather than round.

Enter the following code to create a list of check boxes that lets visitors select their own age group (see Figure 6.5):

```
</pre>
<tt>
<p>What is your field? (<i>Multiple items may be selected.</i>)</p>
<p><input type="checkbox" name="Field" value="Finance" checked>
Finance<br>
<input type="checkbox" name="Field" value="Manufacturing">
Manufacturing<br>
<input type="checkbox" name="Field" value="Agriculture">
Agriculture<br>
<input type="checkbox" name="Field" value="Services"> Services<br>
<input type="checkbox" name="Field" value="Retail"> Retail<br>
<input type="checkbox" name="Field" value="Construction">
Construction<br>
<input type="checkbox" name="Field" value="Technology">
Technology<br>
<input type="checkbox" name="Field" value="Entertainment">
Entertainment<br>
<input type="checkbox" name="Field" value="Education"> Education<br>
<input type="checkbox" name="Field" value="Government">
Government</p>
</tt>
</form>
```

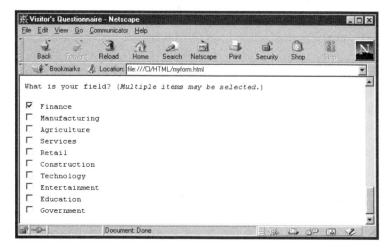

Figure 6.5

Check boxes are
similar to radio
buttons, except
visitors can select
as many as
they want.

As you'll notice in the previous example, the only difference between setting up a check box list and setting up a radio button list is that the TYPE attributes are different. The NAME, VALUE, and CHECKED attributes work exactly the same for both input control types.

Other Input Controls

Besides text boxes, radio buttons, and check boxes, there are a number of additional input controls that you can create with the INPUT tag. Of these, I cover the creation of submit, reset, and image controls later in this session.

There are two other possibly useful input control types: hidden controls and password controls. A *hidden control* is specified by a type="hidden" attribute. If you are putting up more than a single form, you can use hidden controls to help to further identify your different forms. Also, if you're creating a CGI script, hidden controls often specify the address to which the form response is to be sent, as well as which page to display as a confirmation page.

A *password control,* specified by a type="password" attribute, works exactly the same way as a text box control, except the typed text is displayed as a series of asterisks. This control is best used only in a form that is located on a secure server. By itself, it only provides a superficial degree of security. Generally, this control is most useful for creating a simple form that queries for a user name and password in order to give access to a password-protected

site. It also needs to be used in conjunction with a script that can test the entry against a database of user names and passwords, which is beyond the scope of this particular session.

Creating List Menus

By using the SELECT and OPTION tags, you can create a list menu. This type of control initially only displays the first option, whereas clicking on the list menu box then causes the list of options to expand (either dropping down or popping up, depending on the position of the list menu on the Web page). You select an option by clicking on it, after which it is displayed in the collapsed list box. Enter the following code to create an example list menu that queries visitors about how they found out about your site (see Figures 6.6 and 6.7):

```
<tt>
<p>How did you find out about my site?</p>
</tt>
<p><select name="Where_From">
    <option selected>Alta Vista
    <option>Excite
    <option>HotBot
    <option>Infoseek
    <option>Lycos
    <option>WebCrawler
    <option>Yahoo
    <option>Other Search Engine/Directory
    <option>Friend, Relative, or Associate
    <option>Another Web Page
    <option>Magazine/Newspaper
    <option>Radio/Television
    <option>Other
</select>
</form>
```

Figure 6.6

Before a list
menu is clicked,
it displays only
the currently
selected option.

List menu

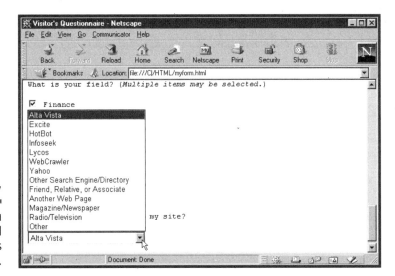

Figure 6.7

After a list menu
is clicked, the full
list of options is
expanded.

Allowing Multiple Selections

By default, a list menu allows visitors to select only a single option. By
including the MULTIPLE and SIZE attributes in the SELECT tag, you can
enable multiple options to be selected from a list menu. This also causes the
list menu to be initially displayed expanded, rather than contracted. To test
this, just edit the previous example by inserting the MULTIPLE attribute
(see Figure 6.8):

```
<p><select name="Where_From" multiple size="13">
```

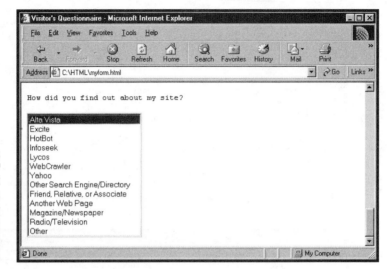

NOTE

Without the SIZE attribute in the previous example, Internet Explorer 5 displays only the first four list menu options, with scroll bars provided to access the remainder. Netscape Navigator 4 by default displays all the options, even when the SIZE attribute is not present. However, if you include a `size="4"` attribute, for instance, both Netscape Navigator and Internet Explorer display only the first four options.

To select multiple options, a visitor just needs to hold down the Ctrl key or the Shift key. By holding down the Ctrl key, visitors can select multiple non-contiguous options. By holding down the Shift key and clicking on two options, visitors select all options that are between the two selected options.

Creating Text Area Boxes

You can use the TEXTAREA tag to create a text area box. A text area box differs from a text box in that it lets visitors enter several lines of text. It can be especially useful for allowing visitors to send you comments or other feedback. Enter the following code as an example of creating a text area box that a visitor can use for typing comments (see Figure 6.9):

```
<tt>
<p>Comments:</p>
<p><textarea name="Comments" rows="5" cols="50"></textarea></p>
</tt>
```

Although not shown in the previous example, you can include default text in your text area box by nesting text between the TEXTAREA start and end tags. This must be straight text with no HTML codes.

Netscape Navigator does not wrap lines typed in the text area box, but scrolls to the right. To type multiple lines of text, you have to press the Enter key to add a hard return at the end of the lines. Internet Explorer, on the other hand, automatically wraps text within a text area box (as shown in Figure 6.10).

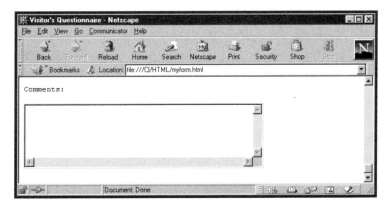

Figure 6.9

A text area box differs from a text box in that it enables visitors to type several lines of text.

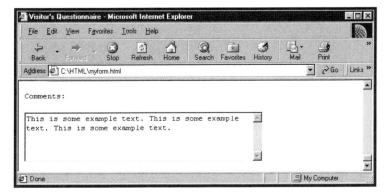

Figure 6.10

Internet Explorer automatically wraps text lines typed in a text area box, but Navigator doesn't.

Creating Submit and Reset Buttons

The last elements you need to create for your form are submit and reset buttons. A submit button, as its name implies, submits the form response, in this case sending it to the e-mail address included in the FORM tag. A reset button lets visitors reset the form, clearing any previous entries. To add submit and reset buttons to your form, enter the following (see Figure 6.11):

```
<p><input type="submit" value="Submit Form"> <input type="reset"
value="Reset Form"></p>
```

Using an Image as a Submit Button

Rather than using the default gray submit button, you can use an image as a submit button. I've included a sample submit button image with the example files that you can use. To add an image submit button to your form, just enter the following (see Figure 6.12):

```
<p><input type="image" src="submit.gif" alt="submit form"
border="0"></p>

</form>
```

It is a good idea to include an ALT attribute to alert users who are unable to view the submit button image, such as users using a text-only or a Braille browser, for instance. The BORDER attribute turns off the display of the border around the image. You can only create a submit button using an image; using this method, you can't create a reset button from an image.

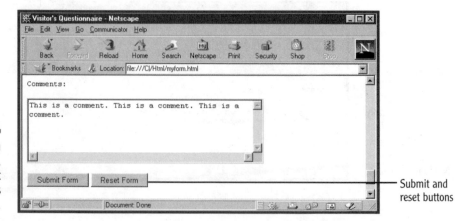

Figure 6.11

The submit button submits the form, whereas the reset button resets the form.

Submit and reset buttons

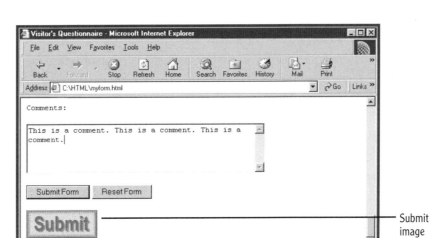

Figure 6.12

You can also use an image as a submit button for your form.

Submit image button

Using the BUTTON Tag

HTML 4 includes a new tag, the BUTTON tag, that potentially provides more versatility when creating submit and reset buttons. At this point, however, the most current version of Netscape Navigator does not support this tag. The most current version of Internet Explorer at best seems only to partially support it. Older browsers do not support it at all. If backward compatibility is a concern (and in most cases it should be), you should probably stick to using the regular submit and reset input controls. For a more detailed description of this tag and its attributes, see Appendix A, "HTML Quick Reference."

Take a Break

This seems like a good place to take a break. You've been at this all weekend, so you deserve a breather! Get up and stretch and grab a quick snack or something cold to drink. If you've got a mate, kids, or a pet, be sure to pay them some attention (they probably haven't seen much of you since Friday evening!). I'll see you back here in ten minutes or so when you'll test your form.

Testing Your Form

To test your form in your browser, fill out or select the different options to see how they work. For instance, type in an imaginary first and last name in the text boxes, select a radio button option, check as many check boxes as you want to, select an option from the list menu, and type a comment. To submit your form, click on the Submit Form button (or click on the submit image button). In both Netscape Navigator and Internet Explorer, you'll get a message warning you that sending the form will reveal your e-mail address to the recipient, as well as send the message unencrypted (because you're sending the message to yourself, however, don't worry about this message). Just click on OK.

Handling Form Responses

Because you're creating a Mailto form, your form responses will be sent directly to the e-mail address you specify in your form's FORM tag. You retrieve your form responses right along with the rest of your e-mail.

For a form sent using Netscape Navigator, a subject line reading "Form posted from Mozilla" is displayed in your inbox. For a form sent using Internet Explorer 4 or higher, a subject line reading "Form posted from Microsoft" is displayed in your inbox.

If you're using Netscape Messenger to retrieve your form messages, just click on the "Part 1" link to a form response sent using Navigator. For a form response sent using Internet Explorer, you can't just click on the link (POSTDATA.ATT) to view the contents. You'll either have to save it as a file and then open it in Notepad, or you can view the message source (with the form response selected, select View, Page Source).

If you're using Outlook Express to retrieve your form responses, you can't directly view your form response in Outlook Express—you have to save the form response attachment and then reopen it in Notepad.

Setting the Content Type

There is a slight problem with Mailto form responses. By default, they're sent in a format that is anything but reader-friendly. Here's an example:

```
First_Name=John&Last_Name=Smith&Title=Vice+President&Company=Smith+%2
6+Sons&Address_1=1111+1st+Street&Address_2=Suite+111&City=Seattle&Sta
te%2FProvince=WA&Country=USA&Zip_Code=98111&E-Mail=jsmith%40
smithsons.com&Web_Address=http%3A%2F%2Fwww.smithsons.com&Age_Group=
50+to+59&Field=Finance&Field=Manufacturing&Where_From=Yahoo&Comments=
This+is+a+comment.+This+is+a+comment.
```

This is because the default content type is what is called "urlencoded," which replaces all spaces and hard returns, for instance, with control codes.

To fix this problem, you can set the content type to plain text. Edit your form's FORM tag, like this:

```
<form method="post" action="mailto:scallihan@earthlink.net"
enctype="text/plain">
```

Now, after submitting and retrieving your form response, the form response is directly displayed in your mail program's message window, with each form field and its content displayed on a separate line—something like this:

```
First_Name=John

Last_Name=Smith

Title=Vice President

Company=Smith & Sons

Address_1=1111 1st Street

Address_2=Suite 111

City=Seattle

State/Province=WA

Country=USA

Zip_Code=98111

E-Mail=jsmith@smithsons.com

Web_Address=http://www.smithsons.com

Age_Group=50 to 59
```

```
Field=Finance
Field=Manufacturing
Where_From=Yahoo
Comments=This is a comment. This is a comment.
```

Using Mailto Form-Processing Utilities

Instead of setting the content type of your form responses to plain text, another alternative is to use a Mailto form-processing utility. Besides translating the Mailto form response into a plain text format, such a utility might also be able to translate your form into a comma-delimited form that then enables you to easily import your form responses into a database or spreadsheet program. For links to several Mailto form-processing utilities, see my Web Tools site at **www.callihan.com/webtools/**.

FIND IT ON ▶
THE WEB

Creating CGI Forms

CGI forms have the advantage of being compatible with both older and newer Web browsers. Someone using Internet Explorer 2.0, for instance, can't use a Mailto form, but they can use a CGI form. A CGI form can also display a confirmation page after the form response has been successfully sent. You can also specify that some form fields are required, which causes visitors to be returned to the form page when they don't fill out a required field.

Using Your Web Host's Form-Processing CGI Script

Your Web hosting company might provide a generic form-processing script that you can use to process your own CGI forms. If so, this is the simplest solution. All you generally have to do is point your form to the location of the form-processing CGI script, as well as include some hidden fields in your form to specify where you want the form responses sent and which page you want to be displayed as your confirmation page after the response has been successfully sent. For instance, the start of your form might look something like this:

```
<form method="post" action="http://www.yourhost.com/cgi-bin/mail.pl">
<input type=hidden name="to" value="yourname@yourhost.com">
<input type=hidden name="return-url" value="http://yourhost.com/your-
name/confirm.html">
```

This example is, of course, fictitious. For specific information on the exact codes you'll need to include in your HTML form, contact your Web hosting company's technical support.

Using a Remotely Hosted Form-Processing CGI Script

If your Web host does not provide access to a form-processing CGI script, there are a number of services available on the Web that let you use their form-processing CGI script to process your forms. For an extensive list of such services, see the CGI Resource Index at **cgi.resourceindex.com/** Remotely_Hosted/Form_Processing/.

FIND IT ON ▶
THE WEB

Creating Your Own CGI Scripts

If you want to create your own CGI form-processing script or to customize an existing one, you need to consider the following:

❂ Your Web hosting company must allow you to create and install your own CGI scripts.

❂ If you're using a UNIX server, your Web hosting company should provide you with Telnet access to your account's folders, so you can then go to the folder where your CGI scripts are stored and set the access permissions using the UNIX chmod command. Some FTP programs might also let you do this. In most cases, you just have to enter chmod 755 (but sometimes "750" or "700") followed by the script's file name, but check with your Web host support to find out the exact "where and what" that you need to do here. (If you don't have a Telnet program, you can download one through TuCows at **www.tucows.com/**).

FIND IT ON ▶
THE WEB

> ✪ Because most CGI scripts are created using the Perl programming language, you might want to develop some familiarity with Perl if you want to be able to customize CGI scripts that have already been created by someone else. Besides Perl, other languages that can be used to create CGI scripts include UNIX Shell scripts, Tool Command Language (TCL), C++, Visual Basic, VBScript, and AppleScript, depending on which OS your Web server is running and which languages are available on it.

Where to Find Form-Processing CGI Scripts

There are lots of form-processing CGI scripts available on the Web that you can download and use. In many cases, you don't even need to customize the script, but only need to insert hidden input controls in your form to specify which features you want to have activated.

Here are a number of resources on the Web where you can learn more about using CGI scripts with forms:

FIND IT ON ▶
THE WEB

> ✪ The CGI Resource Index at **cgi.resourceindex.com/** — You can find an extensive list of CGI scripts for processing forms here (at **cgi.resourceindex.com/Programs_and_Scripts/Perl/ Form_Processing/**).

> ✪ CGI Resources at **www.speakeasy.org/~cgires/** — Includes an introductory tour of using CGI scripts with forms, tips and tricks, and example scripts.

> ✪ CGI Made Really Easy at **www.jmarshall.com/easy/cgi/** — If you have some prior programming experience, you might want to try this tutorial on creating your own CGI scripts for processing form responses.

> ✪ ScriptSearch at **www.scriptsearch.com/** — Bills itself as the world's largest CGI library. Also includes a discussion forum.

For even more links to CGI script resources, see my Web Links site at **www.callihan.com/weblinks/** — just click on the "Programming" link in the sidebar menu.

Software Programs That Create CGI Scripts

There are also a number of form-creation software programs that create CGI scripts for you. Here are two of them:

FIND IT ON ▶
THE WEB

- ✿ WebForms by Q&D Software at **www.q-d.com/**—With WebForms, you need to use it to create your form, but then you can opt to have it create the form as a Mailto or a CGI form. If you choose to create a CGI form, it creates the CGI script for you. An evaluation version is available for download ($34.95 to register).

- ✿ CGI*Star Pro by WebGenie at **www.webgenie.com/**— With CGI*Star Pro, you just need to specify the form for which you want a CGI script created, and it will then create it for you. Registered users who don't have Web hosting accounts that allow the use of CGI scripts can use WebGenie's own CGI hosting facility. An evaluation version is available for download ($99 to register for individual use).

Creating Secure Forms

If you want responses sent by your form to be secure from prying hackers, you need to place your form's HTML file on a secure server. This is especially necessary for order forms, for instance, that ask for credit card numbers or other personal information. Most Web hosting companies have accounts that provide access to secure servers, although expect to pay extra for this.

Besides having access to a secure server, you also need to have access to a digital certificate. A *digital certificate* vouches for you online, so to speak. You don't necessarily need to get your own digital certificate—most Web hosts have accounts that allow you to use their digital certificates. This is usually a lot cheaper than getting your own digital certificate, although it won't necessarily provide as much assurance to your customers, in that they'll be seeing your provider's certificate instead of yours (if you have your own domain name, they might not have any inkling about who your provider is, for one thing). For more information on your digital certificate options, check with your Web hosting company.

Using JavaScript with Forms

You can use JavaScript in conjunction with forms in many different ways. JavaScript can be used to do many of the things that CGI scripts can do, as well. The main disadvantage to using JavaScript with forms is that some earlier browsers either do not recognize JavaScript or are only partially compatible with the latest JavaScript standard. Some surfers also disable JavaScript in their browsers (and some businesses and corporations require that their employees turn JavaScript off). No matter which way you cut it, in other words, some people aren't going to be able to make use of JavaScript.

There are some workarounds that you can use to get around the fact that not everyone can use JavaScript. One is to only use JavaScript to add optional features, so that having JavaScript turned off does not negatively impact the functionality of your form. You can also create an "entrance" page that lets surfers select whether they want to use a JavaScript or non-JavaScript version of your page. Finally, you can use JavaScript to identify surfers who have JavaScript enabled, automatically switching them to the full JavaScript-enabled version of your page (those without JavaScript enabled simply use the initial page). The disadvantage of the last two workarounds is that they require that you maintain two or three HTML files, rather than just one.

That said, you can use JavaScript with forms to do the following and more:

- Provide confirmation that a form response has been successfully submitted.
- Require that certain text boxes be filled out.
- Check that the content of a text box is in the correct format, such as being a valid e-mail address format, for instance.
- Create a pull-down menu that links to other Web pages.
- Disable the submit button after the form response has been submitted, in order to stop multiple duplicate form responses.
- Validate that dates are entered in the preferred format (mm/dd/yyyy, for instance). Also, validate that ZIP codes, phone numbers, or credit card numbers are in a valid format.

These are just some of the things that you can use JavaScript for when working with forms. There isn't space or time available to more fully cover using JavaScript with forms in this session. If you're interested in learning more about using JavaScript with forms, here are some resources that you can check out on the Web:

FIND IT ON ▶
THE WEB

- ✿ The JavaScript Source at **javascript.internet.com/**—Free JavaScript scripts, tutorials, example codes, references, and resources. Includes a list of JavaScript scripts created specifically for use with forms.

- ✿ WebCoder.com at **www.webcoder.com/**—Includes both JavaScript and Dynamic HTML examples.

- ✿ JavaScript.com at **www.javascript.com/**—JavaScript tutorials and free JavaScript scripts.

- ✿ ZDNet Developer: JavaScript at **www.zdnet.com/devhead/filters/ 0,9429,2133214,00.html**—An excellent source of JavaScript examples and resources.

- ✿ Webmonkey: The Web Developer's Resource at **www.webmonkey. com/**—Another excellent resource. Check out their JavaScript code library for scripts you can use in your pages (including scripts for working with forms and data).

Wrapping Up

Wow, you've come a long way! If you've completed both the frames and forms sessions today, you're doing terrific. Even if you skipped the frames session, you've still covered a lot of ground so far this weekend!

If you've completed all the sessions so far, you've had some good practice using all the main features of HTML to create Web pages. Don't expect, however, to become an expert in a single weekend. To keep getting better, you need to keep practicing, and the best way to do that is to create more Web pages. The more you do, the more you'll learn; it is as simple as that.

If your fingers are just getting too stiff and you're having trouble focusing your eyes on the monitor screen, or if the dinner bell has long since rung,

feel free to call it a weekend. You've already done plenty to be able to say, with confidence, "I know HTML!" You can do any remaining sessions or sections you skipped another weekend.

However, if the afternoon hasn't entirely passed yet and you've still got the energy and enthusiasm to learn even more, I've got a bonus evening session, "Working with Graphics," scheduled for this evening. If you want to continue, take a break for dinner, and I'll see you back here in an hour or so, when you'll learn how to create Web art special effects.

SUNDAY EVENING
(BONUS SESSION)

Working with Graphics

- ✿ Creating Interlaced and Transparent GIFs
- ✿ Creating Drop Shadows
- ✿ Creating Gradient and Pattern Fills
- ✿ Creating 3-D Buttons
- ✿ Optimizing Your Web Art Images

Wow, it's Sunday evening! It has been a long haul, if you've managed to follow the schedule so far. I haven't expected you to do everything up to this point—but if you have, you are doing just fantastic!

I've held this session back until Sunday night for a couple of reasons. First, much of what is covered in this session is not strict HTML, but focuses on using graphics to enhance your Web publishing efforts using HTML. Second, graphics, as I've stressed previously in this book, are a value-added enhancement to your Web pages. Therefore, think of them as the frosting on the cake, but not the cake itself. Don't go hog-wild trying to create eye-popping graphics for your Web pages, at least until you've managed to develop their content. Bake the cake first, in other words, and then add the frosting.

What You Need

In this session, you'll be using one of the most popular image editors available on the Windows platform, Paint Shop Pro 6, to learn how to create images using some of the special effects that are particularly useful for creating graphics for the Web. You can find a fully functional evaluation version of Paint Shop Pro 6 on the CD-ROM. For instructions on how to install it from the CD-ROM, see the section "Installing Paint Shop Pro 6" that follows.

FIND IT ON ▶
THE WEB
If you don't have a CD-ROM drive or access to this book's CD-ROM, you can download the latest version of Paint Shop Pro from Jasc Software's site at **www.jasc.com/** (although some procedures to implement features covered in this session might differ in subsequent versions of Paint Shop Pro).

If you've previously installed Paint Shop Pro 6 and exhausted the trial period (30 days, plus a grace period of another 30 days), you can't install Paint Shop Pro 6 from the CD-ROM. If you want to do the Paint Shop Pro sections of this session, your alternatives are to install Paint Shop Pro 6 on a different computer, download a subsequent version of Paint Shop Pro (version 7 or higher) from Jasc Software's site, or purchase Paint Shop Pro.

If you're an Adobe Photoshop user, I've also included tips in this session on how to achieve, in Adobe Photoshop Limited Edition (LE), many of the same special effects you can achieve using Paint Shop Pro 6. Because the LE version is a subset of the full Adobe Phototshop 5.5 version, the steps covered for the LE version should also work for the full version.

If you don't already have Adobe Photoshop, but would like to give it a try, a demo version of Adobe Photoshop 5.5 is included on this book's CD-ROM (you cannot save, export, or print images). There is also, at the time of this writing anyway, a fully functional 30-day trial version of Adobe Photoshop LE 5.0 available for download from Adobe's Web site at **www. adobe.com/products/photoshople/main.html**. It is a biggie, however, at over 74MB.

Installing Paint Shop Pro 6

You can install Paint Shop Pro 6 directly from Prima Tech's interface for the CD-ROM. To install Paint Shop Pro, do the following:

1. Insert the CD-ROM into your CD-ROM drive. If Prima Tech's user interface doesn't automatically run, do the following:

   A. Click on the Start button, and then select Run.

   B. In the Open text box, type *d*:\start.htm (where *d*: is your CD-ROM's drive letter) and click on OK.

2. Read the license agreement and click on "I Accept" to accept its terms.

3. Click on the "Continue to the main page" link.

4. In the CD-ROM interface's Main page, click on the Programs option in the sidebar.

5. Click on the "Paint Shop Pro 6" link, and then click on the "Click here to install software" link.

If Internet Explorer 5 is your default browser, follow these steps:

1. In the File Download dialog box, select the radio button, "Run this program from its current location." Click on OK.

2. At the Security Warning dialog box, a message is displayed that the identity of the publisher, Jasc Software, Inc., is verified by VeriSign and that Jasc asserts that the content is safe. Click on the Yes button. (Earlier versions of Internet Explorer also provide a security warning, although a different one; for those versions, just click on the Open button.)

If Netscape Navigator 4 is your default browser, follow these steps:

1. In the Save As window, click the Save button to save psp602ev2.exe to your My Documents folder.

2. Click the Start button, select the Run option, and then in the Open box, type **C:\My Documents\psp602ev2.exe**. Click on OK.

For both browsers, follow the prompts in Paint Shop Pro 6's install program to install the program.

Running Paint Shop Pro 6

To run Paint Shop Pro 6, just do the following:

1. Click on the Start button, and then select Programs.

2. Select Paint Shop Pro 6, and then select Paint Shop Pro 6 again.

3. Click on the Close button to close the Tip of the Day window. Paint Shop Pro's opening window should now be displayed on your screen.

Starting Your Image

For an example of using the different Web art special effects that are covered in this session, you'll create an example banner image. You can customize this generic banner image later, if you want, and create a more personalized banner image. To start creating your banner image, start a new image in Paint Shop Pro 6:

1. Select File, New.

2. Type **550** in the Width box and **125** the Height box. Make sure that Pixels is selected as the unit of measure.

3. Click on the Background color list and select White as the background color, if it isn't already selected.

4. Leave all the other settings as they are: Resolution (72) and Image type (16.7 Million Colors). Click on OK.

5. Click and drag the Layer Palette and the Tool Options palette so they aren't overlapping your new blank image window. (See Figure 7.1.)

NOTE If you're running in a 640 × 480 screen resolution, all the tool icons on the Toolbox that runs down the left side of Paint Shop Pro's window will not be visible. To reposition the Toolbox, just drag and drop it so that it is horizontally positioned under the Toolbar.

Creating the Banner Text

A banner image is often just a graphical version of your page's title that enables you to select from a much wider range of fonts than is possible using straight HTML. You can also apply many special effects that help your banner graphic

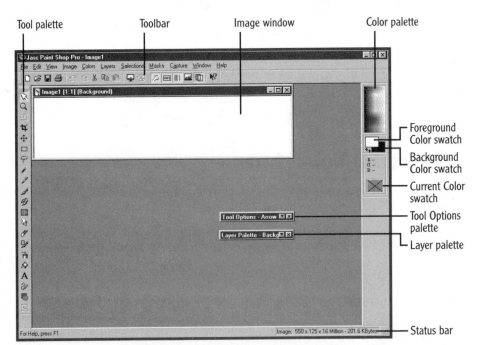

Figure 7.1

Paint Shop Pro 6 is one of the best image editors available for Windows.

stand out from the crowd. For this session's example, you create a generic banner graphic, but feel free to customize it later, in order to create a more personalized look. To add some text to your image, just do the following:

1. First, click on the Foreground Color swatch (in the Color palette) to select a foreground color. In the resulting Color dialog box, choose a color you want to use for your text. For instance, click on the brick red color (third color from the left in the first row of Basic Colors). Click on OK.

2. Click on the Text tool (the "A" icon) in the Toolbox, and then click in the center of the image window. (The Text Entry dialog box should be displayed on the screen; see Figure 7.2).

3. Type **My Banner** as the text for the text banner. Click and drag to highlight the text.

4. From the Name list box, select a font for your text. For instance, select Arial Black. In the Size box, type **64** as the font size. (You can also select a font size from the list.)

TIP To get similarly sized text in Adobe Photoshop LE, you need to select a larger font size. For a bolded Arial Black font, for instance, try specifying 82 pixels as the font size.

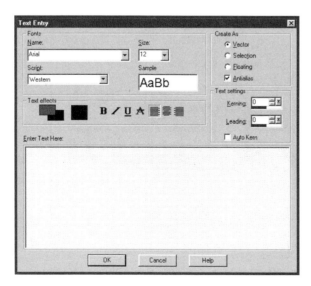

Figure 7.2

In the Text Entry dialog box, you can specify the font, size, color, and content of a text object.

5. In the area labeled "Text effects," click on the brick red foreground color. You'll see the foreground color now displayed in the Color box, as well, which controls the color (brick red) that's applied to your text.

6. To make the font for your text even thicker (which can be handy when creating a banner graphic), you can bold it. If the "B" icon isn't already highlighted in relief, just click on it to turn on bold for the text.

7. Under Create As, select the Floating radio button (not the Vector radio button). Check the Antialias check box. Leave the other options as they are. (See Figure 7.3.) Click on OK.

8. Click and drag the text object to position it in the center of the window. (See Figure 7.4.)

TIP

In Photoshop LE, after inserting your "My Banner" text, to position your text in the center of the image window, first click on the Move tool in the Toolbox (or press Shift+V), and then drag the text to the position where you want it to be.

Figure 7.3

The font, size, and color settings are selected for the "My Banner" text.

Figure 7.4

The text object, "My Banner," is positioned in the center of the image window.

■ ■

TIP If you select the Vector radio button rather than the Floating radio button in the previous steps, you can't use any of the painting tools in the Toolbox (they'll be grayed out).

You can, however, save an image using vector text objects as a bitmap (a JPEG image, for instance) and then reopen it in Paint Shop Pro 6. You then can use any of the painting tools to apply fills or other painting effects to the text.

■ ■

Creating Transparent and Interlaced GIF Images

If you save your image as a GIF, you can choose to save the image with transparency or interlacing.

A transparent GIF image has one color set as transparent (usually the background color). When the image is displayed against a Web page's background color or background image, the page's background will show through the image's transparent color.

There are a couple of ways in which GIF images may be interlaced. Some older image editors created images where only some of the lines of the image are painted in the first pass, with the remaining lines gradually filled in on subsequent passes. This can create a kind of "venetian blind" effect while the image is being downloaded and displayed. More recent image editors insert a rough low-resolution version of the image at the start of the image's data stream, which is then gradually filled in with more detail as the image is further downloaded and displayed, causing the initially blurry image to become sharper and sharper until it is entirely displayed.

Setting a Transparent Color

If you want to set the background color of your image (a white color, in this instance) as transparent, you don't want that color to be present in the body of your image. If it is present, it too is rendered as transparent, which might not be what you want. It is okay to have slight variations of your transparent color present elsewhere in your image (such as a barely off-white color, for instance), because only the specific color selected to be transparent will be transparent.

The first thing you need to do to set a transparent color is to assign the color you want to be transparent to the Background Color swatch in the Color palette:

1. Click on the Dropper icon in the Toolbox (the ninth icon from the top).

2. Right-click inside of the white background of your image to assign its white color to the Background Color swatch.

The next thing you need to do is specify that the assigned background color (the color displayed in the Background Color swatch) is transparent:

1. Select Colors, Set Palette Transparency. At the prompt, to reduce the image to a single background layer, click on the Yes button.

2. At the Decrease Color Depth dialog box, leave the Optimized Median Cut and Nearest Color radio buttons selected (leave all other options as they are), and click on the OK button.

3. At the Set Palette Transparency dialog box, select the second radio button (Set the transparency value to the current background color). (See Figure 7.5.) Click on OK.

4. To view a representation of the transparent color, select Colors, View Palette Transparency. The transparent color is then displayed in a checkerboard pattern (see Figure 7.6).

5. To turn off the transparency view, select Colors, View Palette Transparency again.

Figure 7.5

In the Set Palette Transparency dialog box, you can specify that the background color (the color displayed in the Background Color swatch) be displayed transparently.

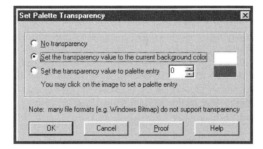

Figure 7.6

When the transparency view is turned on, the assigned transparent color is displayed as a checkerboard pattern.

TIP

To specify the background area of your image as transparent in Photoshop LE, you need to convert your image from an RGB to an indexed-color image, and then export it as a GIF 89a image. (You might also want to first save your image as a Photoshop image—or as a *.psd file—so you can more easily work on it in Photoshop later.)

To convert your image to an indexed-color image, select Image, Mode, Indexed Color. Click on OK to flatten the layers. Click on OK to accept Photoshop LE's recommended indexing scheme: for instance, Palette (Adaptive), Color Depth (8 bits/pixel), Colors (256), and Dither (Diffusion).

To save your image as a transparent GIF, select File, Export, GIF 89a Export. In the GIF 89a Export Options dialog box, the Eye Dropper tool should already be selected. To specify the background of the image as transparent, just click on the background color of the image preview (in this case white). The transparent portion is displayed in the preview area as a gray color. Click on OK. Move to the folder where you want to save the image (C:\Html, for instance), type a file name for the image (such as my_banner.gif—replace Photoshop LE's ".GIF" with ".gif," by the way), and then click on OK to save the image.

Saving Your Image as an Interlaced GIF

In order for the transparency to work when you display the image in a Web browser, you need to save the image as a GIF. Additionally, you can also save your GIF image with interlacing set, which is usually a good idea. To save your image as an interlaced (and transparent) GIF image, do the following:

1. Select File, Save (or Save As).

2. In the "File name" box, type **my_banner** as the file name.

3. From the "Save as type" list, select CompuServe Graphics Interchange (*.gif) as the file type. (You'll notice that a .gif file extension has been added to the end of the file name; see Figure 7.7.)

4. To set interlacing, click on the Options button. Leave the Version 89a radio button selected. Select the Interlaced radio button. (See Figure 7.8.) Click on the OK button.

5. To save my_banner.gif in your working folder (C:\Html), click on the "Save in" list and click on the C drive icon [C:]. In the folder view, double-click on the Html folder. Click on the Save button.

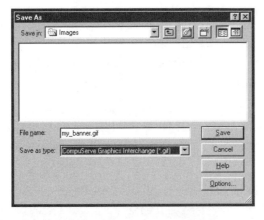

Figure 7.7

The GIF image format is selected.

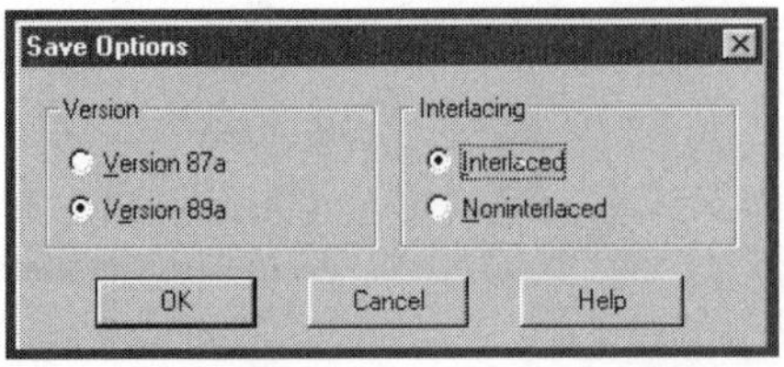

Figure 7.8

You can set GIF interlacing in the Save Options dialog box.

NOTE You need to select interlacing only the first time; it stays selected until you deselect it.

TIP In Photoshop LE, interlacing is set when you export your image as a GIF 89a image. For best results, first convert your RGB image to an indexed-color image: Select Image, Mode, Indexed Color. To export your image as a GIF 89a image, select File, Export, GIF 89a Export.

Checking Out Your Image in Your Browser

In the example files that you installed at the start of the Saturday Morning session, I included an HTML file, my_banner.html, which displays the banner graphic you've just created against a background image, so you can see how the transparency works in action. You can't see the interlacing in action, however, because a local HTML file displays too fast to be able to see the interlacing. To check out your image's transparency, however, just run your browser and open my_banner.html from your working folder (C:\Html). (See Figure 7.9.)

NOTE Just leave my_banner.html open in your browser. You'll be hopping back over again later to check out your banner graphic after you've applied some more special effects.

Figure 7.9

With a transparent GIF, a background image shows through the image's transparent area.

TIP When creating the text object for your banner graphic, you left anti-aliasing on. Anti-aliasing actually blends the edges of the letter forms with the background, so that diagonals and curves are less likely to display what is often referred to as the "jaggies" (or a "staircase" effect). It is usually a good idea to turn anti-aliasing on when creating a headline or text banner where the text is larger than 16 pixels in size. Text smaller than that, however, might appear blurry if anti-aliasing is on. Another negative side-effect that can show up when using anti-aliasing occurs when displaying a transparent GIF image against the background color of an HTML file that differs significantly enough from the image's transparent color. If the Web page's background color is a dark color, but the transparent color in your image's background is a white or light color, for instance, you'll see a thin "halo" around the letters that contrasts visibly with the HTML file's background color. To avoid this halo, either turn anti-aliasing off or synchronize your image's transparent color with the HTML file's background color.

A little later in this session, you learn how to synchronize an image's transparent color with an HTML file's background color or background image. You also learn how to use layers in your images so that you can easily switch your image's transparent color without having to rebuild your image from scratch.

Using Paint Shop Pro's Undo Feature

When you set a transparent color for your image, you had to reduce the color depth of your image, as well as collapse the layers of your image down to a single layer. Because transparency and interlacing are two of the most commonly used effects that can be applied to GIF images, I thought it was important, right off the bat, to show you how to create and save a GIF image using these effects.

Many of the following effects that you'll be learning, however, require that your image have its color depth returned to 16.7 million colors. They also work best when you're working with a multi-layer image. Rather than starting over, you can use Paint Shop Pro 6's Undo feature to back up to the point before you defined the transparent color for your image:

1. Select Edit.
2. Select Undo Set Transparency.

GIF OR JPEG?

Two image formats, GIF and JPEG, are most commonly used to display images on the Web. A GIF image is limited to a 256-color palette, but provides for transparency and interlacing. A JPEG image uses a color palette of 16.7 million colors and uses a compression method to reduce the image's size. A standard JPEG image does not support transparency or interlacing. (A newer type of JPEG image, called a "progressive JPEG," does support a form of interlacing, but is probably best avoided because only more recent browsers can display it.)

Understanding which format is right under which circumstances is one of the keys to becoming an effective Web publisher. Here are some basic pointers to help you decide between these two formats:

- Use JPEG for photographic images or other images that contain continuous tones (or blending of one color or shade into another). These types of images retain a higher quality and achieve smaller file sizes when they're saved as JPEG images.

- Use GIF for line drawings or images composed mostly of flat colors or non-continuous tones, because such images are less likely to require more than 256 colors to be faithfully represented.

- In most cases, use GIF for images that contain text, even when the image contains continuous tones (such as a gradient fill or a drop shadow, for instance), because the compression method used in JPEG images tends to blur sharp edges. Saving your image with an optimized palette can usually counteract many of the problems that accompany displaying continuous-tone areas in images with only 256 colors. However, if your image's quality is unacceptably degraded when saved as a GIF image, even with an optimized palette, consider saving your image as a JPEG, but with a lower compression setting.

A common misconception is that an image saved as a JPEG image will be smaller than the same image saved as a GIF image. That's not necessarily true. If an image isn't a photograph or doesn't include a lot of color blends or continuous-tone areas, or includes 256 or fewer colors to start out with, a GIF image saved with an optimized color palette will usually be smaller than the same image saved as a JPEG.

TIP The shortcut for Undo is Ctrl+Z. If you need to step back through several steps, using Ctrl+Z can be a whole lot quicker than using the Undo menu option.

You should now be back to where you started, before you set the transparency for your image (except that your image is still named my_banner.gif, which is okay).

By using Paint Shop Pro 6's Undo feature, you can always step back through as many steps as you like, even all the way back to the blank image window that you started with. So, if you end up creating an effect that you don't like in Paint Shop Pro 6, just undo it!

TIP

Although Photoshop LE does include an Undo feature, it only enables you to undo the latest command. For that reason, frequently save your image (as a Photoshop *.psd image) while working on it, in case you need to revert to a saved version.

Using Fill Effects

You can use a variety of different fill effects to add additional color and pizzazz to your banner graphic. These include solid color, pattern, and a variety of different gradient fills.

NOTE

In this section, I often refer to a floating palette, the Tool Options palette. This palette lets you choose options to be used with the different tools included in the Toolbox and will be different for each tool that is selected.

Paint Shop Pro 6 uses roll-up floating palettes. After installing Paint Shop Pro 6, the two floating palettes that are initially displayed on the screen are displayed rolled up, so that only their title bars are visible. (Review Figure 7.1.) When you pass the cursor over the floating palette bar, the full palette is then unrolled, letting you choose which options you want to use with the currently selected tool.

If the Tool Options palette bar isn't visible in Paint Shop Pro 6's work area, you might need to turn on its display. To do this, select View, Toolbars, and make sure that the Tool Options Window check box is checked. You can also enable (or disable) automatic roll-ups.

In the instructions, I don't specifically refer to passing the mouse over the Tool Options roll-up bar to unroll it, but assume that action whenever I refer to the Tool Options palette (or any other floating palette).

Using Solid Color Fills

A solid color fill, as its name implies, fills an area with a solid color. To fill the first letter (the "M") in your banner text object with a new solid color, just do the following:

1. Click on the Flood Fill tool (the Paint Bucket icon) in the Toolbox.

2. In the Tool Options palette, if it isn't already selected, select Solid Color from the Fill style list. Leave the other options as they are: Blend mode (Normal), Paper texture (None), Match Mode (RGB Value), Tolerance (20), Opacity (100), and Sample merged (unchecked). (See Figure 7.10.)

3. Click on the Foreground Color swatch to choose a color to be used for the solid fill. In the Color dialog box, click on any of the Basic Colors (other than the brick red color) to select a color for the fill. You can also select a color from the Color Wheel, which gives you a much wider selection of colors. (See Figure 7.11.) Click on OK.

4. Click inside of the letter "M" in the "My Banner" text object. The "M" should now be filled with the new color you assigned to the Foreground Color swatch. (See Figure 7.12.)

TIP　To fill an area with the color currently assigned to the Background Color swatch, with the Flood Fill tool selected, just right-click on the area that you want to fill.

Figure 7.10

The Tool Options palette displays the options for the different tools in the Toolbox.

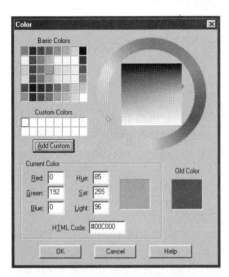

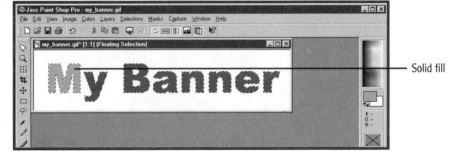

Solid fill

TIP

To fill an area with a solid color in Photoshop LE, first select a foreground color to use for the fill effect, click on the Paint Bucket tool from the Toolbox (or press Shift+K), and then click on the area that you want to fill (the letter "M," for instance). You can also change any of the solid fill options in the Paint Bucket Options palette (such as Opacity and Tolerance options, for instance).

Using Pattern Fills

With a pattern fill, you can fill an area with a pattern based upon a selected image file. Generally, the best images to use for creating pattern fills are background images, in that they're often already set to tile seamlessly. For the following example, you'll be using one of the background images included with the example files in your working folder (C:\Html):

1. First open a background image to use as your pattern. For instance, open b_orange.jpg from C:\Html. Click and drag the background image, if you want, to move it off of your text banner's image window.

■ ■

TIP You can also use Paint Shop Pro 6's Browse feature to open an image. With the Browse feature, you can see thumbnails of all the images in a folder, which can make it easier to find the image that you want to use. To use the Browse feature, just select File and Browse.

■ ■

2. The Flood Fill tool (the Paint Bucket icon) should still be selected. In the Tool Options palette, select Pattern from the "Fill style" list. Leave the other options as they are. (See Figure 7.13.)

3. In the Tool Options palette, click on the second tab with the grid pattern on it (the Fill Options tab). From the "New pattern source" list, select b_orange.jpg. (See Figure 7.14.)

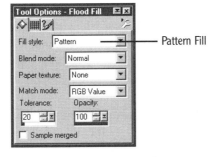

— Pattern Fill

Figure 7.13

The Pattern fill style is selected in the Tool Options dialog box.

Figure 7.14

When the pattern fill is selected, the Flood Fill Options tab enables you to select an open image to be used in creating a pattern fill.

4. Click inside of the letter "B" in your banner text. The letter "B" should now be filled with the pattern you previously selected. (See Figure 7.15.)

NOTE

The example banner graphic you're creating in this session is not intended as an example of excellent design. The purpose of this example is purely to demonstrate how different effects are applied and work, and not to show you what a well-designed banner graphic looks like.

TIP

Photoshop LE doesn't have an exact equivalent to Paint Shop Pro 6's pattern fill feature (although there might be a third-party filter available somewhere). There is a rough workaround that you might want to try, however. First, open a background image (any format) and then save it as a grayscale Photoshop image (*.psd). Select the area (or areas) that you want to fill, or select the layer you want to fill. Select Filter, Render, Texture Fill. Open the grayscale Photoshop image you just saved—the selected area will be filled with it. To add some color to the texture, select an appropriate foreground color and then click inside of the filled area (you might need to adjust the Paint Bucket Options to get the result you want).

For another alternative that lets you add some texture to an area, first select the area you want to affect (for instance, use the Magic Wand tool to select one of the letters in your banner text), and then select Filter and Texture. Just select the Texture option you want to use— the texture will automatically be added to the area you've selected.

Pattern fill

Background image

Figure 7.15

The letter "B" of the banner text is now filled with the selected pattern fill.

Using Gradient Fills

A *gradient fill* blends two or more colors into a single fill effect. There are several kinds of gradient fill effects that you can use: linear, rectangular, sunburst, and radial. In a linear gradient, the colors are blended in a single direction (either left-right, up-down, or at an angle). The other three gradient effects blend their colors in various manners from the inside to the outside of the fill area. For your example banner graphic, you'll be using a linear gradient fill to fill the remaining (unfilled) letters in the banner text. For this example, you'll be creating a gradient fill that blends the currently selected foreground and background colors:

1. Select the colors you want to use for your gradient. First, click on the Foreground Color swatch and pick a color (the carmine red color, fourth over in the first row of the Basic Colors, for instance). Click on OK. Next, click on the Background Color swatch and pick another color (the bright yellow color, first color in the second row of the Basic Colors, for instance). Click on OK.

NOTE If you later plan on resaving your image as a transparent GIF, be sure to reassign the color you want to be transparent to the Background Color swatch, otherwise the transparency won't work.

2. The Flood Fill tool (the Paint Bucket icon) should still be selected. In the Tool Options palette, click on the first tab (the Paint Bucket tab) and select Linear Gradient from the Fill style list. Leave the other options as they are. (See Figure 7.16.)

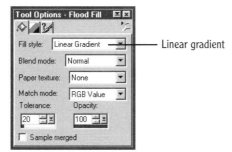

Figure 7.16

The Linear Gradient fill style is selected in the Tool Options dialog box.

3. In the Tool Options palette, click on the second tab (the Flood Fill Options tab) and select Foreground-Background from the Gradient list. (See Figure 7.17.)

4. To reverse the direction of the linear gradient, type **180** in the Angle box (or pull the dial around until it is pointing straight downwards). (See Figure 7.18.)

5. Click in each of the remaining unfilled letters ("y" and "anner"). The letters should be filled with the defined linear gradient. (See Figure 7.19.)

Figure 7.17

When a linear gradient fill style is selected, the Flood Fill Options tab lets you specify the characteristics of the linear gradient fill.

Figure 7.18

The direction of the linear gradient has been turned around 180 degrees.

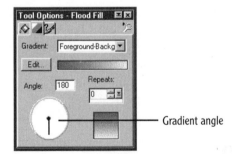

Gradient angle

Figure 7.19

The linear gradient effect blends two colors, in this case the selected foreground and background colors.

▪ ▪

To do a gradient fill in Photoshop LE, first choose the foreground and background colors you want to use to create the gradient fill. Next, select the Magic Wand tool and select the letters that you want to fill—click on the first letter (the "y" letter, for instance), and then hold down the Shift key and click on the other letters ("anner," for instance). (If you don't select anything, the current active layer will be filled with the gradient.) Select the Gradient tool from the Toolbox (or press Shift+G). In the Gradient Tool Options dialog box, you set the options for the fill. To have your gradient fill blend the foreground and background colors, select Foreground to Background from the Gradient list. To specify a linear gradient fill, for instance, select Linear from the Type list. For the other options, you might try Normal, Opacity (100), and Dither (checked).

To apply the vertical gradient, click and hold above the area where you want the gradient to start, pull the cursor straight down until it is positioned below where you want the gradient to end, and then lift off of the mouse button. (You can also do it the other way around, clicking and holding down below the area you want to fill and then drawing it up until it is above the area you want to fill.)

▪ ▪

I don't provide any examples in this session of using the other gradient fills. You don't have all night, after all! The other gradient fills work in a similar fashion to the way the linear gradient fill works, so you shouldn't have any trouble figuring out how to use them. Later, after you've completed the examples included in this session, feel free to experiment with some of the other gradient fills.

Take a Break

This is a good place to take a quick break, if you think you need it. Get up and shake your arms and legs to loosen up and get the circulation flowing. Grab a snack or something to drink, if you're hungry or thirsty. I'll see you back here in five minutes or so, after which you'll learn how to use image layers, drop shadow effects, and optimized color palettes.

Working with Layers

In Paint Shop Pro 6 you can create an image using multiple layers. This lets you assign a color, pattern, or other effect to your image's background layer, while assigning a text object to a separate layer, for example. This can be extremely handy when creating images that use anti-aliased text or other blending effects (such as a drop shadow effect) that you want to display transparently against an HTML file's background image or color. By placing your background and your text object on separate layers, you can easily change the color of the background layer of your image to match an HTML file's background color or image, without having to recreate your text object.

NOTE   The following steps use a new floating palette, the Layer palette. When you install Paint Shop Pro 6, the Layer palette bar is displayed by default, along with the Tool Options palette, in the work area. If the Layer palette isn't displayed, just select View, Toolbars, and make sure that the Layer Palette check box is checked.

To add a new layer to your image, just do the following:

1. To add a layer on top of the background (but under your text object), in the Layer palette, click on the Background bar.

2. In the Layer palette, click on the Create layer icon (first icon in the upper-left corner). In the Layer Properties dialog box, leave the options as they are (see Figure 7.20). Click on OK.

3. To check out the new layer, pass the cursor over the Layer Palette bar to unroll it (see Figure 7.21).

Figure 7.20

The Layer Properties dialog box defines the properties for a new layer.

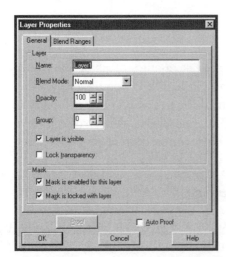

Figure 7.21

A new layer has been added between the Background layer and the text object (Floating Selection).

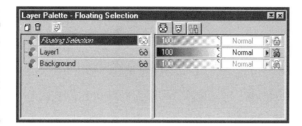

In the Layer palette, you can delete any layer, other than the Background layer, by first selecting it and then clicking on the Garbage Can icon (the Delete Layer icon).

TIP

Layers in Photoshop LE work almost identically to how they work in Paint Shop Pro 6 (actually, Paint Shop Pro 6 pretty much copied this from Photoshop). To create a new layer in Photoshop LE, just click on the Create new layer icon in the Layer palette, for instance.

Creating Drop Shadow Effects

A drop shadow effect can be a great way to set off your text object from the background and give it a 3-D look. To add a drop shadow to your "My Banner" text object, just do the following:

1. The "My Banner" text should still be selected. Select Image, Effects, Drop Shadow.

2. In the Drop Shadow dialog box, click on the Color box to select the color you want to use for the drop shadow. (For instance, in the Color dialog box, select the dark blue-green color, second color over in the fourth row.) Click on OK.

3. Type **85** for the Opacity value, **8** for the Blur value, and **8** for both the Offset values (Vertical and Horizontal). (See Figure 7.22.) Click on OK.

4. The drop shadow effect will now be displayed behind the "My Banner" text object.

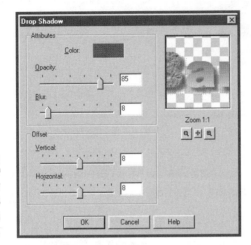

Figure 7.22

The Drop Shadow dialog box defines the properties for a drop shadow effect.

5. To get rid of the selection dashes, so you can get a good look at the effect, select Selections, Select None. (See Figure 7.23.)

6. Select File, and then Undo Select None (to turn the selection back on).

TIP

Photoshop LE doesn't come with a drop shadow effect, although there might be one available as a third-party filter. You can fudge it, however. First, add some text and position it in a blank image window. In the Layer palette, with the text layer (Layer 1) selected, uncheck the Preserve Transparency check box. Next, apply one of the blur filters, such as Gaussian Blur, for instance (select Filter, Blur, and Gaussian Blur). Try setting the Radius value to 4.0 pixels, for instance.

After applying the blur effect, add the same text as before and position it over the blurred text, but up and to the left.

Figure 7.23

A drop shadow effect is displayed behind the "My Banner" text object.

Saving Your Image as a Paint Shop Pro 6 Image

To preserve the layers in an image so you can edit them and their contents later, you need to save your image as a Paint Shop Pro 6 image. If you save your image as a GIF or JPEG image, the layers will be collapsed to a single layer. To preserve the layers in your graphic, just save it as a Paint Shop Pro 6 image (*.psp):

1. Select File and Save As. The C:\Html folder should still be selected (if not, you'll need to change to it).

2. From the "Save as type" list, select Paint Shop Pro Image (*.psp) as the file type.

3. You'll notice that the file name has been automatically changed to my_banner.psp. Click on the Save button.

If you later reopen the image, it will preserve all the characteristics it had when you saved it, including layers, selected areas, and so on.

Creating an Optimized Color Palette

You actually created an optimized color palette earlier, when you specified the background as transparent, before saving your image as an interlaced GIF image. In this section, I cover creating an optimized color palette in a bit more depth. To create an optimized palette, just do the following:

1. Select Colors, Decrease Color Depth, and X Colors (4/8 bit). When prompted to merge the layers in the image, click on Yes.

2. After installing Paint Shop Pro 6, the initial value for the Number of colors box is 200. For this example, type **256** as the number of colors. This will include the maximum number of colors in your image. (Later, in "Optimizing Your Images," I cover finding the optimum number of colors to specify for your GIF image.)

3. Make sure that the Optimized Medium Cut radio button is selected. (This is what creates an optimized, rather than a standard, color palette.)

4. Select the Error diffusion radio button (which will usually give you better results than the Nearest color radio button if your image has a fairly wide range of colors). Also, select the Reduce color bleeding check box (might help, won't hurt). Leave the other check boxes unchecked. (See Figure 7.24.) Click on OK.

5. To check out the new color palette, just click on either the Foreground Color swatch or the Background Color swatch. (See Figure 7.25.) After viewing the new color palette, click on the Cancel button.

Generally, when creating optimized color palettes, I don't recommend that you select the Include Windows Colors check box, because a graphic created for the Web must be displayed on all platforms, not just in Windows.

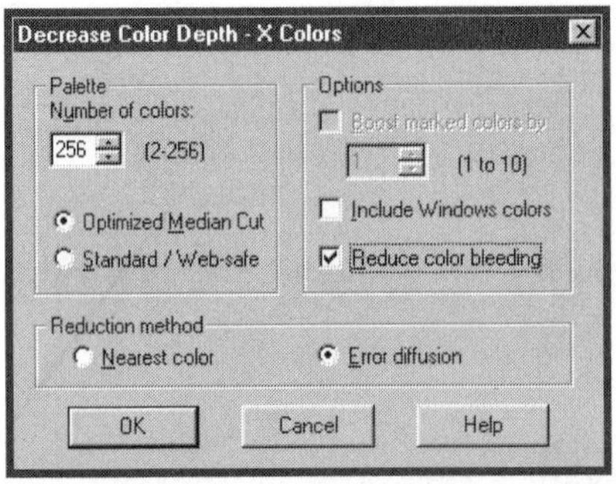

Figure 7.24

The Decrease Color Depth - X Colors dialog box lets you define an optimized color palette.

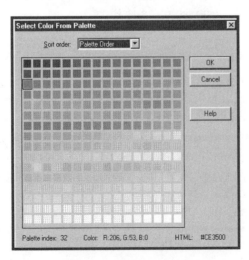

Figure 7.25

When an optimized palette is created, only the colors in the palette are displayed when the Color dialog box is displayed.

The Nearest Color method works by substituting the nearest color included in the optimized palette for a color that has not been included. An image that is reduced from over 3,000 colors, say, to 256 colors will originally contain many more colors than can be contained within an optimized palette. The Error Diffusion method adjusts for the discrepancy between the new color and the old color by adjusting the color of adjacent pixels to diffuse the discrepancy.

For more information on these settings, click on the Help button in the Decrease Color Depth - X Colors window.

When creating an optimized color palette for your image, you want to save your image as a GIF image. If you save it as a JPEG image, your optimized color palette will be converted to a 16.7 million color palette. Don't save your image as a GIF image right now, however. I have you do that a little further on.

Creating Transparent Drop Shadows

Displaying a transparent drop shadow against a background color or background image in a Web browser can create an effective 3-D effect. In the following sections, I'll be discussing how to do this:

- ✪ For use with an HTML file with a light background image (with white as one of its major colors).
- ✪ For use with an HTML file with a non-white background image or color.

Against a Light Background Image with White as a Major Color

In the current example, the color of the image's background is white, meaning that the drop shadow blends to white. As long as you've set the image's background color as transparent and the image is displayed against a light background image, where one of the major colors is white (or near white), the image is displayed transparently against the HTML file's background image.

To check this out, set the background of the image to be transparent and then resave the image as my_banner.gif (in C:\Html):

1. Click on the Dropper tool in the Toolbox and then right-click on your image's white background (close to the edge, away from the drop shadow). You'll notice that the color of the Background Color swatch has turned to white.

2. Select Colors, Set Palette Transparency. In the Set Palette Transparency dialog box, select the second radio button (Set the transparency value to the current background color). Click on OK.

3. To view the transparency, select Colors, View Palette Transparency. (See Figure 7.26.) To turn off display of the transparency, just select Colors and View Palette Transparency again to uncheck the option.

4. Select File, Save As to resave your image as a GIF image (my_banner.gif) in your working folder (C:\Html). Click on the Save button. When prompted if you want to replace the previous copy of my_banner.gif, click on Yes.

5. The Web page, my_banner.html, should still be open in your browser. Use Alt+Tab to hop over to your browser, and then click on the Reload button (in Navigator) or the Refresh button (in Internet Explorer) to update the page. If you earlier closed your browser, re-run it and open my_banner.html from C:\Html. (See Figure 7.27.)

Against a Non-White Background

If you try to display this same image against a background image that does not have white as one of its major colors, or against a non-white background

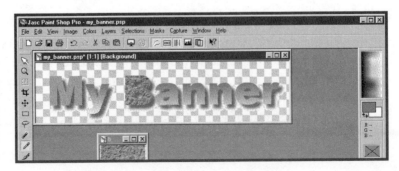

Figure 7.26

The transparency area is shown as a checkerboard pattern.

Figure 7.27

The drop shadow
appears to be
displayed
transparently
against the HTML
file's background
image.

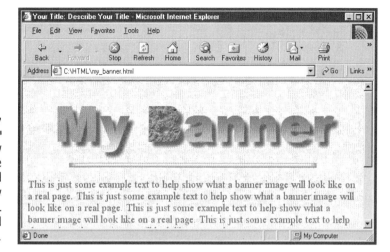

color, you'll notice an undesirable effect—a "halo" effect. The darker the
background image the more noticeable will be the halo. I've included an
HTML file, my_banner2.html, that you can check out to see this in action.
Just run your browser and open my_banner2.html from C:\Html (see
Figure 7.28).

Figure 7.28

If an image with a
white background
is displayed against
a non-white
background, drop
shadow effects will
display a noticeable
halo effect.

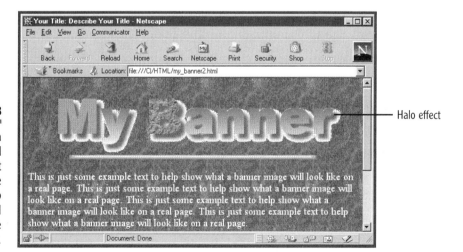

Halo effect

Getting Rid of the Halo Effect Against a Non-White Background Image

To get rid of the halo effect displayed against a non-white background image, you need to replace the white background color in your image with one of the major colors in the background image. To do this, just do the following:

1. First, select Edit and Undo Set Transparency, and then select Edit and Undo Decrease Colors to X. (This will restore the multiple layers and the 16.7 million color palette.)

2. Open the background image that is displayed in your HTML file. For this example, open b_rdmarb.jpg from C:\Html. (Select File, Open, and so on.)

3. Click back on the title bar of my_banner.psp to reselect it. In the Layer Palette, click on the Background layer to select it.

4. Select the Dropper tool from the Toolbox (ninth tool down from the top). Pass the mouse over the background image (b_rdmarb.jpg)—you'll notice that the color directly beneath the Dropper cursor is dynamically displayed in the Current Color swatch (see Figure 7.29).

5. Move the cursor over the background image, and then look for a color, as shown in the Current Color swatch, that is in the mid-range of tones in the image (not too dark, but not too light, in other words). When you see the color you want in the Current Color swatch, just right-click to assign the color to the Background Color swatch.

Figure 7.29

The color beneath the Dropper cursor is dynamically displayed in the Current Color swatch.

6. Select the Flood Fill tool (the Paint Bucket icon) from the Toolbox. In the Tool Options palette, click on the first tab and select Solid Color from the Fill style list. Leave the other options as they are: Blend mode (Normal), Paper texture (None), Match mode (RGB Value), Tolerance (20), Opacity (100), and Sample merged (unchecked).

7. Select Selection, Select None. In the Layer palette, click on the Background bar to select the background layer.

8. Next, position the pointer over the white background of your banner image and right-click to fill the background layer with the color you assigned to the Background Color swatch (see Figure 7.30).

Now that you've filled the background layer of your image with a color that is synchronized with the background image you want to display it against, set the background of the image to be transparent, and then save the image as a GIF image:

1. Select Colors and Set Palette Transparency. When prompted to reduce the image to a single layer, click on Yes.

2. In the Decrease Color Depth - 256 Colors dialog box, leave the Optimized Median Cut and Nearest color radio buttons selected. Click on OK.

3. In the Set Palette Transparency dialog box, select the second radio button (Set the transparency value to the current background color). Click on OK. (To view the transparency, select Colors and View Palette Transparency; repeat to turn it off.)

4. Finally save your image as a GIF image, my_banner2.gif, in C:\Html.

5. Click on Yes to reduce the image to a single layer and to reduce the colors to 256.

Figure 7.30

The background layer of the image has been filled with a color selected from the HTML file's background image.

To check out your new banner image, just open the example HTML file, my_banner3.html, from C:\Html (see Figure 7.31).

After checking out your image in your browser, if you want to revert to a multi-layered image with a 16.7 million color palette, just select File and Undo twice to undo setting the palette transparency and decreasing the color depth. To save your image so you can work on it later, just save it as a Paint Shop Pro image (*.psp), naming it as my_banner2.psp, for instance.

Getting Rid of the Halo Effect Against a Non-White Background Color

To get rid of the halo effect in this instance, you need to closely match the color of your image's transparent background color with the HTML file's background color. You can do this by trial and error, by choosing a transparent background color, saving your image, and then checking it out in your browser.

You can also use Paint Shop Pro 6's Color dialog box to set the hexadecimal color code that is used to set your HTML file's background color. To do this, just click on the Background Color swatch and type the same hexadecimal color code in the HTML Code box that you're using to set your HTML file's background color. Then, just right-click on the white background of the

Figure 7.31

With the image's background color matched to the background image, the halo effect has disappeared.

image to fill it with the new color. (You can't type a color name in the HTML Code box, so if you're using a color name to set your HTML file's background color, to use this technique you either have to switch to using a hex color code or use the trial and error method.)

Take a Break

It's been a long weekend! So, if you feel you're starting to suffer from brain lock, feel free to take a breather.

If it is getting late and you've got to get up early tomorrow to go earn your paycheck, feel free to call it quits at this point. So far in this session, you've learned everything you need to know to create a pretty snazzy banner or logo graphic for your Web pages. You can come back and finish the remainder of this session at another time—like, next weekend, for instance!

On the other hand, if the evening is still relatively young, you're a night owl, or you're not working tomorrow, feel free to hang around for the remainder of this session. I'll see you back here in five or ten minutes, after which you'll learn how to create 3-D buttons and optimize your GIF and JPEG images.

Creating 3-D Buttons

Paint Shop Pro 6 has a handy effect, the Buttonize effect, that you can use to easily create your own 3-D buttons. In this section you'll be using the Buttonize effect, in combination with the Drop Shadow and Cutout effects, to create a 3-D "Home" button.

Starting a New Image

Go ahead and close or minimize any image windows you have open in Paint Shop Pro 6, and then create a new image:

1. Select File and New. Set the Width to 250 and the Height to 100.
2. Leave the other settings as they are: Resolution (72), Background color (White), and Image type (16.7 million colors). Click on OK.

Filling the Background with a Pattern Fill

To give your button image a more textured look, you'll be applying a pattern fill to your button's surface. To do this, just do the following:

1. Open the background image that you want to use for your pattern fill. For instance, open b_wood.jpg from C:\Html. (Feel free later to experiment with other background images.)

2. Select the Flood Fill tool, if it isn't already selected. In the Tool Options palette, select the first tab (the Paint Bucket tab), if it isn't already selected. Select Pattern from the Fill style list, leaving the other options as they are.

3. Click on the second tab (Flood Fill Options), and select b_wood.jpg from the New pattern source list. Then, click inside of the blank image window to fill it with the wood pattern (see Figure 7.32).

Applying the Buttonize Effect

Now you're ready to apply the Buttonize effect:

1. First, click on the Background Color swatch and select a color to use for the 3-D relief effect. For instance, select the dark brown color, second color over in the first row of the Basic Colors. Click on OK.

2. Select Image, Effects, Buttonize. Type **25** as the Height, **35** as the Width, and **50** as the Opacity (you can also select these values using

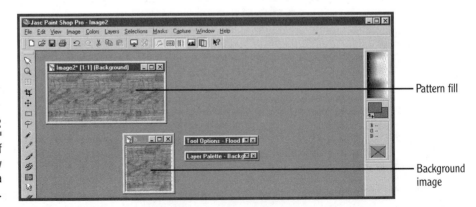

Figure 7.32

The background of the image window is filled with a wood pattern.

the sliders). Leave the Transparent Edge radio button selected. (See Figure 7.33.)

3. Click on OK to see the effect. (See Figure 7.34.)

Creating a Text Label for Your Button

Just a button by itself isn't much use. You need to create a label for the button that'll identify what it's for. For this example, you'll create a "Home" label, which will identify that the button is to be used to link to your home page:

1. Select the Text tool from the Toolbox and click it inside of the button image.

2. In the Text Entry dialog box, type **Home**. Click and drag to re-highlight the text, and then select a font name and font size for your text. For instance, try these selections: Name (Gill Sans Ultra Bold Condensed), Size (52), B (selected), and Create As (Floating and Antialias). Leave the other options as they are.

Figure 7.33

You can specify the height, width, opacity, and edge characteristics of the Buttonize effect.

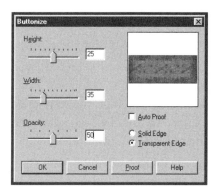

Figure 7.34

The Buttonize effect is applied to the image's wood pattern background, giving it a 3-D look.

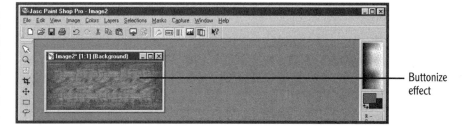

Buttonize effect

NOTE If Gill Sans Ultra Bold Condensed is not available on your system, feel free to choose any other font you want to use. Different fonts have different character widths, however, so you might need to adjust the size of your font up or down to get your text label to fit on your button.

3. In the Text effects area, click on the Color box and select a light color to fill your text. For instance, select the light yellow color, which is next to last in the second row of Basic Colors. Click on OK.

4. Click and drag the "Home" text object to position it in the center of your button (jog it just slightly up and to the left, if you want). (See Figure 7.35.)

Creating 3-D Text Using the Cutout Effect

For a change and to try something new, use the Cutout effect to give your text label a 3-D look:

1. To apply a Cutout effect to your text, select Image, Effects, and Cutout.

2. Check the check box (Fill interior with color) at the top of the dialog box. (If you uncheck this check box, the current fill color or other fill effect will be used for the interior color.)

3. Click on the first color box (Interior color) and select a color: Try the light green color, which is the sixth color over in the third row of Basic Colors. Click on OK. Click on the second color box (Shadow color) and select a color: Try the dark blue-green color, second over in the fourth row of Basic Colors. Click on OK.

4. Set the other settings as follows: Opacity (60), Blur (5), Vertical Offset (-7), and Horizontal Offset (-7). To proof the effect in your image,

Figure 7.35

A light-colored "Home" label has been positioned at the center of the button.

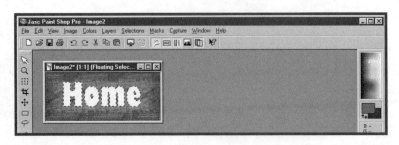

check the Auto proof check box. (To proof the effect, click and drag the Cutout dialog box out of the way, so it isn't overlapping the button image; see Figure 7.36.) Click on OK.

Adding a Drop Shadow Effect

To complete the 3-D look, apply a drop shadow effect to your label text:

1. Select Image, Effects, Drop Shadow. In the Drop Shadow dialog box, click on the Color box and select a color for the drop shadow (try the dark red-brown color, second over in the first row of Basic Colors).

2. Set the other settings as follows: Opacity (100), Blur (10), Vertical Offset (6), Horizontal Offset (6). Click on OK.

3. To get a better look at your 3-D button, choose Selections, Select None. (See Figure 7.37.)

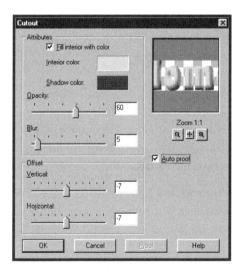

Figure 7.36

You can set the interior and shadow colors for your Cutout effect, along with the degree of opacity, blur, and offset you want to use.

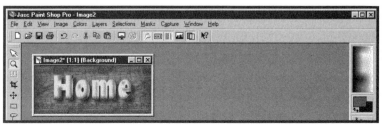

Figure 7.37

A drop shadow is applied behind the button's label text, giving it even more of a 3-D look.

Placing the Label Text on a Separate Layer

It is a good idea to place the label text on a separate layer from the background layer. That way, you can easily come back later and change either the button characteristics or the label text characteristics, independent of each other. That'll let you use this one button image as a template, if you want, to create many other types of 3-D buttons. You've already done this, so it should be pretty much a snap:

1. First, undo turning off the selections: select Edit and Undo Select None. You'll notice that both your text label and the drop shadow effect are now outlined with a dashed line.

2. In the Layer palette, click on the Create Layer icon (the first icon on the upper-left) to create a new layer. In the Layer Property dialog box, just accept the name for the label (it will be either Label1 or Label2). Leave all the other settings as they are and click on OK.

3. Pass the mouse back over the Layer Palette bar again to unroll it. Drag and drop the Floating Selection to place it above the layer you just created (rather than being sandwiched between it and the background layer).

Saving Your Image

First save your image as a Paint Shop Pro image (*.psp), so you can come back and work on it later (or use it as a template for creating other buttons). Save it as my_button.psp, for instance.

Next, save your 3-D button as a GIF or JPEG image. Because your button makes prominent use of text, your best bet is probably to create an adaptive color palette for the image and save it as a GIF image. To do this:

1. Select Colors, Decrease Color Depth, and X Colors (4/8 bit). Click on Yes to collapse the image to a single layer. The following options should still be selected from the last time you did this: Number of colors (256), Optimized Medium Cut, Error diffusion, Reduce color bleeding. Click on OK.

2. Save your image as a GIF image. (Select File, Save As, and select CompuServe Graphics Interchange (*.gif) from the "Save as type" list.)

Using Your 3-D Button in a Web Page

To use your 3-D button in a Web page, just insert it in your HTML file as an image link with the border turned off, like this:

```
<a href="home.html"><img src="my_button.gif" alt="Go to Home Page"
border="0"></a>
```

For this to work, make sure that home.html, my_button.gif, and your HTML file (where you've inserted the 3-D button image link) are saved in the same folder as your HTML file. For guidance on linking to HTML files and images located in separate folders, see Appendix D, "Using Relative URLs."

 NOTE Paint Shop Pro 6 includes many more effects that can be applied to your images. Several of these special effects require that you first select an area or object before applying them. These include the Chisel, Cutout, Drop Shadow, Inner Bevel, and Outer Bevel options. Combining two or more effects can also be effective. Feel free to experiment with some of the other special effects that you haven't tried.

Optimizing Your Images

Most people surfing the Web are still connecting to the Internet at less than stellar speeds—because of slower modems (56Kbps or slower), network congestion, increasingly higher peak demands, and so on. Therefore, to help insure that your pages don't download slower than molasses flows, it is important that you take the issue of optimizing your images seriously.

The goal in optimizing is to create images that are not noticeably inferior in quality, but which are much smaller in bytes, than a non-optimized image. It is often possible to cut an image size by anywhere from 50 to 75 percent or more, depending on the specific image.

Optimizing GIF Images

Optimizing a GIF image involves creating an optimized color palette that includes the minimum number of colors necessary to display the image without a noticeable loss in image quality. The method for doing this involves the following steps:

1. Create and save a 24-bit image that hasn't previously had the color depth reduced.

2. Create an optimized color palette of 256 colors: select Colors, Decrease Color Depth, and X Colors (4/8 bit). After clicking on Yes to reduce the image to a single layer, set 256 as the number of colors and error diffusion as the reduction method. Click on OK. Save your first text image as a GIF image (name it test256.gif, for instance).

3. Select Edit and Decrease Colors to X (or just press Ctrl+Z).

4. Repeat Steps 2 and 3 five or six times, each time reducing the amount of colors an additional amount. For instance, try creating optimized palettes of 192, 128, 96, 64, 48, and 32 colors, saving the images as test196.gif, test128.gif, test96.gif, test64.gif, test48.gif, test32.gif, and test16.gif, respectively.

5. Close the original image that you've been optimizing and then re-open all the images that you've saved. Compare the images, looking for noticeable loss of image quality as the color depth is decreased. Pay especially close attention to any blends or gradients. Use the Magnifier tool to get a closer look, if you want to. (See Figure 7.38.)

6. To compare the relative file sizes of your test images, just select File and Open. In the "Look in" box, select the folder where you saved your test images. Click on the Details button (the fifth icon to the right of the "Look in" box). Scroll, if necessary, to view your test images' file sizes (see Figure 7.39). When you're through comparing the file sizes, click on Cancel.

In the example test that I ran on my_banner.psp (the example image you created in this session), there was very little difference in image quality between test256.gif and test32.gif, meaning that 32 colors (with error diffusion set) were sufficient to display the image without a noticeable loss of image quality. With test256.gif at 21KB and test32.gif at 11KB, that's a 50 percent reduction in size! The test image with the smallest color depth, test16.gif, although it came in at 9KB, wasn't of sufficient quality, however.

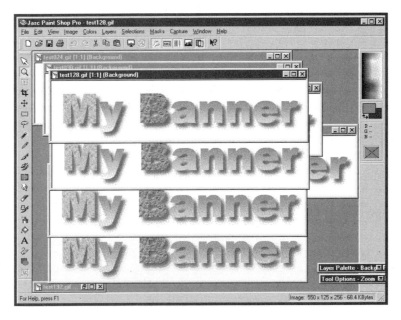

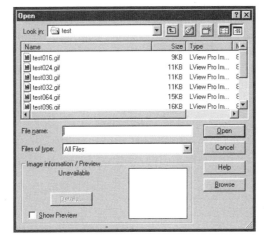

You can do further tests to try to further reduce the file size of your image, although in this case you can't hope to reduce the image size any more than a single kilobyte.

NOTE In Photoshop LE, an optimized palette is called an *adaptive palette*. To create an adaptive palette in Photoshop LE, start out with an RGB image, and then select Image, Mode, Indexed Color. Click on OK to flatten the layers. To create an adaptive palette, select Adaptive from the Palette list. Type the number of colors you want to include in the color palette in the Colors box (or select one of the settings from the Color Depth list). Select Diffusion from the Dither box. After creating your adaptive palette, export your image as a GIF image (File, Export, GIF89a Export).

Optimizing JPEG Images

JPEG images use what is called a *lossy* compression method. This means that color information is subtracted from the image to achieve smaller file sizes, and can't be recovered after the subtraction has been done. The JPEG format's compression method allows it to retain a high degree of image quality in highly complex images containing many colors, while dramatically reducing the file size. (A *lossless* compression method, on the other hand, enables you to undo a compression, but can't achieve the same level of file size savings as a *lossy* method.)

Because JPEG images use a *lossy* method of compression, you should always save your original image in an uncompressed format before saving your image as a JPEG with compression turned on. This can be as a Paint Shop Pro image (*.psp) or a Photoshop image (*.psd), for instance. You can also save your image as an uncompressed JPEG (with a compression level of 1 set in Paint Shop Pro), although that'll also collapse any layers you've created.

The trick to optimizing your JPEG images is simply to find the optimum compression setting for your image, where you'll achieve the maximum amount of reduction in file size while retaining acceptable image quality. This compression setting will vary from image to image.

In Paint Shop Pro 6, you set the compression setting when you save your image as a JPEG:

1. Select File and Save As. In the Save As dialog box, select the JPEG - JIF Compliant (*.jpg, *.jif, *.jpeg) format.
2. Click on the Options button (see Figure 7.40).

Figure 7.40

When you save an image as a JPEG image, you can specify a compression setting to reduce the size of the image.

3. Leave the Standard encoding radio button selected. (Because some earlier browsers are incompatible, it is probably best to avoid selecting the Progressive encoding option.)

4. Use the slider to select a compression setting for your image, or just type in the compression setting you want. Most images can take a compression setting of at least 30 without significant loss in image quality. (See Figure 7.41.) How much higher you'll be able to increase the compression setting without unacceptable loss in image quality depends on the particular image. Click on OK.

You can test for the optimum JPEG compression setting in the same way that you tested for the optimum GIF color palette settings—just save your

Figure 7.41

To reduce the size of a JPEG image, you need to increase the compression setting (but increase it too much and you'll get a splotchy image).

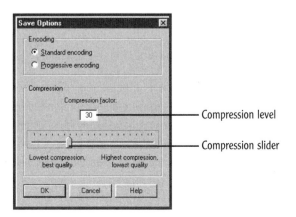

image using a series of progressively higher compression settings. For instance, save images with compression settings of 20, 40, 60, and 80, for instance, saving the images as test20.jpg, test40.jpg, and so on. Then open the images at the same time in your image editor so you can compare them side-by-side. The image with the highest compression ratio, while still retaining acceptable image quality, is the one that wins. Of course, what amounts to "acceptable" image quality will vary depending on the use and purpose of the image. To check out the relative file sizes of your test images, just view the images in the Open dialog box, with the Details button selected.

On a test that I ran on the example banner image you created in this session, I came up with the following results for these compressing settings: 1 (190KB), 20 (43KB), 40 (28KB), 60 (22KB), 80 (14KB).

As with optimizing GIF images, you want to select the compression level that gives you the best combination of image quality and small file size. To further hone in on the optimum compression setting, feel free to save further test images using additional compression settings (65, 70, and 75, for instance, if in your earlier test 60 looks good, but 80 doesn't look so good).

For the test image from which these results were derived, a compression setting of 70, for instance, reduced the size of the image to 18KB.

TIP Photoshop LE uses a scale from 0 to 10 when setting the compression setting for a JPEG image. A setting of 0 corresponds to the lowest image quality (and thus the highest degree of compression), whereas a setting of 10 corresponds to the highest image quality (and the lowest degree of compression).

In Photoshop LE, you set the compression setting for a JPEG image after clicking on the Save button in the Save As dialog box.

CAUTION Some image editors and utilities will recompress an already compressed image, applying a 20 compression setting to an image that has already been compressed at that setting, meaning that the new image gets saved at a 40 compression setting, for instance. You don't have to worry about this in either Paint Shop Pro 6 or Adobe Photoshop LE, but other programs might not be as discerning.

Wrapping Up

If you've completed the whole "Working with Graphics" session, you should be well on your way to becoming a real Web graphics whiz! True, you've only scratched the surface of what can be done, but you should at least now know enough to be able to create some pretty neat graphic effects.

This is the final session of your weekend. If you've managed to complete all the sessions this weekend, you're doing just super. Don't worry, however, if you haven't completed everything that I've thrown at you this weekend. I purposefully included lots of optional material, as well as two whole "bonus" sessions (of which this session was one), in order to allow for a wide range of different learning styles and speeds. Even if you've skipped much, or even all, of the optional or bonus material, you should still be able to say, "I know HTML!" with confidence, as well as be well on your way to becoming even more proficient.

Feel free to come back next weekend to do any of the optional material or bonus sessions you skipped this weekend. If this weekend you skipped the Saturday Evening session ("Working with Tables") or the Sunday Afternoon session ("Working with Forms"), for instance, feel free to do those sessions next weekend (or any other time you want to). Also, feel free to go back over and review any of the material you've covered so far.

I've also included lots of supplementary material in this book's appendixes, including an HTML quick reference, an XML/XHTML compatibility guide, a chart of special characters, plus information and guidance on including relative URLs, cascading style sheets, background sounds, hit counters, guestbooks, GIF animations, image maps, roll-over buttons, streaming media, Java applets, and interactive animations. When you're ready to put your Web site up on the Web, you'll also find a tutorial on using an FTP program, WS_FTP LE, to transfer your Web site's files up onto the Web. Hey, you can easily spend another whole weekend just going through the appendixes!

FIND IT ON ▶
THE WEB

Be sure to check out the Web site I've created for this book—just go to **www.callihan.com/learn3/**. You'll find lots of additional information and resources there, including an FAQ, a page of Web site promotion tips and tricks, a page of links to pages created by readers of my Web publishing books, and more. If you run into a problem not answered in the FAQ, there's a link where you can query me. You'll also find links there to three resource sites I've created, my Web Links, Web Tools, and Web Hosts sites, where you can find updated links to Web publishing resources, Web publishing software tools, and Web hosting options.

When it comes to learning HTML and other related Web publishing techniques and technologies, the learning is never really over. You'll never reach a point at which you "know it all," in other words. But you can, by continuing to learn, become increasingly adept, proficient, and effective in your Web publishing efforts. Don't expect an entirely smooth road (there will be days when you want to pull your hair out), but if you put in a persistent effort, there are very few limits, if any, to what you can learn and do in the area of Web publishing. And don't forget to have fun! Good luck!

HTML Quick Reference

This appendix is a "quick" reference to the tags and attributes included in HTML 4.01, the version of HTML currently recommended at the time of this writing by the World Wide Web Consortium (or W3C).

You can see the full text of the HTML 4.01 specification on the Web at **www.w3.org/TR/html4/**. I've organized the HTML elements according to this order of precedence:

**FIND IT ON ▶
THE WEB**

- ✿ Document and head elements
- ✿ Block elements
- ✿ Inline and other non-block elements
- ✿ Frameset elements
- ✿ General attributes

Attribute Legend

To help you understand the attribute references that follow (and so I don't have to explain them each and every time), here's a legend of what these references refer to:

`attribute="url"`	Absolute or relative URL
`attribute="text"`	Text string
`attribute="n"`	Numerical integer
`attribute="n%"`	Percentage (for example, `"75%"`)
`attribute="#rrggbb"`	Hexadecimal color code
`attribute="MIME type"`	Internet Media Type

A Word about Deprecation

A number of elements and attributes included in HTML 4.01 have been "deprecated." All deprecated elements and attributes have been marked as such in this quick reference. However, just because an element or attribute has been deprecated doesn't mean that you shouldn't use it. That's because deprecation can really have two meanings: either that an element or attribute is on its way toward being "obsoleted" in a future version of HTML or that a more up-to-date alternative exists. Many elements and attributes have been deprecated in favor of using style sheets to achieve the same ends, as is the case with the FONT and BASEFONT elements, for instance. In some other cases, older elements have been deprecated in favor of newer elements (the APPLET element in favor of the OBJECT element, for instance).

I've indicated in the element descriptions what deprecated elements I believe it is safe to continue using and which ones you should avoid. Generally, you should feel free to continue to use any of the elements that have been deprecated in favor of using styles, because styles are only imperfectly supported by current browsers, and not at all by many older browsers. Using styles can also be more complicated to learn and use than is the case with the corresponding deprecated elements.

Document and Head Elements

This section covers the elements that impact the document as a whole. These include the DOCTYPE declaration, as well as the HTML, HEAD, TITLE, BODY, and other elements.

The DOCTYPE Declaration

The latest versions of HTML require that a DOCTYPE declaration be included at the start of an HTML document. This specifies the specific DTD (Document Type Definition) that the document conforms to.

In practice, no current browser requires that a DOCTYPE declaration be included. Nor is it likely that future browsers will do so, considering the very large number of HTML documents present on the Web that do not include DOCTYPE declarations. Most HTML validators, however, do require that a DOCTYPE declaration be present.

The DOCTYPE declaration is inserted at the very top of the page, ahead of any HTML elements (including the HTML tag). There are three DTDs defined for HTML 4.01: Strict, Transitional, and Frameset.

HTML 4.01 Strict Conformance

You can declare this level of conformance for your document if no deprecated elements or attributes are included and no frameset elements are included. Here's an example:

```
<!DOCTYPE HTML PUBLIC "-//W3C//DTD HTML 4.01//EN"
"http://www.w3.org/TR/html4/strict.dtd">
```

HTML 4.01 Transitional Conformance

You can declare this level of conformance for your document if no frameset elements are included. Deprecated elements and attributes, however, may be included. Here's an example:

```
<!DOCTYPE HTML PUBLIC "-//W3C//DTD HTML 4.01 Transitional//EN"
"http://www.w3.org/TR/html4/loose.dtd">
```

HTML 4.01 Frameset Conformance

You should declare this level of conformance if your document includes frameset elements. Here's an example:

```
<!DOCTYPE HTML PUBLIC "-//W3C//DTD HTML 4.01 Frameset//EN"
"http://www.w3.org/TR/html4/frameset.dtd">
```

The "EN" in the previous DOCTYPE example constructs specifies English as the language type of the document. For information on creating HTML documents in languages other than English, see the full HTML 4.01 specification.

The HTML Element

The top-level HTML element. All other HTML elements must be nested inside this element.

Example:

```
<html>

All other HTML elements go here.

</html>
```

The HEAD Element

Nested inside of the HTML element and includes "header" information to be included in the document, such as the title, keywords for search engines, and other information. The TITLE, BASE, ISINDEX, LINK, META, SCRIPT, and STYLE elements are all nested inside the HEAD element.

TITLE

The only required element within the HEAD element. Identifies the title of the HTML document and is usually displayed by a browser in its top title bar.

Example:

```
<html>

<head><title>Type your title here</title>

</head>
```

BASE

An empty element that specifies the *base* URL for an HTML document. Used primarily to indicate the original location of a moved document in order to preserve links using relative URLs.

Attributes:

`href="url"`	Required
`target="frame name"`	Optional

The HREF value must be an absolute URL, not a relative URL. TARGET targets a name of a frame in which the linked document is to be displayed. For more on the TARGET attribute, see the FRAMESET section.

Example:

```
<base href="http://www.domainname.com/foldername/">
```

ISINDEX (Deprecated)

An empty element that prompts the user to perform a keyword search. Not much used anymore. Requires a gateway program to which the user query can be passed. Don't bother, in other words.

Attributes:

```
prompt="text"
```
Optional

LINK

An empty element that specifies the relation of the current document to other documents. Multiple LINK elements can be included to describe multiple relations.

Attributes:

```
href="url"
```
Required

```
rel="link type"
```
Optional

HREF specifies the linked document's URL. REL specifies the type of relationship of the current document to the linked document. No spaces are allowed in the REL value. See **www.w3.org/TR/html4/types.html#type-links** for the list of recommended link types.

Example:

```
<html>
<head>
  <title>Chapter 4</title>
    <link href="../index.html" rel="index">
    <link href="../chapter3/index.html" rel="prev">
    <link href="../chapter5/index.html" rel="next">
</head>
```

META

An empty element that specifies meta-information not included in other HEAD elements. Multiple META elements can be included.

Attributes:

```
name="text"
```
See below

```
http-equiv="refresh"
```
See below

```
content="text"
```
Required

NAME names the meta-information ("author," "date," "keywords," and so on). Many search engine robots recognize the "keywords" value as identifying a list of keywords. HTTP-EQUIV is mainly used to cause another document to load after a set interval, which can be handy if you've moved your page and want to switch visitors automatically from your old URL to your new one. CONTENT is required, in combination with either NAME or HTTP-EQUIV.

Examples:

Here's an example of using the NAME attribute to create a site description and a list of keywords:

```
<meta name="description" content="A site dedicated to providing the latest in  accounting and tax information">

<meta name="keywords" content="accounting, finance, tax, deduction, economy, economics, irs, audit, books, ledger, cpa, depreciation">
```

Here's an example of using the HTTP-EQUIV attribute to cause another page to load in a set interval of time (five seconds):

```
<meta http-equiv="refresh" content="5;url=http://www.myserver.com/mynewpage.html">
```

SCRIPT

Allows the inclusion of client-side scripts, such as those created by JavaScript or VBScript. SCRIPT elements can be placed any number of times in the HEAD or BODY of an HTML document.

Attributes:

type="content type"	Optional
src="url"	Optional

TYPE specifies the type of script: "text/javascript," "text/vbscript," "text/tcl," and so on. SRC specifies the script location. In the absence of an SRC attribute, the script is assumed to be included inside the current SCRIPT element.

NOSCRIPT (4.0)

Provides alternative text in case an otherwise script-aware browser is either not configured to execute scripts or does not support the specified scripting language. A browser that does not support running scripts will display the content of the element.

Commenting Out Scripts

Script-aware browsers will ignore comment tags that are placed above and below a script. Browsers that are not script aware, on the other hand, will ignore anything included within the comment tags.

Example:

```
<script type="text/javascript">
<!- to hide script from old browsers
JavaScript code goes here...
// end hiding script from old browsers ->
</script>
<noscript><p>Non-JavaScript users can <a href="mydata.html">access
the data here</a>.</p></noscript>
```

STYLE

Attaches a style sheet to an HTML document. Although Cascading Style Sheets (CSS1 and CSS2) are the primary style sheet languages developed so far for use with HTML, other style sheet language implementations are possible. When inserted in the HEAD element, a style sheet affects the whole document; when inserted in the BODY element, it has an effect from that point until contravened by another STYLE element.

Attributes:

`type="MIME type"`	Recommended
`media="media type"`	Optional
`title="advisory title"`	Optional

TYPE specifies the style sheet language ("text/css," for instance). MEDIA specifies the destination medium or media; can specify a single media descriptor or a comma-separated list. Allowed media types include: screen, tty, tv, projection, handheld, print, braille, aural, and all. See **www.w3.org/TR/html4/types. html#type-media-descriptors** for descriptions of these media types. Future versions of HTML may introduce additional allowed media types.

TITLE specifies a title for the style sheet. It is common to nest the contents of the STYLE tag inside of a comment, to shield them from search engine robots or from browsers that don't support the STYLE element.

The STYLE *attribute*, not to be confused with the STYLE *element*, can be used to apply inline styles to particular elements.

Example:

Here's an example of using the STYLE element to display all level-one, level-two, and level-three headings in a red Arial or sans serif font (an example of an inline style is also shown):

```
<style type="text/css">
<!–
h1, h2, h3 {font-family: "arial", sans-serif; color: red}
–>
</style>
</head>
<body>
<h1 style="font-size: 28pt; color: blue">
```

The BODY Element

The BODY element is nested directly inside of the HTML element and contains the body of an HTML document. With the exception of the FRAMESET element (which replaces the BODY element), everything not included in the HEAD element must go inside the BODY element.

Attributes:

background="url" (Deprecated)	Optional
bgcolor="#rrggbb|colorname" (Deprecated)	Optional
text="#rrggbb|colorname" (Deprecated)	Optional
link="#rrggbb|colorname" (Deprecated)	Optional
vlink="#rrggbb|colorname" (Deprecated)	Optional
alink="#rrggbb|colorname" (Deprecated)	Optional

These attributes are all deprecated in favor of using styles. BACKGROUND specifies the URL of a background image. BGCOLOR specifies a background color (using a hexadecimal color code or a color name). TEXT, LINK, VLINK, and ALINK assign colors to the base text font, hypertext links, visited links, and activated links, respectively.

Example:

```
</head>
<body background="../images/stucco.jpg" bgcolor="#ffffcc" text="navy"
link="green" vlink="#999933" alink="lime">
Everything to be displayed in the "body" of your Web page goes
here...
```

```
</body>
</html>
```

Block Elements

A block element is displayed in a browser as a separate block, with vertical spacing added above and below to separate the element from other elements. (For a list of inline elements, see the following section, "Inline and Other Non-Block Elements.")

ADDRESS

Adds author and contact information at the end of a document. In most cases, text in an ADDRESS element is italicized. It's common to precede the ADDRESS element with an HR element. Name, email Mailto link, URL, and last date updated are commonly included.

Example:

```
<hr>
<address>
Johnny Appleseed<br>
E-Mail: <a href="mailto:jappleseed@appletrees.com">jappleseed@
appletrees.com</a>
</address>
```

BLOCKQUOTE

Displays a block of text indented in from the left and right margins. It can be used to display an actual block quote or simply as a means of indenting text in from the margins.

Attributes:

cite="URL"   Optional

CITE allows you to specify a URL to designate the source of the quote.

Example:

```
<p>The World Wide Web Consortium refers to HTML as a mother tongue
for publishing information on the Web:
<blockquote cite=" http://www.w3.org/TR/html4/intro/intro.html#h-2.2">
```

```
To publish information for global distribution, one needs a univer-
sally understood language, a kind of publishing mother tongue that
all computers may potentially understand. The publishing language
used by the World Wide Web is HTML (from HyperText Markup Language).
</blockquote>
```

CENTER (Deprecated)

Causes any included text or elements to be centered. This element was originally a Netscape extension to HTML, but has been defined since HTML 3.2 as
equivalent to `<div align="center">...</div>`. Be aware, however, that browsers
not compliant with HTML 3.2 might support the CENTER element, but not
the DIV element.

Example:

```
<center><img src="gcanyon.jpg" width="200" height="350"><br>A photo
of the Grand Canyon<center>
```

DIR (Deprecated)

Because practically all browsers display the DIR element identically to the UL
(Unordered List) element, you should avoid using it and use the UL tag instead.

DIV (Division)

Defines a "division" within an HTML document, which can include any other
HTML block and inline elements.

Attributes:

```
align="left|right|center|justify"              Optional
```

The DIV element, by itself, can only be used to horizontally align (using the
ALIGN attribute) multiple lines of text and elements. In combination with style
sheets, however, it becomes much more powerful. The DIV element should not
be nested inside any element other than the BODY element.

Example:

```
<div align="center">
<h1>Welcome to My Home Page!</h1>
<p>Introductory paragraph...</p>
</div>
```

DL (Definition List)

Allows you to create a definition list (also called a glossary). The DT (Definition Term) and DD (Definition Data) elements are nested inside of the DL element to create the list. Another use of the DL element is to mark up dialogue, with the DT element identifying the speaker and the DD element containing the dialogue.

DT (Definition Term)

Specifies the "term" element in a definition item. It's always nested inside the DL element. The DT element is not an empty element, but a container element that has an implied end tag.

DD (Definition Data)

Specifies the "data" element in a definition item; it contains the actual "definition" that's included in the list. It's displayed indented under the DT item. Normally, it follows a DT element, but can be included by itself. The DD element is not an empty element, but a container element that has an implied end tag.

Example:

Here's an example of using the DL, DT, and DD elements:

```
<dl>
  <dt>Block element
  <dd>A block element is displayed as a separate block in an HTML
document.
  <dt>Inline element
  <dd>An inline element is displayed inline in an HTML document.
</dl>
```

H*n* (Heading Levels)

The H*n* elements, H1 through H6, allow you to define different heading levels.

Attributes:

```
align="left|center|right|justify"
```
Optional

ALIGN horizontally aligns a heading. Left alignment is the default.

Example:

```
<h1 align="center">Level-One Heading</h1>
<p>Introductory paragraph...</p>
<h2 align="right">Level-Two Heading</h2>
```

HR (Horizontal Rule)

Allows you to insert a horizontal rule.

Attributes:

`size="n"` (Deprecated)	Optional
`width="n|n%"` (Deprecated)	Optional
`align="left|right|center"` (Deprecated)	Optional
`noshade` (Deprecated)	Optional

(All these attributes are deprecated in favor of using styles to achieve the same results.) SIZE specifies the height in pixels. WIDTH specifies the width, either in pixels or as a percentage. ALIGN aligns the rule (center alignment is the default). NOSHADE turns off any 3-D shading.

Example:

```
<hr size="8" width="75%" noshade>
```

MENU (Deprecated)

Creates a menu list. Because virtually all browsers display this element identically to the UL element, avoid using this element and use the UL element instead.

OL (Ordered List)

Creates a numbered list. OL elements can be nested inside each other to create a multilevel numbered list. OL elements can also be nested inside of UL (Unordered List) elements, and vice versa.

Attributes:

`type="1|a|A|i|I"` (Deprecated)	Optional
`start="n"` (Deprecated)	Optional

TYPE specifies the type of ordered list. START specifies where the list is to start, other than at 1, a, A, i, or I (such as 2 or C, for instance). TYPE and START are deprecated in favor of using styles.

LI (List Item)

Used in combination with the UL element (and the OL element) to specify the items in a list. The LI element, despite appearances, is not an empty element, but a container element with an implied end tag. Adding the end tag currently has no effect, although HTML 4.0 has specified that adding the end tag should cause additional space to be added following a list item.

Attributes:

type="1|a|A|i|I" (Deprecated)   Optional

value="n" (Deprecated)   Optional

These attributes force a type and value for any list item, with ensuing list items conforming to the new type and number values. You could, for instance, create a list numbered 1, 2, 4, 5 (skipping past 3)—but why would you want to? TYPE and VALUE are deprecated in favor of using styles.

Example:

```
<p>Favorite Jazz Musicians:</p>
<ol type="A">
  <li>Thelonius Monk
  <li>Nat Adderly
  <li>Bill Evans
</ol>
```

P (Paragraph)

Defines a text paragraph. The P element is a container element, although adding the end tag is considered optional.

Attributes:

align="left|center|right|justify" (Deprecated)   Optional

ALIGN specifies that the paragraph is either centered or right-aligned. Left-alignment is the default.

Example:

```
<p>Use the P tag to tag ordinary text.</p>
```

PRE (Preformatted Text)

Used to include a block of text displayed in a monospaced font with all spaces and line breaks translated literally. Prior to the TABLE element, the PRE element was the only way to display tabular or columnar data or information. The IMG, BIG, SMALL, SUB, SUP, and FONT elements are not allowed within a PRE element. Because line breaks are translated literally, you don't need to use P or BR elements, but you should be aware that <p> and <br> codes will be parsed by a browser, rather than presented literally. Also, B, I, EM, STRONG, U, and other text markup elements, as well as character entities, will also be parsed.

Example:

```
<pre>
           1st Qtr        2nd Qtr        3rd Qtr        4th Qtr

1999     $1,055,000     $  800,985     $2,095,300     $1,785,500

1998     $  985,250     $1,225,000     $1,500,600     $  865,900

</pre>
```

TABLE

Displays text or other objects in a tabular format. Tables can also include lists (DL, OL, and UL), paragraphs, forms, images, preformatted text (PRE), and even other tables.

Attributes:

align="left|center|right" (Deprecated)	Optional
width="n|n%"	Optional
border="n"	Optional
cellspacing="n"	Optional
cellpadding="n"	Optional
valign="top|middle|bottom|baseline"	Optional
bgcolor="#rrggbb|colorname" (4.0)	Optional
cols="n" (4.0)	Optional
summary="text" (4.0)	Optional
frame="frame display" (4.0)	Optional
rules="rules display" (4.0)	Optional

ALIGN horizontally aligns the table to the left, center, or right. Left-alignment and right-alignment work similarly to the IMG tag, causing following text or other elements to flow around the table. WIDTH specifies the width of the table in pixels or as a percentage of a browser window. BORDER sets the thickness in pixels of the border around the table. CELLSPACING sets the space in pixels between cells. CELLPADDING sets the space in pixels within cells. VALIGN specifies whether text in a table is top- or bottom-aligned.

BGCOLOR assigns a background color. This works exactly the same as in the BODY element. COLS specifies the number of columns in a table. This is intended to assist browsers to start rendering a table prior to receiving all the data. FRAME specifies which parts of the frame surrounding a table will be visible. Allowed values are "void", "above", "below", "hsides", "vsides", "lhs" (left), "rhs" (right), "box", and "border". RULES specifies which rules within a table will be visible. Allowed values are "none", "groups" (between THEAD, TFOOT, TBODY, and COLGROUP), "rows", "cols", and "all". SUMMARY provides a summary of the table's purpose and structure that can be presented by speech or Braille browsers, for instance.

These elements are nested inside the TABLE element: CAPTION, TR, TH, TD, COLGROUP (4.0), THEAD (4.0), TBODY (4.0), and TFOOT (4.0).

CAPTION

Specifies a caption for a table.

Attributes:

`align="top|bottom|left|right"` (Deprecated)	Optional

ALIGN aligns the caption relative to the top, bottom, left, or right of a table. The default is top. This attribute is deprecated in favor of using styles.

TR (Table Row)

Defines a table row. Every row in a table should start with `<tr>` and end with `</tr>`.

Attributes:

`align="left|center|right|justify|char"`	Optional
`valign="top|middle|bottom|baseline"`	Optional
`char="character"` (4.0)	Optional
`charoff="n"` (4.0)	Optional

ALIGN and VALIGN allow you to horizontally and vertically align the contents of a table row. The CHAR and CHAROFF attributes, as well as the "char" value for the ALIGN attribute, have yet to be supported by either Internet Explorer or Netscape Navigator. Once browsers support this, you'll be able to display columns aligned on a decimal character, for instance. (You can fudge this simply by setting right-alignment, as long as the number of decimal characters are the same.)

TH (Table Heading)

Defines a heading cell within a table and is displayed by a browser in a bold, center-aligned font. The allowable attributes for the TH element are the same as for the TD element that follows.

TD (Table Data)

Defines a data cell within a table. It takes the same attributes as the TABLE element.

Attributes:

`align="left|center|right|justify|char"`	Optional
`valign="top|middle|bottom"`	Optional
`height="n"` (Deprecated)	Optional
`width="n"` (Deprecated)	Optional
`bgcolor="#rrggbb"|colorname"`	Optional
`colspan="n"`	Optional
`rowspan="n"`	Optional
`nowrap` (Deprecated)	Optional
`abbr="header abbreviation"` (4.0)	Optional
`axis="header names"` (4.0)	Optional
`headers="header id's"` (4.0)	Optional
`scope="row|col|rowgroup|colgroup"` (4.0)	Optional

ALIGN, VALIGN, HEIGHT, WIDTH, and BGCOLOR all work as described previously. COLSPAN and ROWSPAN in the TR element allow you to create a cell that spans (encompasses) more than one column or row. COLSPAN and ROWSPAN can be used in the same cell (TH or TD). NOWRAP turns wrapping off. ABBR, AXIS, HEADERS, and SCOPE have no effect in current browsers (for details on what these attributes are supposed to do, see the W3C's HTML 4.01 specification at **www.w3.org/TR/html4/**).

COLGROUP (Column Group) (4.0)

Defines column groups in a table to which styles can be applied.

Attributes:

`span="n"`	Optional
`width="n|n%|0*"`	Optional
`align="left|center|right"`	Optional
`valign="top|middle|bottom"`	Optional

SPAN specifies the number of columns in a group (the default is "1"). WIDTH specifies the width for each column in a group. This can be set either in pixels, as a percentage of the table width, or by assigning a value of "0*", which specifies that the width of any column in the group should be the minimum necessary to display its contents. ALIGN and VALIGN work the same as in the TABLE element.

COL (Column) (4.0)

Nested inside the COLGROUP element and sets SPAN and WIDTH values for cells within a column group. The same attributes applicable to the COLGROUP element are used with the COL element.

Example:

```
<TABLE>
<COLGROUP>
  <COL WIDTH="40"><COL WIDTH="20"><COL WIDTH="0*">
</COLGROUP>
Table body...
</TABLE>
```

THEAD (Table Head) (4.0)

Defines a group of rows as a table header. This element is currently only supported by Internet Explorer 4.0 or greater.

Attributes:

`align="left|center|right|justify|char"`	Optional
`valign="top|middle|bottom|baseline"`	Optional

TBODY (Table Body) (4.0)

Defines a nested group of rows as the body of a table. The TBODY element takes the same attribute values as the THEAD element. This element is currently only supported by Internet Explorer 4.0 or greater.

TFOOT (Table Foot) (4.0)

Defines a nested group of rows as the table footer. The TFOOT element takes the same attribute values as the THEAD and TBODY elements. This element is currently supported by Internet Explorer 4.0 or greater.

Example:

```
<table align="center" width="75%">
<thead>
<tr><th colspan="3">First Qtr Profits</th></tr>
<tr><th>Jan</th><th>Feb</th><th>Mar</th></tr>
</thead>
<tbody>
<tr><td>$1,596</td><td>2,384</td><td>1,893</td></tr>
</tbody>
<tfoot>
<tr><td colspan="3" align="center">All dollar amounts in
000's.</td></tr>
</tfoot>
```

UL (Unordered List)

Creates a bulleted list. UL elements can be nested inside each other to create a multi-level bulleted list. UL elements can also be nested inside of OL (Ordered List) elements, and vice versa.

Attributes:

type="disc|square|circle" (Deprecated)   Optional

TYPE specifies the type of bullet ("disc", "square", or "circle") to be used with the list. (The default is "disc".) It is deprecated in favor of using styles to achieve the same result.

LI (List Item)

Used in combination with the OL element (and the UL element) to specify the items in a list. The LI element, despite appearances, is not an empty element, but a container element with an implied end tag.

Attributes:

`type="disc|square|circle"` (Deprecated)   Optional

TYPE forces a bullet type for a list item and for ensuing list items. TYPE is deprecated in favor of using styles.

Example:

```
<p>Favorite Vacation Destinations:</p>
<ul type="square">
  <li>The Mountains
  <li>The Desert
  <li>The Ocean
</ul>
```

Inline and Other Non-Block Elements

The following elements are either displayed inline in the position where they're inserted or do not independently define a separate block in an HTML document. Although block elements can be nested directly inside of the BODY element (unless it is required that they be nested inside of a particular block element), inline elements should always be nested inside of a block element (such as a P, H1, or ADDRESS element, for instance).

A (Anchor)

Provides a means to insert hypertext links into HTML documents.

Attributes:

`href="url"`	See below
`name="targetname"`	See below
`rel="url"`	Optional
`rev="url"`	Optional
`target="framename"` (4.0)	Optional
`accesskey="character"` (4.0)	Optional

HREF or NAME is required. HREF specifies the link URL. NAME specifies a target anchor that another link can jump to (either from the same or another Web page). TARGET targets a frame, causing the linked document to be retrieved in the named frame (see the FRAMESET element). ACCESSKEY allows you to assign a shortcut key to a link.

Example:

```
<p>Go to the <a href="http://www.w3.org/">World Wide Web
Consortium</a>.</p>
```

ABBR (Abbreviation) (4.0)

Marks an abbreviation and optionally provides the full term. Currently, this element is not supported by the latest versions of either Internet Explorer (5.01) or Netscape Navigator (4.73). Using this element to spell out abbreviations can, however, assist search engine robots in indexing your page.

Attributes:

```
title="full term"
```
Optional

TITLE can be used to specify the spelled-out term.

Example:

```
<p>James P. Randolph, <abbr title="Master of Fine
Arts">M.F.A</abbr></p>
```

ACRONYM (4.0)

Marks an acronym and optionally provides the full term. Currently, this element is not supported by the latest versions of either Internet Explorer (5.01) or Netscape Navigator (4.73). Using this element to spell out acronyms can, however, assist search engine robots in indexing your page.

Attributes:

```
title="full term"
```
Optional

TITLE can be used to specify the spelled-out term.

Example:

```
<p>For great drama programs, you can't beat the <acronym
title="British Broadcasting Corporation">BBC</acronym>.</p>
```

APPLET (Deprecated)

Runs a Java applet from within an HTML document. In HTML 4, the APPLET element is deprecated in favor of the OBJECT element.

Attributes:

`code="classfile"`	Required
`width="n"`	Required
`height="n"`	Required
`codebase="url"`	Optional
`alt="text"`	Optional
`name="applet name"`	Optional
`align="top|middle|bottom|left|right"`	Optional
`hspace="n"`	Optional
`vspace="n"`	Optional

CODE references the file name for the applet's compiled subclass, which must be relative to the applet's base URL. CODEBASE specifies the applet's base URL (if other than the HTML document's URL). ALT provides alternative text. NAME allows applets on the same page to communicate with each other.

PARAM (4.0)

An empty element used to pass named parameters to an applet. It's nested inside the APPLET element.

Attributes:

`name="name"`	Required
`value="text"`	Required

NAME specifies a name token, which must start with a letter (A to Z or a to z) and can be followed by any number of letters, digits, hyphens, or periods. Character entities cannot be included. VALUE contains the parameter that's being passed to the applet.

Example:

```
<applet code="password.class"  width="500" height="32">
  <param name="pass" value="password.html">
  <param name="nopass" value="nopassword.html">
</applet>
```

B (Bold)

Used to turn bold on and off.

Example:

```
<p><b>This line is bolded.</b></p>
```

BDO (4.0)

Allows authors to override the bi-directional algorithm for text phrases. Currently, this element is supported by the latest version of Internet Explorer (5.01), but not Netscape Navigator (4.73).

Attributes:

`dir="ltr|rtl"`	Required
`lang="language code"`	Optional

DIR sets either left-to-right ("ltr") or right-to-left ("rtl") direction. LANG specifies a language code. For further guidance in using this element, see **www.w3.org/TR/html4/struct/dirlang.html**. For a listing of two-character language codes, see **www.unicode.org/unicode/onlinedat/languages.html**.

Example:

```
<p><bdo dir="ltr">0 1 2 3 4 5 6 7 8 9</bdo></p>
<p><bdo dir="rtl">9 8 7 6 5 4 3 2 1 0</bdo></p>
```

BASEFONT (Deprecated)

Used to reset the base font size. You can specify an absolute or a relative value. Multiple BASEFONT elements can be inserted into an HTML document—the new base font size will apply until a new BASEFONT element is inserted. Deprecated in favor of using styles.

Attributes:

`SIZE="n" or "-n|+n"`	Required

SIZE specifies an absolute or a relative base font size. Seven absolute font sizes are available (1 through 7, with 3 as the default). Relative font sizes are set relative to the current base font size (+3 would equal a font size of 6 relative to the default font size of 3).

Example:

```
<basefont size="4">
```

BIG

Displays text in a font that's one size bigger than the base font. To display even bigger fonts, multiple instances of the BIG element can be nested within each other.

Example:

```
This is <big>big</big>. This is really <big><big>big</big></big>.
```

BR (Break)

Inserts a line break. This can be used for formatting lists or lines of poetry—anywhere you want a single line break between lines. (Most "block" elements, such as the P element, are followed by *two* line breaks.)

Attributes:

`clear="left|right|all"` (Deprecated) Optional

CLEAR stops text from wrapping around a left- or right-aligned image, with "left" moving text (or other elements) down until the left margin is clear, "right" until the right margin is clear, and "all" until both the left and right margins are clear. The CLEAR attribute is deprecated in favor of using styles to achieve the same result.

Example:

```
<p>Address:</p>
<p>Rupert Blank<br>
1111 First Street<br>
Seattle, WA 98111</p>
```

or

```
<p><img align="left" src="myimage.gif">
Type text to flow around image here...
<br clear="left"></p>
```

CITE

Renders a citation, typically in italics. Your best bet is to use I or EM instead.

Example:

```
<p>My favorite novel is <cite>The Brothers Karamazov</cite>.</p>
```

CODE (Program Code)

Renders program or computer code. Intended for rendering short phrases or words of code (the PRE tag should be used to render blocks of program code). This element should be displayed in a monospaced font. Your best bet is to simply use the TT tag instead.

Example:

```
<p>The query result was <code>XP 4429</code>.</p>
```

(COMMENT)

In HTML, a "comment" can be inserted by preceding the comment with `<!--` and ending it with `-->`.

Example:

```
<!--
This text is a comment and will not be displayed.
-->
```

DEL (Deletion) (4.0)

Marks text for deletion, which should then be displayed as strikeout text. Currently, only Internet Explorer 4 or higher supports this element (the attributes are ignored, however). If all you want to do is mark strikeout text, your best bet is to use the STRIKE tag, instead, because it is more likely to be supported by earlier browsers.

Attributes:

`cite="url"`	Optional
`datetime="datetime"`	Optional

CITE designates the URL of a source document or message that is cited as the source, reason, or authority for the deletion. DATETIME can take values in the following order: *YYYY* (year), *MM* (month), *DD* (day), *T* (start of time element), *hh* (hour), *mm* (minute), *ss* (second), *z* (Coordinated Universal Time, UCT/GMT), *+hh:mm* (local time relative to UCT; replaces *z*), and *-hh:mm* (local time relative to UCT; replaces *z*). This example corresponds to September 15, 2000, 12:00 p.m. UTC (GMT):

Example:

```
<del datetime="2000-09-15T12:00:00Z">Text to be deleted.</del>
```

DFN (Definition)

Used to display the defining instance of a term. Internet Explorer displays it in italics, but Navigator entirely ignores it. Your best bet is to use I or EM tags instead.

Example:

```
<p>A <dfn>relative URL</dfn> states the location of a link relative
to the location of the linking document.</p>
```

EM (Emphasis)

Emphasizes text by displaying it in italics. This element should always display in a browser identically to the I element—the only difference being that the EM element is a *logical* element, whereas the I element is a *literal* element.

Example:

```
<p>This text is <em>emphasized</em>.</p>
```

FONT (Deprecated)

Sets font size, color, and face properties. Although it has been deprecated in HTML 4.0 in favor of using styles, it's just too handy to ever go away.

Attributes:

size="n" or "+n|-n"	Optional
color="#rrggbb|colorname"	Optional
face="font[,font2][,font3]" (4.0)	Optional

SIZE specifies an absolute or relative font size. A relative font size is specified *relative to* either the default base font size (3) or base font size set previously using the BASEFONT tag.

COLOR sets the font color, either with a hexadecimal color code (#*rrggbb*) or a color name (black, white, aqua, blue, fuchsia, gray, green, lime, maroon, navy, olive, purple, red, silver, teal, and yellow). FACE specifies a font name or a comma-separated list of font names that can be used to display the font.

Example:

```
<p>This is <font size="5" color="red" face="arial, helvetica">
important!</font></p>
```

I (Italic)

Displays text in italics. Is displayed in browsers exactly the same as the EM (Emphasis) tag, but is quicker to type.

Example:

```
<p>This text is <i>italicized</i>.</p>
```

IFRAME (Inline Frame) (4.0)

Lets you insert and dimension an inline frame in a Web page. Currently, no version of Netscape Navigator supports using inline frames. Versions 3.0 and higher of Internet Explorer do, however.

Attributes:

`src="url"`	Required
`height="n"`	Optional
`width="n"`	Optional
`name="framename"`	Optional
`align="horizontal or vertical"`	Optional
`frameborder="1|0"`	Optional
`marginheight=""n|n%"`	Optional
`marginwidth="n|n%"`	Optional
`scrolling="yes|no|auto"`	Optional

SRC gives the inline document URL. HEIGHT and WIDTH specify the dimensions (the default in Internet Explorer is 300 pixels wide by 150 pixels high). NAME assigns a name to the frame that can be targeted by an external link's TARGET attribute (see the FRAMESET element). FRAMEBORDER turns the border off ("0"). MARGINHEIGHT and MARGINWIDTH set the frame's margins. SCROLLING turns scrolling "on" or "off" (the default is "auto").

Example:

```
<iframe src="example.html" width="400" height="500" marginheight="5"
marginwidth="5">

[Your browser does not support display of inline frames. Please
visit

<a href="example.html">the related page.</a>]

</iframe>
```

IMG (Image)

An empty element that allows you to insert an inline image in your Web page.

Attributes:

src="url"	Required
alt="alternate text"	Advised
align="vertical and horizontal"	Optional
height="n"	Advised
width="n"	Advised
border="n"	Optional
hspace="n"	Optional
vspace="n"	Optional
usemap="#map name"	Optional
ismap	Optional

SRC specifies the URL for a GIF, JPEG, or PNG image. ALT provides alternative text for browsers that don't display images. ALIGN specifies vertical alignment ("top", "middle", or "bottom") relative to the baseline of the element, or it specifies horizontal alignment ("left" or "right") with text or other elements wrapping along the other side. The default is "bottom". HEIGHT and WIDTH specify the image dimensions. If the image is inside of an A (Anchor) element (an "image link"), the BORDER attribute can increase or decrease the width of the border around the image. Setting BORDER="0" will turn the border off. HSPACE and VSPACE add space to the left and right or above and below the image, respectively.

USEMAP specifies the name of a MAP element that defines the hotspots for a client-side image map. (See the MAP element.) ISMAP causes the clicked location in the image to be passed to the server, activating a server-side image map.

Example:

```
<center><img src="mybanner.gif" width="400" height="100" alt="My
banner image"></center>
```

INS (Insertion) (4.0)

Marks text as an insertion. How it is to be displayed is left up to the browser. Currently, only Internet Explorer 4.0 (or higher) displays this element (the attributes are not supported, however).

Attributes:

For a description of the attributes that can be used with the INS element, see the DEL element, earlier in this appendix. See the DEL element also for examples of using the INS element (just substitute INS for DEL).

KBD (Keyboard)

Displays text to be entered from the keyboard. The latest versions of both Internet Explorer and Netscape Navigator display it in a monospaced font, although some earlier versions of Internet Explorer also reduce the size of this element. If all you want is monospaced text, your best bet is to use the TT tag instead.

Example:

`<p>Type <kbd>help</kbd> at the prompt to get a list of commands.</p>`

MAP (Image Map)

Defines the hotspots in a client-side image map.

Attributes:

name="map name"	Required

NAME specifies the name of the MAP element that's called by an IMG element being used as an image map. The AREA element is nested in the MAP element.

AREA

An empty element that defines a hotspot within a MAP element.

Attributes:

shape="shape"	Optional
coords="coordinates"	Optional
href="url"	Optional
alt="alternate text"	Recommended
nohref	Optional
target="text"	Optional
tabindex="n"	Optional

SHAPE specifies the shape of the hotspot ("rect", "circle", or "poly"). The default is "rect" (rectangle). COORDS specifies the coordinates of a hotspot. If

COORDS is absent, the image coordinates are used. HREF specifies the URL that's activated by the hotspot. If HREF is absent, the document URL is used. Use of ALT is strongly recommended to provide alternative text for browsers that don't display images. NOHREF specifies that the area has no action. TARGET targets a frame name (see the FRAMESET element). TABINDEX specifies the hotspot's tabbing order position. Here's an example:

Examples:

```
<p align="center"><img src="../navbar.gif" border="0" width="450"
height="75" usemap="#navbar">

<map name="navbar">

<area shape="rect" alt="Back" coords="59,10,141,65" href="../
back.htm">

<area shape="rect" alt="Home" coords="180,10,268,66" href="../
home.htm">

<area shape="rect" alt="Next" coords="307,9,390,66" href="../
next.htm">

<area shape="default" nohref>

</map>
```

OBJECT (4.0)

Provides a single source for inserting different objects into an HTML document, including image, sound, video, animation, program (such as Java and ActiveX), and other files. This tag is ultimately intended to replace the IMG, APPLET, and EMBED tags (for guidance on using the EMBED tag, which is a Netscape extension that has not been included in HTML 4.0, to play background music, see Appendix F, "Completing Your Wish List"). The OBJECT tag is currently supported to a limited extent by recent versions of Internet Explorer and Netscape Navigator. My take on this tag is that it replaces three relatively simple solutions with one relatively complicated one. For a full description of this tag and its attributes, along with examples of its use, see **www.w3.org/TR/html40/struct/objects.html**.

Q (Quote) (4.0)

Displays quoted text. Theoretically, browsers should be able to render this differently depending on the document's language. This is also supposed to be a "smart" element that desists from inserting quotation marks if they are already present. Currently, neither Internet Explorer nor Netscape Navigator supports this element.

Attributes:

```
cite="url"                              Optional
lang="language[-country] code"          Optional
```

CITE provides the Web address of the quote. LANG specifies the language of the quote, so appropriate quote marks can be rendered. For listings of two-character language and country codes, see **www.unicode.org/unicode/onlinedat/languages.html** and **www.unicode.org/unicode/onlinedat/countries.html**.

Example:

```
<p>Peter said, <q lang="en-us">Let me do it!</q></p>
```

S (Strikethrough) (Deprecated) (4.0)

Renders text in strikeout. Originally a proposed HTML 3.0 element that didn't make it into HTML 3.2, but was included in HTML 4.0 (and deprecated at the same time in favor of the DEL tag). Because of wider support in older browsers, you should use the STRIKE tag instead.

Example:

```
<p>This text is <s>struck out</s>.</p>
```

SAMP (Sample)

Renders "sample" text or any other string of literal characters. All browsers render it identically to the TT tag, which should be used instead.

Example:

```
<p>Type your title in the third line (<samp>Vice President</samp>,
for instance).</p>
```

SCRIPT

Can be inserted either in the HEAD or BODY element. For more information on the SCRIPT element, see its listing under the HEAD element.

SMALL

Reduces the font size by one size, relative to the base font size. Can be nested inside itself to reduce the font size down two levels (or more, if the base font size has been increased).

Example:

```
This is <small>small</small> text. This is even <small><small>
smaller</small></small> text.
```

SPAN (4.0)

Similar to the DIV element, except that it's a text element instead of a block element. By itself, the SPAN element does absolutely nothing—only when you use it as a vehicle for applying styles to "spans" of text does it comes to life (see the STYLE element). Both Internet Explorer 4.0 or greater and Navigator 4.0 or greater support applying style characteristics to the SPAN element.

Example:

```
<style type="text/css">
<!--
span {font-family: sans-serif; font-size: 1.5em; color: green}
-->
</style>
</head>
<body>
<p>This is the <span>spanned text</span>.</p>
```

STRIKE (Deprecated)

Was originally a Netscape extension for marking strikeout text that was included in HTML 3.2, but has since been deprecated in HTML 4.0 in favor of the new DEL tag. All the same, the STRIKE tag is much more likely to be supported by older browsers—use it instead of the DEL or S tags.

Example:

```
<p>This text is to be <strike>struck out</strike>.
```

STRONG (Strong Emphasis)

Marks text as "strongly emphasized" and is displayed in a bold font, indistinguishable from the B element.

Example:

```
<p>This text is <strong>strongly emphasized</strong>.</p>
```

SUB (Subscript)

Marks text as subscripted. Internet Explorer 3.0 and Navigator 4.0 display subscripts and superscripts in a smaller font, but earlier versions of these browsers do not.

Example:

```
<p>I'd like a drink of H<sub>2</sub>O.</p>
```

SUP (Superscript)

Marks text as superscripted. To allow for nonsupporting browsers, you might want to put superscripted text inside of parentheses.

Example:

```
Try Goober's Hair Grease<sup>(TM)</sup>!
```

TT (Teletype Text)

Often referred to as the "Typewriter Text" element. Is displayed in a smaller, monospaced font by all browsers and is the preferred element for rendering monospaced text.

Example:

```
<p><tt>This text is displayed in a monospaced font.</tt></p>
```

U (Underline)

Marks text as underlined. Be aware that versions of Netscape Navigator 3.0 and earlier do not support this element. Generally, if you want to add emphasis to an HTML document, you should use the I or EM tags or the B or STRONG tags.

Example:

```
<p>This text is <u>underlined</u>.</p>
```

VAR (Variable)

Used to render a program variable. All browsers should display this element in an italic font. Your best bet is to use I or EM instead.

The FRAMESET Element (4.0)

Allows you to define a multiple-frame Web page, where each frame contains and displays its own HTML document. Frames can be scrolled and resized by the user, unless scrolling and resizing is turned off.

Attributes:

`rows="n,n,..."`	Optional
`cols="n,n,..."`	Optional

ROWS specifies row dimensions in a FRAMESET element, whereas COLS specifies column dimensions. Pixel, percentage, or relative dimensions can be specified:

- ✿ **Pixel dimensions**—You can define columns or rows within a FRAMESET element using absolute pixel dimensions. For instance, `<FRAMESET ROWS="80,400">` defines two rows, with the top row being 80 pixels high and the bottom row being 400 pixels high. To allow for different screen resolutions (and browser window dimensions), you shouldn't set all rows or columns in a FRAMESET element as absolute pixels.

- ✿ **Percentage dimensions**—You can define columns and rows as percentages of the total height or width of the browser window. For instance, `<FRAMESET ROWS="80%,20%">` defines two rows, with the top row filling 80 percent and the bottom row filling 20 percent of the total height of the browser window.

- ✿ **Relative dimensions**—You can combine either pixel or percentage row or column dimensions with the wildcard character (*). For instance, `<FRAMESET ROWS="*,100">` defines the top row as a "relative" row that would expand or contract depending on the total space available in the browser window, whereas the bottom row would remain fixed at a height of 100 pixels.

FRAME (4.0)

Nested inside the FRAMESET element. It's used to define frames that are included in the frame page.

Attributes:

`src="url"`	Usually
`name="framename"`	Recommended
`frameborder="1|0"`	Optional
`marginheight="n"`	Optional

`marginwidth="n"`	Optional
`noresize`	Optional
`scrolling="yes|no|auto"`	Optional

SRC specifies the frame document's URL. NAME names a frame so it can be targeted from hypertext links located in other frames. FRAMEBORDER turns the border of a frame off or on ("0" turns it off; "1" is the default). MARGIN-HEIGHT and MARGINWIDTH set the amount of left and right and top and bottom margin spaces, respectively (the minimum value is "2"). NORESIZE stops the manual resizing of a frame. SCROLLING determines how scroll bars are treated in a frame. A "no" value turns off scroll bar display, even if the document extends beyond the dimensions of the frame. You might want to do this, for instance, in the case of the space that's added below an H1 element or other block element causing scroll bars to appear, even though no text actually extends beyond the frame. The default SCROLLING attribute value is "auto", which will automatically cause scroll bars to be added to a frame if they're required.

 NOTE Don't try creating "seamless" frames using the standard attributes. It can't be done. It can be done, however, by using a combination of attributes that are Netscape and Microsoft extensions. For more information on how to do this, see the Sunday Morning session, "Working with Frames."

NOFRAMES (4.0)

Provides content in a frame page that will be displayed by non-frames-capable browsers (or by frames-capable browsers where frames have been turned off). Should be nested inside the top-level FRAMESET tag. A non-frames-capable browser will ignore the FRAMESET element, whereas a frames-capable browser will ignore the contents of the NOFRAMES element.

Example:

This is an example of a simple two-column frame page:

```
<html>
<head><title>Title goes here</title>
</head>
<frameset cols="25%,75%">
  <frame name="Side_Bar" src="sidebar.html">
  <frame name="Main_Window" src="front.html">
```

```
<noframes><p>A frames-capable browser is required to view this page.
Please click the link to go to my <a href="front.html">front
page</a>.</p></noframes>
</frameset>
</html>
```

In this example, one FRAMESET tag is nested inside another FRAMESET tag to create a combination row-column frame page:

```
<frameset rows="150,*">
    <frame name="Masthead" SRC="masthead.html>
    <frameset cols="75,*"
        <frame name="Left_Bar" SRC="left_bar.htm">
        <frame name="Main_Window" SRC="front.htm">
    </frameset>
</frameset>
```

Instead of nesting a frameset inside of another frameset, you can nest a frame linking to another frameset. This allows you to use links to swap out one frameset for another. Here's an example of the first frameset:

```
<frameset rows="*,75">
    <frame name="Nest_Frame" src="nest_frame.html">
    <frame name="Bottom_Bar" SRC="bot_bar.html">
</frameset>
```

Here's the page, nest_frame.html, containing the nested frameset:

```
<html>
<frameset cols="85,*">
    <frame name="Sidebar" SRC="sidebar.html">
    <frame name="Main" src="main.htm">
</frameset>
</html>
```

Controlling Frames

The TARGET attribute of the A element is used to control frame content. If you don't include a TARGET attribute in a link that is located within a frame, the object of the link will be displayed in the same frame as the link. By using the TARGET attribute to target a frame name, you can use a link in one frame to control the content of any other frame in your frameset.

In addition to targeting the name of a frame, there are a number of standard TARGET attribute values you can use:

- ✿ `target=_top` displays the link object in the top-level browser window (outside of the frameset).
- ✿ `target=_blank` displays the link object in a new blank browser window. This opens a second browser window, which `target="_top"` does not.
- ✿ `target=_self` displays the link object in the same frame where the link is located (the default).
- ✿ `target=_parent` displays the link object in the parent frame of the frame where the link is located.

Some earlier, but otherwise frames-capable, browsers may flub up if you put quotes around these TARGET attribute values, so it's better to leave off the quotes in these instances.

◆◆

CAUTION Be aware that others might not look kindly to having *their* Web pages displayed inside a frame in *your* frameset. When linking to external Web sites from within a frameset, you should *always* include a `target=_top` or `target=_blank` attribute in your link, so that the linked page will be displayed in its own browser window and not inside your frameset.

◆◆

Example:

To have a link located in any of the other frames in the previous frame examples link to the "Main" frame (`name="Main"`), just include `target="Main"` in the link, like this:

```
<a href="page2.html" target="Main">Page 2</a>
```

Note that frame names and link targets are case-sensitive. In other words, if you've got `name="main"` in the FRAME tag, but `target="Main"` in the link's A tag, or vice versa, the link won't work. The NAME and TARGET attributes must match exactly.

General Attributes

There are a number of attributes in HTML 4.0 that can be generally applied to most HTML elements. I haven't listed these previously, unless they were critical or important to the function of the element.

Element Identifiers

HTML 4.0 added two "element identifiers": the ID and CLASS attributes. These attributes can be used to individually identify an element or assign an element to a class:

```
id="name"
class="element class or classes"
```

ID assigns a document-wide name for a specific instance of an element. This must be a unique name, and it should not be duplicated in more than one element. This name should start with a letter and can be followed by any number of letters, numbers, hyphens, and periods, but nothing else. Note that the ID name will replace any instance of the NAME attribute used within an element.

CLASS assigns a class or classes to an element. A class is a group of elements that can have styles attached to the entire group. An element can belong to more than one class. Any number of elements can be assigned the same class name or names. In a CLASS attribute, multiple classes are separated by spaces.

Other Multi-Element Attributes

There are several other attributes that can be applied generally to many HTML elements. Some of these have been already described in certain elements where they performed a critical or important function. These attributes are:

```
style="inline style"
title="element title"
align="left|center|right|justify"
lang="language code[-country code]
dir="trl|ltr"
```

For information on using the STYLE attribute to apply inline styles to elements, see the STYLE element section. TITLE can be used to create an advisory title for an element. Browser may display this, for instance, when the cursor is passed over an element. Search engine robots can also use the content of this element in indexing your site. ALIGN can be used to horizontally align block elements.

Intrinsic Events

"Intrinsic event" attributes in HTML 4.0 allow elements to trigger scripts based on specific events (such as clicking on, passing the cursor over, and so on). They can be applied to most elements. Here's a list of these new attributes along with some short descriptions of what they're supposed to do:

- ✿ onload="script"—Triggered when a window or frame finishes loading. (BODY and FRAMESET only.)

- ✿ onunload="script"—Triggered after a window or frame finishes unloading. (BODY and FRAMESET only.)

- ✿ onclick="script"—Triggered after the mouse (or other pointing device) is clicked on the element. (Most elements.)

- ✿ ondblclick="script"—Triggered after the mouse is double-clicked on the element. (Most elements.)

- ✿ onmousedown="script"—Triggered when the mouse button is held down on the element. (Most elements.)

- ✿ onmouseup="script"—Triggered when the mouse button is released over an element. (Most elements.)

- ✿ onmouseover="script"—Triggered when the mouse is moved over an element. (Most elements.)

- ✿ onmousemove="script"—Triggered when the mouse is moved at all. (Most elements.)

- ✿ onmouseout="script"—Triggered when the mouse is moved out of an element. (Most elements.)

- ✿ onfocus="script"—Triggered when an element "receives focus," either via a mouse or tabbing navigation. (Used with BUTTON, INPUT, LABEL, SELECT, and TEXTAREA.)

- ✿ onblur="script"—Triggered when an element "loses focus," either via a mouse or tabbing navigation. (Used with same elements as ONFOCUS.)

- ✿ onkeypress="script"—Triggered when a key is pressed and released on an element. (Most elements.)

- ✿ onkeydown="script"—Triggered when a key is held down on an element. (Most elements.)

- ✿ onkeyup="script"—Triggered when a key is released over an element. (Most elements.)

- ✿ onsubmit="script"—Triggered when a form is submitted. (FORM only.)

- ✿ onreset="script"—Triggered when a form is reset. (FORM only.)

- ✿ onselect="script"—Triggered when a user selects text in a text field. (INPUT and TEXTAREA only.)

- ✿ onchange="script"—Triggered after a control has been modified and has lost focus. (INPUT, SELECT, and TEXTAREA only.)

For more information on using both intrinsic event handlers and element identifiers, see the W3C's section on scripts in the HTML 4.01 specification at **www.w3.org/TR/html4/interact/scripts.html**.

XHTML/XML Compatibility Guide

You might be wondering what is involved in transitioning from HTML to the new XHTML (Extensible HyperText Markup Language) and XML (Extensible Markup Language) standards. In most cases, you shouldn't need to worry about this, in that the W3C has committed itself to maintaining the character of HTML as a "language that the ordinary person can use" and its accessibility to individuals who "still find value in writing their own HTML from scratch." It is expected, in other words, that most individual Web publishers, especially those who want to write their own code from scratch, will be sticking with using straight HTML to create their pages. You should have no fear that future browsers will cease to support regular HTML.

XHTML, it must be stressed, is also a version of HTML and is not fundamentally different. XHTML is a reformulation of HTML in conformance with XML. XML is an umbrella-language (or meta-language) that sets rules, in compliance with SGML (Standardized General Markup Language), for any number of additional markup languages that may be grouped under its head, including XHTML, MathML, SMIL, and so on. For a fuller discussion of the characteristics of XML, see the Friday Evening session, "Getting Oriented."

Web publishers working within a corporate setting or for larger organizations, however, might need to be mindful of the requirements for transitioning from HTML to XHTML. The capability of XHTML to mark up a single document for presentation in multiple media (on the Web, on paper, for pre-press, on WebTV, on wireless devices, for speech synthesization, in Braille browsers, and so on) is bound to appeal to corporations and larger organizations that have large amounts of traditional paper documents and printed material that they also want to present on the Web and through other non-paper media.

This appendix shows you how to make your HTML documents XHTML-friendly, so that if you do decide in the future to convert your HTML documents to XHTML, the task will be less daunting. The same guidelines apply if you want to start working in XHTML, but want your XHTML documents to still be displayable in today's HTML-supporting browsers.

FIND IT ON ▶ THE WEB To learn more about XHTML and XML, go to the W3C's sites at **www.w3. org/TR/xhtml1/** and **www.w3.org/XML/**.

Main Differences between XHTML 1.0 and HTML 4.01

Here is a summary of the main differences between the two markup languages:

- ✿ Although implied end tags are allowed for several HTML tags, end tags must be included in XHTML and can't be implied.

- ✿ Empty tags must include the / character at the end of the tag. The HTML `<br>` must be written as `<br />` in XHTML, for instance.

- ✿ Although in HTML you can type HTML elements and attributes any way you want (`<html>`, `<Html>`, and `<HTML>` all being the same tag), all XHTML elements must be typed in all lowercase. (In this book I've stressed typing elements and attributes in lowercase.)

- ✿ In HTML, quoting attribute values is often optional, but in XHTML it is required. Thus, whereas `align=right` is allowed in HTML, in XHTML this must be written as `align="right"`. (In this book I've stressed quoting attribute values.)

⚙ HTML allows including minimized attributes, such as the NOSHADE attribute of the HR tag, but XHTML disallows this. What can be written in HTML as `<br noshade>`, for instance, must be written in XHTML as `<br noshade="noshade" />`.

⚙ The NAME attribute in HTML is superseded by the ID attribute in XHTML. Whereas `<a name="section1"></a>` can be used to define a target anchor in HTML, `<a id="section1"></a>` should be used in XHTML. The NAME attribute has been included in XHTML for transition purposes, but will be obsoleted in a future version of XHTML.

⚙ The LANG attribute in HTML is superseded by the XML:LANG attribute in XHTML. Whereas `lang="en"` can be used to specify English as the language in HTML, `xml:lang="en"` should be used in XHTML. The LANG attribute has been included in XHTML for transition purposes, but will be obsoleted in a future version of XHTML.

• •

NOTE Including guidelines or directions for creating XHTML 1.0-compliant documents is not part of the purpose of this appendix. If you're interested in writing XHTML 1.0-compliant documents, you should first thoroughly read the W3C's recommendation at **www.w3.org/ TR/xhtml1/**.

• •

Guidelines for Making Your HTML Documents XHTML-Friendly

The following guidelines do not ensure that your HTML documents will be XHTML-compliant, but can be used in writing your HTML documents in a form that will lessen the number of changes you'll have to make if you do decide to convert them to XHTML. (These same guidelines can be used by XHTML authors to ensure that their XHTML documents will be displayable in HTML browsers.)

⚙ Do not use implied tag endings. Although leaving off end tags for some elements, such as the `</p>` end tag, for instance, is allowed in HTML, end tags must be included in XHTML documents.

⚙ In empty elements, always include a trailing / character in the tag. To ensure that HTML browsers will read this correctly, include a space in front of the / character, like this: `<br />`. (HTML browsers will simply ignore the / character.)

- To conform to XHTML, all minimized attributes (compact, nowrap, ismap, declare, noshade, checked, disabled, readonly, multiple, selected, noresize, and defer) should be expanded (to `nowrap="nowrap"`, for instance). Note, however, that although this will not cause any problems in HTML 4.0-compliant browsers, some older browsers may fail to recognize the expanded attribute.

- Use external style sheets or scripts if <, &, or]] are included, or make sure that these characters are not included. (XHTML browsers may seek to parse these characters, whereas HTML browsers will not.)

- When specifying languages, use both LANG and XML:LANG attributes: `<p lang="fr" xml:lang="fr">`, for instance. (HTML browsers will simply ignore the XML:LANG attribute.)

- When using a "fragment identifier" in a link to jump to a target anchor in the same or another HTML file, include both the NAME and ID attributes in the target anchor. For instance, if the link reads `<a href="page2.html#sect2">...</a>`, the target anchor (in page2.html) should read `<a name="sect2" id="sect2"></a>`.

- When specifying the character encoding for a document, use both an XML declaration (`<?xml version="1.0" encoding="EUC-JP"?>`, for instance) at the top of the document and a META tag HTTP-EQUIV statement (`<meta http-equiv="Content-type" content'text/html; charset="EUC-JP'" />`, for instance) nested in the HEAD element. In XHTML, the XML declaration will take precedence, whereas it will be ignored by HTML browsers.

- Avoid including ampersands (&) in attribute values, or include them in the form of character entity references (`&amp;`).

- When creating tables, don't rely on the TBODY element being inferred. In HTML, a TBODY style will automatically be applied to the body of a table in the absence of THEAD or TFOOT elements, but XHTML requires that the TBODY element be present in a table if its style characteristics are to be applied.

Non-Keyboard Characters

The ISO 8859-1 character set is the official character set for Web pages, at least as far as Western languages (English, French, German, and so on) are concerned. It is an 8-bit character set, which allows for 256 code positions. The code positions 000 through 031 and 127 are assigned as control characters (line feed, space character, and so forth). Positions 032 through 126 correspond to the US-ASCII characters that you can type in at the keyboard. Code positions 128 through 159 are designated as "unused" in ISO 8859-1, although both the Macintosh and Windows systems assign characters to many of these positions.

The only characters that are officially specified by the ISO 8859-1 character set as okay to use in a Web page correspond to positions 160 through 255. Windows and UNIX systems display all these characters because the ISO 8859-1 character set is also their native character set. However, 14 of the officially sanctioned characters are missing from the Macintosh native character set (which is a different character set than the ISO 8859-1 character set).

In the following sections, you'll find tables showing the reserved, unused, and special characters included in the ISO 8859-1 character set.

Reserved Characters

These are the numerical and named characters that are reserved for formatting HTML tags and codes.

Number	Name	Description	Character
"	"	Double quotation	"
&	&	Ampersand	&
<	<	Left angle bracket	<
>	>	Right angle bracket	>

You should only type < or > (left or right angle brackets) into your HTML documents to designate the start or end of an HTML tag; to use these characters "as is," you need to type in the numerical or named entity code (< and >).

Double quotations and ampersands, on the other hand, generally need only be replaced in an HTML file if they are part of an HTML code that you want to display "as is."

CAUTION

◆ ◆

You should use character entity names with caution, because versions of Netscape Navigator prior to 4.0 only recognize the following character entity names:

✿ All the reserved character entity names (", &, <, and >).

✿ The copyright (©), registered (®), and non-breakable space ( ) entity names.

✿ All the accented characters (starting with À and ending with ÿ), with the exception of the Y-acute and y-acute characters (Ý and ý), which should be avoided altogether because they aren't included in the Macintosh character set.

For inserting all other characters, you should stick to using numerical entity codes.

◆ ◆

Unused Characters

Both Windows and the Macintosh assign characters to many of the code positions that the ISO 8859-1 character set designates as unused, and 12 of these extra characters are dissimilar on the two systems.

CAUTION

◆ ◆

There's no guarantee that any of these "unused" characters will display on other platforms. Generally, it is best to avoid using these characters in an HTML file. A possible exception is the trademark symbol (`&#153;`), which displays on Macintosh, Windows, and most UNIX systems. However, if for legal reasons you want to insure that your trademark symbol displays on *all* platforms, you should use `<sup>(TM)</sup>` instead. (The trademark's entity name, `&trade;`, should be avoided, however, because no version of Netscape Navigator supports it.)

◆ ◆

Number	Name	Description	Character
`&#128;`		Unused	
`&#129;`		Unused	
`&#130;`		Single quote (low)	‚
`&#131;`		Small Latin f	ƒ
`&#132;`		Double quote (low)	„
`&#133;`		Ellipsis	…
`&#134;`		Dagger	†
`&#135;`		Double dagger	‡
`&#136;`		Circumflex	ˆ
`&#137;`		Per mile sign	‰
`&#138;`		S-caron	Š (not Mac)
`&#139;`		Left angle quote	‹
`&#140;`		OE ligature	Œ
`&#141;`		Unused	
`&#142;`		Unused	
`&#143;`		Unused	
`&#144;`		Unused	
`&#145;`		Left single quote	'
`&#146;`		Right single quote	'
`&#147;`		Left double quote	"

Number	Name	Description	Character
”		Right double quote	"
•		Bullet	•
–	–	En dash	–
—	—	Em dash	—
˜		Small tilde	˜
™	™	Trademark	™
š		s-caron	š (not Mac)
›		Right angle quote	›
œ		oe ligature	œ
		Unused	
ž		Unused	
Ÿ		Y-umlaut	Ÿ

Displayable Characters

The following characters, 160 through 255, are part of the ISO 8859-1 character set. These are the only characters that are officially designated for use in HTML documents. They should generally be available on any operating system that uses the ISO 8859-1 character set.

CAUTION   You should be aware, however, that 14 of these otherwise allowable characters, as well as two additional "unused" characters, are absent from the Macintosh's default character set and might not be displayable on that platform. The latest versions of Internet Explorer for the Macintosh do display these characters, but only by substituting the Latin 1 (or ISO 8859-1) character set. Other Macintosh browsers, however, will not display these characters (Navigator displays question marks in place of the missing characters). In the character tables, these characters are marked with "(not Mac)" and should not be used.

Number	Name	Description	Character
		Non-breakable space	[] (brackets added)
¡	¡	Inverted exclamation	¡
¢	¢	Cent sign	¢
£	£	Pound sign	£
¤	¤	Currency sign	¤

Number	Name	Description	Character
¥	¥	Yen sign	¥
¦	¦	Broken vertical bar	¦ (not Mac)
§	§	Section sign	§
¨	¨	Umlaut	¨
©	©	Copyright	©
ª	ª	Feminine ordinal	ª
«	«	Left guillemet	«
¬	¬	Not sign	¬
­	­	Soft hyphen	—
®	®	Registered	®
¯	&hibar;	Macron	¯
°	°	Degree	°
±	±	Plus/minus sign	±
²	²	Superscripted 2	² (not Mac)
³	³	Superscripted 3	³ (not Mac)
´	´	Acute accent	´
µ	µ	Micro sign	µ
¶	¶	Paragraph sign	¶
·	·	Middle dot	·
¸	¸	Cedilla	¸
¹	¹	Superscripted 1	¹ (not Mac)
º	º	Masculine ordinal	º
»	»	Right guillemet	»
¼	¼	1/4 fraction	¼ (not Mac)
½	½	1/2 fraction	½ (not Mac)
¾	¾	3/4 fraction	¾ (not Mac)
¿	¿	Inverted question mark	¿
À	À	A-grave	À
Á	Á	A-acute	Á
Â	Â	A-circumflex	Â
Ã	Ã	A-tilde	Ã
Ä	Ä	A-umlaut	Ä
Å	Å	A-ring	Å

Number	Name	Description	Character
Æ	Æ	AE ligature	Æ
Ç	Ç	C-cedilla	Ç
È	È	E-grave	È
É	É	E-acute	É
Ê	Ê	E-circumflex	Ê
Ë	Ë	E-umlaut	Ë
Ì	Ì	I-grave	Ì
Í	Í	I-acute	Í
Î	Î	I-circumflex	Î
Ï	Ï	I-umlaut	Ï
Ð	Ð	Uppercase Eth	Ð (not Mac)
Ñ	Ñ	N-tilde	Ñ
Ò	Ò	O-grave	Ò
Ó	Ó	O-acute	Ó
Ô	Ô	O-circumflex	Ô
Õ	Õ	O-tilde	Õ
Ö	Ö	O-umlaut	Ö
×	×	Multiplication sign	× (not Mac)
Ø	Ø	O-slash	Ø
Ù	Ù	U-grave	Ù
Ú	Ú	U-acute	Ú
Û	Û	U-circumflex	Û
Ü	Ü	U-umlaut	Ü
Ý	Ý	Y-acute	Ý (not Mac)
Þ	Þ	Uppercase Thorn	Þ (not Mac)
ß	ß	Sharp s (German)	ß
à	à	a-grave	à
á	á	a-acute	á
â	â	a-circumflex	â
ã	ã	a-tilde	ã
ä	ä	a-umlaut	ä
å	å	a-ring	å
æ	æ	ae ligature	æ
ç	ç	c-cedilla	ç

Number	Name	Description	Character
è	è	e-grave	è
é	é	e-acute	é
ê	ê	e-circumflex	ê
ë	ë	e-umlaut	ë
ì	ì	i-grave	ì
í	í	i-acute	í
î	î	i-circumflex	î
ï	ï	i-umlaut	ï
ð	ð	Lowercase Eth	ð (not Mac)
ñ	ñ	n-tilde	ñ
ò	ò	o-grave	ò
ó	ó	o-acute	ó
ô	ô	o-circumflex	ô
õ	õ	o-tilde	õ
ö	ö	o-umlaut	ö
÷	÷	Division sign	÷
ø	ø	o-slash	ø
ù	ù	u-grave	ù
ú	ú	u-acute	ú
û	û	u-circumflex	û
ü	ü	u-umlaut	ü
ý	ý	y-acute	ý (not Mac)
þ	þ	Lowercase Thorn	þ (not Mac)
ÿ	ÿ	y-umlaut	ÿ

FIND IT ON ▶
THE WEB

For additional information on the ISO 8859-1 character set, see A. J. Flavell's page on ISO 8859-1 at **ppewww.ph.gla.ac.uk/~flavell/iso8859/**.

Unicode Characters

The Unicode Worldwide Character Standard, usually just referred to as Unicode, makes many more characters available that can be inserted in Web pages. The current standard, Unicode 3.0, potentially allows for the inclusion of over 49,000 Unicode characters, covering the main languages of the Americas,

Europe, the Middle East, Africa, India, Asia, and the Pacific, as well as various sets of mathematical, technical, and other symbols. Characters from additional languages will be added as time goes by.

However, whether a particular Unicode character will display in your browser depends on whether you have a Unicode-supporting font installed on your system that includes that character. That you're able to view a particular Unicode character in your browser doesn't mean that someone else will be able to view the same character. For instance, if you have a Unicode-supporting Russian font installed on your system, you'll be able to view Cyrillic Unicode characters inserted in a Web page, but someone else without a Unicode-supporting font installed that includes Cyrillic characters will not be able to view the same characters.

FIND IT ON ▶ THE WEB To test which Unicode characters are viewable on your system, go to A. J. Flavell's Unicode Test page at **ppewww.ph.gla.ac.uk/~flavell/unicode/** (click the "test tables" link).

FIND IT ON ▶ THE WEB 32-bit versions of Windows use Unicode-supporting core fonts—Arial, Times New Roman, and Courier New. These fonts use the 652-character WGL4 characters set, which includes many Unicode characters. To see characters (and their decimal values) included in the WGL4 character set, see Alan Wood's page on the WGL4 character set at **www.hclrss.demon.co.uk/demos/wgl4.html** (Navigator users see the following tip before attempting to view the Unicode characters in this page).

TIP

■ ■

If you're using Navigator, unless the author has set the HTML document's character set to UTF-8, you can't automatically view Unicode characters in that document. You can, however, manually set the UTF-8 character set yourself. In Navigator 4.0 or higher, just select View, Character Set (or Encoding), and Unicode (UTF-8).

■ ■

FIND IT ON ▶ THE WEB Support for Unicode on the Macintosh platform is just in its infancy. Support for Unicode has been built into the Mac since OS 8.5. Currently, the Symbol font on the Mac platform has support for many Unicode Greek and other symbol characters. The Mac also has support for Unicode characters in its MacRoman character set—to see which characters are included in this character set, along with their Unicode decimal values, see Alan Woods' page on the MacRoman character set at **www.hclrss.demon.co.uk/demos/macroman.html**. You can insert extended (non-keyboard) characters from this character set, using their decimal Unicode values with assurance that Macintosh users will also be able to view your characters.

Generally, Unicode characters from the following Unicode decimal value ranges should be available on both 32-bit Windows and Macintosh computers (running Mac OS 8 or higher): Greek characters: 913-937, 945-969, 977-978, and 981-982; Punctuation: 8211-8212, 8216-8218, 8220-8222, 8224-8226, and 8230; Letterlike Symbols: 8482 and 8486; Arrows: 8592-8597, 8629, and 8656-8660; Mathematical Operators: 8706, 8710, 8719, 8721-22, 8725, 8730, 8734, 8745, 8747, 8776, 8800-8801, and 8804-8805; Geometric Symbols: 9632, 9650, 9660, 9674, and 9679; and Miscellaneous Symbols: 9824, 9827, 9829, and 9830.

However, you should be mindful that just because a character is available to Windows and Mac users, doesn't mean that it will be available to UNIX or Linux users, for instance.

■■■

Microsoft Office 2000 comes with a font, Arial Unicode MS, which includes all 40,000 characters and symbols defined by the Unicode 2.1 standard. If you have MS Office 2000, but didn't install the Arial Unicode MS font when you installed Office, you can install it from the Office 2000 CD. (You should be aware, however, that this font is very large and might slow your system down if installed, although you can uninstall it, if you want.) To install this font, just reinstall Office 2000 and select Add or Remove Features, click the plus sign (+) next to Office Tools, click the plus sign next to International Support, click the icon next to Universal Font, and then select the installation option you want.

There are a number of fonts available online that support varying parts of the full Unicode character set. Two sources are the Alan Woods' Unicode Resources page at **www.hclrss.demon.co.uk/unicode/** and the Unicode Consortium's Useful Resources page at **www.unicode.org/unicode/onlinedat/resources.html**. If you're going to include Unicode characters in your page, you might want to include these links in your page, or include other links to where viewers of your page can download an appropriate Unicode-supporting font.

■■■

Setting the UTF-8 Character Set (Required for Navigator)

In order for Unicode characters to display in Netscape Navigator, you need to set the character set to UTF-8. To do this, insert the following META tag in your page's HEAD element:

```
<head><title>Type your title here</title>
<meta http-equiv="Content-Type" content="text/html;charset=utf-8">
</head>
```

Inserting Unicode Characters in Web Pages

Unicode characters are inserted in the same fashion as the ISO 8859-1 characters, except that the codes begin at 256 and go up (whereas the ISO 8859-1 characters stop at 255). You can enter a Unicode character code using either a decimal or a hexadecimal value.

The first two Unicode character ranges (Basic Latin and Latin-1 Supplement) are the same characters included in the ISO 8859-1 character set.

For instance, here are a few random examples of Unicode decimal and hexadecimal character codes:

 NOTE Currently, versions of Internet Explorer 4.0 or greater support inserting Unicode characters using hexadecimal codes, but Netscape Navigator only supports inserting Unicode characters using decimal codes. For that reason, unless your audience will be restricted only to Internet Explorer users, you should stick to using Unicode decimal codes.

Decimal	Hex	Description
&#916;	&#x0394;	Greek Capital Delta
&#946;	&#x03B2;	Greek Small Beta
&#1048;	&#x0418;	Cyrillic Capital I
&#1488;	&#x05D0;	Hebrew Alef
&#8364;	&#x20AC;	Euro Currency Sign
&#8482;	&#x2122;	Trademark Symbol
&#8594;	&#x2192;	Right Arrow
&#8734;	&#x221E;	Infinity Symbol
&#9829;	&#x2665;	Heart Suit Symbol

Using Relative URLs

In the tutorial and work sessions of this book, I had you save your HTML files and image files all in the same folder. This is primarily for convenience's sake, so you can get your feet wet before diving into the deep end of the pool. By saving your files all in the same folder, you only have to include the file name as the URL for a hypertext link or an inline image.

However, if you begin creating more complicated Web sites, organized into separate projects, for instance, each with its own main page and subpages, you'll definitely start to outgrow simply saving all your files in the same folder. You'll then want to organize your separate Web page projects in their own separate folders. You might also want to create a separate folder just to hold your images (this way, different Web page projects can share many of the same images, as well). In order to do this, you'll need to learn how to use *relative URLs*.

What Is a Relative URL?

A *relative URL* states the location of a link object (another HTML file, an inline image, and so on) *relative to* the location of the linking HTML file. You've actually already been using one form of a relative URL when you've used only a file name in an A (Anchor) tag's HREF attribute or an IMG tag's SRC attribute. Specifying only the file name as the link object means that both it and the linking HTML file are located in the same folder.

A relative URL is contrasted with an *absolute URL*. An absolute URL states the location of a link object absolutely (or relative to the Web, itself). You've also already used or seen some examples of these kinds of URLs in this book's work sessions. The URL for this book's Web site is an absolute URL:

```
http://www.callihan.com/learn3/index.html
```

A relative URL is also sometimes called a *partial URL*, whereas an absolute URL is sometimes called a *full URL*. That's because with a relative URL you only have to state that *part* of the object's Web address that is not common to both the linked and linking file. An absolute URL, however, includes the *full* Web address of the linked file.

Benefits of Using Relative URLs

When linking to files that are internal to your own Web site, always use relative URLs, rather than absolute URLs. Here are the reasons:

- Using relative URLs lets you test your site offline on your local computer.

- After testing your site offline on your local computer, you can then go online and transfer your site's folders and files up to your Web site's folder on a Web server, without having to change any of the links.

- Using relative URLs also makes it much easier if you decide to move your site to another server, get a domain name, and so on. Because the root server is not included in a relative URL, you won't need to change any of your links.

- If you want to reorganize your site, your task will be much easier if you're using relative URLs. For instance, if you decide to rename or move a project folder, you'll only need to fix the links that are external to that folder. Any links that are between files within that folder (and its subfolders) can remain as they are.

Examples of Using Relative URLs

In this section, I present a hypothetical multi-folder Web site and then show you some examples of using relative URLs to link between locations within it.

Figure D.1 shows a hypothetical Web site organized into folders and subfolders. In the following explanations, I refer quite often to the different folders illustrated in this figure, so be sure to refer back to it frequently to refresh your mental picture of what's going on.

Getting Your Terms Straight

In order to help you visualize them, in the following explanations I'll be describing the relationships between folders in terms of familial relationships.

The phrase *child folder* refers to a folder that is inside (a child of) the linking file's folder. This folder can also be referred to as a *subfolder* of the linking file's folder. In Figure D.1, for instance, the images, products, and support folders are all child folders (or subfolders) of the My Pages folder.

The phrase *parent folder* refers to the folder within which a linking file's folder is located. In Figure D.1, for instance, the My Pages folder is the parent folder of the images, products, and support folders.

Figure D.1

The My Pages folder contains the images, products, and support folders, and the support folder contains the technical and sales folders.

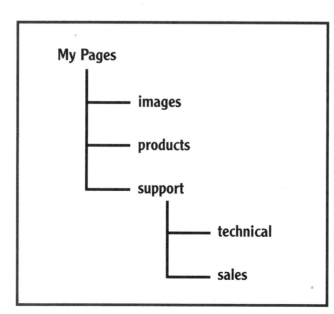

The phrase *grandparent folder* refers to the parent folder of a parent folder. In the illustration, for instance, the My Pages folder is the grandparent folder of the technical and sales folders. The phrase *grandchild folder*, on the other hand, refers to the opposite relation—in the figure, the technical folder is a grandchild folder of the My Pages folder.

The phrase *sibling folder* refers to child folders located in the same parent folder. Other relationships can be set up here, such as between two cousins, between an aunt or uncle and a niece or nephew, and so on.

NOTE   Although the terms *parent folder* and *child folder* are commonly used technical terms describing the relationships in question, the other familial terms I'm using in this appendix (*grandparent folder, grandchild folder, sibling folder, cousin folder,* and so on) are not common. They are used only in order to help describe the "extended" relationships that are involved.

Be sure to frequently refer back to Figure D.1 for a visual representation of the relationships described in the following sections.

Linking to a File in the Same Folder

You've already been doing this. To link to a file in the same folder, you only need to refer to its file name in the link, like this:

```
<img src="headline.gif">
```

Linking to a File in a Child Folder

Now, suppose you want to link from your home page (My Pages > index.html) to an inline image stored in the images folder (My Pages > images > headline.gif). In that case, the IMG tag only needs to include the following:

```
<img src="images/headline.gif">
```

Linking to an HTML file in a child folder works exactly the same way. Suppose you want to link from your home page (My Pages > index.html) to a product catalog you've saved in the products folder (My Pages > products > catalog.html). In that case, the hypertext link needs to look like this:

```
<a href="products/catalog.html">
```

CAUTION

◆ ◆

You'll notice in the previous URLs that no forward slash (/) precedes the images or products folder. Although all versions of Internet Explorer and more recent versions of Netscape Navigator let you get away with starting a relative URL with a forward slash, earlier versions of Netscape Navigator—and likely other browsers, as well—don't let you get away with this.

You might also be tempted to use backward slashes (\), rather than forward slashes. Although the Windows versions of Internet Explorer let you get away with this, no other browser that I know of does (including the Macintosh versions of Internet Explorer).
If you don't want many visitors to your site to get broken links and images that aren't displaying, do not precede relative URLs with forward slashes or use backward slashes.

◆ ◆

That's pretty simple. If you want to link to a file that is in a child folder (or subfolder) of the linking file's folder, you only need to include the name of the child folder, a forward slash, and the file name of the file you're linking to.

Linking to a File in a Grandchild Folder

But what if you want to link to a file that's located in a subfolder of a subfolder (a grandchild folder, in other words) of the linking file's folder? Suppose that you want to link from your home page (My Pages > index.html) to a page of support phone numbers you've saved in the technical folder (My Pages > support> technical > numbers.html). In that case, the hypertext link needs to look like this:

```
<a href="support/technical/numbers.html">
```

Linking to a File in a Parent Folder

Linking back up from a child folder to a parent folder gets a little trickier. For instance, assume that you want to create a link in your catalog page (My Pages > products > catalog.html) to your home page (My Pages > index.html). In that case, the hypertext link needs to look like this:

```
<a href="../index.html">
```

Notice the two dots and the forward slash (../). This originates from UNIX, which is where the Web and HTML were born, and refers to a parent folder of the current folder. So this URL tells the browser to step up one level (to the parent folder of the linking file's folder), and then to open index.html.

Linking to a File in a Grandparent Folder

What if you want to link back up to a file stored in a parent of the parent of the linking file's folder? For instance, suppose you want to create a link in your page of support numbers (My Pages > support > technical > numbers.html) that links back to your home page (My Pages > index.html). In that case, the link needs to look like this:

```
<a href="../../index.html">...</a>
```

In other words, for each level you want to step back up to, you just insert two dots and a forward slash (../).

Linking to a File in a Sibling Folder

What about linking between files located in separate child folders of the same parent folder? Assume, for instance, that you want to add a link to your product catalog page (My Pages > products > catalog.html) that links to an FAQ page, faq.html, that you've saved in the support folder (My pages > support > faq.html). That requires stepping up one level (to the parent folder) and then stepping back down one level (to the sibling folder). To do this, the link needs to look like this:

```
<a href="../support/faq.html">...</a>
```

 **CAUTION** In the 32-bit versions of Windows (all except for Windows 3.1 or earlier) you can create folder and file names with spaces in them. Although Internet Explorer lets you get away with including spaces in folder and file names, Netscape Navigator and likely other browsers, as well, do not. Make sure that there are no spaces in the names of folders or files included in your Web site—you can substitute underscores (_) for spaces if you want. (This doesn't apply to your Web site's root folder on your local computer, because when you transfer your pages and other files onto the Web, you'll be transferring the contents of that folder, but not the folder itself.)

Linking to a File in a Child Folder of a Sibling Folder

What if you want to link to a file located in a child folder of a sibling folder (that is, to a nephew or niece folder)? Assume, for instance, that you want to create a link in your product catalog page (My Pages > products > catalog.html) to a page of technical support numbers, numbers.html, that you've saved in the technical folder (My Pages > support > technical > numbers.html). In that case, the link needs to look like this:

```
<a href="../support/technical/numbers.html">...</a>
```

Now, assume that you want to make a link in the other direction, from numbers.html (in My Pages > support > technical) to catalog.html (in My Pages > products). That link needs to look like this:

```
<a href="../../products/catalog.html">...</a>
```

Here you're actually stepping back up two levels (../../) on the tree, and then walking down another branch (the products folder).

Linking to a File in a Cousin Folder

Suppose you want to link to a file located in another grandchild folder of the grandparent folder of the linking file's folder. In other words, to a cousin folder. You won't see this relationship illustrated in Figure D.1, but if you use a little imagination you should be able to picture it for yourself. Assume that the linking file is a list of prices (prices.html, for instance) located in a prices folder (not shown in Figure D.1) that is inside of the products folder (My Pages > products > prices > prices.html). You want to include a link in it that links to a list of technical support numbers (numbers.html, for instance), located in the technical folder that is inside of the support folder (My Pages > support > technical > numbers.html). In this case, the relative URL looks like this:

```
<a href="../../support/technical/numbers.html">...</a>
```

CAUTION

◆ ◆

When typing folder and file names in URLs, you need to be aware that folder and file names are case-sensitive on UNIX servers (and most Web servers still run UNIX). Thus, if folder and file names in URLs don't exactly match the actual folder and file names, you'll end up with broken links or images not displaying after transferring your site up to a UNIX server.

What I do is try to make sure that the names of files or folders included in my site are all typed using all lowercase letters, and then I uniformly refer to them that way in my URLs. See also Appendix G, "Transferring Your Pages to the Web," for pointers on how to use WS_FTP LE to force the conversion of transferred folder and file names to all lowercase.

◆ ◆

Using Cascading Style Sheets

I f you've worked with word processing or desktop publishing programs that use *styles* (user-configurable tags), you should have at least a working familiarity with the basic paradigm that underlies using cascading style sheets on the Web. In straight HTML, a browser decides what an H2 tag will look like, for instance, but by defining a style for the same element, you can determine what an H2 tag will look like in browsers that support cascading style sheets. True, you can do somewhat the same thing by applying FONT tags to set the size, color, and face of sections of text. By using styles, however, you only need to define a style once for it to be applied in every instance for a particular element. Define a style for the H2 tag and every instance of that tag will display the characteristics you set.

Besides being able to globally control the look of elements in your page, you can also easily swap different style sheets in and out to give your pages an entirely different look. You can also utilize a single style sheet to specify the display features of several, or even all, of your pages.

Cascading Style Sheets, level 1 (CSS1), the initial W3C recommendation, was released in December 1996. Of current browsers, only Internet Explorer and Opera substantially support CSS1. The current version of Netscape Navigator (4.x) only partially supports CSS1, although the next full version of that browser is expected to fully support CSS1. At this time, the only browser that fully supports CSS1 is Internet Explorer 5 for the Macintosh.

Cascading Style Sheets, level 2 (CSS2), was released in May 1998. CSS2 builds on CSS1 by providing support for media-specific style sheets. User agents other than standard visual Web browsers, such as wireless devices, WebTV, speech browsers (or aural agents), Braille browsers, printing routines, and so on, can utilize CSS2 to assist in presenting information included in HTML documents. Besides support for media-specific presentation, CSS2 also provides support for content positioning, downloadable fonts, table layout, and other features. Current browsers only provide minimal support for CSS2, but new browser versions should be adding more support for CSS2 features.

In this appendix, I stick to showing you how to implement some of the CSS1 style sheet features in your Web pages. The features covered all work in the current versions of Internet Explorer, Netscape Navigator, and Opera. I also show you how to use a resource on the Web to make sure that your Web pages using styles are cross-browser compatible.

The STYLE Element

The STYLE element allows you to define a style sheet for your page. The STYLE element is nested inside the HEAD element:

```
<html>
<head>
<title>Style Sheet Example Page</title>
<style type="text/css">
Style declarations are inserted here...
</style>
</head>
```

Shielding the Contents of the STYLE Element

If you include a STYLE element in the HEAD element of your page, some search engines might seek to index its contents along with the remainder of your page, causing your page to fall in their rankings. They might also display the contents of the STYLE element as their description of your page, instead of the start of your first paragraph, which is not likely to encourage others to visit your page. The fix for this is to nest the contents of the STYLE tag inside of a comment, like this:

```
<style type="text/css">
<!--
Style declarations are inserted here...
-->
</style>
```

Browsers that recognize styles will entirely ignore these comment tags, whereas search engines and browsers that don't recognize styles should ignore the commented-out content of the STYLE tag.

Typing Style Declarations

It is important to understand the basic format that is used to type style declarations. You type a style declaration in the following format:

```
element { property1: value; property2: value; }
```

NOTE Those are "squiggly" parentheses ({ and }) being used, not regular ones ((and)). Use of regular, rather than squiggly, parentheses is one of the main reasons for style sheets not working. You should also notice that a colon is used to separate a property from its value, whereas a semicolon is used to separate the properties (with their values). Getting these mixed up is also a common reason why style sheets don't work.

Creating a Simple Style Sheet

The best way to learn is just to jump in and start doing it. The following example creates a simple style sheet that specifies the presentation characteristics of some of the more commonly used HTML tags:

```
<html>

<head>

<title>Style Sheet Example Page</title>

<style type="text/css">

body {background-color: #003300; color: white;}

p {font-family: sans-serif; font-weight: 600;}

h1 {color: #ffcc00; font-weight: bold; text-align: center;}

h2, h3, h4 {font-family: monospace; font-style: italic; color:
#99ffff;}

a {color: #99ff00; font-weight: 600;}

ul {list-style: square; font-family: sans-serif; color: white;}

li {color: #ffffcc;}

address {color: aqua; text-align: center;}

</style>

</head>
```

Next, create the codes for the body of your page. Following is an example you can use:

```
<body>

<h1>Style Sheet Examples</h1>

<p>This is just some text to show what styles can do. This is just
some text to show what styles can do. This is just some text to
show what styles can do. This is just some text to show what styles
can do. This is just some text to show what styles can do.</p>

<h2>Level-Two Heading</h2>

<p>This is just some text to show what styles can do. This is just
some text to show what styles can do. This is just some text to
show what styles can do. This is just some text to show what styles
can do. This is just some text to show what styles can do.</p>

<h3>Links:</h3>

<ul>

<li><a href="http://www.w3.org/">The World Wide Web Consortium
(W3C)</a> — Sets standards for the Web.

<li><a href="http://www.isoc.org/">The Internet Society (ISOC)</a> —
Sets standards for the Internet.

<li><a href="http://www.icann.org/">The Internet Corporation for
Assigned Names and Numbers (ICANN)</a> — In charge of setting domain
name policies.
```

```
</ul>

<hr>

<address>

Type Your Name Here<br>

E-Mail: <a href="mailto:yourid@yourmail.com">yourid@yourmail.com</a>

</address>

</body>

</html>
```

You'll notice that there are no background, text, or link colors set in the BODY tag, nor are there any FONT tags or ALIGN attributes included inside of the BODY element.

Checking It Out in Your Browser

Go ahead and save your style sheet example file as mystyles.html in C:\Html and then open it in your browser. What you see should look similar to what's shown in Figure E.1 (although you'll be able to see the colors).

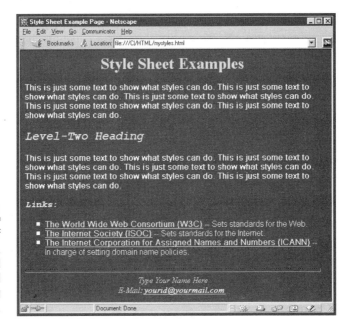

Figure E.1

The formatting of this page (colors, alignment, and weights) is created entirely by using styles.

TIP

■ ■

If you're using Netscape Navigator 4.x, in order to see the style examples in your browser window, JavaScript must be turned on. Turning JavaScript off in Navigator also turns off display of styles. To turn JavaScript on, select Edit and Preferences, click the Advanced category, and then make sure that the Enable JavaScript check box is checked. (The Enable style sheets check box should also be checked.)

■ ■

Understanding the Style Sheet

The following breaks down the style sheet, line by line, so you can get a good grasp of what's included.

```
body {background-color: #003300; color: white;}
```

A background color and a foreground color are set for the body of the Web page. The foreground color should be applied to all elements (all elements nested inside of the BODY tag). In this case, a dark green background color is set (#003300) and a white foreground color. You can use any of the 16 standard color names or you can use a hexadecimal color code to specify the color (see the Saturday Afternoon session for information on using color names and hexadecimal color codes).

Even if you decide not to set a background color for your page, if you want to make sure that the background color of your page is displayed as white, you should specify `background-color: white;` in the BODY element declaration. This causes browsers that otherwise default to a gray background color, for instance, to display a white background.

```
p {font-family: sans-serif; font-weight: 600;}
```

The font for the paragraph element is set to a sans-serif font. Because this font is to be displayed against a dark background color, the weight of the font has been increased to 600 to make it easier to read. Browsers display their default sans-serif font, which might be Arial in Windows or Helvetica on the Mac, for instance. You can also specify a font name, a list of font names, or a combination of the two: `font-family: Verdana, Arial, Helvetica, sans-serif;`. There are five generic font names you can choose from: serif, sans-serif, cursive, fantasy, and monospace. In most cases, browsers should display Times (for serif), Arial or Helvetica (for sans serif), and Courier (for monospace), or close variants. Browsers are supposed to display a script or calligraphic font, such as Zapf-Chancery, for instance, for a cursive font and a fancy display font, such as Western, for instance, for a fantasy font. Because the fonts displayed in different browsers vary greatly when a cursive or a fantasy font is specified, you're probably best off avoiding specifying those generic font families.

```
h1 {color: #ffcc00; font-weight: bold; text-align: center;}
```

For a level-one heading (H1), a golden-yellow color, a bold font-weight, and center-alignment is specified.

```
h2, h3, h4 {font-family: monospace; color: #99ffff;}
```

Three elements (H2, H3, and H4) are grouped so they can share the same style declaration. In this case, a monospaced font and a light-blue color are specified for the H2, H3, and H4 elements.

```
a {color: #99ff00; font-weight: 600;}
```

Here, the color of hypertext links is set to a lime-green color, whereas the font-weight is increased a notch. For the font-weight property, you can choose from four descriptive values: normal, bold, bolder, and lighter. You can also choose from nine "stepped" values: 100, 200, 300, 400, 500, 600, 700, 800, and 900. The value of normal should be the same as 400, whereas bold should be the same as 700, for instance. In this case, the font-weight is slightly less than what is displayed when a bold value is specified.

```
ul {list-style: square; font-family: sans-serif; color: white;}
li {color: #ffffcc;}
```

The UL declaration specifies that an unordered (or bullet) list should be displayed using a square bullet and a sans-serif font. The LI declaration specifies that the color of the list item text should be a light-yellow color. The square bullet displays in Navigator for the Macintosh as a hollow square bullet, but in other browsers this displays generally as a solid square bullet.

Internet Explorer and Navigator, however, do handle this slightly differently. On the Windows platform, in Navigator, the bullet for the list item is displayed in the color set for the LI element, while the list item text is displayed in the color that is set for the UL element. In Internet Explorer, both the bullet and the list item text are displayed in the color set for the LI element (light-yellow). On the Macintosh platform, in Navigator, both the bullet and the list item text are displayed in the color set for the UL element, whereas in Internet Explorer they are both displayed in the color set for the LI element. (If you want this to be consistent across browsers, just set the same color for both the UL and LI tags.)

In addition to the square value, other list-style values that can be applied to unordered lists include circle and disc. Although this example style sheet does not include an OL (Ordered List) declaration, the list-styles that can be applied to that element include decimal, lower-roman, upper-roman, lower-alpha, and upper-alpha.

Although this doesn't work in Netscape Navigator, you can also specify the URL for an icon bullet. Here's an example: ul {list-style-image: url(icon.gif);}. (As long as your style sheet is included inside of your HTML file, this assumes that icon.gif is located in the same folder as your HTML file. This can get trickier, however, when you're using an external style sheet, but I'll cover that later.)

Adding to Your Style Sheet

The example style sheet that you just created is pretty basic, although in many instances it'll give you everything that you want. If you want to get fancier, however, there's lots more you can do using style sheets.

Specifying a Background Image for Your Page

You've specified a background color for your page, but a background image would be nice. That's easy—just edit the BODY element declaration like this:

```
body {background-image: url(b_pool.gif); background-color: #003300;
color: white;}
```

This assumes that you're using an internal style sheet (as you've created in this example) and your HTML file and the background image is saved in the same folder (C:\Html, in this instance). Now, if you resave your HTML file and hop over and refresh your browser, what you should see should look pretty similar to what's shown in Figure E.2.

When setting a background image for your page, you should always set a background color of a similar hue and tone. That way, if someone is surfing with the display of images turned off, they can still see the background color you've set.

Indenting the First Line of a Paragraph

Indenting the first line of your paragraphs is easy to do using styles. Just edit the P element declaration in your style sheet, like this:

```
p {font-family: sans-serif; font-weight: 600; text-indent: 1em;}
```

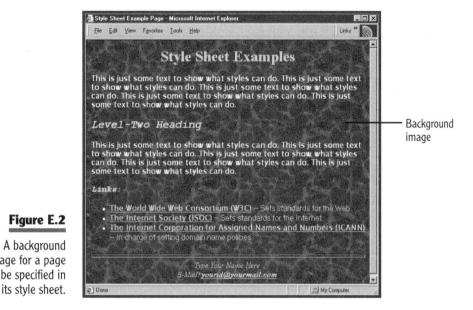

Background image

Figure E.2

A background image for a page can be specified in its style sheet.

This causes the first line to be indented one em (see Figure E.3). An *em* is a relative unit of measurement (roughly equivalent to the width of the letter "M") that scales up or down in size relative to the font size of the text in which it is located. An em space included on a line of 24-point text should be wider than an em space included on a line of 14-point text, for instance.

Other units of measurement that can be used include: in (inches), cm (centimeters), mm (millimeters), pt (points), pc (picas), px (pixels), ex (ex units), and % (percentage). Of these, in addition to em units, you should use only pixels, ex units, or percentages, avoiding using the others. That's because you can't be certain at what resolution or in which font sizes a Web page will be displayed, so you want to use relative units of measurement that will scale, rather than absolute units of measurement that stay fixed in size.

Setting the Page Margins

Setting the margins for your page can be a good way to give your page a bit of a different look. Here's an example of setting a one-percent width for the top and bottom margins and a three-percent width for the left and right margins (see Figure E.4):

```
body {background-image: url(b_pool.gif); background-color: #003300;
color: white; margin: 1% 3%;}
```

First line indent —

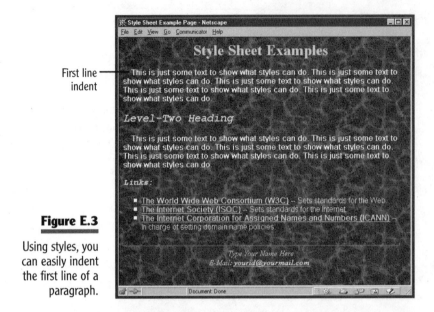

Figure E.3

Using styles, you can easily indent the first line of a paragraph.

Left margin —

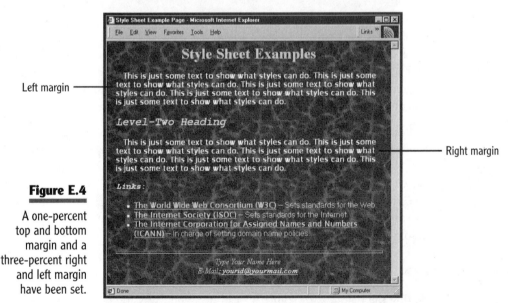

Right margin

Figure E.4

A one-percent top and bottom margin and a three-percent right and left margin have been set.

To set a uniform margin, say of three percent, around the whole page, you'd just need to include `margin: 3%;`. To set all four margins, just include `margin: 1% 3% 2% 5%`. This example sets a one-percent top margin, a three-percent right margin, a two-percent bottom margin, and a five-percent left margin.

You can also use the margin-left, margin-right, margin-top, and margin-bottom properties to individually specify any of the margins.

Setting Element Margins

You can also set margins for specific elements. For instance, to set the left and right margins for the paragraph element, edit its declaration, like this (replace the text-indent property):

```
p {font-family: sans-serif; font-weight: 600; margin-left: 2%;
margin-right: 2%;}
```

As shown in Figure E.5, each of the paragraph elements is now further indented in, on the left and right, from the overall margin that was set for the page.

Using the SPAN Tag

HTML 4 includes a new element, the SPAN tag, that is used with styles to specify the display features for *spans* of text. This can be handy, for instance, when you want to add special emphasis to a word or phrase. First, edit your style sheet to add a SPAN declaration, for instance:

```
span {color: #ff99ff; font-size: 1.25em;}
```

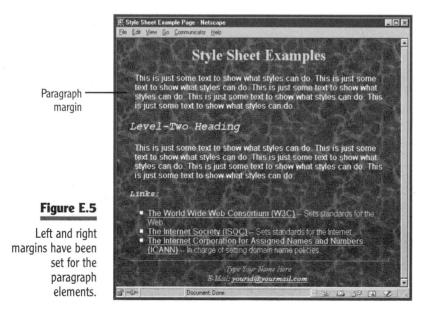

Paragraph margin

Figure E.5

Left and right margins have been set for the paragraph elements.

You'll notice that a new style property, font-size, is used in this style declaration.

Next, edit the body of your HTML file, bracketing the text you want to emphasize with the SPAN tag. Like this, for instance (see Figure E.6):

```
<h1>Style Sheet Examples</h1>

<p>This is just some text to show what styles can do. <span>This
text is SPANNED.</span> This is just some text to show what styles
can do. This is just some text to show what styles can do....
```

Adding Boxes and Borders

Adding boxes and borders can really snazz up your page. In the following example, I show you how to create a blue box with a wood-colored border around it that'll surround the example link list. First, edit your style sheet to add the following style declaration (see Figure E.7):

```
.box {font-family: sans-serif; background-color: #003399; background-image: url(b_rdmarb.jpg); padding: 0.5em; margin-left: 1em;
margin-right: 1em; margin-top: -1em; border-style: groove; bordercolor: #ff9900; border-width: 0.75em; float: center;}
```

Next, edit the body of your HTML document, bracketing the UL tag with the following DIV tag:

```
<h3>Links:</h3>
<div class="box">
<ul>
```

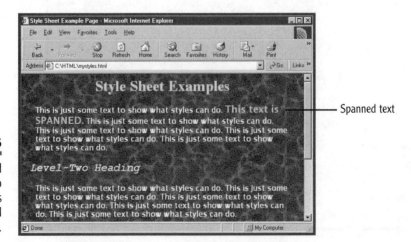

Figure E.6

You can add special emphasis to words or phrases by using the SPAN tag with styles.

Spanned text

```
<li><a href="http://www.w3.org/">The World Wide Web Consortium
(W3C)</a> — Sets standards for the Web.
<li><a href="http://www.isoc.org/">The Internet Society (ISOC)</a> —
Sets standards for the Internet.
<li><a href="http://www.icann.org/">The Internet Corporation for
Assigned Names and Numbers (ICANN)</a> — In charge of setting domain
name policies.
</ul>
</div>
```

First, notice that this style is different from the ones you've created before, in that it starts with a period (.box). This signifies that this style defines characteristics that can be applied to a *class* of elements. The DIV tag that you just inserted in the body of your HTML document contains a `class="box"` attribute that identifies it as belonging to the class of elements (the `"box"` class) that takes formatting characteristics from the .box style. Other things to notice about this style are:

✿ `background-color: #003399;` — Sets the background color of the DIV element to a dark blue color.

✿ `padding: 0.5em;` — Sets extra padding of one-half em around the element.

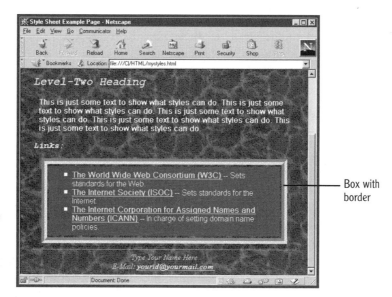

Figure E.7

Creating a box with a border can be a great way to snazz up your page.

Box with border

- ⚙ `margin-left: 1em; margin-right: 1em; margin-top: -1em;` — Sets margins outside of the left, right, and top sides of the box. Notice that the margin-top property is actually set to a negative value, which has the effect of closing up the space above the top of the box.

- ⚙ `border-style: groove; border-color: #ff9900; border-width: 0.75em;` — Sets the border style, as well as the color and the width of the border. In addition to the groove border style, you can choose from these border styles: dotted, dashed, solid, double, ridge, inset, outset, and none. The default is none.

- ⚙ `float: center;` — Don't leave this out! Without this, your box and border won't display correctly in Netscape Navigator, which otherwise does not like having both the padding and the margin properties set at the same time. This specifies the DIV element as a "floating" element, allowing it, in this case, to float in the center of the element's space. Note: You can flow text and other elements around a box by specifying `float: left;` or `float: right;`.

There is one Navigator quirk you should know about. When including other elements within a floating box, Navigator seems to lose track of the order of inheritance that, for instance, otherwise would assign a white foreground color defined in the BODY tag to any other tags nested inside of the BODY tag. The result is that in Navigator, after surrounding an element by a box, you might suddenly find text color both within and outside of the box reverting back to what the default color would be (black) if no text colors were set. If that happens, the fix is simply to directly set the foreground color (`color: white;`, for instance), for any affected elements.

You may also wonder why you don't just insert the `class="box"` attribute inside of the UL tag, rather than inside of the DIV tag. The reason is that the UL tag is indented, by default, in from the left, leading to the box being off-center if you use the UL tag as the base for the box.

You should also be aware of a possible undesirable consequence of setting the measurements in this style using em units. Because em units are sized relative to the element's text size, applying the .box style to another element with a larger font size (such as the H1 element, for instance) will cause all of the em unit measurements to scale up correspondingly. So, if you want to apply this style to elements using different text sizes, you should probably use pixels (px) instead of em units (em). You can also just clone the .box style, creating a second style, .box2, that uses pixels instead of ems. Figure on about 12 pixels per em.

Displaying a Background Image Inside the Box

Besides displaying a background color inside the box, you can also display a background image. To display the background image, b_rdmarb.jpg, inside the box, edit the .box style, like this (see Figure E.8):

```
.box {font-family: sans-serif; background-color: #003399;
background-image: url(b_rdmarb.jpg); padding: 0.5em; margin-
left: 1em; margin-right: 1em; margin-top: -1em; border-style:
groove; border-color: #ff9900; border-width: 0.75em; float: center;}
```

Finding Out More about Styles

This appendix just scratches the surface of using styles. To find out more about styles, check out these resources on the Web:

FIND IT ON ▶
THE WEB

- ✿ Cascading Style Sheets by the W3C at **www.w3.org/Style/CSS/**—Has the very latest on CSS-enabled HTML editing tools. You'll also find the official recommendations for CSS1 and CSS2 here.

- ✿ Cascade Style Sheets Guide by webreview.com at **style.webreview.com/**— Features the Browser Compatibility Charts. See how different browser versions of Internet Explorer, Netscape Navigator, and Opera support different features of CSS. A "don't miss" for anyone serious about using styles.

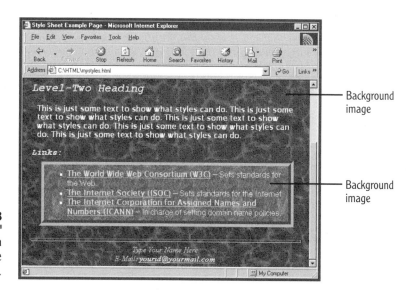

Background image

Background image

Figure E.8

You can display a background image inside of a box.

- Guide to Cascading Style Sheets by Web Design Group (WDG) at **www.htmlhelp.com/reference/css/**—An excellent collection of articles on using CSS in your Web pages.

- Get Started With Cascading Style Sheets by CNET Builder.com at **builder.cnet.com/Authoring/CSS/**—Has lots of good information on the evolution of style sheets, practical examples, as well as a rundown on the positioning of objects using styles. (Although this article is dated back a ways, the material it covers is still valid.)

- CSS Reference Table by CNET Builder.com at **builder.cnet.com/ Authoring/CSS/table.html**—A handy reference to all the properties and values included in CSS1.

- Steve Knoblock's Style Sheet Cookbook at **home.att.net/~knoblock/ cookbook/index.html**—Includes a CSS tutorial and a gallery of style examples.

- CSS Bugs and Workarounds by the CSS Pointers Group at **css.nu/ pointers/bugs.html**—Includes pointers on CSS bugs and workarounds gathered from the collective wisdom of expert posters to the CSS news-group (**comp.infosystems.www.authoring.stylesheets**).

Completing Your Wish List

This appendix is a kind of grab bag that covers a number of oft-requested and popular features that you can add to your pages. After you've learned and become comfortable with straight HTML, you might want to experiment with implementing some of the features covered here:

- Adding background sound
- Adding a hit counter
- Adding a guestbook
- Adding a message board
- Adding GIF animations
- Adding image maps
- Adding a search form

- Adding JavaScript scripts
- Adding Java applets
- Adding interactive animations

Adding Background Sound

One of the most frequent questions I get from readers is how to add background sounds to their pages. The main difficulty with getting background sounds to work is that Internet Explorer and Netscape Navigator use different methods to do this. Internet Explorer uses the BGSOUND tag, which is a Microsoft extension to HTML, and Netscape Navigator uses the EMBED tag (Internet Explorer also supports using the EMBED tag). In the following, I briefly cover how to use these two tags, plus how to get the two tags to work together on the same page.

Some Caveats

Nothing says that you *have* to add background sound to your Web site. It can add significantly to the amount of time your site takes to download and display, for instance, and seldom adds any informational value to your site. I personally do not include any background sound clips in my site and don't particularly care for them while I'm surfing. More often than not, background sound just makes me dive for the Back button. Silence is golden, in other words.

So, why tell you how to do it? Well, for one thing, I'm not into telling people what they should or should not be doing. I'll try to tell you why you might not want to do something, and I'll try to tell you how to most appropriately do it if you decide you must do it, but ultimately I'll leave the decision up to you.

No matter how you cut it, however, because non-standard tags and competing methods of implementation are involved, there are going to be a significant number of people who aren't going to be able to hear your background sound anyway.

If you do decide to include background sound to your site, here are some recommendations:

- Stick to using short sound clips that don't consume very much bandwidth.
- Do not indefinitely loop a background sound clip, unless you're also displaying the plug-in player console on your page, so a visitor can easily turn off the music.

- Check the volume of your sound clip before posting it to your site. Check all your system's audio volume controls, to make sure you don't have them turned way up or way down. If you're going to include a background sound clip, you don't want it to be barely audible, on the one hand, or blast a visitor out of their chair, on the other.

- Remember that your personal taste in music or audio effects might not match the taste of others.

- Finally, realize that many music and audio clips that are widely available over the Web contain copyrighted material. If you put up a copyrighted music clip on your personal site, at worst the owner might ask (or demand) that you take it down. If you put it up on your business site, you could get sued.

TIP Don't know where to find sound clips so you can experiment playing background sound clips in your pages? You might have some sound clips right on your computer that you can check out. Just use the Find command (click the Start button and select Find) to do a search for either WAV (*.wav) or MIDI (*.mid) files on your own hard drive.

There are also many repositories of WAV, MIDI, and other sound files available on the Web. For a great collection of classical music clips, for instance, check out the Classical Midi Archives at **www.prs.net/midi.html**.

NOTE Feel free to try out in your browser any of the examples provided in this section. Chances are that you already have the capability of playing the most common audio formats. If you don't, see "Getting a Plug-In Player" at the end of this section.

Using the BGSOUND Tag

The BGSOUND tag plays background sounds in Internet Explorer. You can insert the BGSOUND tag either in the HEAD or in the BODY element. Here's an example (you'll need to substitute the file name of the actual sound file you want to use):

```
<bgsound src="mysound.wav">
```

In most cases, this should play the sound file, mysound.wav, once when your page is loaded, although some players might loop the sound clip indefinitely. It is a good idea to specifically set your sound clip to play only a set number of times. Here's an example of setting your background sound to play only once:

```
<bgsound src="mysound.wav" loop="1">
```

To make sure that your background sound loops indefinitely, just add a `loop="infinite"` attribute, although I don't generally recommend that you do this. (I personally find indefinitely looping background sounds to be a bit irritating.)

Using the EMBED Tag

If you want to include a background sound clip that will play automatically in both Netscape Navigator and Internet Explorer, you have to use the EMBED tag, not the BGSOUND tag. The EMBED tag is inserted in the BODY element. Here's an example of using the EMBED tag:

```
<embed src="mysound.mid" width="200" height="65" autostart="true">
```

Looping a Background Sound

If you want to play your background sound indefinitely, just add a `loop="true"` attribute, like this:

```
<embed src="mysound.mid" width="200" height="65" autostart="true"
loop="true">
```

If you do decide to loop your background sound indefinitely, I recommend that you do not turn off display of the plug-in console. By leaving the console visible, you give your visitor the option of turning your background sound off, just in case your taste in music doesn't complement theirs. Also, indefinitely looping music can get to be irritating after a couple of loops.

TIP

MIDI (*.mid) files are generally better for playing music clips than WAV (*.wav) files, and they're usually smaller as well. It is also more common, however, that a visitor to your site won't have a plug-in player installed for playing MIDI files. If you're going to include MIDI files in your site and you want to make sure that everyone has the chance to hear your music, include a link to where a plug-in player can be downloaded. One of the best MIDI players is Crescendo, which can be downloaded from **www.liveupdate.com/**. They even have download buttons you can add to your site.

Figure F.1 shows a hypothetical Web page, the Jones Family page, which shows how the display of a plug-in player, in this case the Crescendo player, can be worked into the overall design of a page.

Don't depend, however, on any one plug-in player being displayed. What shows up on someone else's screen is whatever plug-in they've got designated to play the type of sound clip you've embedded.

Hiding the Console

You might decide that displaying the plug-in console just doesn't fit into your design plans, but you still want to play some background music when your page is opened. If you want to do this, I recommend that you don't loop your music indefinitely. Make it a relatively short music clip and play it only once.

You can hide the plug-in console by specifying a width of zero and a height of two pixels:

```
<embed src="mysound.mid" width="0" height="2" autostart="true"
loop="false">
```

Don't try to use `hidden="true"` to hide the player console. Although this does work for some player consoles, it doesn't work for others.

At least one player I know of, the QuickTime 4.0 for Windows player, however, will not play the background sound in the previous example.

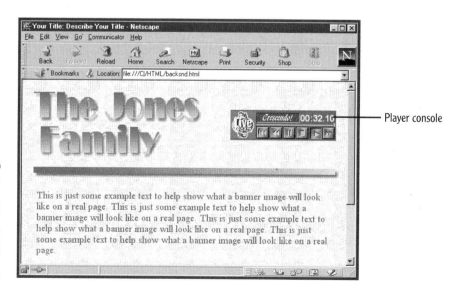

Figure F.1

If you're going to loop your music, display the plug-in player on-screen, so visitors can turn off the music if they don't like it.

Player console

The QuickTime 4.0 player, according to Apple's own site, is supposed to accept a HIDDEN attribute, by itself, to hide the player console, but this also does not work in the QuickTime 4.0 player for Windows. It will play only when both the HEIGHT and WIDTH attributes are set to a minimum value of 2, like this:

```
<embed src="mysound.wav" width="2" height="2" autostart="true"
loop="false">

</body>
```

Thus, if you're concerned about having everybody (or as many people as possible) hear your background audio, stick to setting both the HEIGHT and WIDTH attributes to 2. The problem with this is that it might muck up your page's layout, because it occupies both vertical and horizontal space. One solution is to insert the EMBED tag for your background sound at the bottom, rather than at the top, of your page. By being at the bottom of your page, following after any other elements within the BODY element, the 2 × 2 square shouldn't have any effect on your page's layout. This has the added benefit of letting the remainder of your page load and display before the sound file has to be downloaded and played.

The remaining problem is that the background of the player console dimensions will also show up as a 2 × 2 white dot against any background color or background image you may have set in your page. You can include a BGCOLOR attribute in the EMBED tag that'll work for the QuickTime player, and which may work as well for other players. If you set a background color in the EMBED tag that matches (or is at least pretty close to) your Web page's background color or one of the colors included in its background image, the 2 × 2 remnant of the player console will be rendered completely invisible in players that support this attribute (the QuickTime player does).

Here's a rundown of some of the other attributes that can be assigned to the EMBED tag:

- **LOOP**: Values: true (for infinite loop), false (to not loop).
- **ALIGN**: Values: top, right, left, middle, and bottom. To center, nest the EMBED tag inside of a CENTER tag.
- **VOLUME**: Values: 0 to 100; the default volume is 100.
- **PLUGINSPAGE**: Value: URL where appropriate plug-in can be downloaded. Examples:
  `pluginspage="http://www.apple.com/quicktime/download/"` (for the QuickTime player) or `pluginspage="http://www.liveupdate.com/dl.html"` (for the Crescendo player).

Using the NOEMBED Tag

The NOEMBED tag lets you include content in your page that will be seen only by visitors using browsers that don't recognize the EMBED tag. A common use for this tag is to include a regular hypertext link to the sound file, so the visitor can click on it and, if they have the correct player installed, play the sound clip. Here's an example of using the NOEMBED tag:

```
<embed src="mymusic.wav" width="2" height="2" autostart="true"
loop="false">

<noembed><p>Your browser does not support the EMBED tag. Click on
the link if you would like to download and listen to the <a
href="mymusic.wav">background music</a> that accompanies my
site.</p></noembed>
```

Finding Out More About Embedding Audio

If you want to find out more about using the EMBED tag to include background and other audio files in your Web pages, check out these places on the Web:

- ✪ Embedding QuickTime for Web Delivery at **www.apple.com/quicktime/authoring/embed.html**.
- ✪ Crescendo Netscape Plug-In Authoring Information at **www.liveupdate.com/cpauth.html**.
- ✪ Audio for HTML Using the EMBED tag at **www.world-voices.com/resources/addaud.html**.

Getting a Plug-In Player

Before downloading a plug-in player, test out in your browser some of the previous EMBED tag examples with different audio files on your local system. Just make sure that your HTML file and any audio files you want to test are in the same folder. Also be sure to add the appropriate file extension (.wav for WAV files, .au for AU files, .aif for AIFF files, and .mid for MIDI files) and eliminate any spaces from the file names. Chances are that you already have the capability of playing the most common audio formats.

MIDI (*.mid) files are generally better for playing music clips than WAV (*.wav) files, and they're usually smaller as well. It is also more common, however, that a visitor to your site won't have a plug-in player installed for playing MIDI files. In that case, you might want to include a link to where a plug-in player can be downloaded. You can also include the PLUGINSPAGE attribute in your EMBED tag.

One of the best MIDI players is Crescendo, which can be downloaded from **www.liveupdate.com/dl.html**. They even have download buttons you can add to your site.

For Windows users, you might want to recommend that they download the Windows Media Player, which should be able to handle most audio file types. The Windows Media player can be downloaded from **www.microsoft.com/windows/windowsmedia/**.

For Mac users, you might want to recommend that they download the Quick-Time player. The QuickTime player plays not only MIDI audio files, but also AIFF, AU, and WAV audio files. The latest version of the QuickTime player can be downloaded from **www.apple.com/quicktime/download/**.

Don't depend, however, on any one plug-in player being displayed. What'll show up on someone else's screen will be whatever plug-in they've designated to play the type of sound clip you've embedded.

Adding a Hit Counter

A hit counter is probably the most popular thing people want to add to their Web pages. A hit counter counts "hits" (or visits) to a Web page. One reason hit counters are a much-desired feature is that they give you concrete assurance that people are actually visiting your page. Having a high hit count can also impress visitors with how popular your page is with other visitors (but a low hit count can leave the opposite impression).

The first place to check is your Web space provider, many of which provide free hit counters that you can easily add to your pages. Just follow their instructions to add the proper code to your pages. Figure F.2 shows a counter that I've added to my own pages that is provided by my Web space provider.

If your Web space provider does not provide a hit counter or guestbook, free hit counters are available on the Web. These usually involve some form of advertising that accompanies the hit counter.

There are many sources of free hit counters on the Web. Here are some places where you can start your search for the perfect hit counter for your site:

FIND IT ON ▶
THE WEB

✪ TheCounter.com at **www.thecounter.com/**. They promise not to put any advertising on your site. In addition to the free counter, they also provide free site statistics.

✪ Being Seen's Hit Counters at **www.beseen.com/beseen/free/counters.html**.

Figure F.2

Your Web space
provider might
provide a free hit
counter you can
add to your pages.

- WebCounter at **www.digits.com**.
- LiveCounter Classic at **www.chami.com/counter/classic/**. This is a Java counter that displays up-to-the-minute hit counts, like an odometer.
- CounterGuide.com at **www.counterguide.com/**. This provides reviews of free and other counter sites.

Adding a Guestbook

A guestbook can be a great addition to your site. Unlike an e-mail link, you can share the feedback you get with anyone else who cares to take a look. A guestbook can also be a great substitute for an e-mail link, preventing spammers from grabbing your e-mail address from your page.

A guestbook is usually displayed on your page in the form of a couple of links, inviting visitors to either sign or view your guestbook, sometimes along with accompanying graphics to call attention to it. If visitors choose to sign your guestbook, they can type a message to you and post it to your guestbook. If they choose to view your guestbook, they can scroll through and read any of the messages that have been posted to your guestbook.

There's no shortage of free guestbook providers on the Web, so you should be able to find one that suits you. Here are some places to start looking:

FIND IT ON ▶
THE WEB

- GuestWorld at **saturn.guestworld.tripod.lycos.com/**.
- GuestBook from MyComputer.com at **guestbook.mycomputer.com/**.
- Guestbook4free.com at **www.guestbook4free.com/**.
- Dreambook at **www.dreambook.com/**.
- Alx' Free Guestbook Service at **www.alxbook.com/**.

Adding a Message Board

The message board takes communication one step further by allowing others not only to provide feedback to you, but also allowing them to interact with each other. There can be some pitfalls to hosting your own message board, such as boorish or flaming posters, but it can also be a lot of fun. Check out these sites for free message boards that you can add to your site:

- NetForum at **members.tripod.com/~Dobrolyubov/**. This program lets you add a message board to your Web site, without having to use any CGI. It works by using an e-mail link to download messages to your inbox, and then it uploads the messages to your site to update the message board. The downside is that messages are not updated immediately, but the upside, besides not requiring CGI, is that it is free.

- Delphi Forums at **www.delphi.com/**. Create your own discussion forum in seconds.

- Boardhost at **www.boardhost.com/**. Get set up in seconds!

- Creationcenter.com at **www.creationcenter.com/**. Free message boards, guestbooks, and Tell-a-Friend service.

- Free Message Boards by Freebiescenter.com at **www.freebiescenter.com/ webmaster/mess.html**. This lists and ranks free message board providers.

Adding GIF Animations

The GIF 89a format enables you to include multiple images, or *frames*, in a single GIF image to create a GIF animation. You can't create or view a GIF animation, however, in an image editor. To create and preview a GIF animation, you need a GIF animation editor. You can also, of course, view the result in your browser.

A GIF animation is inserted in your page just like a regular inline image: `<img src="myanim.gif">`, for instance.

Finding GIF Animations

You don't have to create your own GIF animations just to be able to add them to your site. Here are some places on the Web where you can find GIF animations that you can download and use:

- Animation Library at **www.animationlibrary.com/**.

- Animation Factory at **www.eclipsed.com/**.

✿ Rose's Animated Gifs at **www.wanderers2.com/rose/animate.html**.

Creating Your Own GIF Animations

Creating your own GIF animations isn't all that difficult, so you shouldn't necessarily shy away from doing this, especially if you want to add unique dynamic content to your pages that can't be found anywhere else. The more adept you are at creating your own graphics, of course, the more professional your results will look, because the frames included in a GIF animation are just regular images. Besides letting you include multiple image frames in a GIF image, GIF animation editors can also let you add transition effects, manipulate color palettes, and more.

Two of the best GIF animation editors are included on the CD-ROM:

✿ GIF Construction Set Professional 2.0 by Alchemy Mindworks is a shareware application that includes an easy-to-use animation wizard, which makes creating your own GIF animations a breeze. If you like it, the cost to purchase it is only $20. For more information, see **www. mindworkshop.com/alchemy/gifcon.html**.

✿ Animation Shop 2 by Jasc Software is bundled with Paint Shop Pro 6. During the evaluation period, you can try out both programs. Animation Shop also includes an easy-to-use animation wizard. The cost of Paint Shop Pro 6 (including Animation Shop 2) is $99. For more information, see **www.jasc.com/**.

Using GIF Construction Set

GIF Construction Set's Animation Wizard makes it a snap to create GIF animations. After installing GIF Construction Set from the CD-ROM, go ahead and run it. Just follow these steps to use its Animation Wizard:

1. Select File and Animation Wizard. At the Animation Wizard's Welcome dialog box, click on Next.

2. Leave the Yes, for use with a Web page radio button selected. Click on Next.

3. Leave the Loop indefinitely radio button selected. Click on Next.

4. Select the Dithered to super palette radio button. Click on Next.

NOTE When creating the images for your animation, create an optimized palette for each image that includes as few colors as possible, while still retaining acceptable image quality. This helps reduce the amount of dithering required to render the images inside of the GIF animation.

5. Select 20 hundredths in the Delay list. Click on Next.

6. Click on the Select button. Click on the "Look in" list box, and then click on the C drive icon [C:]. In the folder view, double-click on the HTML folder.

7. In the folder view, click on anim1.gif, and then hold down the Shift key and click on anim4.gif. All four example images should now be highlighted. Click on Open, and then click on Cancel to close the Open dialog box.

TIP You're not limited to only selecting GIF images to be included in your animation. By changing the "Files of type" selection to All Files, you can also choose from among JPEG, BMP, PCX, TGA, and PNG images.

8. The four example animation images should now appear in the "Selected files" box. Click on Next.

9. Click on the Done button to generate your animation. (See Figure F.3.)

Previewing and Saving Your Animation

To preview your animation in GIF Construction Set, select Block and View, or you can click on the "sunglasses" icon on the toolbar. (See Figure F.4.)

To close the animation preview window, just click on the close button ("x"). If you want to make any changes, such as speeding up the delay rate, for instance, just rerun the Animation Wizard, changing the relevant settings.

To save your animation, select File and Save (or Save As). For the file name for your animation, type **animhome.gif**. Click on the Save button.

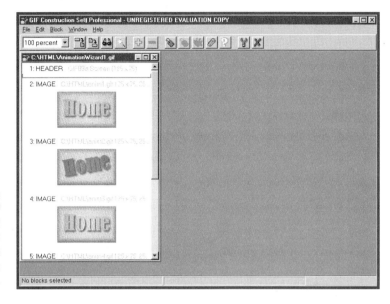

Figure F.3

GIF Construction Set's Animation Wizard has generated a finished animation.

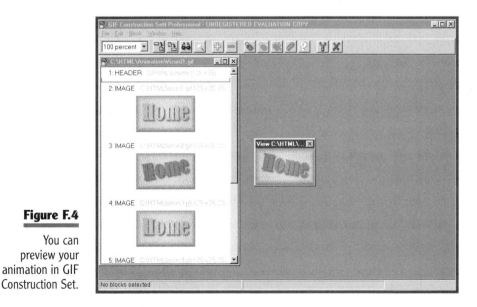

Figure F.4

You can preview your animation in GIF Construction Set.

To include your GIF animation in a Web page, just insert it as a regular inline image: `<img src="animhome.gif">`. You can also insert it as an image link: `<a href="index.html"><img src="animhome.gif"></a>`.

Adding Image Maps

An *image map* is an inline image, either a GIF or JPEG file, in which hotspots have been defined. A *hotspot* is an area in the image that works as a link—click on the hotspot and the object of the link is activated. The object of the link can be anything that can be linked to (for example, a Web page, a graphic, a sound file, and so on).

In this section, I briefly cover using two image map editors: Mapedit and Map This! Mapedit is a trialware program that you have 30 days to evaluate, whereas Map This! is a freeware program.

Choosing an Image Map Editor

There are many image map editors available on the Web. Two very good ones are included on the CD-ROM:

○ Mapedit by Boutell.com makes creating image maps a breeze. An evaluation version is included on the CD-ROM. If you like it, it only costs $25 to purchase. For more information, see **www.boutell.com/mapedit/**.

○ CoffeeCup Image Mapper is also an excellent image map editor. If you like it, it only costs $20 to purchase. For more information, see **www. coffeecup.com/**.

For links to even more image map editors that you can download and try out, see my Web Tools site at **www.callihan.com/webtools/**.

Getting Ready to Create an Image Map

Before creating your image map, you need to do a few things:

○ Create the image you'll be using for your image map.
○ Create an HTML file and insert the image map as an inline image.
○ Create any HTML or other files that will be linked to the image map.

To help save you some time, I've already created "dummy" examples of these files that you can use. You'll find them included with the example files. These include an example image map image (imagemap.gif), an example HTML file (imagemap.html) for displaying the image map, and four additional files (home.html, products.html, services.html, and contact.html) that will be linked to the image map. Normally, however, you'd first have to create these files before going on to create your image map.

Using Mapedit

To create an image map in Mapedit, follow these steps:

1. Create the image that you want to use for your image map and then create an HTML file with the image inserted as an inline image. (I've already included an example image map image and HTML file with the example files that you can use.)

2. Run Mapedit. At the Open dialog box that Mapedit starts at, open the HTML file that includes the inline image you want to use for your image map. To use the example image map HTML file I've created for you, go to C:\HTML and open imagemap.html.

3. You'll see a list of the inline images included in imagemap.html. Double-click on imagemap.gif to select it as your image map image.

4. Double-click on imagemap.gif to select it as your image map image. (See Figure F.5.)

Drawing a Rectangular Hotspot

The easiest type of hotspot to draw is a rectangular hotspot. To do this:

1. Click on the Add Rectangles tool on the toolbar. Read the First Time Hints prompt, which describes what you need to do to draw a rectangular hotspot. Click on OK.

2. Click above and to the left of the Home button, drag the mouse until it is to below and to the right of the Home button, and then click again to draw the hotspot. Once again, read the First Time Hints prompt, which describes the next step in the process. Click on OK. The Object URL dialog box is displayed.

3. In the URL for clicks on this object box, type **home.html**. (I've included this file with the example files.)

4. In the Alternate [ALT] Text box, type **Link to Home Page**. For this example, leave the other options blank. Click on the OK button.

Figure F.5

The image that'll be used to create the image map is displayed in Mapedit's window.

You'll now see a rectangular box drawn around the Home button, which defines the hotspot.

Testing and Editing Your Hotspot

To edit or delete a hotspot, click on the Test and Edit Hotspots tool (the first tool in the third group of tools). After reading the First Time Hints prompt, just click on OK. Then, click on the hotspot you just drew. The hotspot will be highlighted in inverse colors (that's the "test" part) and the Object URL dialog box will reopen (that's the "edit" part). (See Figure F.6.) Just click on OK to close the Object URL dialog box.

Drawing the Other Hotspots

Just repeat the previous steps to create the other hotspot buttons. For the second hotspot button ("Products"), in the Object URL dialog box, type **products.html** and **Link to Products Page**, respectively, in the top two text boxes. For the third hotspot button ("Services"), type **services.html** and **Link to Services Page**. For the fourth button ("Contact"), type **contact.html** and **Link to Contact Page**.

Using the Other Drawing Tools

You can also use the Add Circles tool and the Add Polygons tool to draw circular and irregular (polygonal) hotspots.

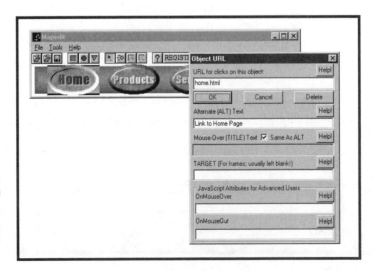

Figure F.6

You can test, edit, or delete a hotspot that you've already created.

To draw a circular hotspot using the Add Circles tool, click the cursor in the center of the area you want to define as the hotspot, and then draw the cursor outwards until the circle encloses the area. Just click the mouse again to create the hotspot and open the Object URL dialog box.

To draw a polygonal hotspot using the Add Polygons tool, click the cursor at the edge of the area you want to define as a hotspot, and then just continue clicking along the edge of the area. When you've drawn the irregular area all around the area you're defining, just right-click the mouse (or press the Enter key) to create the hotspot and open up the Object URL dialog box.

Adding a Default URL

You can also add a default URL that will be activated whenever someone clicks outside any of your hotspots. To do this, first click on the Test and Edit Hotspots tool, and then click anywhere that is clearly outside of any of the hotspot areas you've already drawn. In the Default URL dialog box, you can then type a default URL for your image map.

Saving Your Image Map's HTML File

After drawing your hotspots, when you save your image map's HTML file, Mapedit writes the HTML codes required to activate the image map and then resaves the HTML file. To do this, click on the Save HTML Document tool (third tool in the first group). You might see the hard drive light flicker, but otherwise you won't see anything else indicating that the file has been saved.

Checking It Out in Your Browser

To check your new image map out in your browser, just open imagemap.html from C:\Html. When you click on any of the hotspot areas you've defined, you should jump to the page that you specified as that hotspot's object.

Adding a Search Form

Another often-requested feature is the search form. It lets visitors search the contents of your site. Here are a few free search form providers on the Web that make adding one a snap:

✪ PicoSearch at **www.picosearch.com/** — Three plans are available — Free, Professional, and Premium. Using PicoSearch, you can have your own search engine up and running in minutes.

○ FreeFind at **search.freefind.com/**—Add a free search engine to your site in fewer than ten minutes. Automatically produces a site map and what's new list, tracks visitors' searches, and more.

Adding JavaScript Scripts

Adding JavaScript scripts can be an excellent way to add interactive and dynamic content to your site. You don't necessarily need to know JavaScript to add it to your site. There are lots of sites that provide scripts that you can cut and paste into your page. Here are some places you can check out:

○ The JavaScript Source at **javascript.internet.com/**. Includes over 600 JavaScript scripts you can cut and paste into your pages.

○ WebCoder.com at **www.webcoder.com/**. Your home for JavaScript and Dynamic HTML on the Web. Includes how-to, reference, demos, and a "scriptorium."

○ Programming: JavaScript by Webmonkey at **hotwired.lycos.com/webmonkey/programming/javascript/**.

○ The JavaScript Weenie from Web Developer's Journal at **www.webdevelopersjournal.com/JavaScriptWeenie.html**. Includes tips and tutorials, as well as discussion groups and mailing lists.

Adding JavaScript Roll-Over Buttons

I'm sure you've run across these on the Web. You pass the cursor over a button, and the button changes the text, color, and so on, to indicate a hotspot. When you move the cursor off of the button, it changes again. That's called a roll-over button. Roll-over buttons are actually easy to create, once you know what codes to use. First, insert the JavaScript inside of the HEAD element (I've bolded the parts you can change):

```
<script type="text/javascript">
    if (document.images)
    {
    image1 = new Image;
    image2 = new Image;
    image1.src = "home1.gif";
    image2.src = "home2.gif";
    }
```

```
    function newImg(name, image)
  {
   if (document.images)
      {
       document[name].src = eval(image+".src");
      }
  }
</script>
```

Next, in the body of your page where you want the roll-over button to appear, add the intrinsic event attributes, onMouseOver and onMouseOut, to an image link, like this:

```
<p><a href="http://www.callihan.com/" onMouseOver='newImg("enter",
"image2")'
  onMouseOut='newImg("enter", "image1")'><img name="enter"
  src="home1.gif" border="0" alt="Come on in!"></a></p>
```

To set this up, first make sure that the image files you want to use are located in the same folder as the HTML that includes the script. In the previous code examples, for home1.gif and home2.gif, substitute the file names of the images you want to use for the roll-over effects.

You also need to substitute the Web address to which you want your roll-over button to link to. You can use an absolute URL (http://www.callihan.com/, for instance) or a relative URL (../personal/homepage.html, for instance).

One of the nice things about a JavaScript roll-over button is that if JavaScript is turned off or someone is using an older browser that doesn't support JavaScript, if you've set up the roll-over button as an image link (as with the previous example), it simply functions as a regular link.

To see this roll-over button example in action, just open example.html in your browser from C:\Html, scroll down to the bottom of the page, and then pass the cursor over and off of the button (see Figures F.7 and F.8).

Adding Java Applets

Java applets are another good way to spice up your page. A Java applet is a software program that is actually downloaded and run on your computer. Many kinds of Java applets are available on the Web, from relatively simple Java animations to more sophisticated full-feature applications.

Figure F.7

Pass the cursor over the button and the image rolls over to another image (a green Home button).

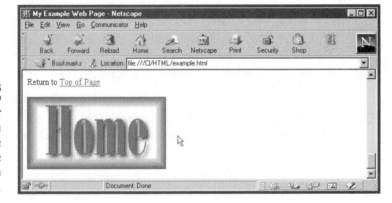

Figure F.8

Pass the cursor off of the button and the image rolls back to the original image (a red Home button).

◄◄◄◄◄◄◄◄◄◄◄◄◄◄◄◄◄◄◄◄◄◄◄◄◄◄◄◄◄◄◄◄◄◄◄◄◄◄

BUZZ WORD

A *Java applet* is a small program (thus the word "applet") created in the Java programming language that can be downloaded with a Web page and executed by any Java-enabled browser. All current Web browsers support running Java applets.

◄◄◄◄◄◄◄◄◄◄◄◄◄◄◄◄◄◄◄◄◄◄◄◄◄◄◄◄◄◄◄◄◄◄◄◄◄◄

Generally, the source of the Java applet should provide you with the HTML code required to insert the applet in your page, as well as all the files and folders that compose the applet. In many cases, you can just copy the HTML code for the applet and then paste it into your page, rather than having to retype it. Here's an example of doing that:

1. View the applet's page source. In either Internet Explorer or Netscape Navigator, just right-click on the applet's Web page, and then click on View Source.

2. Highlight the applet code (everything starting with `<applet>` and ending with `</applet>`) and press Ctrl+C to copy the code. Use Ctrl+V to paste it into the HTML file.

3. You might need to edit the code slightly. For instance, if you are placing all the Java applet files in the same folder as the applet's HTML file, delete any "codebase" attribute values included in the APPLET tag.

Finding Java Applets

You can find Java applets to use in your Web pages on the Web. Here are some Web sites where you can find Java applets:

- ✪ The Java Boutique at **www.javaboutique.internet.com/**.
- ✪ The JavaBoutique at **javaboutique.webdeveloper.com/**.
- ✪ Applet Depot at **www.ericharshbarger.com/java/**.
- ✪ Gamelan: The Official Directory for Java at **developer.earthweb.com/ dlink.index-jhtml.72.1082.-.0.jhtml**.
- ✪ Coding/Java by ZDNet Developer at **www.zdnet.com/devhead/ filters/0,,2133223,00.html/**.
- ✪ Java by About.com at **html.about.com/compute/html/msubjava.htm**. Includes free applets you can download and use.
- ✪ Programming: Java by Webmonkey at **hotwired.lycos.com/webmonkey/ programming/java/**.

There are a few issues you need to be aware of before trying to use Java applets in your pages:

- ✪ Performance issues. Including a Java applet in your page can significantly increase the amount of time that it takes your page to download and display. Visitors using browsers that don't support Java or who have Java turned off cannot see your applet. Java applets can also cause compatibility problems with some browsers. Nothing says you *have* to include Java applets in your pages.

- ✪ The minimal installs for the latest versions of Internet Explorer 5 for Windows do not include support for Java. Users of the minimum install are prompted if they want to download Microsoft's Java Virtual Machine the first time they encounter a Java-enabled Web site.

- ✪ The latest version of Internet Explorer 5 for the Macintosh also does not automatically include support for a Java Virtual Machine. If a version of the Mac OS Runtime for Java (MRJ) earlier than version 2.1 is installed, a visitor to your site will get a confusing error message, saying that "MRJ 2.1 or later" is required in order to run Java. Because absolutely no other information is provided and "MRJ" is not spelled out, many visitors who find themselves in this situation will be totally stumped.

Microsoft is obviously trying to put roadblocks in front of people being able to offer cross-browser accessible Java applets on their sites. If you want to use Java applets in your pages, it's best to provide links to where visitors to your site can download and install a Java virtual machine if they need one:

- ✿ Windows users who visit your site can download and install Microsoft's latest Java Virtual Machine for Internet Explorer 5 from **www.microsoft. com/java/vm/dl_vm40.htm**. It is compatible with Internet Explorer 4.01 and later. For more info on Microsoft's support for Java, they can also visit the Microsoft Technologies for Java page at **www.microsoft. com/java/**.

- ✿ Macintosh users who visit your site can download and install the latest version of MRJ (currently MRJ 2.2.2) from **developer.apple.com/java/ text/download.html**. For more info, they can also visit Apple's Mac OS Runtime for Java page at **developer.apple.com/java/**.

Be sure to include links for both Windows and Macintosh users. Just because you're running in Windows, for instance, doesn't mean that you don't have a significant number of visitors who are running a Mac.

Adding Dynamic HTML Effects

The development of Dynamic HTML has largely been stymied because Microsoft and Netscape support different document object models (DOMs). This should all change once the next generation of browsers comes along, which should all support the same DOM. If you want to learn more about using Dynamic HTML in your pages, check out these sites:

- ✿ Dynamic HTML by About.com at **html.about.com/compute/html/ msubdhtml.htm**.

- ✿ WebCoder.com at **www.webcoder.com/**. Your home for JavaScript and Dynamic HTML on the Web.

- ✿ Dynamic HTML Index at **www.all-links.com/dynamic/**.

Adding Streaming Media

Adding streaming media can be a great way to keep visitors to your site coming back for more. There are several media formats that can be streamed across the Web, including RealMedia (*.ra and *.ram), Windows Media Format (*.wmf), Active Streaming Format (*.asf), QuickTime (*.mov), and other formats.

Some streaming media formats require server-side support, whereas others don't. RealMedia (RealAudio and RealVideo), for instance, requires installation of the RealMedia Server. Other media types require that servers be configured to recognize their MIME type. Before trying to implement streaming media on your site, check to see whether your Web hosting service supports it.

One free Web hosting service, Yahoo! GeoCities at **geocities.yahoo.com/home/**, includes the capability to stream up to 5MB of RealMedia (RealAudio or RealVideo) for a one-time setup fee of $4.95. If you want to offer more than 5MB of streaming media, the cost is $5/month for each additional 100MB of streaming media. When you sign up for a Yahoo! GeoCities account and choose to include streaming media on your site, you can download a version of Real-Network's RealProducer that has been customized especially for creating streaming media for use with Yahoo! GeoCities.

Creating Your Own Streaming Media

There are several free or inexpensive software tools that you can use to create your own streaming media:

- ✿ Creating Streaming Media by RealNetworks at **www.realnetworks. com/developers/index.html**—Descriptions and download links for all RealNetworks' streaming media creation tools. Three free tools are available: RealProducer Basic, RealSlideshow Basic, and RealPresenter Basic. See also Yahoo! GeoCities at **geocities.yahoo.com/home/**, which includes the capability to stream RealMedia and provides a customized version of RealProducer that you can use to create your own RealMedia files.

- ✿ Microsoft Windows Media Encoder 7 at **www.microsoft.com/windows/ windowsmedia/en/WM7/encoder.asp**—Converts both live and prerecorded audio, video, and computer screen captures Windows Media Format (*.wmf) files for streaming delivery over the Web.

- Microsoft Windows Media On-Demand Producer at **www.microsoft. com/windows/windowsmedia/en/features/on-demand/default.asp**— Simplifies the creation of streaming audio and video media.

- TrueSpeech Internet Player at **www.dspg.com/player/main.htm**—The Windows Sound Recorder is the only tool you need to encode WAV audio files into TrueSpeech files. The free TrueSpeech Player is available for both Windows and Macintosh. The TrueSpeech Converter is available for Windows. For instructions on how to use the Windows Sound Recorder to create TrueSpeech audio files, see **www.dspg.com/player/ voice.htm**.

- AudioActive Production Studio at **www.audioactive.com/**—Available for Windows 95/98/NT. Encode WAV audio into MP3, ASF, SWA (Shockwave), and compressed WAV audio formats. AudioActive Production Studio costs only $34.95, whereas AudioActive Production Studio Professional costs $149.95.

- QuickTime Pro from Apple at **www.apple.com/quicktime/upgrade/**— This is a $29.99 upgrade for the free QuickTime Player and is not only a streaming media player, but also allows you to create Web-ready audio and video, apply special effects and filters to your movies, and export audio and video to over a dozen formats.

TIP You can use the EMBED tag to embed QuickTime video and audio files in your pages. For instance, to embed a video, mymovie.mov, that is 240 pixels high, just insert the following code:

```
<embed src="mymovie.mov" width="320" height="256">
```

To embed a QuickTime audio file, just set the height to 16 pixels, like so:

```
<embed src="mymovie.mov" width="216" height="16">
```

If you also set the width to 16 pixels, the controller will be minimized to a single Play/Pause button. Never set the height or width to fewer than two pixels.

- Adobe LiveMotion at **www.adobe.com/products/livemotion/**—Imports multiple audio formats, exporting them as MP3 files. Also functions as a full-feature image editor and animation program, exporting images and animations in Flash, JPEG, Animated GIF, PNG, and Photoshop file formats, and generating JavaScript roll-over buttons. Versions are available for both Windows and Macintosh—works seamlessly with Adobe GoLive, Photoshop, and Illustrator. A try-out version is available for download ($299 to purchase).

✿ CoolEdit 2000 and CoolEdit Pro from Syntrillium Software at **www. syntrillium.com/cooledit/index.html**—One of the best Windows-based audio editing utilities. Record through your sound card from a microphone, CD-ROM, or other source, read and write MP3, and more. Shareware demo is available. CoolEdit 2000 is $69 and CoolEdit Pro is $399.

If you plan on adding streaming media to your site, you'll also want to include links to where visitors to your site can download a streaming media player if they don't already have one. Here are some of the main ones:

✿ Windows Media Player at **www.microsoft.com/windows/ windowsmedia/EN/default.asp**

✿ Yahoo! Player at **player.broadcast.com/**

✿ QuickTime Player at **www.apple.com/quicktime/**

Adding Interactive Animations

One way to juice up your site is to include interactive animations. Be aware that software tools for creating interactive animations are sophisticated applications that can take considerable time and effort to master. They also aren't cheap. That said, here's a quick rundown on some of the software tools you can use to create multimedia interactive animations for your site:

✿ Macromedia Flash at **www.macromedia.com/software/flash/**. The Flash player is built into Netscape Navigator 4.0+ and Windows 98, but some users might have to download a plug-in to see the animations. Trial version is freely available ($399 to purchase).

✿ Adobe LiveMotion at **www.adobe.com/products/livemotion/main.html**. Use an object-oriented timeline to create interactive multimedia animations. Exports Flash animations (*.swf) and MP3 audio. ($299 to purchase.)

Transferring Your Pages to the Web

Once you've learned some HTML and fashioned your first Web site on your local machine, you're going to want to put it up on the Web so that the rest of the world can see your handiwork. This is a two-part process involving the following:

- ✿ Finding a Web host for your Web pages.
- ✿ Using an FTP client to transfer your pages up to your folder on a Web server.

Finding a Web Host

The first step is to find a server to host your page. There are two basic options for this: finding a free Web host or paying for a Web space account.

Finding a Free Web Host

There are lots of options when it comes to finding free Web space. Here are some of the options:

- ✿ If you're a student, check to see whether your school provides you with a free account on their Web server. (Realize, though, that once you graduate, you'll probably lose your Web space.)

- ✿ Check with provider of your dial-up access to the Internet (your ISP, or Internet Service Provider). Most ISPs these days provide anywhere from 3 to 10MB, or even more, of free Web space to their customers. Many also charge reasonable rates if you decide you need more space than they've allotted.

- ✿ There are also many free Web hosts on the Web that you can use. These accounts usually mean having some advertising displayed with your page, either in the form of a banner ad or a pop-up window. For lots of links to where you can find out about free Web hosting services on the Web, see my Web Host page at **www.callihan.com/webhosts/**.

AOL USERS

If you're an AOL user, here are some resources on setting up an AOL Web site that you'll find especially useful. First, go to the keyword "My Place" in AOL; for help in using My Place to publish your files, select Frequently Asked Questions. You can get additional information on how to use My Place at these Web sites:

- ✿ "AOL: Uploading your web page" at **www.patmcclendon.com/aol.html**

- ✿ "Web Site Design by AWEBPAGE.COM" at **www.awebpage.com/upload.html**

- ✿ "How Do I?" at **members.aol.com/ftpmaster/faqs.htm**

Finding a For-Pay Web Host

There are many reasons why you might want to investigate finding a for-pay Web host on the Web:

- You might need a higher Web space or traffic allotment than is available through a free Web host. This can be because you plan on creating a more graphic-intensive site with lots of images or other media, for instance.

- You might want extra services that are not available through a free Web host. These might include additional e-mail addresses, support for streaming media, custom CGI scripts, virtual FTP folders, mailing lists, e-commerce services, and more.

- If you're planning on creating a business site, or just want to establish your own unique identity on the Web, you'll probably want to get your own domain name. Most for-pay Web hosts will register and maintain your domain name for you at a reasonable cost.

How Much Does It Cost?

The cost of a for-pay Web space account can run anywhere between $5 a month and $25 a month, depending on the provider and the mix of services that are included. Generally, you should expect to pay $20 a month or less for a virtual host account (an account that includes the registration and maintenance of a domain name). A one-time setup fee might also be charged, running anywhere between $5 and $35 or slightly more, depending on the services included or whether you're registering a domain name.

For lots of links to where you can find out about affordable for-pay Web hosting services on the Web, see my Web Host page at **www.callihan.com/webhosts/**.

Registering a Domain Name

If you're creating a business site or just want to establish your own unique identity on the Web, you'll want to look into registering your own domain name. There are several ways of going about doing this:

- The most trouble-free way of registering your domain name is to first sign up with a Web hosting service to host your pages and then to have them register your domain name for you. This, however, might not be the cheapest way to do this, in that you'll probably have to pay the top price, which is $35 for the first year, and $35 a year thereafter.

POINTERS ON CHOOSING A FOR-PAY WEB HOST

Deciding what is the best Web host for you can be a confusing and sometimes frustrating experience. Here are some pointers on what to look for when shopping for a Web host:

- Plenty of space. Most for-pay Web hosts offer at least 30MB of space and often as much as 50MB.

- A healthy traffic allowance. This is one of the most important considerations. Don't settle for less than 2GB per month. More is better. (For comparison purposes, my Web host provides a traffic allowance of 200MB a day, which roughly equals 6GB per month for a virtual host account that costs $20 a month.) Don't believe promises of "unlimited traffic"—there's no such thing.

- Extra features and add-ons. Look for any special features you might need to have, either free or at a reasonable cost. For instance, if you're going to want to set up additional e-mail boxes, you should make sure that's included or is at least available at a reasonable cost. Other desired features might also include virtual FTP, autoresponders, custom CGI scripts, mail lists, shopping carts, e-commerce solutions, and so on.

- An upgrade path. You want to avoid paying for features that you don't need now, but have them available at a reasonable cost if you might need them later. For instance, you might not currently be planning on selling products online, but if you might later decide to do so and want to be able to accept online credit card orders, you'll want to make sure that you can upgrade to an account, at a reasonable cost, that includes access to a secure server and e-commerce solutions (shopping cart application, database support, and so on).

- The cheapest way of registering your domain name is to first shop around to find the domain name registrar that is offering the best deal. You can find domain name registrars, for instance, that will register your domain name for you for as little as $15 a year. This, however, might not be the most trouble-free way of doing this, in that if you decide to have someone else host your pages, you'll have to go through the hassle of transferring your domain name to your new host. This can cause a delay in the amount of time it'll take to get your Web site up and running under your domain name.

So, which way is right for you? That depends. If saving $20 a year, for instance, is not important to you, you should probably make selecting the right Web host for your pages your top priority, and then have them register your domain name for you. If your Web host goes through Network Solutions to register your domain name, you'll be billed separately by them for $35 to cover the first year, and then $35 a year after that. This will be over and above whatever your Web host is charging to host your pages. If they go through a different registrar to register your domain, the cost might be less.

On the other hand, if you're not planning on selecting a Web host for your pages for a while and you're worried that others might first grab the domain names you might want, or you just want to save money, your best bet might be to look

SEARCHING FOR A DOMAIN NAME

Although you might decide to have a Web host register a domain name of your choice for you when you sign up for a virtual domain account, you might first want to see what domain names are available. That way, when you sign up for your Web hosting account and tell them what domain name you want, you can be sure that you've chosen the domain name you really want, rather than making a decision off the top of your head.

You can use Network Solution's search form to search to see if a domain name you want is available or not. Just go to **www.networksolutions.com/** and use their search form to see if a *.com, *.net, or *.org domain name is available. If the exact domain name that you want is not available, Network Solutions suggests other similar domain names that are available. You can also play around with inserting hyphens, for instance, to come up with a close variant of your preferred domain name. Take the time to think through what kind of domain names are best for you and to find out which ones are available that work for you. If you're not going to be registering your domain name right away, you might want to come up with two or three variants that work for you, just in case your top choice isn't available later.

If you do find that the one perfect domain name for you is still available and you're afraid that it'll be grabbed from under your nose before you get around to registering it, you should try to register it as quickly as possible. If you've already decided on the Web hosting service you want to use, sign up for your account right away and ask them to register your domain. You can also go ahead and register your domain name yourself right away, either through Network Solutions or another domain name registrar. Don't make an instant decision, however, unless you're certain it's right— once you've bought it, you've got it (at least for a year, anyway).

for the best domain name registration deal you can find right away. You can then park your domain name with them until you've decided on which Web host service you're going to use. For links to lots of domain name registrars, as well as other domain registration resources, see the Domain Name Resources Directory at **www.dnresources.com/**. You can also check out Yahoo's directory for domain name registration at **dir.yahoo.com/Business_and_Economy/ Business_to_Business/Communications_and_Networking/Internet_and_ World_Wide_Web/Domain_Registration/**.

Transferring Your Web Pages to a Server

You transfer your Web site files to your folder on your Web server using FTP (File Transfer Protocol). Your Web host should provide you with FTP access to your site. This means providing you with a user ID and a password, as well as assigning you a password-protected folder on its server where you can store your HTML and other files. You might also be assigned an account name, although usually not. This allows you to use an FTP program to access your Web site's folder on the Web (and any folders you create within that folder) so you can transfer your Web site files from your local machine to your server.

What You Need to Know

When you sign up for your Web space account, your Web host should provide you with all the information you need to connect to your Web space folder using an FTP program. This will likely include the following:

- **Host name.** Your Web host should provide you with the host name (or address) of the Web server where your Web space will be located. This will be in the form of *server.domain.category* (srv2.yourhost.net, for instance). If you have a domain name, you might also be able to access your Web space folders by using your domain name. I can access my Web space folders, for instance, just by specifying my domain name, callihan.com.

- **Host type.** You should need to know this only if you have trouble connecting to your server account. In most cases, your FTP program should be able to auto-detect what the host type is.

- **User ID.** This is your user name. If you have received your Web space from a local ISP or a commercial online service, this will likely be the same as the user name you use to log on. If not, it will be the user name you requested and/or had assigned to you when you signed up for your account. (Your user ID is case-sensitive.)

✪ **Password.** Your password will keep others from accessing your Web site folders. As with your user ID, if you have received your Web space from a local ISP or a commercial online service, your password will likely be the same as the password you use to log on to the Internet. If not, it will be the user name you requested and/or had assigned to you when you signed up for your account. (Your password is case-sensitive.)

In the vast majority of cases, that is all you'll need to access your Web site folders on your Web host's server using an FTP program. You should be automatically switched to your Web site folder when you connect.

● ●

In rare instances, a Web host might also provide an account name, in addition to your user ID, that you'll need to connect to its server. An occasional Web host won't automatically switch you to your Web site folder, in which case you'll need to know the remote directory path to your folder on its server. Your Web host should let you know if either of these are required.

If your Web site folder is located behind a firewall (most aren't), your Web host should let you know what other settings you'll need to connect to your site.

● ●

For additional information on using FTP to transfer your HTML files to the Web, see FTPplanet.com at **www.FTPplanet.com.**

Choosing an FTP Program

There are lots of different FTP programs available that you can use to connect to your Web site folder on the Web. Here are a few you might want to check out:

✪ WS_FTP by Ipswitch at **www.ipswitch.com/**—There are two versions available, WS_FTP LE and WS_FTP Pro. WS_FTP LE is free if you are 1) a student, faculty, or staff member at an educational institution, 2) a U.S. federal, state, or local government employee, or 3) going to be using WS_FTP LE exclusively at home for non-commercial purposes. WS_FTP Pro is available in an evaluation version ($39.95 to register). A little later in this appendix, you'll find a hands-on tutorial on using WS_FTP LE.

✪ CuteFTP by GlobalSCAPE.com at **www.cuteftp.com/**—This is a popular FTP program that uses a Windows Explorer–style interface. An evaluation version is available ($39.95 to register; includes their CuteHTML HTML editor, a $19.95 value).

- ✿ **FTP Voyager** by RhinoSoft.com at **www.ftpvoyager.com/** — An award-winning FTP client that also uses a Windows Explorer–style interface. An evaluation version is available ($49.95 to register; includes two years of upgrade protection).

- ✿ **CoffeeCup Direct FTP** by CoffeeCup Software at **www.coffeecup.com/** — Includes a built-in WinZip archive utility. An evaluation version is available ($30 to register).

- ✿ **FreeFTP** by Brandyware Software at **members.aol.com/brandyware/main.htm** — This is a freeware FTP client.

- ✿ **FTP - Commander** by Vista at **www.vista.ru/** — This is another freeware FTP client.

Using WS_FTP LE to Transfer Your Web Page Files

The following covers using WS_FTP LE to transfer your Web page files to your Web server folder. Earlier versions of WS_FTP LE should be quite similar, except the arrangement of the Properties and Options menus might be somewhat different. Other FTP programs should work in a similar fashion, although their interfaces will differ, of course.

If you're a qualified non-commercial user, you can download WS_FTP LE directly from the Ipswitch Web site at **www.ipswitch.com** and use it for free. If you're not qualified to use WS_FTP LE, you can download the evaluation version of WS_FTP Pro.

At this point, I am assuming that you have a connection to the Internet, that you have some space on a Web server to store your Web pages, and that you have password-protected access to your site's folders. I'm also assuming that you know the information detailed earlier under "What You Need to Know" and that you have installed WS_FTP LE (or WS_FTP Pro).

Running WS_FTP LE

To run WS_FTP LE, click on the Start button, and then select WS_FTP LE and WS_FTP LE again. You should also be able to double-click on the WS_FTP LE icon on your Desktop.

Using the Session Properties Window

You use the WS_FTP's Session Properties window to set up your connection to your Web space account.

The General Tab

The General tab is displayed automatically when you run WS_FTP LE. In this section, you specify the general characteristics of your FTP connection, including the host name, your user name and password, and so on:

1. In the Profile Name box, type a profile name for the connection to your site. This can be whatever you want. For instance, you might type **My Web Site** as your profile name. Just make it something you can remember.

2. In the Host Name/Address box, type either the name of the server where your Web site is located or your domain name (if you have one). Your Web space provider should have provided you with this information.

3. In the Host Type box, to have WS_FTP LE auto-detect the host type, just leave "Automatically detect" selected—in most cases, WS_FTP LE should be able to detect your host type. If that doesn't work, try "UNIX (standard)" because the majority of Web servers are still UNIX machines. In most cases, one or the other of these two settings should work. If neither works, you need to find out from your Web space provider the actual host type you should choose here.

4. The Anonymous check box should be unchecked, because you'll be using a user name and password to log in to your server account. To have WS_FTP LE save your password so that you won't have to type it in every time you log in, click on the Save Pwd check box to check it.

◆◆

Checking the Save Pwd (Save Password) check box causes your password to be saved to your hard drive in an encrypted form. If you're on a network connected to the Internet, or have an "always on" DSL connection to the Internet, you should be aware that this might be a security hazard. A hacker, for instance, might conceivably be able to gain access to your computer, search for any passwords stored on your computer's hard drive, and then use readily available tools to decrypt them. So, take your pick: security or convenience. If you choose to not save your password, you'll have to type it in each time you connect to the Internet.

If you are not on a network, however, security shouldn't be as much of an issue because a hacker has to be sitting at your keyboard to get at your password.

◆◆

5. In the User ID box, type your user name. This is case-sensitive, so you should type it exactly, including any uppercase letters. Your Web space provider should have provided you with this information. If you're using free Web space provided to you by your dial-up provider, this will likely be the same user name you use to log in to the Internet.

6. In the Password box, type your password. If you enabled Save Password, it appears as a row of asterisks. (Note: Don't type a row of asterisks!) Your Web space provider should have provided you with a password. If you're using free Web space provided to you by your dial-up provider, this will likely be the same password you use to log in to the Internet.

7. Leave the Account box blank unless your Web host has provided you with an account name (which isn't likely).

Figure G.1 shows the General tab of the Session Properties window filled out to connect to a free Web space account I set up at Yahoo! Geocities.

The Startup Tab

You can click on the Startup tab to specify additional characteristics for your connection, including initial remote and local folders:

1. For now, just leave the Initial Remote Site Folder box blank. Some Web space providers connect you first to a root folder for your site, but the folder where your Web site files need to be transferred is actually a folder within that folder. For instance, for my site, the files for my Web site are actually stored in a folder, www, that's located within the root folder for my site. To have WS_FTP LE automatically connect to the www folder in my site, I just specify www in the Initial Remote Site Folder box.

2. In the Initial Local Folder box, type the path to the local folder on your hard drive where your Web page files are located. For instance, if your Web page files are stored in a My Pages folder on your C drive, you just need to type **C:\MyPages** in the Initial Local Folder box to have WS_FTP LE automatically display the contents of that folder after you've logged in to your Web space account. (See Figure G.2.)

Figure G.1

In the Session Properties window, a profile name, host name, user name, and password for a hypothetical FTP connection have been specified.

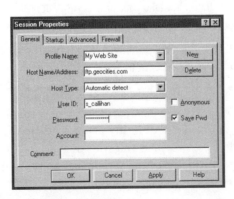

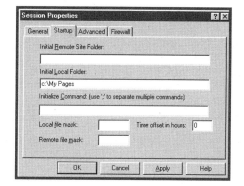

Figure G.2

In the Startup tab of the Session Properties window, you can specify which remote and local folders you want to be initially displayed by WS_FTP LE.

3. Leave all the other options blank. Click on the Apply button to save your new session profile. (In some earlier versions of WS_FTP LE, this is a Save button.)

The Advanced and Firewall Tabs

You should only have to deal with these tab sections if you are having trouble connecting to your Web space account or you're trying to connect from behind a firewall. If you have trouble connecting to your site, you can check with your Web space provider to find out what settings they recommend be selected under the Advanced tab. If you're located behind a firewall, you should check with your network administrator to find out what settings you need to make under the Firewall tab. For more information on the contents of these two tab sections, click on their Help buttons.

Connecting to Your Site

To connect to your site, just click on the OK button. Figure G.3 shows the WS_FTP LE window after it has connected to the free Web space account I set up at Yahoo! Geocities.

If this hasn't worked, you'll need to go back to the drawing board. You might need to specify a specific host type (you'll probably have to e-mail your Web host to find out what this is). Make sure that the host name of your Web server is correct. You should double-check that your user ID and password are correct.

If it still doesn't work, under the Advanced tab, try increasing the Network Timeout amount or the number of connection retries. If none of this works, you'll have to check with your Web host to make sure you're using the correct

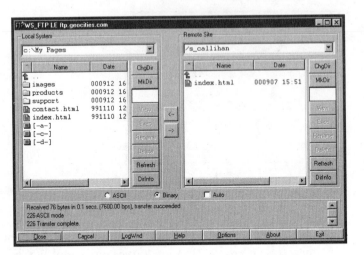

Figure G.3

If you successfully connect to your site, you'll see the local folder you specified on the left and the remote folders for your Web site on the right.

host name, host type, user name, password, and so on. If you're trying to connect at work, check with your network administrator to find out what settings you might need to specify under the Firewall tab.

As mentioned previously, for some Web space accounts, you might need to open an additional folder located in your site's root folder to get to the actual folder to which your Web site files need to be transferred. For my Web site, for instance, the folder where my Web site files are stored is a www folder that is located in my site's root folder. At my Web site, I've also got an ftp folder that is located in my site's root folder, which provides me with a virtual FTP server.

You'll also notice in Figure G.3 that an index.html file is already located in the folder displayed in WS_FTP LE's right frame. That is actually a file that has been created by the Web space provider I've used for this example (Yahoo! GeoCities). Most Web space providers do the same. If you want to check out the starting page that your Web space provider has created for you, just use your browser to access your site's Web address. If you want to keep it as an example, just rename it. To have the home page that you've created for yourself load automatically when your site is accessed, you'll need to create your own index.html and transfer it to your site (you can also use the Rename button to rename it after you've transferred it).

Hopefully, you should now be connected to your Web site and can start transferring files from your site's local folder (C:\My Pages, for instance) to its remote folder on the Web. (If your Web page files are actually located in a subfolder of your root folder, such as a www folder, for instance, go ahead and double-click on that folder in WS_FTP LE's right frame to open it.)

NOTE Although index.html is the most common file name used for an "index" page on the Web (or a page that will automatically be displayed in a browser without having to be typed in a URL), your Web server might use a different file name for this. Other common index file names include default.html, welcome.html, main.html, for instance. Your Web server might also accept several of these, although it will recognize one over the others if more than one is located in your site's folder.

Figure G.3 shows a hypothetical Web site displayed in WS_FTP LE's left frame that I've set up to transfer. Don't worry if your local Web folder contents look different—you might not yet have organized your site into subfolders and might still be storing all your files for your site in a single folder, for instance.

Navigating WS_FTP LE's Main Window

Navigating WS_FTP LE's main window, you can do the following:

- ✪ You can move up or down the folder structure in either frame. To open a folder, just double-click on it. Clicking on the green bent arrow icon will take you back to the parent folder of the current folder. You also can use the ChgDir button in either window to change the directory.

- ✪ You can use the MkDir button to create a new folder in either frame. To delete a folder, just click on it and click on the Delete button.

- ✪ You use the -> and <- buttons to actually transfer your files. For instance, to transfer a file from your local computer to a remote folder in your Web site, just click on the file you want to transfer in the left frame and then click on the -> button to transfer it to the remote folder that's displayed in the right frame.

- ✪ Of the remaining buttons, you're most likely to use the Rename and Delete buttons, which can be used to rename or delete a selected file or folder. For information on the function of the other buttons, click on WS_FTP's Help button.

Transferring a File

Transferring a file to your Web site is fairly simple. Just follow these steps:

1. In WS_FTP LE's left frame, make sure that the folder from which you want to transfer the file is displayed. (To move down the folder tree, just double-click on a subfolder; to move back up the folder tree, double-click on the green bent arrow icon.)

2. In WS-FTP LE's right frame, make sure that the folder to which you want to transfer the file is displayed.

3. Click on the file in the left frame that you want to transfer to your Web site. If the file is an HTML file or other text file, select the ASCII radio button. If the file is a binary file, such as a JPEG or GIF image, select the Binary radio button. Click on the -> button to transfer the file. (See Figure G.4.)

You can transfer more than one file at a time. To select multiple files to transfer, click on the first file to highlight it, and then hold down the Ctrl key and click on the other files you want to transfer. (You can also hold down the Shift key to select a range of files to transfer.)

Be patient. If you are copying several files, or if any of them are large (such as a banner graphic file, for instance), it might take a little bit before the files have been transferred. You'll see a message, "Transfer complete," in the lower frame, when the transfer of your file or files is complete.

To transfer a file from your Web site's remote folders to your local computer, just do it the other way around. Select the folders in the right and left frames that you want to transfer the file between, select the file you want to transfer in the right frame (the remote folder), and then click on the <- button to transfer it to the folder displayed in the left frame (the local folder). (Generally, however, I only do it the other way around, because I do all my Web page creation on my local computer; there's also a danger that you'll overwrite a later version of the file.)

Forcing Lowercase File Names

If you're transferring your files to a UNIX server, there's one gotcha you've got to look out for—file names on UNIX servers are case-sensitive. Thus, **Whacko.html** and **whacko.html** on a UNIX system represent two *different* files. To avoid this problem (getting the wrong case), I set WS_FTP LE to force lowercase file names when transferring files to my server. I then make sure that all hypertext links in my Web pages are also all lowercase. To set up WS_FTP LE to do this, first log in to your Web site, and then in the WS_FTP LE window, follow these steps:

1. Click on the Options button. Under the Session tab (Session Options in earlier versions of WS_FTP), check the next to last check box, Force Lowercase Remote Names. (See Figure G.5.)

2. Click on the Set as default button, and then click on OK.

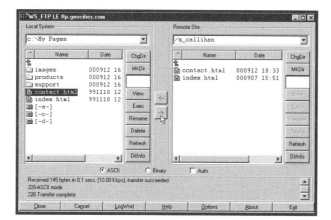

Figure G.4

An HTML file, contact.html, has been transferred to the example Web site.

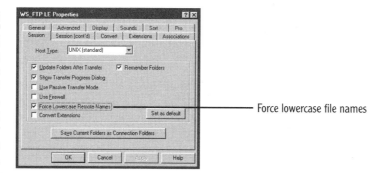

Figure G.5

You can force all files transferred to your Web server to be converted to all lowercase letters, which will keep you from tripping over UNIX's case sensitivity.

Force lowercase file names

Transferring Folders and Their Contents

You can batch-transfer a whole folder simply by clicking on the folder you want to transfer, checking the Auto check box, and then clicking on the -> button to transfer the folder and its contents. When prompted if you want to transfer the selected folder and its contents, just click on the Yes button. Figure G.6 shows a folder, the images folder, after it has been transferred.

Identifying ASCII File Types

The example images folder I transferred, as shown in Figure G.6, contained only GIF and JPEG images, which are both binary file formats. When you use the Auto check box to batch-transfer a whole folder and its contents, WS_FTP will automatically transfer all files as binary files, unless their file extensions are listed under the Extensions tab of WS_FTP LE's Options window. By default, only the *.TXT file extension is listed. If you want your HTML files, or any other

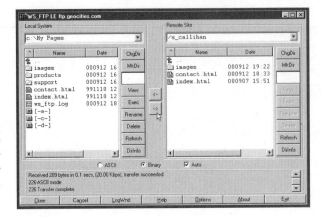

Figure G.6

You can transfer
a whole folder
and its contents to
your Web site.

ASCII format files you want to transfer, to also be automatically recognized
as ASCII files, you need to specify their file extensions under the Extensions tab
of the Options window:

1. Click on the Options button, and then click on the Extensions tab.

2. To add an ASCII file extension, first type the file extension (.**HTML**, for
   instance), and then click on the Add button to add it. Repeat to add
   .HTM and .JS (for JavaScript files). Figure G.7 shows the .HTM, .HTML,
   .JS, and .TXT file extensions listed as ASCII file types. Click on OK.

Closing and Exiting WS_FTP LE

When you are through transferring files to or from your server, you should
always close your FTP session before exiting WS_FTP LE. To do this, just click
on the Close button, wait for the Goodbye message to be displayed in the lower
activity window, and then click on the Exit button. After exiting WS_FTP LE,
log off the Internet, if you want.

Figure G.7

You can identify
any file types of
ASCII text files so
WS_FTP LE will
transfer them as
ASCII files when
using the Auto
check box.

What's on the CD-ROM

On the CD-ROM that accompanies this book, you'll find:

- All the example files used in this book's work sessions.
- A set of HTML templates created by the author that you can customize for your own pages.
- A wide range of software programs that you can install and try out, including HTML editing, text editing, image editing, FTP, animation, and other shareware and trialware programs.
- Links to HTML and Web publishing resources on the Web.

Running the CD-ROM Interface

Because no install routine is required to use the CD-ROM, running the CD-ROM is a breeze, especially if you have Auto Insert Notification ("autorun") enabled for your CD-ROM drive. Simply insert the CD-ROM in your CD-ROM drive, close the tray, and wait for the CD-ROM user interface to open in your browser.

 NOTE The following instructions assume that you are using Windows 95/98, NT, 2000, or Me. If you are not a Windows user, you can still install the example files and the HTML templates from the CD-ROM, but you cannot install any of the software programs, all of which are specific to Windows. For information on how to install the example files and HTML templates if you are not a Windows user, open readme.txt in your text editor or word processor from the root folder of the CD-ROM.

If the CD-ROM interface does not automatically run, follow these steps:

1. From the Start menu, select Run.
2. Type **d:\start.htm** (where *d* is your CD-ROM drive letter) and press the Enter key (or click on OK).

The Prima Tech License

Take a moment to read the agreement, and then click on the I Agree link to accept the license and proceed to the user interface. If you do not agree with the license, click on the I Decline link and then close the browser window (or exit your browser).

 NOTE After you accept the license agreement, a page is displayed notifying you that you must be using a 32-bit version of Windows (95/98/NT/2K/Me) to run any of the software on the CD-ROM or to use the CD-ROM interface to install any of the example files, HTML templates, or software programs.

If you're using a 32-bit version of Windows, just click on the "Continue to the Main page" link.

If you're not using a 32-bit version of Windows, just click on the "Read the nowindow.txt file" link for directions on how to install the example files and the HTML templates to your hard drive.

The Main Page

From the Main page, you have the following options:

- ⚙ **Programs.** Click on this option to install any of the software programs from the CD-ROM.

- ⚙ **Examples.** Click on this option to install all the example files used in this book's work sessions.

- ⚙ **Templates.** Click on this option to install a collection of HTML templates created by the author.

- ⚙ **Links.** Click on this option to check out HTML and Web publishing resources on the Web.

- ⚙ **Main.** Click on this option at any time to return to the main page.

● ●

The example files, HTML templates, and most of the software programs included on the CD-ROM use executable installation files (*.exe).

When using the HTML CD-ROM interface to install these files, if you choose to run (or open) these installation files, rather than save them, you'll be presented with a security warning.

Some of the software programs include a digital certificate that authenticates that the producer of the software also produced the executable install program. Be aware, however, that many software install programs do not include digital certificates, so you shouldn't be overly concerned if an install program lacks one. All the software install programs included on this book's CD-ROM were created by the company or author who produced the software.

● ●

Installing the Example Files

All the example files used in this book can be easily installed from the CD-ROM:

1. Click on the Examples option in the sidebar.

2. Click on the link "Click Here to Install the Example Files to Your Hard Drive."

3. You might be asked whether you want to run (or open) the example files' self-extracting file, examples.exe, or whether you want to save it. You may also simply be prompted to save it.

    A. If you choose to run (or open) examples.exe, you might get a security warning (see previous note). Click on Yes if you want to continue;

click on No if you want to quit. (Note: The file examples.exe is a self-extracting file created by the author.)

B. If you choose to save examples.exe, just save the file on your hard drive and then use the Windows Run command (Start, Run) to run it.

C. You might also simply be prompted to save examples.exe, without being given the option of running (or opening) it. Just save it on your hard drive and then use the Windows Run command (Start, Run) to run it.

4. At the WinZip Self-Extractor window, click the Unzip button to install the example files to an HTML folder on your C drive (C:\Html). (If you want to install these files to a different drive or folder, just edit the "Unzip to folder" box.)

5. After the files have been unzipped, click the OK button, and then click the Close button. To close the CD-ROM interface, select File, Close. To exit your browser, select File, Exit.

If you installed the example files to the default drive and folder, you'll find them in an HTML folder on your C drive (C:\Html).

Installing the HTML Templates

I've created a collection of HTML templates and included them on the CD-ROM. Feel free to use any of these templates in creating your own pages. To install the HTML templates to your hard drive:

1. Click on the Templates option in the sidebar.

2. Click on the link "Click Here to Install the HTML Templates to Your Hard Drive."

3. You might be asked whether you want to run (or open) the HTML templates' self-extracting file, template.exe, or whether you want to save it. Or you might simply be prompted to save it.

A. If you choose to run (or open) template.exe, you might get a security warning (see previous note). Click on Yes if you want to continue; click on No if you want to quit. (Note: The file examples.exe is a self-extracting file created by the author.)

B. If you choose to save template.exe, just save the file on your hard drive and then use the Windows Run command (Start, Run) to run it.

C. You might also be prompted to save template.exe, without being given the option of running (or opening) it. Just save it on your hard drive and then use the Windows Run command (Start, Run) to run it.

4. At the WinZip Self-Extractor window, click the Unzip button to install the HTML templates to an Html\templates folder on your C drive (C:\Html\templates). (If you want to install these files to a different drive or folder, just edit the "Unzip to folder" box.)

5. After the files have been unzipped, click on the OK button, and then click on the Close button. To close the CD-ROM interface, select File, Close. To exit your browser, select File, Exit.

If you installed the HTML templates to the default drive and folder, you'll find them in an Html\template folder on your C drive (C:\Html\template).

The Software Programs

This section gives you a brief description of the shareware and evaluation software you'll find on the CD.

• •

NOTE The software included with this publication is provided for your evaluation. If you try this software and find it useful, you must register the software if that is a requirement for its continued use (as discussed in its documentation). Prima Publishing has not paid the registration fees for any shareware or evaluation software included on the CD-ROM.

• •

◆ ◆

CAUTION Because many of the programs included on this CD-ROM will cease functioning after their evaluation periods are over, you should wait to install a program until you're actually ready to try it out.

If you previously downloaded and installed from the Web an evaluation program included on the CD-ROM, you might not be able to evaluate it again unless the program on the CD-ROM is a later version than the one you previously evaluated. You can also check the vendor's Web site to see whether a later version has been released.

◆ ◆

AceFTP. This is an FTP program you can use to transfer your Web page files onto the Web.

AceHTML 4. This is a freeware HTML editor that you can use to create your own HTML files.

Adobe Acrobat Reader. This is a free program from Adobe that you can use to view documents in PDF (*.pdf) format. PDF files are becoming an increasingly popular way of offering DTP-like formatted documents over the Web.

CuteFTP. This is another FTP program you can use to transfer your Web page files onto the Web.

Drag and Zip. A handy utility that integrates a ZIP compression/decompression utility into Windows. Many downloadable files on the Web are offered in ZIP format, which compresses files to allow for smaller file transfer sizes. A couple of the programs provided on this CD-ROM are also in ZIP format.

Dreamweaver 3. A great HTML editor/Web publishing suite from Macromedia with many extra goodies. Supports creating Web pages using cascading style sheets, Dynamic HTML, JavaScript behaviors, image maps, and much, much more.

Dreamweaver UltraDev. A Web page application development environment from Macromedia. Designed to let you quickly connect Web pages to databases; preview live data in the workspace with Live Data Preview; and easily add server-side logic, navigation, and interactivity. Designed specifically for application development, Macromedia Dreamweaver UltraDev is a new product that's based on the Dreamweaver core architecture.

EditPad Classic. This is a free text editor that you can use instead of Notepad to create your own HTML files. You can try EditPad Classic for a short while, but if you want to keep on using it, you are kindly requested to say "thank you" to the author by sending him a nice postcard or a used phone card.

Fireworks 3. Macromedia's suite of design, illustration, image editing, JavaScript, and animation tools can create everything for your Web site, without the annoyance of jumping from application to application. Automates the creation of JavaScript roll-over buttons and exports Flash 4 animation files.

Flash 4. A program from Macromedia that lets you create your own Flash 4 animations, which have become the ad-hoc standard for publishing Web animations.

GIF Construction Set Professional 2.0. A GIF animation editor that makes producing your own GIF animations a snap.

Note: The GIF Construction Set Professional 2.0 software included with this publication is provided as shareware for your evaluation. If you try this software and find it useful, you are requested to register it as discussed in its documentation and in the About screen of the application. The publisher of this book has not paid the registration fee for this shareware.

HTML Editor. An excellent HTML editor from CoffeeCup Software, which features highlighted tags, integrated FTP uploading and downloading, an image gallery (including 3-D background images), animated GIFs, JavaScripts, a frame designer, support for cascading style sheets and Dynamic HTML, and much, much more.

Image Mapper. An excellent image map editor from CoffeeCup Software that you can use to create your own client-side image maps with hotspots linked to other HTML files or Web sites.

Mapedit. This is another excellent image map editor from Boutell.com. Mapedit makes creating client-side image maps a breeze.

Paint Shop Pro 6. A great image editor from Jasc Software that you can use to create your own customized Web graphics. Animation Shop, a GIF animation editor, is included with Paint Shop Pro.

PhotoLine 32. This is another image editor that you can use to create your own Web graphics. (You can try the software, but any saved images are marked with a "Demo" notice.)

Photoshop 5.5. From Adobe, this is the image editing tool-of-choice among design professionals.

Premiere. From Adobe, a video-editing tool for producing broadcast-quality movies for video, multimedia, or the Web.

RTF to HTML Version 4. A great tool that converts word processing documents to HTML documents. Just save your document as a Rich Text Format file (*.rtf) and RTF to HTML will convert it to an HTML file.

StyleSheet Maker. From CoffeeCup Software, this is a style sheet editor that can be used to create HTML files utilizing cascading style sheets.

Installing the Software Programs

To install any of the included software programs, just do the following:

1. Click on the Programs option in the sidebar.

2. Click on the link for the program you want to install and then click on the "Click here to install software" link.

3. You might be asked whether you want to run (or open) the program's install program or whether you want to save it. You might also be prompted to save it.

    A. If you choose to run (or open) the program's install program, you might get a security warning (see previous note). Click Yes if you want to continue; click No if you want to quit.

    B. If you choose to save the program's install program, just save the program on your hard drive and then use the Windows Run command (Start, Run) to run the program.

    C. If prompted to save the program's install program, without being given the option of running (or opening) it, just save the program on your hard drive and then use the Windows Run command (Start, Run) to run the program.

What happens next depends on the kind of installation file that's being run. If a straight installation file, the install program for the software will run directly. If a self-extracting ZIP file, the contents of the ZIP file should first be extracted, and then the install program for the software should run directly. If a regular ZIP file, the file will be opened in your default file compression utility, if you have one. You'll then need to extract the contents of the ZIP file to a folder (preferably an empty one) on your hard drive.

 NOTE Only one of the software programs included on the CD-ROM, Edit Pad Classic, utilizes a ZIP format install file. To open and extract the contents of the ZIP file, you need to have a file compression utility that can decompress ZIP files. If you don't have one, I recommend that you download and install WinZip from **www.winzip.com/**.

Glossary

absolute URL. A complete path, or *address*, of a file on the Internet (such as **http://www. someserver.com/somedir/somepage.html**). Also called a *complete URL*. See also *relative URL*.

adaptive palette. A color palette for an image that has been reduced to only the colors present in the image. Also referred to as a *customized palette* or an *optimized palette*.

alternative text. Text describing an image that is included in an IMG (Image) tag using the ALT attribute.

anti-aliasing. The blending of colors to smooth out the "jaggies" along diagonals and curved edges in bitmap images. Applied most commonly to font characters inserted into a graphic image.

applet. A client-side program, usually Java or ActiveX, that is downloaded from the Internet and executed in a Web browser.

ASCII. American Standard Code for Information Interchange. Defines a standard minimum character set for computer text and data.

bandwidth. The transmission capacity of a network, but also the amount of capacity being consumed by a connection.

binary file. A non-text file, such as an image or program file.

BinHex. The standard method on the Macintosh of converting a *binary file* into *ASCII* (text) so it can be transferred as an e-mail attachment.

bitmap. An image composed of pixels, sort of like a pointillist painting. GIF and JPEG images are bitmap images, for instance.

bookmarks. A means, in Netscape Navigator, for "bookmarking" the URLs of favorite Web sites so they can easily be returned to. See also *favorites*.

cascading style sheets. A means for defining styles, using the STYLE tag, to control the display of HTML elements.

CGI. Common Gateway Interface. An interface to a gateway through which a Web server can run programs and scripts on a host computer.

client. A computer on a network that makes a request to a server.

client-side. A process or program that is downloaded and run by a user agent (or browser). See also *server-side*.

crippleware. See also *shareware* or *demoware*.

customized palette. See *adaptive palette*.

definition list. A glossary list in HTML that's created using the DL (Definition List) tag.

demoware. A term describing demo software programs that have certain key functions (such as saving and printing) turned off. Sometimes also called *crippleware*. See also *shareware*.

dithering. To create a new color by interspersing pixels of multiple colors so that the human eye "mixes" them and perceives the intended color. Used to display colors that are not available on a system (such as with 256-color systems).

DOM. The Document Object Model, which is an interface model that allows programs and scripts to dynamically access and update the content, structure, and styles of an HTML or XHTML document. The key component for enabling *Dynamic HTML*.

domain category. A grouping of domain names identified by their extension, such as .com, .org, .net, .edu, .mil, and .gov.

domain name. An alphanumeric alternative to an IP address. Both are registered with InterNIC (Internet Network Information Center).

download. To transfer files from a server to a client. See also *upload*.

Dynamic HTML. Various means of providing dynamic Web content to respond interactively to user actions.

end tag. The end of a non-empty HTML element (</P>, for example). See *start tag*.

FAQ. Frequently Asked Questions. Generally a compilation of common questions and their answers within a particular technical area.

favorites. A feature in Microsoft Internet Explorer that is similar to Netscape Navigator's bookmarks feature, allowing you to save a list of your favorite sites.

firewall. A gateway device or software program designed to protect non-public areas of a network from being penetrated by unauthorized visitors (or hackers).

frames. An extension to HTML, pioneered by Netscape, and incorporated into HTML 4.0. Allows HTML documents to be presented inside multiple frames in a browser window.

freeware. A software program that can be freely used.

FTP. File Transfer Protocol. The protocol used for downloading or uploading ASCII and binary files on the Internet.

GIF. Graphic Interchange Format. A 256-color image format developed by CompuServe that is one of the most popular ways (along with JPEG images) to display images over the Web. Supports interlacing, transparency, and multiple frames (animation). See also *JPEG*.

GIF animation. A GIF image file containing multiple images.

hotlink. See *hypertext link*.

HTML. HyperText Markup Language. A markup language for preparing documents for display on the World Wide Web. The current version is HTML 4.01 (previous versions were HTML 1.0, HTML 2.0, HTML 3.2, and HTML 4.0).

HTML editor. A software program that edits HTML files, usually with the aid of pull-down menus, toolbars, and wizards.

HTML element. Includes everything that is nested within a tag, in the case of a container tag. A stand alone tag is both a tag and an element.

HTML tag. Either a stand alone tag, such as <hr>, or a container tag, such as <p>...</p>. Generally, the term "tag" references both the start and end tag in a container tag, whereas the term "element" references everything in between as well.

HTTP. HyperText Transfer Protocol. The protocol used to exchange Web pages and other documents across the Internet.

hyperlink. See *hypertext link*.

hypermedia. The interlinking of multiple media (text, images, sound, animation, and video).

hypertext. A means of providing for non-sequential linking of information.

hypertext link. A link between an HTML document and another HTML document or object file on the Web, allowing for the non-sequential browsing of multiple information sources.

image link. An inline image inserted inside a hypertext link, often displayed with a blue border to show that it's an active link.

image map. An image displayed in a Web browser that has hidden "hotspots" that link to their designated URLs.

in-context link. A hypertext link inserted within a paragraph or other text, rather than in a separate list or menu of links.

inline image. An image (GIF, JPEG, or PNG) that's displayed *inline* ("in a line") on a Web page.

interlaced GIF. A GIF image that is displayed in several passes, with only some of the image lines displayed each time, until all the lines have been displayed.

Internet. A set of protocols for transmitting and exchanging data among networks.

IP address. Internet Protocol address. A unique number, such as 185.35.117.0, assigned to a server on the Internet.

IPP. Internet Presence Provider, also often called a Web host or Web space provider. A company that rents out Web space.

ISP. Internet Service Provider, also often called an *access provider*. A company that provides dial-up access to the Internet.

Java. A computer language developed by Sun Microsystems for the delivery of cross-platform, client-side *applets* over the Internet.

JavaScript. A scripting language developed by Netscape for the execution by a browser of client-side scripts embedded in a Web page.

JPEG. Joint Photographic Expert Group, an acronym used to designate JPEG-format images that can display colors selected from a palette of up to 16.7 million colors. See also *GIF*.

keyword. A word used in an Internet or Web search.

link. See *hypertext link*.

link list. A list of hypertext links, sometimes also called a *hot list*.

link text. The text displayed in a hypertext link, usually in blue and underlined.

MathML. Mathematical Markup Language. The proposed standard for displaying equations and mathematical symbols on the Web.

Microsoft extension. An extension to HTML originally developed and supported by Microsoft in its Internet Explorer browser. The MARQUEE tag, for instance, is a Microsoft extension. See also *Netscape extension*.

MPEG. Moving Pictures Expert Group. A means of compressing video and audio files.

Netscape extension. An extension to HTML originally developed and supported by Netscape in its Navigator browser. Many Netscape extensions have been incorporated into HTML 3.2 and 4.0, including the FONT and FRAMESET tags, for instance, or are supported by other browsers. See also *Microsoft extension*.

offline browsing. Browsing HTML files on a local hard drive without connecting to the Internet.

optimized palette. See *adaptive palette*.

ordered list. A numbered list in HTML.

plug-in. An application that provides a Web browser with the ability to display or play additional types of media, such as streaming audio or video.

PNG. Portable Network Graphics. A newer graphics format for the display of images on the Web that supports a 48-bit color depth (JPEG supports a 24-bit color depth).

POP3 server. Post Office Protocol, Version 3. An "incoming mail" server. See also *SMTP server*.

QuickTime. A method developed by Apple Computer for delivering video, animation, and audio files.

refresh. To update the display of a Web page (using the Refresh button in Internet Explorer or the Reload button in Netscape Navigator).

relative URL. The location of a linked object within a Web site that is stated *relative to* the linking object. See also *absolute URL*.

search engine. A Web site that has compiled a searchable index of sites on the Web, such as AltaVista or Lycos.

server. A computer on a network that responds to requests from clients. See also *client*.

server-side. A process or program that is executed from the server, rather than being downloaded and executed by a user agent (or browser). See also *client-side*.

servlet. A server-side Java applet. See also *applet*.

SGML. Standard Generalized Markup Language. The parent markup language of HTML.

shareware. A means for freely distributing software so users can try it to see whether they like it. Users are encouraged to share the software with others, thus the term. If they like it, they're supposed to purchase it. Originally described software that had no time-out, but now loosely describes any software that users can evaluate before buying. See also *freeware, trialware,* and *demoware.*

SMIL. Synchronized Multimedia Integration Language. (Pronounced "smile.") An HTML-like language for describing multimedia presentations.

SMTP server. Simple Mail Transfer Protocol. An "outgoing mail" server (e-mail is sent to an SMTP mail server). See also *POP3 server.*

start tag. The start of a non-empty HTML element (<P>, for instance).

style sheet. A set of descriptions of how elements in a Web page should be displayed by a browser that can display styles. See also *Cascading Style Sheets.*

SVG. Scalable Vector Graphics. A new standard being developed for displaying vector-based graphics over the Web.

target anchor. A hypertext anchor that defines the "landing spot" for a link.

transparent GIF. A GIF image that has one color designated as transparent.

trialware. A software program that provides a trial period (most commonly 30 days) during which users can freely try out a program, after which the program stops running.

unordered list. A bulleted list in HTML.

upload. To transfer files from a client to a server.

URI. Universal Resource Identifier. A more recent variant of *URL* that the W3C prefers to use.

URL. Universal Resource Locator. An address on the Web.

user agent. Any client utilized to present data and information from the Web and the Internet. A browser is a user-agent, for instance, but so might be a TV set-top box.

WAP. Wireless Application Protocol. A protocol that enables the creation of Web-based applications for wireless devices.

Web browser. A software program that browses HTML and other files on the World Wide Web. See also *user agent.*

Webmaster. System operator for a server on the World Wide Web, but also often used to refer to a person in charge of creating a Web site.

WebTV. A means of interactively browsing the Internet and the Web using a TV set, from Microsoft.

World Wide Web. The WWW or the Web. Termed these days by Tim Berners-Lee, the inventor of the World Wide Web, as "the universal space of all network-accessible information."

XHTML. Extensible HyperText Markup Language. A reformulation of HTML as conforming to *XML.*

XML. Extensible Markup Language. A meta-language that sets the standard for creating SGML-compatible mark-up languages for display over the Web (XHTML, SMIL, MathML, and so on). (A "meta-language" is a language that sets the rules for other languages.) A key to enabling multi-modal publishing (Web, print, voice, Braille, and so on) from a single document.

XSL. Extensible Stylesheet Language. The specification for style sheets in XML documents.

INDEX

3-D buttons (Paint Shop Pro), 259
    Buttonize effect, 260–261
    Cutout effect, 262–263
    drop shadow effect, 263
    pattern fill background, 260
    text labels, 261–262

A

A (anchor) tag, 58–64, 291–292
ABBR (Abbreviation) tag, 44, 292
absolute font sizes, 106–107
absolute URLs, 399
AceHTML, 396
ACRONYM tag, 44, 292
adaptive palette, 399
address block, 8
    centering, 75
ADDRESS tag, 72–75, 281
Adobe Acrobat Reader, 396
Adobe Photoshop, 228
Adobe Type Manager, 116
ALIGN attribute, 38–39, 70
alignment, 11

    address book, centering, 75
    captions (tables), 135
    cell contents (tables)
        horizontal, 138–139
        vertical, 140–141
    horizontal, 38–39
        images, 85
    images, vertical, 70
    PRE tag and, 50
    side-by-side tables, 156–157
    tables, centering, 135–136
ALT attribute, 68–69
alternative text, images and, 68–69, 399
anchors, 8
    NAME, 60
animations
    GIF, 358–361
    interactive, 373
anti-aliasing, 238, 399
AOL (America Online), Web hosting, 376
APPLET tag (deprecated), 293
applets, 399
    Java, 11, 367–370

ASCII (American Standard Code for Information Interchange), 399

Asymmetrix Toolbox, 5

attributes (tags), 26, 274

ALIGN, 38–39, 70

ALT, 68–69

BACKGROUND, 149–151

BGCOLOR, 146–147

BODY, 117

BORDER, 94, 132

CELLPADDING, 133

CELLSPACING, 133

COLSPAN, 141–142

element identifiers, 309

FACE, 114–116

HEIGHT, 69–70

HREF (hypertext reference), 59

HSPACE (horizontal space), 90–91

intrinsic events, 309–310

MAXLENGTH, 204

MULTIPLE, 211

NAME, 203

ROWSPAN, 142–143

SIZE, 106–110

SRC (source), 67

START, 100

TYPE, 203, 207

VALUE, 100

WIDTH, 69–70

B

B (bold) tag, 41–42, 294

background

color, 116–119

tables, 146–148

transparent, 234

images, 11, 119–121

boxes, 347

frames, 195

style sheets, 340

tables, 149–151

light with white as major color, 253–254

non-white, 254–259

halo effect, 256–259

two-column background image, 158

BACKGROUND attribute, 119–121, 149–151

bandwidth, 399

banner images, 82–84

transparent, 123–124

two-column layouts, 160

banner text, 230–233

base font size, 109

BASE tag, 276

BASEFONT tag (deprecated), 109, 294

BDO tag, 294

BGCOLOR attribute, 146–147

BGSOUND tag, 351–352

BIG tag, 110, 295

binary files, 399

BinHex, 399

bitmaps, 399

blank lines

BR and, 40–41

P and, 37–38

block elements, 25

ADDRESS, 281

BLOCKQUOTE, 281–282

CENTER (deprecated), 282

DIR (deprecated), 282

DIV (division), 282

DL (definition list), 283

Hn (heading levels), 283–284

HR (horizontal rule), 284

MENU (deprecated), 284

OL (ordered list), 284–285

P (paragraph), 285

PRE (preformatted text), 286

TABLE, 286–290

UL (unordered list), 290–291

block quotes, 48–50

BLOCKQUOTE tag, 48–50, 281–282

blur effect (Paint Shop Pro), 250

BODY tag, 31–32, 280–281

attributes, 117

bold text, 9, 41–42

bookmarks, 400

frames, 168

BORDER attribute, 94

tables, 132

borders

images, 11

links, 94

style sheets, 344–346

tables, 132–133

color, 152

removing, 148–149

boxes

background images, 347

style sheets, 344–346

BR (break) tag, 39–41, 295

breaks, line breaks, 39–41

browsers, 8, 22

files, opening, 34

frames and, 172–174

moving between text editor and, 36

voice browsers, 17

bulleted lists, 8, 52–53

custom, 98–99

nesting, 53–54

BUTTON tag, 215

Buttonize effect, 3-D buttons, 260–261

buttons

3-D, 259

radio buttons, 206–208

Submit buttons, images as, 214–215

C

CAPTION tag, 134–135

captions (tables), 134–135

cascading style sheets, 12, 16, 333, 400. *See also* styles

borders, 344–346

boxes, 344–346

creating, 335–340

indented paragraphs, 340–341

margins, 341–343

case-sensitivity, elements, 26
CD-ROM, 391–398
    example files, 23–24
CELLPADDING attribute, 133
cells (tables)
    columns, spanning, 141–142
    content alignment
        horizontal, 138–139
        vertical, 140–141
    rows, spanning, 142–143
    spacing, removing, 148–149
CELLSPACING attribute, 133
CENTER tag (deprecated), 282
centering
    address block, 75
    tables, 135–136
CGI (Common Gateway Interface), 400
    form-processing CGI script, 218–219
        downloading, 220
        remotely-hosted, 219
    forms, 200
    scripts
        form-creation software, 221
        writing, 219–220
check boxes, 208–209
child folders, 327, 328–329, 330–331
CITE (citation) tag, 44, 295
client-side, 400
clients, 400
CODE (program code) tag, 44, 296
color
    background, 116–119
    fonts
        color names, 111–112
        RGB hex codes, 112–114
        tables, 145
    links, visited, 118

optimized color palette (Paint Shop Pro), 251–253
    tables
        background, 146–148
        borders, 152
    transparent, 234–235
    white as major color, 253–254
color names, 111–112
COLSPAN attribute, 141–142
columns
    spacer images, 158–159
    tables, 131–132
        cells, spanning, 141–142
        headings, 134
        width, 139–140
    two-column background image, 158
comments, 48, 296
containers, 25
content, responses, 217–218
counters, 356–357
cousin folders, 331
crippleware, 400
custom lists, bulleted lists, 98–99
customized palette, 400
CuteFTP, 396
Cutout effect, 3-D buttons, 262–263

D

DD (definition description) tag, 56
definition lists, 56–57, 400
DEL (delete) tag, 44, 296
demoware, 400
deprecated elements, 110, 274
DFN (definition) tag, 44, 297
digital certificates, security and, 221
DIR tag (deprecated), 282
displayable characters, 318–321

dithering, 113, 400

DIV (division) tag, 282

DL (definition list) tag, 56–57, 283

DOCTYPE declaration, 275

document elements, 274–281

docuverse, 4

DOM (Dynamic Object Model), 13, 16, 400

domain category, 400

domain name, 400

    registering, 377–380

downloading, 400

Drag and Zip, 396

Dreamweaver 3, 396

Dreamweaver UltraDev, 396

drop shadow effects (Paint Shop Pro), 249–250

    3-D buttons, 263

    transparent, 253–259

drop-cap text, 92

DT (definition term) tag, 56

Dynamic HTML, 370, 400

E

e-mail, 200

EditPad Classic text editor, 396

element identifiers, 309

elements, 25–27. *See also* specific elements

    attributes, 26, 274

    block, 25

    case sensitivity, 26

    containers, 25

    deprecated, 110

    empty, 25

    end, 30

    implied, 26

    inline, 25

    margins, 343

    nesting, 27

    overlapping, 27

    stand-alone, 25

    start, 30

    structure, 25

EM (emphasis) tag, 41, 297

EMBED tag, 352–355

empty tags, 25

end tag, 30, 400

example files, installing from CD-ROM, 393–394

F

FACE attribute, 114–116

FAQ (frequently asked questions), 400

favorites, 400

file transfer, Web server, 380–382

files

    linking to, 59–60, 64, 328–331

    linking within, 60–63

    new, 29–32

    opening in browsers, 34

    saving, 27–29, 76, 82, 130–131

fills (Paint Shop Pro), 240

    gradient fills, 245–247

    pattern fills, 242–244

        3-D buttons, 260

    solid color, 241–242

firewalls, 400

Fireworks 3, 396

Flash 4, 396

flowing images between images, 91

flowing text

    images

        around, 87–90

        between, 89–90

        spacing, 90–91

    tables, 154–155

        side-by-side, 155–156

folders

child, 327, 328–329, 330–331

cousin, 331

grandparent, 328, 330

parent, 327, 329

sibling, 328, 330–331

subfolders, 327

FONT tag (deprecated), 106–110, 145, 297

fonts

Adobe Type Manager, 116

color

color names, 111–112

RGB hex codes, 112–114

tables, 145

faces, 114–116

headings, level-one, 122–123

sans-serif, 123

serif, 123

size, 10, 11

absolute, 106–107

base size, 109

relative, 108

tables, 145

FORM tag, 202

form-processing CGI scripts, 218–219

downloading, 220

forms

CGI, 200

INPUT, 207

input controls

check boxes, 208–209

hidden controls, 209

password controls, 209

radio buttons, 206–208

text boxes, 202–206

JavaScript, 222–223

list menus, 210–212

Mailto, 200

responses, 216–218

content type, setting, 217–218

search forms, 365–366

security, 221

starting page, 201–202

testing, 216

text area boxes, 212–213

fragment identifiers, 60

FRAME tag, 305–306

frames, 12, 400

background images, 195

browsers, 172–174

column width, 174–175

controlling, 307–308

links outside frame, 177–178

NOFRAMES, 177

pros/cons, 167–169

row/column combo, 183–186

nested, 187–195

seamless, 176

sidebar menus, 171–172

top bar menu, 179–180

two-column pages, 178

two-row pages, 178–182

frameset files, saving, 171

FRAMESET tag, 170–171, 305–308

controlling frames, 307–308

FRAME, 305–306

NOFRAMES, 306–307

freeware, 400

FTP (File Transfer Protocol), 400

WS_FTP LE FTP software, 382–393

G

GIF animations, 358–361, 401

GIF Construction Set, 359–361, 396

GIF images, 67, 120, 400–401
    interlaced, 233–234, 236–237, 401
    optimizing, 265–268
    transparent, 233–234, 234–235
    versus JPEG, 239
glossary lists, 8
gradient fills (Paint Shop Pro), 245–247
grandparent folders, 328, 330
graphic rules, 85–86
    resizing, 86–87
graphics. *See also* images
    banner graphics, 230–233
guestbooks, 74, 357

H

H2 tag, 33
H3 tag, 33
halo effect
    non-white background color, 258–259
    non-white background image, 256–258
HEAD tag, 30
    BASE, 276
    ISINDEX (deprecated), 277
    LINK, 277
    META, 277–278
    SCRIPT, 278–279
    STYLE, 279–280
    TITLE, 276
head tags, 274–281
headings, 33–35
    alignment, 38–39
    level-one, 122–123
    tables
        columns, 134
        rows, 137–138

HEIGHT attribute, 69–70
    tables, 143–144
hidden controls, 209
hierarchical structure, 9
highlighting text, 41–45
hit counters, 356–357
H*n* (heading levels) tags, 283–284
horizontal alignment, 38–39
    images, 85
horizontal rules, 71. *See also* graphic rules
    ADDRESS tag and, 73
hotlinks, 401
hotspots, 363–365
    roll-over buttons, 366–367
HR (horizontal rule) tag, 71, 284
HREF (hypertext reference) attribute, 59
HSPACE (horizontal space) attribute, 90–91
HTML (Hypertext Markup Language), 3, 401
    documents, XHTML compliant, 313–314
    Dynamic HTML, 370
    early versions, 8–9
    elements (*See* specific elements)
    Microsoft extensions, 9–10
    Netscape extensions, 9–10
    tags (*See* tags)
    version 2.0, 9
    version 3.0, 10
    version 3.2, 11–12
    version 4.0, 12–13
    version 4.01, 13
    XHTML differences, 312–313
HTML Editor, 397, 401
HTML tag, 29–30, 276, 401
HTTP (HyperText Transfer Protocol), 401
HyperCard system, 4–5

hyperlinks, 401

hypermedia, 4, 401

hypertext, 4–5, 401

    anchors, 8

    links (*See* links)

I (italic) tag, 41–42, 298

icons

    link lists, 102–106

        tables, 152–153

    navigational, 95

IFRAME (inline frame) tag, 298

image links, 401

Image Mapper, 397

image maps, 362–365, 401

    hotspots, 363–365

    Mapedit, 363–365

images. *See also* graphics

    alignment

        horizontal, 85

        vertical, 70

    alternative text, 68–69

    as Submit buttons, 214–215

    background, 119–121

        boxes, 347

        frames, 195

        style sheets, 340

        tables, 149–151

    banner images, 82–84

    borders, 11

    flowing images between, 91

    GIF, 67, 120

        interlaced, 233–234, 236–237

        optimizing, 265–268

        transparent, 233–234, 234–235

    inline, 9, 66–70, 401

    JPEG, 67

        optimizing, 268–270

    links, 93–94

        borders, 94

        thumbnails, 95–97

    saving in Paint Shop Pro format, 251, 264

    size, 11, 69–70

    spacer images, columns, 158–159

    SRC, 67

    tables, 140

    text flow, 11, 87–90

        spacing, 90–91

    tiling, 119

IMG tag, 10, 66–70, 299

implied elements, 26

in-context link, 401

indents

    block quotes, 48–50

    icon link lists, 104–106

    paragraphs, 340–341

inline elements, 25

    A (anchor), 291–292

    ABBR (Abbreviation), 292

    ACRONYM tag, 292

    alignment, 70

    APPLET (deprecated), 293

    B (bold), 294

    banner images, 82–84

    BASEFONT (deprecated), 294

    BDO, 294

    BIG, 295

    BR (break), 295

    CITE (citation), 295

    CODE (program code), 296

    comments, 296

inline elements *(continued)*

DEL (delete), 296

DFN (definition), 297

EM (emphasis), 297

FONT (deprecated), 297

I (italic), 298

IFRAME (inline frame), 298

images, 66–70

IMG tag, 299

INS (insert), 299–300

KBD (keyboard), 300

MAP, 300–301

OBJECT, 301

Q (Quote), 301–302

S (strike) tag, 302

SAMP (sample text), 302

SCRIPT, 302

SMALL, 302–303

SPAN, 303

STRIKE (strikethrough), 303

STRONG (strong emphasis), 303

SUB, 304

SUP, 304

TT, 304

U (underline), 304

VAR (variable), 304

inline images, 9, 401

input controls

check boxes, 208–209

hidden controls, 209

password controls, 209

radio buttons, 206–208

text boxes, 202–206

default values, 205–206

INPUT tag, 203

forms, 207

INS (insert) tag, 44, 299–300

inserting

images in tables, 140

paragraphs, 101–102

installing Paint Shop Pro, 228–229

interactive animations, 373

interlaced GIF images, 233–234, 236–237, 401

Internet, 401

intrinsic events, 309–310

IP address, 401

IPP (Internet Presence Provider), 401

ISINDEX tag (deprecated), 277

ISO 8859-1 character set, 45

ISP (Internet Service Provider), 401

italic text, 9, 41–42

J

jaggies, 238

Java, 401

Java applets, 11, 367–370

JavaScript, 401

forms and, 222–223

scripts, adding, 366–367

JPEG images, 67, 120, 402

optimizing, 268–270

versus GIF, 239

K

KBD (keyboard) tag, 44, 300

keywords, 402

L

Latin1 character set, 45

layers (Paint Shop Pro), 247–249

label text, 264

text labels, 264

level-one headings, fonts, 122–123

LI (list item) tag, 54–55

line breaks, inserting, 39–41
LINK tag, 277
links, 57–58, 401–402
  A tag, 58–64
  frames and, 177–178
  icon link lists, 102–106
    tables, 152–153
  images, 93–94, 401
    borders, 94
    thumbnails, 95–97
  lists, 65, 402
    descriptions, 66
  loop-back, 62–63
  Mailto, 73
  netiquette, 60
  reciprocal, 60
  to files, 59–60, 64, 328–331
  visited, color, 118
  within files, 60–63
list menus, 210–212
  multiple selections, 211–212
lists
  bulleted lists, 52–53
    custom, 98–99
  definition, 56–57
  icon link lists, 102–106
    tables, 152–153
  link lists, 65–66, 402
  mixing, 55–56
  numbered, 54–55
  ordered lists, 402
  outlines, multi-level, 99–101
loop-back links, 62–63

M

Mailto form-processing utilities, 218
Mailto forms, 200

Mailto links, 73
MAP (image map) tag, 300–301
Mapedit, 363–365, 397
margins, style sheets, 341–343
  element margins, 343
markup languages, 5–6
MathML (Mathematical Markup Language), 16–17, 402
MAXLENGTH attribute, text boxes and, 204
memex, 4
MENU tag (deprecated), 284
menus, list menus, 210–212
message board, 358
META tag, 277–278
  frames, 168
Microsoft HTML extensions, 9–10, 402
mobile access, 17
monospace characters, 9
  embedding, 42–43
MPEG (Moving Pictures Expert Group), 402
multi-level outlines, 99–101
MULTIPLE attribute, 211

N

NAME anchor, 60
NAME attribute, 203
named entity codes, 45
navigation bar, row/column frameset page, 184
navigational icons, 95
nesting
  bulleted lists, 53–54
  elements, 27
  paragraphs, 36–37
  row/column combo frameset page, 187–195
netiquette, links and, 60
Netscape HTML extensions, 9–10, 402
NOFRAMES tag, 177, 306–307

non-keyboard characters, 45–46, 315–324

　　displayable, 318–321

　　reserved characters, 316

　　Unicode characters, 321–324

　　unused characters, 317–318

　　UTF-8 character set, 324

non-white background, 254–259

　　halo effect, 256–259

Notepad, Word Wrap, 29

numbered lists, 9, 54–55

numerical entry codes, 45

O

OBJECT tag, 301

offline browsing, 402

OL (ordered list) tag, 54–55, 284–285

　　nesting, 99–100

opening files in browsers, 34

optimized color palette (Paint Shop Pro), 251–253, 402

optimizing images

　　GIF, 265–268

　　JPEG, 268–270

ordered lists, 402

outlines, multi-level, 99–101

Outlook Express, 200

P

P (paragraph) tag, 35–38, 285

　　blank lines, 37–38

　　end element, 37

padding, tables, 133

Paint Shop Pro, 227–228, 397

　　blur effect, 250

　　drop shadow effects, 249–250

　　　　3-D buttons, 263

　　fills, 240

　　　　gradient fills, 245–247

　　　　pattern fills, 242–244, 260

　　　　solid color, 241–242

　　images, saving, 251

　　installation, 228–229

　　layers, 247–249

　　optimized color palette, 251–253

　　Undo, 238–240

paragraph tag, 9

paragraphs, 35–38

　　alignment, 38–39

　　indents, 340–341

　　inserting, 101–102

　　nesting, 36–37

parent folders, 327, 329

partial URLs, 326. *See also* relative URLs

password controls, 209

pattern fills (Paint Shop Pro), 242–244

　　3-D buttons, 260

PDAs (personal digital assistants), 80

PhotoLine 32, 397

Photoshop 5.5, 397

pixels, jaggies, 238

plug-in players, sound, 355–356

plug-ins, 402

PNG images, 120, 402

POP3 server, 402

PRE (preformatted text) tag, 50–52, 286

preformatted text, 50–52

Premiere, 397

Prima Tech license agreement, 392

proportional fonts, 42

Q

Q (Quote) tag, 44, 301–302

QuickTime, 402

quotes, block quotes, 48–50

R

radio buttons, 206–208

RealMedia, 371

reciprocal links, 60

refresh, 402

relative font sizes, 108

relative URLs, 84, 402

  benefits of, 326

  examples of, 327–328

  partial URLs, 326

reserved characters, 46–48, 316

responses to forms, 216–218

  content type, setting, 217–218

returns, 41

RGB hex codes (colors), 112–114

roll-over buttons, 366–367

row/column frameset page, 183–186

  navigation bar, 184

  nested, 187–195

rows (tables), 131–132

  cells, spanning, 142–143

  columns, spanning, 142–143

  headings, 137–138

  height, 143–144

ROWSPAN attribute, 142–143

RTF to HTML Version 4, 397

rules, 71–72

  graphic, 85–87

S

S (strike) tag, 44, 302

SAMP (sample text) tag, 302

sans-serif fonts, 123

saving

  files, 27–29, 76, 82, 130–131

  images in Paint Shop Pro format, 251, 264

scratch pad approach, 27

SCRIPT tag, 278–279, 302

scripts

  CGI

    form-creation software, 221

    writing, 219–220

  JavaScript, 366–367

seamless frames, 176

search engines, 402

search forms, 365–366

security

  digital certificates, 221

  forms, 221

serif fonts, 123

server-side, 402

servers, 402

servlets, 402

SGML (Standardized General Markup Language), 5, 312, 402

shading, rules, 72

shareware, 402–403

sibling folders, 328, 330–331

side-by-side tables, 155–156

  alignment, 156–157

sidebar menu pages, 171–172

SimpleText text editor, 22

SIZE attribute, 106–110

  text boxes, 203

SMALL tag, 110, 302–303

SMIL (Synchronized Multimedia Integration Language), 17, 403

SMTP (Simple Mail Transfer Protocol) server, 200, 403

software programs on CD-ROM, 395–398

solid color fills (Paint Shop Pro), 241–242

sound, 350–351
    BGSOUND tag, 351–352
    EMBED tag, 352–355
    looping, 352–353
    plug-in players, 355–356
spacer images, columns, 158–159
spacing, 41
    banner images, 83
    tables, 133
        cells, removing, 148–149
    text flow around images, 90–91
spaghetti code, 6–7
spam, 74
SPAN tag, 303, 343–344
special characters
    displayable characters, 318–321
    non-keyboard, 45–46, 315–324
    reserved characters, 46–48, 316
    Unicode characters, 321–324
    UTF-8 character set, 324
SRC (source) attribute, 67
stand-alone elements, 25
START attribute, 100
start element, 30, 403
start.html template, 81–82, 130
streaming media, 371–373
STRIKE (strikethrough) tag, 44, 303
STRONG (strong emphasis) tag, 41, 303
style sheets, 403. *See also* cascading style sheets
    background images, 340
    borders, 344–346
    boxes, 344–346
    creating styles, 335–340
    indented paragraphs, 340–341
    margins, 341–343
    SPAN tag, 343–344
    style declarations, 335

STYLE tag, 279–280, 334–335
Stylesheet Maker, 397
SUB tag, 43–44, 304
subfolders, 327
Submit buttons, images as, 214–215
subscript, 10, 43–44
SUP tag, 43–44, 304
superscript, 10, 43–44
SVG (Scalable Vector Graphics), 17, 403

T

TABLE tag, 131, 286–290
tables, 11, 12
    background color, 146–148
    background images, 149–151
    borders, 132–133
        color, 152
        removing, 148–149
    captions, 134–135
    cells
        content alignment, 138–139, 140–141
        spacing, removing, 148–149
        spanning columns, 141–142
        spanning rows, 142–143
    centering, 135–136
    columns, 131–132
        cells, spanning, 141–142
        headings, 134
    flowing text around, 154–155
    fonts, 145
    icon link lists, 152–153
    images, 140
        background, 149–151
    padding, 133
    rows, 131–132
        cells, spanning, 142–143
        headings, 137–138

height, 143–144

side-by-side, 155–156

alignment, 156–157

spacing, 133

two-column layout and, 158–163

width, 136

columns, 139–140

tabs, 41

tag elements, 25

tags, 3

target anchor, 403

TD (table data) tag, 131–132

TeachText text editor, 22

templates, 32–33

installing from CD-ROM, 394–395

start.html, 81–82, 130

text

banner text, 230–233

bold, 9, 41–42

color, 121

drop-caps, 92

highlighting, 41–45

italic, 9, 41–42

monospace characters, 9

embedding, 42–43

non-keyboard characters, 45–46

preformatted, 50–52

reserved characters, 46–48

text area boxes, 212–213

text boxes, 202–206

default values, 205–206

MAXLENGTH attribute, 204

SIZE attribute, 203

text editors, 7, 21–22

moving between browser and, 36

SimpleText, 22

TeachText, 22

text flow, 11

images, 87–90

spacing, 90–91

side-by-side tables, 155–156

tables, 154–155

text labels

3-D buttons, 261–262

layers, 264

TEXTAREA tag, 212–213

TH (table heading) tag, 134

thumbnail images, links, 95–97

tiling images, 119

TITLE tag, 30–31, 276

top bar menu, frames, 179–180

TR (table row) tag, 131–132

transparent banner images, 123–124

transparent drop shadows (Paint Shop Pro), 253–259

transparent GIF images, 233–234, 234–235, 403

trialware, 403

TT tag, 304

two-column frame pages

column layout, 170

column width, 174–175

NOFRAMES, 177

seamless frames, 176

sidebar menus, 171–172

two-column layout

background images and, 158

banner images and, 160

spacer images, 158

tables and, 158–163

vertical spacing, 160

two-row frame pages, 178–182

top bar menu, 179–180

TYPE attribute, 203

forms, 207

U

U (underline) tag, 44, 304

UL (unordered list) tag, 52–54, 290–291

Undo (Paint Shop Pro), 238–240

Unicode Worldwide Character Standard characters, 321–324

unordered lists, 403

unused characters, 317–318

uploading, 403

URI (Universal Resource Identifier), 403

URLs (Uniform Resource Locators), 403

  relative, 84

    benefits of, 326

    examples, 327–328

    partial, 326

user agents. *See* browsers

UTF-8 character set, 324

utilities, Mailto form-processing utilities, 218

V

VALUE attribute, 100

VAR (variable) tag, 44, 304

vertical alignment

  banner images, 83

  images, 70

  two-column layout, 160

vertical button menu, two-column layout, 160–161

voice browsers, 17

VSPACE (vertical spacing) attribute, 104–106

W

W3C (World Wide Web Consortium), 10

WAP (Wireless Application Protocol), 403

Web, 5

Web browsers. *See* browsers

Web hosting, 375–380

Web publishing programs, 7

Web server, transferring Web page to, 380–382

Webmaster, 403

WebTV, 403

western European languages, 45

white as major color, 253–254

WIDTH attribute, 69–70

  tables, 136, 139–140

word processors, 22

Word Wrap, Notepad, 29

World Wide Web, 403. *See* Web

WS_FTP LE FTP software, 382–393

WYSIWYG (What You *See* Is What You Get), 6

X

Xanadu, 4

XHTML (Extensible HyperText Markup Language), 15, 311–312, 403

  differences between HTML, 312–313

  HTML documents, compliance, 313–314

XML (Extensible Markup Language), 14–15, 311–312, 403

XSL (Extensible Stylesheet Language), 403